CARIBBEAN CHILDREN'S LITERATURE, VOLUME 1

Salvador

Turks and
Caicos Is. (U.K.)

Great Inagua I.
tánamo
DOMINICAN REPUBLIC
Santo Domingo
Puerto Rico (U.S.)
San Juan
Main Passage
Virgin Is. (U.K.)
Anguilla (U.K.)
St.-Barthélemy (Fr.)
Virgin Is. (U.S.)
Basseterre
ANTIGUA AND BARBUDA
Saint John's
ST. KITTS AND NEVIS
Montserrat (U.K.)
Guadeluope (Fr.)

SEA

Roseau
DOMINICA
Martinique (Fr.)
Fort-de-France
SAINT LUCIA Castries

Aruba (Neth.)
Curacao (Neth.)
Bonaire (Neth.)

Kingstown
**ST. VINCENT AND
THE GRENADINES**
BARBADOS
Bridgetown

allinas
GRENADA
Saint George's
Isla de Margarita

Maracaibo Caracas
Port of Spain
Valencia
Cumaná
TRINIDAD AND TOBA
Maturín
Pico Bolívar
5007 m
Ciudad Bolívar
Ciudad Guayana
rida
Orinoco
Georgeto
San Cristobal
Nieuw A
VENEZUELA

Children's Literature Association Series

CARIBBEAN CHILDREN'S LITERATURE

VOLUME 1

History, Pedagogy, and Publishing

Edited by **BETSY NIES** and **MELISSA GARCÍA VEGA**

University Press of Mississippi / Jackson

The University Press of Mississippi is the scholarly publishing agency of
the Mississippi Institutions of Higher Learning: Alcorn State University,
Delta State University, Jackson State University, Mississippi State University,
Mississippi University for Women, Mississippi Valley State University,
University of Mississippi, and University of Southern Mississippi.

www.upress.state.ms.us

The University Press of Mississippi is a member
of the Association of University Presses.

Frontispiece map courtesy of Dreamstime.

Chapter 6: Blackness, Imperialism, and Nationalism in
Dominican Children's Literature by Stacy Ann Creech
originally appeared in *International Research in Children's Literature*,
Volume 12, Issue 1, pp. 47–61. It is reproduced here
with permission of the Licensor through PLSclear.

Copyright © 2023 by University Press of Mississippi
All rights reserved

First printing 2023

∞

Library of Congress Cataloging-in-Publication Data

Names: Nies, Betsy L., 1959– editor. | García Vega, Melissa, editor.
Title: Caribbean children's literature / edited by
Betsy Nies and Melissa García Vega.
Other titles: Children's Literature Association series.
Description: Jackson : University Press of Mississippi, 2023– | Series:
Children's Literature Association series |
Includes bibliographical references and index.
Identifiers: LCCN 2023001752 (print) | LCCN 2023001753 (ebook) | ISBN
9781496844514 (hardback) | ISBN 9781496844521 (trade paperback) | ISBN
9781496844538 (epub) | ISBN 9781496844545 (epub) | ISBN 9781496844552
(pdf) | ISBN 9781496844569 (pdf)
Subjects: LCSH: Children's literature—History and criticism. | Caribbean Area.
Classification: LCC PN1009.A1 C328 2023 (print) | LCC PN1009.A1 (ebook) |
DDC 809/.8928209729—dc23/eng/20230309
LC record available at https://lccn.loc.gov/2023001752
LC ebook record available at https://lccn.loc.gov/2023001753

British Library Cataloging-in-Publication Data available

Dedicated to all the readers out there.
—B. N.

For all the children I have been blessed to read with
as well as those readers I have yet to meet.
—M. G. V.

CONTENTS

Acknowledgments... xiii

Introduction... 3

Part 1: Histories of Caribbean Children's Literature

Chapter 1. Language, Authenticity, and Representation
in Dutch Caribbean Children's and Young Adult Literature 35
Florencia V. Cornet

Chapter 2. Children's Literature and the Theme of Childhood
in the Francophone Caribbean: An Overview......................... 53
Louise Hardwick

Chapter 3. Anglophone Caribbean Children's Literature: A Snapshot...... 72
Betsy Nies

Chapter 4. Before and After the Revolution: An Exploration
of the Trajectory of Cuban Children's Literature..................... 83
Zeila Frade

Chapter 5. Puerto Rican Children's Literature on the Archipelago 91
María V. Acevedo-Aquino

Chapter 6. Blackness, Imperialism, and Nationalism in Dominican Children's Literature 100
Stacy Ann Creech

Chapter 7. A Brief History of Costa Rican Children's Literature 118
Ann González

Part 2: Decolonizing Children's Literature in the Anglophone Caribbean and Its Diaspora

Chapter 8. Back to *Backfire*: The Pedagogical Impact of the Giuseppis' Caribbean Short Story Collection in the Secondary School System of Trinidad and Tobago from the 1970s to the Present 125
Geraldine Elizabeth Skeete

Chapter 9. Creole vs. Standard English: Negotiating Voice in Caribbean Children's Literature 153
Karen Sanderson-Cole and Barbara Lalla

Chapter 10. Tradition and Modernity: Grace Hallworth and a Vision of the Caribbean for British Readers 170
Karen Sands-O'Connor

Chapter 11. Reading Words, Reading Worlds: Understanding the Value of the Literary Experience in the Process of Reading Caribbean Children's Books in the Jamaican Primary School System. 184
Aisha T. Spencer

Chapter 12. Seriously! Reading and Righting Images of the Caribbean in the American Classroom. 211
Consuella Bennett

Part 3: Picture Books and Publishing

Chapter 13. Publishing Children's Literature in the Caribbean: Four Authors' Perspectives 239
Betsy Nies and Melissa García Vega

Chapter 14. Creating Picture Books: Reflections of
Edwidge Danticat, Olive Senior, and Junot Díaz 258
Betsy Nies and Melissa García Vega

Chapter 15. Making Memories or *Pesadillas*? Junot Díaz's *Islandborn* 266
Megan Jeanette Myers

About the Contributors 287

Index 291

ACKNOWLEDGMENTS

Many thanks to the faculty of the University of North Florida (UNF), who provided supportive feedback during the drafting process—Jenni Lieberman, Laura Heffernan, Chris Gabbard, Stephen Gosden, Sarah Provost, Nicholas de Villiers, and Tru Leverette. I am grateful to the UNF alumni who also supported the editorial process: Paige Perez, Dyllan Cole, Natasha Kane, and Chelsea Hawthorne; and Keith Cartwright, chair of the Department of English, for his ongoing encouragement. I also acknowledge that UNF played a significant role in the production of these two volumes through their award to me of the Faculty Enhancement Grant in 2019 and a sabbatical in fall 2020, both of which made the volumes possible.
—*Betsy Nies*

Thank you to Yarisa Colón Torres, a student at the Center for Advanced Studies on Puerto Rico and the Caribbean, and Rosa M. Marrero Laureano, a retired Puerto Rico Department of Education Spanish middle and high school teacher, for your review and insight on Spanish translations in chapter 13 in volume 1.
—*Melissa García Vega*

CARIBBEAN CHILDREN'S LITERATURE, VOLUME 1

INTRODUCTION

Betsy Nies and Melissa García Vega

Caribbean children's literature finds its roots in the folktale, the legend, the proverb, the riddle, in what Cynthia James refers to as "orature." Evolving from African and indigenous-based beliefs and interwoven with the languages and cultures of colonizers and subsequent immigrants, Caribbean children's literature has reached critical mass, well deserving of scholarly attention. Historically influenced by colonial education systems—and resistance to those systems—Caribbean children's literature has matured in ways yet to be recognized in the academic world. Simultaneously, its presence in classrooms and local libraries remains impacted by the long gaze of colonialism, which privileges books for children as primarily pedagogical tools instead of sites of reading pleasure. Caribbean teacher preparatory programs rarely integrate and evaluate local literatures in ways that honor the growing body of trade books now available for primary and secondary students, aside from those already established within the Caribbean literary canon. Children's literature courses at the university level regionally overlook Caribbean children's literature as a valuable site of investigation.[1] Caribbean young adult literature also has now emerged as an important genre, but one that certainly remains unrecognized in school systems in the region and beyond.

The purpose of this project is to support and build engagement with the children's literature of the region and its diaspora both locally and globally. The collaboration on this project—between regional and international scholars (including former primary and secondary teachers) and children's book authors of multiple linguistic backgrounds—honors the shared cultural links between Caribbean islands and across language traditions. Caribbean theoretical hermeneutics reflecting a Caribbean literary aesthetic is present throughout this two-volume anthology. In 1975, Kamau Brathwaite, in "Caribbean Man in Space and Time," called early upon the need for "content/curriculum research and its relationship to the embodying culture" (6), certainly still a clarion call for educators at all levels, despite the significant advances in curricula following the political and ideological distancing from colonial powers.

The significance of Caribbean literature has many facets, one primary feature being how the region reflects the literary roots of a twenty-first-century pluralistic society, particularly in the major Western countries with prominent Caribbean diasporas, namely the US, Canada, and the United Kingdom. One only has to look at the substantial body of literary scholarship focused on original works as well as critical theory to recognize the imprint Caribbean discourse has had on literary ideology. For example, the comprehensive three volumes of *A History of Literature in the Caribbean* (Arnold 1994, 1997, 2001) present a comparative study of the Caribbean as a literary region including four major European languages (Dutch, English, French, and Spanish). Understanding the legacy of Caribbean literature throughout each volume affords a deeper understanding of the literary roots, themes, techniques, and patterns specific to the region.

Most recently, *Caribbean Literature in Transition* (2021), with three volumes covering the period 1800–2020, magnifies our appreciation and invites us to reflect on how we discuss the Caribbean region's literary existence as it continues to evolve. The vitality of change is consistently present amid story patterns that capture the details of rich lives existing beyond mere survival. One of the aims of this two-volume anthology is to broaden the dialogue by reflecting specifically on literature written for children of the Caribbean region and its diaspora. And while the makeup of the Caribbean is complex, with influences of the original indigenous people and white Europeans as well as people imported from throughout the Asian continent as cheap labor, a main thread of literary influence reflects the cultural impact of the many enslaved people coming from a variety of places across the African continent. As with Caribbean literature for the adult community, it is important to examine Caribbean children's literature in academic scholarship because of its twofold subversive commitment. Despite historical attempts to eradicate and/or silence people who are not white across the island nations as well as to limit the concept of the child to its European Romantic legacy, Caribbean children's literature reflects the potential for a transnational, transgressive body of work to ignite the interest of multilingual learners.

Sylvia Wynter provides a theoretical framework for understanding the cultural importance of such literature. She builds on Frantz Fanon's exploration of racialized subjectivities in *Black Skin, White Masks* (1952) and reviews Fanon's redirection of the late nineteenth-century focus on phylogeny (the evolution of a group of organisms) and the ensuing emphasis on ontogeny (the developmental history of an individual organism) toward sociogeny (or what she calls the "sociogenetic principle"), which looks at the origin and development of a person or thing as a result of social factors (31). Wynter locates human consciousness as formed by social forces yet capable of dismantling prescribed cultural scripts that denigrate Black and brown bodies. She argues that we can reshape the narratives we inherit, much like Fanon, who deconstructs his otherness as a French Caribbean Black man, assigned to him by the metropole. Drawing on the works of anthropologist Jacob Pandian, Wynter distinguishes evolving conceptions of humanity: first as the medieval Christian self, then the secularized, rational Renaissance "Man." Set up in the European imaginary in opposition to such concepts, indigenous people of the US and Caribbean occupied an antithetical position as "savages." Emerging evolutionary theories of Darwinism and natural selection located people of African descent as subhuman, as occupying a missing evolutionary link between human and animal species (43–44). In response, Wynter proposes the "After Man," arguing that the "study of words" or "the study of the *rhetoricity* of our human identity" generates a play space where humans can revise their ideological scripts and inherited conceptions of humanity injurious to mental and physical well-being (60). Poetics then can propel individuals to envision the new into existence. Caribbean children's literature, an extension of orality, offers the potential for all readers but especially children to listen, read, and learn about shape-shifting play that provides a mirror or window on who they are through reflections of their own cultural experiences as well as national and diasporic histories (Bishop).

Paulo Freire's *Pedagogy of the Oppressed* (1970) addresses Fanon's call for an education that is anticolonial and completely new. Wynter's proposal of the "After Man" formed by bios and mythoi ("we are *simultaneously* storytelling *and* biological beings"; McKittrick 29; italics in original) negates and ends the existence of a so-called Man defined in "Western Europe's matrix Judeo-Christian genre of the human" (McKittrick 93). Likewise, inspired and led by Freirean critical literacy, an ecosocialist pedagogy aims to counter "an ideological image of humanity [that] has served to functionally oppress all that has been deemed Other than human" (Kahn 10). The legacy of Caribbean literature is its continued transversal movement disrupting ideas of the Other. Stories for children and young adults engage in this dialogue with depictions of diverse experiences, languages, and ancestral heirlooms central to celebrating humanity in the contemporary.

For the purposes of this study, the Caribbean region encompasses all islands near the Caribbean Sea, as well as countries and areas along the South and Central American coast that politically and/or culturally bear ties to the region, including Guyana, Belize, Suriname, and French Guiana. Choosing a wide geographical definition of the region allows for inclusion of a range of language backgrounds and an exploration of the various historical and cultural continuities between nations, territories, and dependencies already recognized in scholarly literature. Political and economic challenges endemic to the region have led to the widespread influence of printed material for children produced by larger countries or colonizing powers. And while some large publishing houses have a Caribbean subsidiary, depictions of Caribbean life in trade books on the library shelf remain limited. The availability of locally produced, high-quality children's books outside the range of pedagogically crafted material promoted and adopted for classroom use remains restricted, aside from the ongoing attention to folklore. While Caribbean literature written for adult audiences has been widely adopted in secondary curricula, young adult literature that targets both middle-grade readers and older teens lacks visibility and availability to local readers.[2]

Teachers in the Caribbean need to have at their disposal a variety of literature produced within the region. Teacher preparatory programs and children's literature classes must attend to the complexity that exists in these texts in terms of how they draw on oral traditions and local folk culture, or showcase linguistic characteristics and the varied realities of growing up in the Caribbean today. These texts can support teachers engaging students with local history and highlight the ways historical characters can set an example for a Caribbean future. Latoya Teague describes how the African diaspora "combines people with complex histories of slavery yet separates them by culture and language related to their new geographic location as a result of forced migration" (37). Although many colonies within the Caribbean region saw postwar independence, the decolonization process is still ongoing. Central to this decolonization are cultural identity formations. People reading, at any age, in the Caribbean must see aspects of themselves and their location reflected in books that speak to their specific interests and lived experience.

Yahaya Bello, in "Caribbean American Children's Literature," makes the case for "all of us, especially educators, to have some familiarity with the culture and literature of the region" due to mass migration and changing demographics. The population of the region, over 44 million in 2019, contributes to strong immigrant populations in its diapora. For example, in the US, Caribbean immigrants totalled 4.5 million in the same year, forming 10 perent of the US's immigrant population (Lorenzi and Batalova). Today, the population of Latin America and the Caribbean together is approximately 650 million. Angie Zapata and colleagues address the consistent movement between borders and worlds as defining the purpose of a transnational children's literature (6). The extension and expansion of Caribbean studies in a neocolonial global context further connects as well as legitimizes Caribbean literature among global literatures. Language, skin color, and cultural identities inform a transnational experience, and all of these factors are present in Caribbean literature written specifically for children.

The late Édouard Glissant theorizes, from a Caribbean cultural perspective, an interconnection of all phenomena and therefore a futility of domination. Furthermore, he links identity with community via the community seeking a legitimate right to a place or territory through the "revealed word" (*Poetics of Relation* 13). The mutually dependent relationship between the land and its colonized people is evident in many literary works that have come out of the Caribbean. Afro-Caribbean religiosity, based in the region but with roots in Africa, tells the story of a people whom Isidore Okpewho describes as "transplanted Africans and their progeny [who] confronted the host environment and built a life for themselves" (xiv).

In *The Trickster Comes West: Pan-African Influence in Early Black Diasporan Narratives* (2009), Babacar M'Baye argues that traditional tales and figures such as Anansi and Br'er Rabbit are "ubiquitous in the cultures" of the Americas (4). He looks at how Black diaspora writers in the eighteenth and nineteenth centuries "utilized African cultural, religious, and ideological symbols and concepts as means of resistance against oppression in their specific locations in the Western world ... [and] drew from African ancestral traditions" (4). M'Baye identifies how "traditional African folklore [was] an active agent" (6) in Black resistance. Such folkloric discourse as well as other forms of contemporary discourse can challenge what Sujin Huggins highlights as neocolonial discourse in children's literature. She argues that there remains a "campaign for assimilation and acceptance of the way of life of the majority" in international children's literature, a field that impacts the Caribbean through the widespread importation of Western literature for children (7). In an Australian context, Clare Bradford examines indigenous portrayals in children's literature, noting how "children's texts by Indigenous and non-Indigenous producers who afford diverse, self-conscious, and informed representations of Indigenous cultures comprise a crucial intervention in processes of decolonization across settler societies" (227).

Enrique Pérez Díaz acknowledges the impossibility of separating history from culture in children's literature: after five centuries "of the New World being a meeting-place of cultures ... literature specifically for children first appeared in the Latin American and Caribbean countries only between the middle of the nineteenth century and the beginning of the twentieth" (883). Pérez Díaz divulges his perspective in his overview of published picture books associated with the Caribbean. Without a connection to metropolitan trade and production routes, namely in the United Kingdom, the US, and Canada, local projects often die on the vine, constricting the organic development of independent local viewpoints. Instead, a mirror of previous colonial relationships and patterns, in a supposedly postindependence environment, is what dominates the literacy options for most children reading in the Caribbean. Yet authors such as Imam Baksh, Tracey Baptiste, and Lynn Joseph translate to paper the oral stories passed from one generation to another in the Caribbean. For example, in *A Wave in Her Pocket* (1991), Joseph captures the manner and custom of a *tantie* or elder woman, telling stories to children at gatherings. Cultivating culture is analogous to Wynter's comparison of small parcels of land to large plantations. The small parcel or "plot" focuses on the local and is not driven solely by profit, whereas the plantation is based upon a distant cultivation purely for consumerism. The role of small publishing houses as well as the option to self-publish are a central theme in addressing circulation and availability issues that are analogous to a local harvest.

In discussing people(s) who fall under the heading of the Other, Glissant describes, in "The Cultural Creolization of the World," the Caribbean as an archipelago that extends to the diaspora, therefore changing who is the Self and who is the Other. Glissant's proclamation in *Poetics of Relation* (1997) that "the relationship between the center and the periphery will be completely different" is also seen in Antonio Benítez-Rojo's description of creolization as the

> product of the plantation (the big bang of the Caribbean universe), whose slow explosion throughout modern history threw out billions and billions of cultural fragments in all directions—fragments of diverse kinds that, in their endless voyage, come together in an instant to form a dance step, a linguistic trope, the line of a poem, and afterward repel each other to reform and pull apart once more, and so on. (55)

Caribbean literature for adults as well as for young children reflects the population's growing presence in the three central countries for Caribbean-themed publishing: the US, the United Kingdom, and Canada. As global literatures gain momentum as topics of study, children's world literatures are likewise attracting scholarly attention. As regional and international scholars, we bring to the forefront children's literature by Caribbean writers both in the islands and in the diaspora. In volume 1, we address the ways history, pedagogy, and publishing have impacted the production and content of this literature. In volume 2, we analyze a range of genres for young audiences including historical, speculative, and environmental fiction. Contemporary theoretical approaches—childhood studies, ecopedagogy, postcolonialism, and poststructuralism among others—form the groundwork of such analyses.

Peter Hunt, in his introduction to *Understanding Children's Literature*, argues that the underpinnings for the study of children's literature involve three main groups: the audience, the child, and the reader. Hunt notes that the study of how stories are told orally contributes to our understanding of how stories and communication work together as an amalgamation process, concluding that very often stories do several things at the same time, such as expanding the imagination (including general and/or specific social attitudes) as well as dealing with issues or coping with problems. We use this description of the three groups that must be considered when discussing children's literature as a guide to examine what texts are available for the child, as reader and audience, in the Caribbean region. Hunt identifies this list as a matrix in which subtle meanings are generated.

This anthology focuses primarily on works written in English. The domination of the British in the colonial process and the current emphasis on English as a global language has spurred many educators across the region to stress the importance of Standard English as the gold standard for global citizenry. So while some have advocated a multilingual and multicultural literary effort over the past thirty years to reflect the range of languages—in particular creole languages—in the Caribbean and its diaspora in literature for children, English remains the dominant language, in part through the strength of the publishing market in English-speaking countries. However, the anthology does provide important coverage of the growth of children's literature in all four language regions—Dutch, French, Spanish, and English—in volume 1, part 1, on literary histories, revealing language's role in the formation of national identities and the lingering effects of colonial history on publishing markets, school curricula, and teaching practices. Volume 1 also addresses the treatment of creoles in children's literature, their presence an important mark of postcolonial resistance to the colonial denigration of vernaculars of everyday speech. Works published in English, however, dominate the anthology's two volumes, correlating with the past and much of the present publishing power within a global context.

We have separated volume 1 into three parts. Part 1 provides general coverage of the history of children's literature in the regions where the four major colonial powers have left their imprint. While not a part of the Caribbean, Costa Rica has been included in this section; with its Caribbean coastline, it serves as the home to books featuring Afro-Caribbean protagonists and the major Afro-Caribbean children's writer Quince Duncan. Part 2 addresses intersections between pedagogy and children's literature in the Anglophone Caribbean, covering the integration of literature into the classroom, social discourse via teacher preparation programs, and the role of pedagogical curriculum standards and administration. It offers recommendations for using such literatures creatively both in local curricula and abroad. Part 3 explores the challenges of producing and publishing picture books and engages with local authors familiar with the terrain. It closes with interviews and analytical coverage of the work of internationally known writers of the diaspora who have turned from writing for adults to penning picture books for children. Edwidge Danticat, Junot Díaz, and Olive Senior join in conversation to talk about their transition from text-heavy literature for adults to the beautiful world of illustrated texts.

Caribbean children's literature as a field remains buffeted by several factors: limited local publishing opportunities, a lack of inclusion of Caribbean trade books in teacher and administrative training programs, and ongoing issues of access to such books for children in classrooms, libraries, and bookstores. In response, this collection offers deep background information for educators, scholars, and administrators about Caribbean children's literature, emphasizing the richness of what has emerged post-1960. It provides regional and global educators with a place to learn more about the complicated but intertwined histories of these island nations, territories, and dependencies. Caribbean literature for children deserves visibility and a place in local and international conversations within the field.

Literature Review

The Anglophone Caribbean region has received more scholarly attention than the other language regions. In 2005, Cynthia James offered a rare survey of the transformation of oral culture into children's literature in Trinidad and Jamaica, providing insight into the impact of British colonialism on attitudes toward folklore and folklore-based literary traditions. Karen Sands-O'Connor, with her monograph *Soon Come Home to This Island: West Indians in British Children's Literature* (2008), laid the groundwork for examining the literature of the so-called Windrush generation who emigrated to Great Britain between 1948 and 1971. This group included many writers who brought Caribbean literature to the global forefront in the 1960s such as Barbadian Kamau Brathwaite, Trinidadian John La Rose, and Jamaican Andrew Salkey. Forming the Caribbean Arts Movement in 1966, this group played an influential role in supporting artists and authors who produced the first children's literature in Great Britain featuring representations of Caribbean children.

Additionally, scholars have begun the process of theorizing Caribbean children's literature. In 2006, the University of Puerto Rico opened its doors to El Centro para el Estudio de la Lectura, la Escritura y la Literatura Infantil (Center for the Study of Reading, Writing, and Children's Literature) with a six-thousand-volume collection. Three doctoral students (Ada Haiman,

Melissa García Vega, and Carmen Milagros Torres-Rivera) produced scholarly work using theoretical approaches—childhood discourse analysis, ecopedagogy, and critical race theory—to examine children's literature of the English- and Spanish-speaking Caribbean. In 2012, the first anthology on concepts of the child in Caribbean literature was published, titled *The Child and the Caribbean Imagination*, edited by University of the West Indies professors Giselle Rampaul and Geraldine Skeete. In 2018, two Caribbean scholars—Jarrel De Matas and Aisha Spencer—added to the field, De Matas through his study of "child noir" in two young adult Caribbean texts and Spencer through her examination of middle-reader trade books. Spencer argued that Caribbean children's literature offers "a new kind of *poetics* and *politics* for representing and reading the nations of the Caribbean" (115).

One library study deserves mention as it puts into relief issues that inform the field of contemporary Caribbean children's literature. Sujin Huggins, a librarian at the Port of Spain Children's Library of the National Library of Trinidad and Tobago from 2004 to 2006, focused her 2012 University of Illinois dissertation on the contents and use of a dedicated local children's literature collection within the Children's Library. Mandated by the government, this 302-book collection—roughly 3 percent of the entire Children's Library—contained children's books written by Caribbean authors living in the region. Librarians faced several problems indicative of larger issues in the field. In their search for the children's literature of Trinidad and Tobago, librarians could find only self-published children's literature of variable quality (about twenty-seven books, or 9 percent of the collection's total) due to the lack of local publishing opportunities (with Trinidad's publishers concentrating on the predictable educational market) (Huggins 25). Fourteen percent of the collection consisted of leveled readers, with 8 percent classified as "language/grammar," accounting then for 22 percent of the collection (90), indicative of broader trends that see literature primarily as a tool to gain literacy. Over half of the collection was folklore or nonfiction with a focus on travel and history (200), with few chapter books or books appropriate for middle-grade readers. With the majority of books published overseas (68 percent), Huggins's study raises questions about what constitutes "local" literature (70). Macmillan Caribbean published 21 percent of the dedicated collection—sixty-six books—with fifty-three published by its educational division (70). Huggins found little interest among library patrons in the collection (perhaps due the bookshelves' obscure location and limited signage) except for three parents who expressed an interest in folklore, a result of their own early reading experience (81–82). She found a disconnection between local schools and the library, with teachers unaware of so-called local literature as an option for in-school use (80–81).

Huggins cites Jamaican children's author Diane Browne, who, in her 2003 master's thesis, reached the same conclusion. After working with urban primary schoolteachers in Jamaica, Browne found that they lacked an awareness of local children's literature. After introducing them to such books, the teachers recognized the importance of providing students with self-representation; they saw the motivational aspects of such literature, its importance for interdisciplinary study, and the need for high-quality illustrations. Summer Edward also concurs with the results of Huggins's study, noting that many people in the region lack a general knowledge of Caribbean children's literature; most see folktales as occupying this slot, with little awareness of literature outside of school readers. Seeking to address this issue, Edward published *Anansesem: News, Ideas, Arts, and Letters from the World of Caribbean Children's & YA Publishing*, launched online in 2010. She showcased local authors, books, histories, and issues, offering a significant resource for readers, teachers, and scholars of Caribbean children's literature.

In the Dutch Caribbean, scholars have researched the history of children's literature. As Florencia Cornet notes in this volume's first chapter on this linguistic region, Wim Rutgers offered *Bon dia! Met wie schrijf ik? Over Caraïbische jeugdliteratuur (Good Morning! Who Am I Writing With?)*[3] in 1988; it covers the history of the children's literature tradition—even if nontraditional in its attention to religious texts for children in the nineteenth century. Aart G. Broek followed with his study of literature for children by the Catholic Church published in the local Creole from the late 1800s to 1940. In the field of Francophone Caribbean children's literature, Louise Hardwick, Molly Krueger Enz, and Kiera Vaclavik have highlighted the work of Maryse Condé (Guadeloupe) and Dany Laferrière (Haiti/Canada). Spanish literature scholar Ann González offers research on works of children's literature from the Spanish-speaking Caribbean in her book *Resistance and Survival: Children's Narrative from Central America and the Caribbean* (2009). González notes the marginality of Spanish-language Caribbean children's literature, typically left out of the purview of Latin American studies. She finds coverage of such literature in scholarly works "sketchy at best," restricted to national educational studies for curriculum development in Caribbean countries (2). Significantly, she notes that local children's literature has played an important role in national battles for independence; now, she argues, Caribbean Spanish children's literature has entered a new phase, fighting against the monochromatic effects of globalization. She writes, "Rather than a cohesiveness induced by globalization, a new cohesiveness based on belonging to the immediate community, local culture and ethnicity is emerging within the periphery to maintain a sense of identity" (3). The rise of technology and the ongoing presence of US media in the Caribbean islands has made local children's literature that much more important. Regional voices have been advocating for a recognition of such literatures, a salve against the importation and recirculation of globalized images and stories.

Part 1: Histories of Caribbean Children's Literature

Part 1 of this volume treats the history of children's literature by language, in the Dutch-, French-, English-, and Spanish-speaking nations and territories. All four language regions share important similarities. Beginning with Christopher Columbus's arrival in 1492, competing European powers decimated indigenous populations—the Taíno, the Island Caribs of the Lesser Antilles, and the Guanahatabey of western Cuba—through disease, warfare, and slavery. Beginning in the sixteenth century, Africans were forcibly brought as slaves to the region; scholars estimate that altogether more than five million Africans (and their descendants) were enslaved, coming to form the region's majority population (Lambert). Following emancipation in the nineteenth century, contract labor helped fill labor shortages, with workers arriving primarily from Asia. Migratory flows from Latin America, the US, Canada, and Europe continue to inform the changing population. Majority languages typically feature a mix of the colonial language(s) (with many islands colonized repeatedly and alternately by competing powers) with the languages of forced and voluntary migration, producing various creoles. Often unacknowledged in educational settings, these creoles have gained some traction in terms of formal acceptance in nations resistant to colonial pedagogies. Other factors—local government investment, natural disasters, the development of school libraries and children's libraries, internet access, and teacher preparatory programs—all figure into the availability of local children's literature for public consumption. The evolution of children's literature in the Dutch Caribbean serves as an important example of the intersectionality of colonialism, language use, and the accessibility of children's literature to the majority populations.

The Netherlands Antilles, originally composed of Dutch colonies—the Leeward Islands (Aruba, Bonaire, and Curaçao) and the Windward Islands (Sint Maarten, Sint Eustatius, and Saba)—together with the colony of Suriname on the South American continent, became nominatively equal members of the Kingdom of the Netherlands in 1954. Resistance to embedded hierarchies of color that excluded Afro-Caribbean people from full participation in government activities emerged during a revolt in 1969 in Curaçao, the most populated island of the archipelago, sparking reevaluations of the relationships between the kingdom and its members. In 1975, Suriname seceded from the kingdom and gained independence. While not immediately recognized, Aruba became its own constituent country of the Kingdom of the Netherlands in 1986, with Curaçao and Sint Maarten following suit in 2010. The remaining islands chose to become municipalities, governed by a national Caribbean Dutch council in charge of education and other administrative matters. While Dutch remains an official language of the archipelago, several other languages now share this status. Such language diversity and colonial history influence the language of available literature for children in both libraries and educational systems.

As Monique Alberts-Luijdjens notes in her review of the Dutch-instituted library system, in the early twentieth century, libraries served as repositories for the colonial elites and as sites of acculturation for citizens expected to read material in Dutch, mandated by law for use in the schools in 1907 (35–36). Earlier, the Leeward Islands were heavily influenced by Venezuelan settlement and included the establishment of colleges (with Spanish instruction) in the nineteenth century; Catholic Venezuelan priests rans schools, which included instruction in Papiamentu, the local Portuguese-based Creole (in contrast to the Spanish-based Creole Papiamento of Aruba).[4] But the Dutch decided to reassert their cultural presence in the twentieth century with the conversion of all instruction to Dutch at all levels in 1907. In the nineteenth century, libraries were separated according to language, with both Dutch- and Spanish-language-based libraries in existence (Alberts-Luijdjens 34–35). Dutch-language libraries suffered in terms of clientele. Only a small percentage of citizens used them, with colonial libraries closing temporarily in the predominately English-speaking Windward Islands due to lack of membership in the 1930s. They were staffed by volunteers until the 1950s, when the Netherlands first sent trained librarians (37). Not until the 1980s did such libraries gain traction with local patrons with the establishment of the Antillean Public Library Association, which offered training to local librarians in multilingual literatures. The government investment in library buildings in the same decade in Curaçao, Aruba, and Sint Maarten, and the expansion of the language base of these library collections to include creoles, has attracted patrons (37). Such movements coincide with the greater acceptance of Papiamentu/o in public education, impacting then the growth and availability of multilingual children's literature.

In the 1960s, when educators and school administrators born locally started to outnumber their European counterparts, the use of Dutch as the language of instruction became a contentious issue, linked to deepening cultural interest in strengthening local identity but also spurred by high attrition rates of the majority non-Dutch-speaking students (Frank 112). A 1976 UNESCO study indicated that the Dutch-mandated instruction served as a roadblock to literacy for local populations. Many educators argued that the dropout rates—up to 50 percent before graduation in 2001—were due to the difficulty of learning to write and read in a foreign language before even speaking it (Dijkhoff and Pereira 244). By the mid-1980s, Papiamentu/o gained status as a subject area in primary schools throughout the Antilles; by the 1990s teachers began training in teaching the language, and with gradual adoption of standardized orthographies—while differing between islands—Papiamentu/o become the language of instruction at the lower levels (Eckkrammer 84). Such an educational shift has coincided with the growth of the children's literature industry, whose locally known authors now write in multiple languages—Papiamentu/o, Spanish, English, and Dutch. Historically, as Marta Dijkhoff and Joyce Pereira note, Papiamentu/o has been denigrated as the language of enslavement, with Dutch the language of status (240, 244); increased distancing from colonial rule and political resistance to both language and color hierarchies, including the adoption of Papiamentu/o in popular media and news outlets, paved the way for the emergence of local talent mindful of the language and content needs of their citizens. Cornet provides coverage of this transition in chapter 1, "Language, Authenticity, and Representation in Dutch Caribbean Children's and Young Adult Literature."

Other language regions have faced similar transitions, struggling to recognize and integrate Creole into education programs to supplement the language of official instruction, part and parcel of the break from the ideologies of colonial education. In Haiti, for example, the adoption of the French-based Creole, literally translated as "Creole" (Kreyòl), as an official language in 1987 has led to some instructional flexibility, impacting the production of children's literature in Creole and bilingual texts. Like the colonial situation in the Dutch Caribbean, the colonizer's French serves as the language of instruction and all official and government business. The majority of monolingual Creole speakers (95 percent, with only 5 to 10 percent French-receptive) have little avenue for public engagement outside of their language communities (Zéphir 123). While advocacy for educational reform started in the 1970s, citizens remain resistant to having students learn in Creole because of its second-class status (Zéphir 121). Since the 2010 earthquake and the rebuilding of educational institutions, there has been a new push to integrate Creole to increase literacy, measured in 2006 at 70 percent for those aged fifteen to twenty-four, with an increase to 83 percent in 2016 (UNESCO Institute for Statistics). In the US, Educa Vision provides a large sampling of English/Creole, Creole, and French educational books for children.

In the broader Francophone region, literature for children remains shaped by adult traditions, or so argues Louise Hardwick in chapter 2, "Children's Literature and the Theme of Childhood in the Francophone Caribbean: An Overview." In French overseas departments—Guadeloupe, Martinique, and French Guiana—and overseas semiautonomous collectivities Saint Martin (sharing the same island as Sint Maarten) and Saint Barthélemy, French remains the language of instruction. Caribbean writers well known for their work for adults—Gisèle Pineau (Guadeloupe/France), Maryse Condé (Guadeloupe), Patrick Chamoiseau (Martinique/France), and Dany Laferrière (Haiti/Canada)—now write children's and young adult books, deepening and enhancing a children's literary tradition through their awareness of literary debates central to the neocolonial condition. These writers for children offer keen insights into the hardships faced by children—the *restavek* children of Haiti (children from poor families lent out, or trafficked, frequently to urban families to work as slaves), the persecution of young Haitians in other island nations if they are able to escape from Haiti, and other elements of difficulty typically not represented in Western children's literature. Some writers, in their adult fiction, deeply critical of colorism and sexism, also address the persecution of women, all issues echoed in literature for young people.

School libraries can also play a role in introducing children to local literatures, but their presence in the Caribbean has been impacted by colonial histories, local economies, and the ongoing threat of natural disasters, whether that be hurricanes, floods, or earthquakes. Such events destroy power grids and buildings, damaging collections through mold and water, with such frequency that accessibility to books and computers can remain limited.[5] School libraries were developed in haphazard ways under colonialism. For example, throughout the Anglophone region, comprising eighteen nations and territories, Great Britain established libraries beginning in the 1940s with in-school collections, but the British did not formally provide actual rooms or library personnel until the 1970s, according to Cherrell Shelley-Robinson (97). These collections were not connected to any curricula, or accorded space or supervision; they were simply housed in classrooms or on a bookshelf in a hallway (97). These beginnings, Shelley-Robinson argues, account for the ongoing lack of interest and economic investment in such libraries in the Anglophone region, with the exception of a few nations: Trinidad and Tobago, Jamaica, and Antigua and Barbuda have all developed sophisticated school libraries with trained staff, facilities, and computer access (97). Other language regions have established connections between local libraries and schools, such as in (Francophone) Martinique and Guadeloupe, where librarians coordinate literacy initiatives between schools and public libraries, according to Louise Hardwick (see chapter 2 of this volume). The economic status of each island plays a crucial role in developing and sustaining its educational institutions and public resources. The Anglophone Caribbean remains heavily influenced by Great Britain—but also has seen significant changes in the content of its libraries with many books, published both locally and abroad, featuring representations of local children and settings instead of those of the former colonizers. Betsy Nies explores these literary transitions in chapter 3, "Anglophone Caribbean Children's Literature: A Snapshot."

Among the Spanish-speaking countries in the Caribbean region, Puerto Rico and Costa Rica nationalized their school library systems in the 1980s (Figueras). While Cuba remains the most literate nation in the Americas—with 98 percent of its population receiving at least an eighth-grade education and the highest percentage of teachers per capita in the world—its extensive library system remains encumbered by the datedness of its print material, due to the US embargo and the government's restriction of internet service. Additionally, while all schools have libraries with a professional staff, materials are tied to a highly structured state curriculum (Hamilton 4). Regardless of ideological restrictions, Cuban literature for children has undergone changes worth reviewing. Zeila Frade, in chapter 4, "Before and After the Revolution: An Exploration of the Trajectory of Cuban Children's Literature," explores these shifts and current expansion of themes of Cuban children's literature, which now treats such controversial issues as divorce and voluntary departures of Cubans for the US. Additionally, many Cuban writers and descendants of Cubans in exile produce outstanding material, published and circulating across borders. Joel Franz Rosell (France/Cuba), Alma Flor Ada (US/Cuba), and Margarita Engle (US/Cuba) are a few of the most prolific. The award-winning Cuban-born author Cristina García (US) also now writes for children.

Access to local literatures for children also requires, importantly, an introduction to such literature via teacher preparation programs, curriculum planners, and school administrators. Aisha Spencer contends that "theoretical discussions on the distinctive Caribbean textual features in and the unique literary experience of Caribbean children's literature continue to be insufficient" (see chapter 11 of this volume). She argues that this academic reality impacts the use of such literature by teachers and administrators in Jamaica's school system. While folklore has been integrated into curricula at the primary levels, Jamaican schools offer little in terms of contemporary Caribbean children's literature, Spencer argues. Colonial relationships have impacted territories as well. For example, in Puerto Rico, following the US invasion in 1898 and the subsequent reorganization of schools, local teachers were fired and English-speaking US teachers hired, to acclimatize and teach students to be US citizens (Stokas-Gonzalez 49–50). Even today, teachers are instructed in educational philosophies tied to US rhetoric and literatures in English (Stokas-Gonzalez 51). Carmen Milagros Torres-Rivera, who teaches adolescent and children's literature at the University of Puerto Rico, writes,

> At present, teacher educators in Puerto Rico rely on texts written for an American educational setting such as *Charlotte Huck's Children's Literature* (Children's Literature in the Elementary School) edited by Barbara Kiefer; the only work that addresses local literature is *Un siglo de literatura infantil Puertorriqueña/A Century of Puerto Rican Children's Literature* written by Flor Piñeiro de Rivera (1987), which is out of print. ("Unsilencing the Voices")

In chapter 5 of this volume, "Puerto Rican Children's Literature on the Archipelago," María Acevedo-Aquino provides insights into Puerto Rico's children's literary history and the inevitable waves of resistance to colonization, occupation, and territorial status. Similarly, Stacy Ann Creech traces the impact of colonial history on racial representation in children's literature in the Dominican Republic and recent efforts to challenge the hegemonic reverence for whiteness in chapter 6, "Blackness, Imperialism, and Nationalism in Dominican Children's Literature." In chapter 7, "A Brief History of Costa Rican Children's Literature," Ann González reviews the interrelationship between Costa Rica's children's literary history, its national identity, and its Caribbean coastline; characters and folk heroes of indigenous or Afro-Caribbean ancestry play important roles in these books. Quince Duncan, born of Jamaican and Barbadian parents, remains a widely heralded writer for children with his stories of the Atlantic coast and his experiences of racism as an Afro-Caribbean.

Part 2: Decolonizing Children's Literature in the Anglophone Caribbean and Its Diaspora

A review of the history of the Anglophone Caribbean, sometimes referred to as the Commonwealth Caribbean (all countries and territories formerly colonized by Great Britain), provides insight into the nuances of the complex relationship between colonialism, the emergence of local literatures, and language variation in such literatures, in particular the use of Creole. The region includes ten independent island nations, two mainland nations (Belize and Guyana), and five territories. Other English-speaking nations outside of the Commonwealth but within the Anglophone Caribbean include the US Virgin Islands, Puerto Rico (nominally, with English imposed as an official language), and Sint Maarten.[6]

With independence, the transformation of children's literature and its pedagogical function was shaped by competing interests: a desire to increase literacy rates by teaching children Standard English *and* to replace the colonial curricula with material that reflected local cultures and populations. For example, after gaining independence in 1962, Trinidad and Tobago formulated an educational plan for 1968–1983 seeking to right the wrongs of colonial education that had denigrated island citizens through their very invisibility. The government of Trinidad and Tobago sought to encourage national identity formation through education:

> Full national independence and identity will be achieved and secured only on the basis of an educational system which does not rely on foreign assumptions and references for its existence and growth. Every component of the system would require to have, as the foundation of its validity, its relevance to the needs of the peoples it serves. (Organization of American States)

Such aspirational goals, however, often competed with ingrained biases favoring colonial curricula that had educated the very people seeking such reforms. Since independence, many Caribbean countries have developed curricula that reflect local culture, even as they retain the language and often the values of the colonizer.

Prolific Jamaican children's author and linguist Jean D'Costa provides an excellent example of this tension when she investigated having her first children's book, *Sprat Morrison* (1972), adopted in Jamaica's primary school system. Following Jamaica's independence in 1962, D'Costa sought the blessing of the Jamaican Ministry of Education regarding the incorporation of local language—including Jamaican Creole—into her book. As D'Costa writes in her recollection of this incident,

> If the book was to pass the censorship of the Ministry of Education, the teaching profession, and the parent group, then there could be no overt trace of Creole or dialect anywhere in it. Senior education officers whom I consulted in 1969 laid down these rules. *The ministry would not introduce any text containing the smallest trace of nonstandard into any classroom or school library.* (76; italics in original)

To accommodate these strictures, D'Costa had to remove her protagonist from informal peer interactions such as the "street, market, playground, backyard, back-fence, and joke-telling episodes" that require language registers unacceptable to this mandate (76). While she did use informal Standard Jamaican English to connect with her audience, her plight when writing this book reflects the decades of struggle that Caribbean writers for children face both in trade book publication and in the inclusion of such work in educational settings.

At the secondary level, writers also encountered challenges including vernaculars in school readers following emancipation. Educator John Figueroa of the University of the West Indies' Department of Education advocated early on for the transformation of the literature curricula. At the 1961 Conference of the Association of Caribbean Headmasters and Headmistresses, he argued that students should "become familiar with their heritage," including "the greater study of West Indian Literature" (17, 18). As historian Gail Low notes,

> Critiques of the Anglophilic orientation of Caribbean high schools also became more vociferous with the election of the premiers of Independent Jamaica and Trinidad and Tobago, Norman Manley and Eric Williams [in 1959 and 1962, respectively]. Both argued for a break with Cambridge which they represented as central to an outmoded colonial regime. (108)

Movements toward a local pan-Caribbean regulatory agency for testing spurred overseas publishers to produce cheap readers for the growing secondary school population in Anglophone territories and nations (Low 110). A spate of readers featuring Caribbean literature followed, such as Cecil Gray's *Response: A Course in Narrative Comprehension and Composition for Caribbean Secondary Schools* (1969) with stories by writers such as Michael Anthony, Monica Skeete, Merle Hodge, and Victor Reid.[7] Longman, Collins, Macmillan, and Heinemann all appointed Caribbean editors to build curricula in the 1960s (Low 111). Anne Walmsley of the UK, who taught in Jamaica from 1959 to 1962, was finally able to publish *The Sun's Eye: West Indian Writing for Young Readers* (1968) with Longman, after the Jamaican Ministry of Education rejected the reader based on objections to the inclusion of Sam Selvon's "The Village Washer," which included Creole (Walmsley 76). Working with Figueroa in 1968, Heinemann established its Caribbean Writers series, which included three books deemed appropriate for use in secondary schools: V. S. Naipaul's *Miguel Street* (1959), George Lamming's *In the Castle of My Skin* (1953), and Michael Anthony's *A Year in San Fernando* (1965) (Low 115). The advent of the Caribbean Examinations Council in 1973 legitimized such a curricular transformation.

Barbadian poet and academic Kamau Brathwaite contributed to the conversation when he coined the term "nation language" in 1984 as a positive term for the language of the majority, part of the nation-building rhetoric popularized postindependence:

> We in the Caribbean have a . . . kind of plurality: we have English, which is the imposed language on much of the archipelago. It is an imperial language, as are French, Dutch, and Spanish. . . . We have also what is called nation language, which is the kind of English spoken by the people who were brought to the Caribbean, not the official English now, but the language of slaves and labourers, the servants who were brought in. (*History of the Voice* 5–6)

Condemning the use of the term "dialect" as a pejorative term for Creole, Brathwaite instead honored the African roots that inform the grammatical structures and phonemes of most creoles throughout the region. He continues,

> Nation language is the language which is influenced very strongly by the African model, the African aspect of our New World/Caribbean heritage. English it may be in terms of some of its lexical features. But in its contours, its rhythm and its timbre, its sound explosions, it is not English, even though the words, as you hear them, might be English to a greater or lesser degree. (*History of the Voice* 13)

Brathwaite's "nation language" gained in popularity as a tool for political change.

During the 1960s and after, writers for adults broke the language barrier, increasing their use of the vernacular, including Creole, in fiction and poetry. This sea change was informed by publicly embraced orature for children. For example, Louise Bennett, more affectionately called by one of her public personas in her dramatic monologues—the opinionated "Miss Lou"—hosted a children's show called *Ring Ding* on Jamaica's National Broadcasting Service from 1968 to 1980, speaking and writing in Brathwaite's nation language. The visibility of such performances raised acceptance of the use of patois as a sign of Jamaican pride; her poetry, including her well-known "Colonization in Reverse" (an ironic take on the emigration of Jamaicans to Great Britain), was integrated into school curricula. Trinidadian storyteller, poet, and comedian Paul Keens-Douglas, an admirer of Bennett, similarly wrote poetry and told stories in talk tent performances (held outside in tents often at carnivals or festivals) and made recordings intended for family audiences in the 1970s and 1980s. Works by writers for adults were integrated into secondary schools—Anthony, Selvon, Hodge, and Earl Lovelace in the 1970s—were followed in the

1980s and 1990s by prominent female writers such as Bennett, Olive Senior, Erna Brodber, and Zee Edgell who also used vernacular in their fiction.

Geraldine Skeete, a former student and teacher at the primary, secondary, and tertiary levels in Trinidad (currently a lecturer at the University of the West Indies), discusses the impact on students and teachers of the integration of Caribbean-based readers in Trinidad's junior secondary classrooms in this volume's chapter 8, "Back to *Backfire*: The Pedagogical Impact of the Giuseppis' Caribbean Short Story Collection in the Secondary School System of Trinidad and Tobago from the 1970s to the Present." While previously, secondary schools served only the lucky few with high test scores and scholarships—or the ability to pay tuition—independence brought the opening of public junior secondary schools, free to all. Elements of Creole are included in some stories in the Giuseppis' reader, demonstrating a progressive attempt to represent the linguistic variety and daily speech of the population. The short stories of this reader reflect the daily lives of students with familiar situations and sayings, and is accessible to those without strong literacy skills, an important stepping stone to more advanced material.

But the battle over the use of Creole in schoolbooks and trade books remains in play across the region. In a review of the use of nation languages in Caribbean trade books for children aged nine through sixteen, Karen Sanderson-Cole and Barbara Lalla explore Creole's presence (or absence) in such literature dating back to the late 1950s in chapter 9, "Creole vs. Standard English: Negotiating Voice in Caribbean Children's Literature." They discover that Creole use, through the 1980s, is restricted to folklore figures, the aged, and lower-class characters without an education. Only in the past few decades has Creole been represented in a fluid manner, reflective not only of group sensibilities but also of individual speakers who code-switch according to the situation. In recent young adult books, Creole can signify empowerment and self-actualization, a notable change since D'Costa wrote her first book for children in the late 1960s. Sanderson-Cole and Lalla introduce a range of young adult works from Barbados, Belize, Jamaica, Trinidad, and Guyana, noting that picture books for children still rely on Standard English.

In chapter 10, "Tradition and Modernity: Grace Hallworth and a Vision of the Caribbean for British Readers," Karen Sands-O'Connor discovers similar patterns in language use in her examination of Hallworth's work. A Trinidadian librarian who immigrated to the US, Canada, and Great Britain, Hallworth wrote and produced children's literature anthologies and books.

In 1977, she launched a collection of Caribbean stories titled *Listen to This Story* in primarily Standard British English. By 1990, she more comfortably included a range of vernaculars in *Cric Crac: A Collection of West Indian Stories*, as Sands-O'Connor notes, without apology. She joins a bevy of writers in the United Kingdom, such as Jamaican-born Christine Craig, who authored the first fully illustrated book featuring Jamaican children, *Emanuel and His Parrot* (1970), followed by *Emanuel Goes to Market* (1971), illustrated by Jamaican Karl "Jerry" Craig. Other British-based Caribbean authors publishing after 1970 include Guyanese-born writers John Agard and Grace Nichols, and Benjamin Zephaniah, born to Jamaican and Barbadian parents. All vacillate between Standard British English and Caribbean Englishes in their poetry and prose for children and young adults, showing wider use of the vernacular as the decades progress.[8]

In chapter 11, "Reading Words, Reading Worlds: Understanding the Value of the Literary Experience in the Process of Reading Caribbean Children's Books in the Jamaican Primary School System," the aforementioned Aisha Spencer, who served as a secondary school teacher for eighteen years in Jamaica before becoming a faculty member at the University of the West Indies, Mona, argues that the colonial legacy still affects Jamaican lower-level teaching and school administration. In her exploration of primary teachers' attitudes toward teaching reading, Spencer believes that the colonial stigma attached to illiteracy and fears about student success still inform pedagogical practices. She argues that anxieties about testing stem from a colonial background that encourages teachers to teach for such simple skills as recall and pronunciation, ignoring then the context of reading, rendering it an act of performance rather than of comprehension. The continued use of basal readers at the lower levels that do not represent their readership or highlight the oral structures of the target population renders the search for meaning difficult. Spencer reviews several Caribbean picture books, pointing out ways students can experientially connect to content in addition to understanding the intricacies and nuances of literary language.

Learning abroad, Caribbean immigrant schoolchildren face similar challenges connecting with curricular material when not provided with language arts material that represents their home countries. With the current emphasis on multiculturalism and diverse literatures in the US education system, Caribbean and Caribbean American children's literature is not featured in book lists with such emphasis, or so notes Consuella Bennett in chapter 12,

"Seriously! Reading and Righting Images of the Caribbean in the American Classroom." In her review of current multiethnic curricula, she notes that the absence of Caribbean literature can impact new immigrant populations who seek to connect to reading material or find a context suggestive of home. She outlines a series of books by authors of the Caribbean and its diaspora, including Andrew Salkey's *Hurricane* (1964) and more recent works such as *Before We Were Free* (2002) by Dominican American Julia Alvarez and *The Jumbies* (2015) by Trinidadian American Tracey Baptiste. Bennett sees bringing such fictional narratives into the US classroom as one step toward dismantling popular conceptions of the Caribbean as simply sun, sea, and sand. She also inventively pairs these works with other international texts to encourage teachers and young people to think globally and broaden their often limited horizons.

Part 3: Picture Books and Publishing

Part 3 examines the publishing challenges for local writers and the contributions to picture books by writers of the diaspora. While prominent writers of adult fiction who are internationally known may not have difficulty finding an established publishing house with its bevy of illustrators to produce their work, those within the region who write solely for children face a different battle. Publishers in the region publish primarily for educational purposes, leaving the complex and costly work of hiring illustrators to create highly polished picture books a financial burden difficult to lift. While certainly many Caribbean writers find international publishers—and local publishers do publish some trade books—they may instead write for educational reading programs instead of pursuing their own creative arc.[9] In this section, local children's authors converse about the children's literature publishing industry in the Caribbean, followed by attention to the works of authors with international visibility. In chapter 13, "Publishing Children's Literature in the Caribbean: Four Authors' Perspectives," Joanne Gail Johnson of Trinidad, editor of Caribbean Macmillan's tween Island Fiction series and writer and director of the family film *Sally's Way* (2015), dialogues with other Caribbean children's authors: Diane Browne of Jamaica; Puerto Rican playwright, puppeteer, and television producer Tere Marichal-Lugo; and Ada Haiman, professor emeritus of the University of Puerto Rico and author of *Tulipán: The Puerto Rican Giraffe*, part of a picture book series.

In chapter 14, "Creating Picture Books: Reflections of Edwidge Danticat, Olive Senior, and Junot Díaz," three authors of worldwide acclaim gather in conversation to discuss their approach to writing picture books. Danticat, winner of multiple awards, has published children's fiction since 2002; her works include three picture books, one children's novel, and three young adult novels. Her picture books include *Eight Days: A Story of Haiti* (2010), illustrated by Alix Delinois; *Mama's Nightingale: A Story of Immigration and Separation* (2015), with Leslie Staub; and *My Mommy Medicine* (2019) with Shannon Wright. Senior, winner of the Commonwealth Writers' Prize for a book used in Caribbean secondary schools—*Summer Lightening and Other Stories* (1987)—began publishing picture books in 2012. While Danticat addresses the trauma of the 2010 earthquake and US detention, Senior's picture books draw on remembrances of her rural Jamaican childhood. They include *Birthday Suit* with Eugenie Fernandes (2012); and *Anna Carries Water* (2014) and *Boonoonoonous Hair* (2019), both illustrated by Laura James. Díaz, who won the Pulitzer Prize for Fiction in 2008 for *The Brief Wondrous Life of Oscar Wao* (2007), published his first picture book, *Islandborn* (2018), with illustrator Leo Espinosa. He integrates memories of a Dominican American community, which include references to the brutal Dominican dictator Rafael Trujillo through symbolism. The three authors dialogue about this transition—from writing for adults about trauma to writing for young readers who are visually minded, offering them hope among the wreckage. The interplay between text and image takes on new dimensions in a medium with so few words. Megan Jeanette Myers, in chapter 15, "Making Memories or *Pesadillas*? Junot Díaz's *Islandborn*," analyzes Díaz's take on historical trauma, examining the interplay between text and image. These authors offer their readers a sense of community even if they have never been to their ancestral homes.

♦ ♦ ♦

Both volumes of the present anthology aim to build an awareness of the tripwires and tipping points of contemporary Caribbean children's literature as a field, showcasing the ways it has surged forward to provide children with the representation they need, or has developed more quietly, struggling to be recognized. Current children's literature has moved beyond the content of the colonial literature of parent countries with their snow-covered landscapes and groves of apple trees. Caribbean books now mirror Caribbean daily life or local fantasies that include regionally based folklore figures. Children ride bikes, gather coconuts, engage in adventures, and unpack mysteries that emerge in response to local incidents linked to storytelling or myths, to be solved by journeying through island landscapes. The characters live in urban or rural spaces, often in comforting homes with multiple relatives present. These scenes stand in opposition to colonial fantasies about the Caribbean depicted in British and French literature for children. In these European works, women are erotically fashioned, wearing fruit baskets on their heads, a common colonial trope. Peasants find themselves easily duped by other, more worldly characters, a version of the trickster story but also indicative of European views of peasants as illiterate and ignorant. Locally written contemporary Caribbean children's literature, in contrast, depicts familiar scenes yet also addresses local issues—the need for code-switching between Creole and Standard languages to navigate social interactions, practices for surviving a hurricane, and ways to preserve the environment and fight the dangerous effects of climate change. Such books may include elements of the orature of the people, the proverbs and stories of previous generations. Nation language has made its way into young adult books, with the vernacular also finding some representation in material for lower grades. The field of transnational children's literature should draw its riches not from surface-level multicultural representations, but rather from the deep cultural dive Caribbean children's literature offers.

Notes

1. See Aisha Spencer's "Reading Words, Reading Worlds: Understanding the Value of the Literary Experience in the Process of Reading Caribbean Children's Books in the Jamaican Primary School System," chapter 11 in this volume; and Diane Browne, in conversation with other local writers in chapter 13 of this volume.

2. This is not to overlook or understate the importance of writers for children who contribute in ongoing ways to the development of curricula through the publication of series books such as Carlong's Sand Pebbles Pleasure Series.

3. Florencia V. Cornet's translation; see chapter 1 of this volume.

4. As Cornet notes, "Curaçao and Bonaire speak and write Papiamentu while Aruba speaks and writes Papiamento (though we can all understand and communicate with each other). There is a clear difference between the spoken and written forms in the

Portuguese-based Papiamentu and the Spanish-based Papiamento" (side note on a draft version of chapter 1 of this volume).

5. For coverage of issues facing Puerto Rican public libraries, see Mariela Santos-Muñiz's article "Puerto Rican Librarians Call for Greater Investment in Library Sciences and Infrastructure to Serve Public Needs"; and George M. Eberhart's "Hurricane Maria: The Aftermath."

6. Despite its status as a Dutch possession, Sint Maarten's everyday language of communication is English, which is also the first language of most of the territory's residents. Most Sint Maarteners learn Dutch as a second language.

7. Other anthologies include Kenneth Ramchand, *West Indian Narrative: An Introductory Anthology* (1966); G. R. Coulthard, *Caribbean Literature* (1966); O. R. Dathorne, *Caribbean Narrative: An Anthology* (1966); O. R. Dathorne, *Caribbean Verse: An Anthology* (1967); John Figueroa, *Caribbean Voices: An Anthology of West Indian Poetry* (1966); Andrew Salkey, *Caribbean Prose* (1967); Anne Walmsley, *The Sun's Eye: West Indian Writing for Young Readers* (1968); and Therese Mills, *Great West Indians: Life Stories for Young Readers* (1973).

8. See Sands-O'Connor, *Soon Come Home to This Island*, 159–64, for an analysis of language use by these authors in their poetry for young adults.

9. Educational publishers who also publish trade books include Caribbean Reads of Saint Kitts and Nevis; Blue Banyan Books and LMH Publishing of Jamaica; Editorial Gente Nueva of Cuba; and Éditions Jasor, Éditions Nestor, and PLB Éditions of Guadeloupe. Several small publishing houses of the diaspora also carry lines for children that emphasize Caribbean authorship: Campanita Books (Spanish/English) and Little Bell Caribbean, both imprints of Editorial Campana in New York; and Peepal Tree Press of the United Kingdom.

Works Cited

Alberts-Luijdjens, Monique. "Historical Development of Libraries in the Netherlands Antilles and Aruba." *Caribbean Libraries in the 21st Century: Changes, Challenges, and Choices*, edited by Cheryl Peltier-Davis and Shamin Renwick, Information Today, 2007, pp. 31–40.

Arnold, A. James, editor. *A History of Literature in the Caribbean*. Vol. 2, *English- and Dutch-Speaking Regions*. John Benjamins, 2001.

Arnold, A. James, editor. *A History of Literature in the Caribbean*. Vol. 3, *Cross-Cultural Studies*. John Benjamins, 1997.

Arnold, A. James, Julio Rodriguez-Luis, and J. Michael Dash, editors. *A History of Literature in the Caribbean*. Vol. 1, *Hispanic and Francophone Regions*. John Benjamins, 1994.

Bello, Yahaya. "Caribbean American Children's Literature." *Teaching Multicultural Children's Literature in Grades K–8*, edited by Violet J. Harris, Christopher-Gordon Publishers, 1992, pp. 245–65.

Benítez-Rojo, Antonio. "Introduction: The Repeating Island." *The Repeating Island: The Caribbean and the Postmodern Perspective*, Duke UP, 1996, 1–32.

Bishop, Rudine Sims. "Mirrors, Windows, and Sliding Glass Doors." *Perspectives: Choosing and Using Books for the Classroom*, vol. 6, no. 3, Summer 1990, pp. ix–xi. https://scenicregional.org/wp-content/uploads/2017/08/Mirrors-Windows-and-Sliding-Glass-Doors.pdf.

Bradford, Clare. *Unsettling Narratives: Postcolonial Readings of Children's Literature*. Wilfrid Laurier UP, 2007.

Brathwaite, Edward Kamau. "Caribbean Man in Space and Time." *Savacou*, nos. 11–12, September 1975, pp. 1–11.

Brathwaite, Edward Kamau. *History of the Voice: The Development of Nation Language in Anglophone Caribbean Poetry*. New Beacon Books, 1984.

Broek, Aart G. "Ideological Controversies in Curaçaoan Publishing Strategies (1900–1945)." *A History of the Literature in the Caribbean*, vol. 2, *English- and Dutch-Speaking Regions*, edited by A. James Arnold, John Benjamins, 2001, pp. 375–85.

Browne, Marguerite Diane. "'I Will Not Look at Books the Same Way Again': Teachers' Opinions about the Use of Caribbean Children's Literature." 2003. U of the West Indies, Mona Campus, master's thesis.

Cummings, Ronald, and Alison Donnell, editors. *Caribbean Literature in Transition*. Vol. 3, *1970–2020*. Cambridge UP, 2021.

Dalleo, Raphael, and Curdella Forbes, editors. *Caribbean Literature in Transition*. Vol. 2, *1920–1970*. Cambridge UP, 2021.

D'Costa, Jean. "The Caribbean Novelist and Language: A Search for a Literary Medium." *Caribbean Literary Discourse: Voice and Cultural Identity in the Anglophone Caribbean*, edited by Barbara Lalla, Jean D'Costa, and Velma Pollard, U of Alabama P, 2014, pp. 68–92.

De Matas, Jarrel. "Adopting the Shadows: Caribbean Childhood Noir in Kevin Jared Hosein's *The Repenters* and Ezekiel Alan's *Disposable People*." *Tout Moun: Caribbean Journal of Cultural Studies*, vol. 4, no. 2, November 2018, pp. 1–14.

Dijkhoff, Marta, and Joyce Pereira. "Language and Education in Aruba, Bonaire and Curaçao." *Creoles in Education: An Appraisal of Current Programs and Projects*, edited by Bettina Migge, Isabelle Léglise, and Angela Bartens, John Benjamins, 2010, pp. 237–72.

Eberhart, George M. "Hurricane Maria: The Aftermath." American Libraries, January 2, 2018. americanlibrariesmagazine.org/2018/01/02/hurricane-maria-aftermath-caribbean-libraries/.

Eckkrammer, Eva Martha. "Papiamentu, Cultural Resistance, and Socio-Cultural Challenges: The ABC Islands in a Nutshell." *Journal of Caribbean Literatures*, vol. 5, no. 1, Summer 2007, pp. 73–93.

Edward, Summer. "Caribbean Literary Culture's Gatekeeping of Caribbean Children's Literature." May 16, 2015. www.summeredward.com/2015/05/caribbean-literary-cultures-gatekeeping_61.html.

Enz, Molly Krueger. "The Haitian Flight for Freedom in Maryse Condé's *Rêves amers* and Marie-Célie Agnant's *Alexis d'Haïti*." *Contemporary French and Francophone Studies*, vol. 22, no. 5, December 2018, pp. 553–61.

Fanon, Frantz. *Black Skin, White Masks*. Translated by Charles L. Markmann, Grove Press, 1967.

Figueras, Consuelo. "Library Services to Youth in Some Latin American Countries." *School Libraries Worldwide*, vol. 3, no. 1, January 1997, pp. 61–70.

Figueroa, John. *Staffing and Examinations in British Caribbean Secondary Schools*. Evans, 1964.

Frank, Francine Wattman. "Language and Education in the Leeward Netherlands Antilles." *Caribbean Studies*, vol. 13, no. 4, January 1974, pp. 111–17.

Freire, Paulo. *Pedagogy of the Oppressed*. Translated by Myra Bergman Ramos, Herder and Herder, 1970.

García Vega, Melissa. *Living Legacies: Folkloric Characters Forge Environmental Awareness in Caribbean Children's Literature*. 2016. U of Puerto Rico, PhD dissertation.

Glissant, Édouard. "The Cultural Creolization of the World: Interview with Edouard Glissant." Interview by Tirthankar Chanda. *Label France*, no. 38. ehess.

modelisationsavoirs.fr/lubat/creolisation/the-cultural-creolization-of-the-world.-interview-with-edouard-glissant_6589.pdf.
Glissant, Édouard. *Poetics of Relation*. Translated by Betsy Wing, U of Michigan P, 1997.
González, Ann. *Resistance and Survival: Children's Narrative from Central America and the Caribbean*. U of Arizona P, 2009.
Haiman, Ada. *The Discourses of Childhood: A Child-Centered Critique of Anglo-Caribbean Literature*. 2006. U of Puerto Rico, PhD dissertation.
Hamilton, Stuart. "Librarians or Dissidents? Critics and Supporters of the Independent Libraries in Cuba Project." *Progressive Librarian*, nos. 19–20, Spring 2002, pp. 3–46.
Hardwick, Louise. *Childhood, Autobiography and the Francophone Caribbean*. Liverpool UP, 2013.
Huggins, Sujin. *How Did We Get Here? An Examination of the Collection of Contemporary Caribbean Juvenile Literature in the Children's Library of the National Library of Trinidad & Tobago and Trinidadian Children's Response to Selected Titles*. 2012. U of Illinois, PhD dissertation.
Hunt, Peter, editor. *Understanding Children's Literature: Key Essays from the Second Edition of the International Companion Encyclopedia of Children's Literature*. Routledge, 2009.
James, Cynthia. "From Orature to Literature in Jamaican and Trinidadian Children's Folk Traditions." *Children's Literature Association Quarterly*, vol. 30, no. 2, Summer 2005, pp. 164–78.
Joseph, Lynn. *A Wave in Her Pocket: Stories from Trinidad*. Clarion Books, 1991.
Kahn, Richard. "From Education for Sustainable Development to Ecopedagogy: Sustaining Capitalism or Sustaining Life?" *Green Theory and Praxis: The Journal of Ecopedagogy*, vol. 4, no. 1, June 2008, pp. 1–14.
Lambert, David. "An Introduction to the Caribbean, Empire and Slavery." British Library, West India Regiments, November 16, 2017. www.bl.uk/west-india-regiment/articles/an-introduction-to-the-caribbean-empire-and-slavery.
Low, Gail. "'Read! Learn!' Grobalisation and (G)localisation in Caribbean Textbook Publishing." *The Global Histories of Books: Methods and Practices*, edited by Elleke Boehmer, Rouven Kunstmann, Priyasha Mukhopadhyay, and Asha Rogers, Palgrave Macmillan, 2017, pp. 99–127.
Lorenzi, Jane and Jeanne Batalove. "Caribbean Immigrants in the United States. Migration Information Source July 7, 2022. www.migrationpolicy.org/article/caribbean-immigrants-united states.
M'Baye, Babacar. *The Trickster Comes West: Pan-African Influence in Early Black Diasporan Narratives*. UP of Mississippi, 2009.
McKittrick, Katherine, editor. *Sylvia Wynter: On Being Human as Praxis*. Duke UP, 2015.
O'Callaghan, Evelyn, and Tim Watson, editors. *Caribbean Literature in Transition*. Vol. 1, *1800–1920*. Cambridge UP, 2021.
Okpewho, Isidore. Introduction. *The African Diaspora: African Origins and New World Identities*, edited by Isidore Okpewho, Carole Boyce Davies, and Ali A. Mazrui, Indiana UP, 1999.
Organization of American States. "Planning the Growth of Secondary Education." The Educational Portal of the Americas. www.educoas.org/Portal/bdigital/contenido/interamer/BkIACD/Interamer/Interamerhtml/Alleynehtml/AllCh6.htm.
Pérez Díaz, Enrique. "Central and South America and the Caribbean." *International Companion Encyclopedia of Children's Literature*, edited by Peter Hunt and Sheila G. Bannister Ray, Routledge, 1996, pp. 871–82.

Rampaul, Giselle, and Geraldine Elizabeth Skeete, editors. *The Child and the Caribbean Imagination*. U of the West Indies P, 2012.

Rutgers, Wim. *Bon dia! Met wie schrijf ik? Over Caraïbische jeugdliteratuur*. Charuba, 1988.

Sands-O'Connor, Karen. *Children's Publishing and Black Britain, 1965–2015*. Palgrave Macmillan, 2017.

Sands-O'Connor, Karen. *Soon Come Home to This Island: West Indians in British Children's Literature*. Routledge, 2008.

Santos-Muñiz, Mariela. "Puerto Rican Librarians Call for Greater Investment in Library Sciences and Infrastructure to Serve Public Needs." *Prism*, July 13, 2022. prismreports.org/2022/07/13/puerto-rican-librarians-investments-library-infrastructure/.

Shelley-Robinson, Cherrell. "School Libraries in the Caribbean: A Jamaican Case Study." *Caribbean Libraries in the 21st Century: Changes, Challenges, and Choices*, edited by Cheryl Peltier-Davis and Shamin Renwick, Information Today, 2007, pp. 95–118.

Spencer, Aisha. "'Breaking the Mirror': Reshaping Perceptions of National Progress through the Representation of Marginalized Cultural Realities in Caribbean Children's Stories." *The Routledge Companion to International Children's Literature*, edited by John Stephens, Routledge, 2017, pp. 114–22.

Stokas-Gonzalez, Ariana. "Teacher Formation and the Epistemic Suppression of Borinquen." *Philosophy of Education Yearbook*, edited by Eduardo Duarte, Philosophy of Education Society, 2015, pp. 46–54.

Teague, Latoya. "Not American Enough: African Diaspora, Unfinished Migrations, and Transnational Children's Literature." *Journal of Children's Literature*, vol. 47, no. 2, Fall 2021, pp. 35–47.

Torres-Rivera, Carmen Milagros. "Puerto Rican Children's Literature and the Need for Afro–Puerto Rican Stories." *Bookbird: A Journal of International Children's Literature*, vol. 52, no. 3, July 2014, pp. 81–85.

Torres-Rivera, Carmen Milagros. "Unsilencing the Voices of Afro–Puerto Rican Children and Young Adult Literature." 2020. U of Puerto Rico, unpublished manuscript.

UNESCO Institute for Statistics. "Literacy Rate, Youth Total (% of people ages 15–24)." World Bank, June 2022. data.worldbank.org/indicator/SE.ADT.1524.LT.ZS.

Vaclavik, Kiera. "'Damaging Goods? Francophone Children's Books in a Postcolonial World." *International Research in Children's Literature*, vol. 2, no. 2, December 2009, pp. 228–42.

Walmsley, Anne. "Sam Selvon: Gifts." *Kunapipi*, vol. 17, no. 1, 1995, pp. 76–77.

Wynter, Sylvia. "Towards the Sociogenic Principle: Fanon, Identity, the Puzzle of Conscious Experience, and What It Is Like to Be 'Black.'" *National Identities and Sociopolitical Changes in Latin America*, edited by Mercedes F. Durán-Cogan and Antonio Gómez-Moriana, Routledge, 2013, pp. 30–66.

Zapata, Angie, Thomas Crisp, Mary Napoli, and Vivian Yenika-Agbaw. "A Focus on Transnational Experiences in Children's Literature." *Journal of Children's Literature*, vol. 47, no. 2, Fall 2021, pp. 6–7.

Zéphir, Flore. "Challenges and Opportunities for Haitian Creole in the Educational System of Post-Earthquake Haiti." *International Journal of the Sociology of Language*, no. 233, April 2015, pp. 119–30.

PART 1

HISTORIES OF CARIBBEAN CHILDREN'S LITERATURE

CHAPTER 1

Language, Authenticity, and Representation in Dutch Caribbean Children's and Young Adult Literature

Florencia V. Cornet

The Complex Aesthetics of a People: Dutch Caribbean Literary Ontology

Within the rich body of literary works from the Dutch Caribbean, a selection of literary pieces focuses on the developing and maturation stages of protagonists. These children or young adults navigate the influences and experiences on their island or between the multiple countries that constitute the Dutch Kingdom. The writers who produce these types of literature expose the youth to picture books, poetry, drama, fantasy, and realism that reflect their social realities and conditions from the perspective of a Dutch Caribbean ontology.

When alluding to Dutch Caribbean children's and young adult literature, I am situating works produced by writers who are native to the islands that constitute the Dutch Caribbean and Caribbean Dutch. This chapter provides a brief overview of children's and young adult literature from the region. The focus is primarily on literature from Curaçao but extends to works produced by writers from Aruba, Bonaire, and Sint Maarten due to the established cultural, historical, insular, and interregional connections between the residents of these islands.

Since most Dutch Caribbean writers are prolific in multiple languages, including the native Creole language, Papiamentu/o, language of expression remains central to this review. Although the official languages have expanded to include English and Papiamentu/o, Dutch still remains a key language on the islands, particularly in Aruba, Bonaire, and Curaçao. Furthermore, because all Dutch Caribbean islands retain some form of neocolonial bond with the Netherlands, islanders not only traffic interregionally but they also tend to move to the Netherlands for higher education and economic opportunities. Travel between the center and the periphery continues to be a constant and ongoing feature of the islanders' reality. Hence, a proficiency in Dutch is required. Moreover, many people still associate progress, success, and social mobility with the Dutch language—this notwithstanding the slow and continued headway made toward decolonization.

Currently, Curaçao, Aruba, and Sint Maarten (the CAS islands) are autonomous countries within the Dutch Kingdom, while Bonaire, Sint Eustatius, and Saba (the BES islands) are special municipalities of the Netherlands. The CAS islands are identified as *Dutch Caribbean*, whereas the BES islands are recognized as *Caribbean Dutch*. These differences in signification are directly related to the islands' constitutional relation with the European metropolis after 2010, when the Netherlands Antilles ceased to exist. It is a center-periphery association that still foregrounds the Netherlands at the center, regardless of the Dutch Kingdom's constitutional suggestions of equal distribution of power between the nations. The historical trajectory of Dutch Caribbean literature then includes writers who produce works geared toward insular, local, European, and/or international audiences. This is also the case in the production of children's and young adult literature.

Moreover, Dutch Caribbean literature can be produced by a Euro-Dutch writer who might have spent some time on any one of these islands. But for the purposes of this chapter, native-born and local writers who are a part of the intertwined literary histories between the islands and the Netherlands remain front and center. The intention is to capture an "authentic" ontology in Dutch Caribbean children's and young adult literature by tracing the past and present cultural aesthetics presented in the works of writers who originate from these islands. Indeed, by providing an overview of Dutch Caribbean children's and young adult literature by native and local writers, I seek at once to introduce the aesthetic consciousness of a postcolonial people grappling with a linguistic and cultural identity that is tacitly still informed by "the gaze" of the metropolis. Regardless of the cultural politics in the Dutch Kingdom, Dutch Caribbean writers of children's and young adult literature negotiate the coloniality of power and seek to introduce a subjectivity and "living culture" sensed and authorized on Dutch Caribbean soil.

Language and Representation from 1881 through 1945

Some of the critical debate about young adult literature, especially during the mid- to late twentieth century, regards the language through which the stories are shared. Young adult works were mostly published in Dutch, while the majority of children's literature was published in Papiamentu/o. Even prior to the discussions on literary language of representation, popular Bonairean novelist Cola Debrot (1902–1981) argued in favor of a more creolized representation in Dutch Antillean literature. As scholar and literary critic Aart G. Broek mentions in *The Colour of My Island* (2009), Debrot advocated in the 1930s for writings that would take "local needs and desires into account" (44). Broek shows how Debrot's argument persisted even as he produced his most popular works with themes of creolization in the Dutch language. Some of the most popular local novelists up until the 1950s did not include the Papiamentu/o language in their presentation of a Dutch Caribbean ontology for young adults. As mentioned earlier, Papiamentu/o was the language of choice for children's literature in the Dutch Antillean Leeward Islands[1] but not necessarily the language of choice in the later production of young adult literature. Hence, a schism emerged concerning the question of language of authenticity in children's versus young adult literature. One can argue that much of this disparity has to do with local cultural developments and publication opportunities for books about children and young adults.

Broek writes in *The Colour of My Island* that creolization and the Papiamentu/o language were twin sisters in poetry, oral narratives, and the dramatic arts (45). Here we see signs of writings and expressions for children in Papiamentu/o. Critical literature suggests that children's writings in Curaçao developed in ironic and nuanced ways. Literary critic and specialist in Dutch Caribbean literary history Wim Rutgers has published works that research children's and young adult literature from the Dutch Caribbean. His publications provide a portal for the analysis of the most prominent writers of this style. His groundbreaking book *Bon dia! Met wie schrijf ik?*

Over Caraïbische jeugdliteratuur (*Good Morning! Who Am I Writing With? About Caribbean Children's and Young Adult Literature*; 1988)[2] introduces the most active writers of Dutch Caribbean children's and young adult literature in the early to late twentieth century. Rutgers's text also offers an extensive overview of the history of children's and young adult literature from the Dutch Caribbean in the twentieth century.

Rutgers makes clear that literature for children in Papiamentu/o, the native Portuguese and Spanish Creole spoken in Aruba, Bonaire, and Curaçao (referred to as the ABC islands), could be spotted even before the 1900s (*Bon dia!* 14). His research led him to the early religious publication of short stories and poems composed to provide children with moral and ethical lessons as assigned by the Catholic Church. These publications, original works as well as some Dutch translations, date from 1881 through the 1940s. Even though, as Rutgers notes, the writings produced in the late 1800s do not necessarily represent children's literature in the traditional sense, they still provide evidence of an attempt at cultural moralization in the psyche of local children (*Bon dia!* 14–16). Broek also writes of these contradictory developments in children's literature from Curaçao. He notes how the Roman Catholic Church, which dominated religious traditions on the island, used the local language as a tool for "civilization" all while growing their religious and cultural hold from the late 1800s through the 1940s ("Ideological Controversies" 377).

It was useful for the Dutch European colonizer, from the abolition of slavery in 1863 through the period leading to autonomy in 1954, to insert Catholic values in the psychosocial and cultural production of the Antillean landscape. This then speaks, in part, to why children's stories, songs, rhymes, and literature in Papiamentu/o held a dominant position in the early educational and developmental process on Curaçao from the late 1800s through the 1940s. I contend that at the very least, these early works in children's literature show an acknowledgment of the importance for youngsters to hear and see themselves in what they read. The idea that an auto-ethnographic and transcultural approach to writings for children should be entertained is central here. It was in fact children's literature in Curaçao that inadvertently used Papiamentu/o as a pattern for resistance and self-determination during the early period from emancipation to autonomy (Clemencia 437–40). So, Papiamentu/o's usefulness as a tool of cultural moralization through western European and Judeo-Christian values, ironically, served an unintended secondary purpose of local resistance and protest to colonial indoctrination of youngsters from an early age. Works for children were often lifted from the oral tradition, performed through storytelling, rhyme, or song (Broek, *The Colour of My Island* 33; Broek, "Ideological Controversies" 380–83; Rutgers, *Bon dia!* 15; Clemencia 437; Allen 424).

The early children's literature beyond church magazines and pamphlets produced in the late 1880s and early 1900s also follows this trajectory of writings in Papiamentu/o (*Bon dia!* 15). As Rutgers notes in *Bon dia! Met wie schrijf ik?*, "Dutch only temporarily took over the children's literary scene in the Dutch Caribbean, particularly during the processes leading towards a more Dutch leaning education system" (15). However, over time, consequent to the constitutional changes in 1954 and the mobilization for heightened insular cultural consciousness, Papiamentu/o remained the solid language of publication of children's literature on the ABC islands. Still, as children grew older, Dutch became the modus operandi in schools. This was part of an early twentieth-century development in which laws were introduced, starting in 1907, supporting Dutch as the language of instruction in the education system (Alberts-Luijdjens 34–35; Rutgers, *Beneden en boven de wind* 135). Progress and success were, in part, measured by one's ability to fluently speak, read, and write Dutch. This contributed partially to the stagnation of Papiamentu/o in the production of young adult literature.

This is not to say that the discussions on language and cultural authenticity ceased. The ponderings evident from the time of emancipation in 1863 leading up to autonomy in 1954 only intensified. A few popular writers from Curaçao patterned the Creole linguistic tradition from children's literature in their adult narratives and poetics in the 1920s, 1930s, and 1940s (Broek, "Ideological Controversies" 382). Linguistic representation remained a fundamental component in the markedness of a postcolonial Dutch Caribbean people and their literary production. This continued to be the case throughout the struggle for a greater sense of independence and autonomy of representation in the Dutch Kingdom.

Children's and Young Adult Literature after 1954

There were times when developments in the publication of children's and young adult literature paralleled the many turning points in the decolonization process of the region. The year 1954 marks a crucial time. The

Charter of the Dutch Kingdom was established, giving the colonies a level of self-governance that made them equal partners in the kingdom. This new level of representation translated into a different visibility and literary focus within the kingdom, especially after World War II. Rutgers explains how Dutch European attention to literature about their colonies in the Americas grew during this time, particularly for Surinamese literature (*Bon dia!* 9–10). However, the European attempt to "write" the Caribbean experience was limited to a perspective that patterned travel writing—inscribing from without as opposed to within the islands' cultures. This made for a nonauthentic and rather ethnographic approach to Dutch Caribbean literature.

According to Rutgers, among the Dutch European writers, only Miep Diekmann (1925–2017) managed to embody an authentic Antillean experience in her Dutch-language works about Dutch Caribbean children and young adults (*Bon dia!* 9). She especially made a name for herself with titles like *De boten van Brakkeput* (*The Boats of Brakkeput*; 1956), *Padu is gek* (*Padu Is Crazy*; 1957), and, later, *De dagen van Olim* (*The Days of Olim*; 1971). Diekmann was born in the Netherlands in 1925. She lived and visited on and off in Aruba and Curaçao from 1934 through the late twentieth century. Her literary spirit was coached and nurtured from her experiences as an "outsider-within" on these islands (Rutgers, *De Caraïbische jeugdboeken*). Her literary success was acknowledged with multiple literary prizes that she garnered both on the islands and in the Netherlands. Diekmann played a crucial role in the future visibility of a few canonical native Dutch Caribbean writers of children's and young adult literature in subsequent decades (Heuvel and Van Wel).

After the 1950s, we see a continued overall increase in the publication of children's and young adult literature by native writers, though many still had difficulty navigating the processes of getting published. It was still not uncommon to see self-published works, or publications by small printing companies of low quality and subpar distribution strategies (Rutgers, *Bon dia!* 32). Writers would often have to navigate every level of the entire production process of their books (Rutgers, *Bon dia!* 32). This was especially the case for publications in Papiamentu/o. Although many writers of this classification continued to produce in Papiamentu/o, various authors generated their work in Dutch or in multiple languages. It was a matter of publisher interest, the language used in the education system, and the desired audience.

In the mid-1950s, Curaçaoan and Aruban writers and poets such as Sonia Garmers and Ernesto Rosenstand produced an increased number of literary pieces for children in Papiamentu/o (Rutgers, *Bon dia!* 16). Garmers dominated the children's literary scene in this decade with publications like *Tantan Nini ta conta* (*Telling Stories with Auntie Nini*; 1955), *Cuentanan pa mucha* (*Children's Stories*; 1956), *Conta cuenta* (*Telling Stories*; 1957), and *Un makutu yen di cuenta* (*A Basket Full of Stories*; 1960). These works were locally produced and published through local printing companies. Still, in the case of Curaçao, not until the time leading up to and after the historical events of the late 1960s, when appreciation for Dutch Caribbean creolization and self-actualization significantly increased, was young adult literature highlighted in all local artistic forms in general.

The May 30, 1969, uprising of the working-class Afro-Curaçaoan population allowed a new level of self-respect and appreciation for everything local. As Broek notes, during this time, "Papiamentu vernacular was held as living proof of a unique Antillean development strongly rooted in an African past" (*The Colour of My Island* 49). This authentic Creole language of the Leeward Dutch Antilles sustained the self-confidence of the locals. Papiamentu/o proved to be a pillar in the aesthetic production of local culture through literature. As the pushback against colonial influences strengthened on Curaçao, so too did publications for children and young adults grow in number. Groups of writers patterned the style of the pre–World War II Papiamentu/o poets by continuing to use this native Creole in their literature and poetry, to heighten and support self-actualization and self-worth in new ways. As Rutgers notes, Pierre Lauffer and Elis Juliana, two prominent Curaçaoan poets, continued to promote and produce children's literature in Papiamentu/o during the 1960s (*Bon dia!* 16).

Particularly in Curaçao, the linguistic critique stems from the reality that most of the ABC Dutch Caribbean population live, speak, feel, and think in Papiamentu/o, and so, local cultural organizations and popular writers and artists, even prior to the publication of the first *true* literary pieces for young adults, believed that "[w]esternization that does not take local needs and desires into account should be opposed" (Broek, *The Colour of My Island* 44). This opposition to literary cultural production from "without" is still evident in twenty-first-century Curaçao. This is especially demonstrable in the continued promotion of children's and young adult literature in Papiamentu/o in various local institutions. The Frank Martinus Arion National Public

Library in Curaçao has, since the 1980s, played a crucial role in cataloguing and promoting reading and literary works for children and young adults in all languages, but primarily works by local writers who have in some way acknowledged Papiamentu/o in their literature. For example, the successful annual Siman Di Ban Lesa, a children's book week festival organized at the library, encourages reading among children and young adults while at the same time promoting the works of local Papiamentu/o writers of this literary category.

Though in different ways, Aruba also underwent a cultural and political consciousness process in literary production for young adults and children. The Aruba National Public Library and publisher Charuba were instrumental in promoting the visibility of this literary classification in both Dutch and Papiamentu/o, particularly during the 1980s. Charuba is based in Aruba and was established in association with Leopold, a Dutch publishing house in the Netherlands equally geared toward children's literature. Contemporary Aruban writers such as Desiree Correa, Josette Daal, Frances Kelly, and Richard Pieternella were all being published by Leopold/Charuba at the time. Presently, Charuba is less focused on children's and young adult books and moving toward a variety of publications beyond the earlier literary grouping (LM Publishers). The publishing company now promotes a cooperative approach with multiple agencies and institutions. The Union di Organisacionnan Cultural Arubano (UNOCA) has also gotten involved with funding the publication of books. The National Public Library participates in these collaborations as well. Although a broad range of solid publishing companies with a focus on books for children and young adults would be preferred, self-publishing remains a viable option on the island. And so, many writers for children and young adults continue producing books that speak to the experiences of the locals.

Several contemporary writers of children's literature in Aruba believe like the earlier Curaçaoan writers that Papiamentu/o should be the language to reflect Aruban authenticity currently and in the future. Furthermore, some of these writers contend that even though publishers may not offer editorial advice, editorial expertise on the island has been developed over time by writers who study the art of storytelling through literature (Kock). One such Aruban writer is Olga Buckley, with her popular children's series about the character Bencho published between 2005 and 2020. Her fourth book in the ongoing five-part series is entitled *Bencho i e gran crusada* (*Bencho and the Great Crusade*; 2020). Here we see Bencho traveling to Venezuela on an adventurous stint as part of his emancipation into his teenage years (Rutgers, "Olga J. Buckley"; Buckley; Kock). Other writers such as Munye Oduber-Winklaar, who is originally from Bonaire but grew up and still lives in Aruba, also highlights the importance of Papiamentu/o as the communicative writing tool for authentic children's stories (Kock), regardless of the education system, which in many ways still centers on the Dutch language. Both Buckley and Oduber-Winklaar produce children's stories that critically inform youngsters about their development in an Aruban environment, culture, and history.

In the case of Dutch Antillean Windward Islands Sint Eustatius, Sint Maarten, and Saba (the SSS islands),[3] much like in the case of the ABC Dutch Leeward Islands, children's and young adult literature originated in the oral tradition (Albus 447; Badejo 676–79; Rutgers, *Bon dia!* 15). Furthermore, literary projects authentic to these islands, according to Fabian Badejo, have mostly been expressed through poetry (676–79). This continues to be the primary literary form on the three islands (Albus 443–49; Badejo 676–79). Furthermore, the language question has also influenced literary development particularly as it pertains to children's literature on the SSS islands. It has been difficult for the Dutch language to penetrate the everyday vernacular on these islands. The locals have been forceful in maintaining English as their living language of choice.[4]

With the flourishing of tourism since the 1980s, there has also been a growing influx of immigrants establishing themselves on Sint Maarten to the point that the island's population and authentic culture are at times unrecognizable. Consequently, although English remains dominant, multiple languages, including Spanish, have become significant in daily communications. Young adults tend to communicate in multilingual ways. The literature has come to reflect this social operation in parallel languages. Also, the art of dual language representation in texts has permeated some of the works produced for children.

It is not uncommon to see literature produced in English, Dutch, and/or Spanish by immigrants living in Sint Maarten. Findings provided by the Sint Maarten Philipsburg Jubilee Library indicate that there are a few known native-born writers who produce children's or young adult literature.[5] The House of Nehesi Publishers (HNP), a Sint Maarten–based publishing company established on the island in 1986, has played some role in the publication of a few children's books.⁶ For example, the children's book *Lizzy Lizard* by Robin Boasman, published in 2013, was the second book in this category published by HNP. It is the story of a lizard daring to move beyond the confines of her comfortable environment to explore friendship with other animals much different from her in the capital of the country. The introduction of reptiles in this Sint Maarten children's book is not an uncommon feature in Caribbean children's literature in general. These creatures reflect some of the first animals that Caribbean kids encounter when growing up, thus shaping the imagination of many. And so, to use these creatures as symbols to introduce life lessons and capture broader themes of concern on a particular island makes sense. Jocelyne Arnell, another native Sint Maarten writer, uses common island animals in their natural environment in her children's books, which are printed with Xlibris, indicating her choice for self-publishing.

According to information obtained from the Jubilee Library, Arnell's children's book series about Ignacio the iguana has been very popular among young readers. The first book in the series is titled *Ignacio and the Mysterious Egg* (2015), followed by *Ignacio the Iguana and Chichi Bird* (2018). This second book in particular explores adaptive ways of moving forward after the traumatic experience of a natural disaster, a theme much explored by other writers from Sint Maarten after Hurricane Irma impacted the island in 2017. *Ignacio the Iguana and Chichi Bird* features Ignacio and a bird who are forced to live anew in a shared environment where natural disaster has upset the ecology. These staple animals of Caribbean islands tackle the trauma of this experience by fashioning a collaborative friendship. Clearly, this book offers Sint Maarten's children authentic ways of dealing with life after Hurricane Irma. Thus, here too, like in Curaçao and Aruba, we see writers speaking to children's tangible experiences through fiction. These books help children learn and understand how they inform the environment and how the environment in turn informs them.

Loekie Morales, a native Curaçaoan residing in Sint Maarten since 2000, is another signature writer. Morales is an interregional Dutch Caribbean writer who has transferred her love of writing children's and young adult literature from the Leeward to the Windward Dutch Caribbean. Although she is not the first to contribute to the literary traditions of both the Leeward and Windward Islands, her trajectory reflects the post-1980s socioeconomic, political, and cultural developments that impacted migration between Curaçao and Sint Maarten. Furthermore, Morales echoes the tradition of

Dutch Caribbean women writers having a stronghold on children's and young adult literature on the majority of the Dutch islands.

The Centrality of Women Writers in Fostering Children's and Young Adult Literature

Euro-Dutch writer Miep Diekmann, introduced earlier in this chapter, played a role in boosting the visibility of native Curaçaoan and Aruban writers of children's and young adult literature. Diekmann helped formalize Charuba in association with Leopold in 1984; Leopold published the majority of Diekmann's literary works about the Dutch Caribbean. Diekmann also encouraged and, to some degree, fostered the early works of a few canonical writers of children's and young adult literature. Sonia Garmers, Diana Lebacs, and Josette Daal, among others, were all at some point in their career coached by Diekmann (Heuvel and Van Wel). Charuba would publish original children's and young adult literature in Papiamentu/o and Dutch, while also sanctioning the translation of literary works between the two languages. Diekmann was crucial in mentoring Lebacs with tips and strategies on producing the first official work for young adults by a Dutch Caribbean native (Rutgers, *Bon dia!* 100–102).

Lebacs (1947–2022) is remembered as one of the foremost writers of young adult literature in the Dutch Caribbean. Her works are required reading for anyone seeking a window into Dutch Caribbean children's and young adult literature spanning the ABC islands. Her novel *Sherry: Het begin van het begin* (*Sherry: The Beginning of a Beginning*) was published by Leopold in 1971. This novel, as with all her young adult literary pieces, speaks to the historical time in which it was produced. It highlights a central feature in Curaçaoan culture, namely the continued search for identity within a colonial and neocolonial existence. Furthermore, much like Lebacs's other young adult works, it introduces parallel developments in the sociocultural history of Curaçao, the Netherlands, the rest of the Dutch Antilles, and the Caribbean in general. The novel was published just a short time after the May 1969 revolt for social and economic justice of the Black working class in Curaçao, which led to increased levels of self-affirmation as well as cultural, economic, and political power. *Sherry* is the story of a young girl growing into self-assertion of her Blackness and local culture (Cornet). She travels to the Netherlands for higher education and returns to Curaçao after the May 1969 revolt, developing agency that benefits herself and her society. As Lebacs notes, Sherry is symbolic of all Antillean girls (Rutgers, "Diana Lebacs werkt"; Cornet), meaning that the novel reflects along situational, emotional, and social lines the maturation process of Black Dutch Caribbean girls. It also highlights the role of youth, particularly young women, in building the country.

Sherry was followed by a four-part novel series published during the period 1975–1982. Nacho, the protagonist of the series, a male youth from Bonaire, travels between Curaçao and Bonaire as part of his growth and developmental process. Much of Nacho's experiences speak to the history and social relations between the two islands particularly during the 1950s and 1960s, when Bonaireans migrated to Curaçao for higher education and better opportunities.

Lebacs's novel *Sugarcane Rosy* (1983) serves as another bildungsroman, in which the main character, Rosy, travels from her native island, the fictional Irbisca, to Curaçao for employment opportunities and a better life. The economic and familial linkages among multiple Caribbean islands are apparent, as some of Rosy's family members have also moved to Aruba and Sint Maarten for employment. This, too, is a realistic fiction with emotional and situational authenticity. It highlights the substantial migration of people from the English-speaking Caribbean islands to Curaçao, which had begun modernizing after the establishment of a Shell oil refinery in the early twentieth century.

Lebacs's literary trajectory in young adult literature continuously introduces young adult main characters who travel interregionally or internationally as part of their developmental process. This speaks specifically to the Caribbean diasporic experience whereby citizens emerge into adulthood, in part, by way of forced or circumstantial migration. These young adult novels also highlight the psychological and identity development of Dutch Antillean people: a constant grappling with the process of "becoming" within a neocolonial construct in which issues of gender, race, ethnicity, cultural citizenship, and mother-daughter-father-son and other familial relationships, coupled with migration, frame these realistic fictional pieces. One can argue that these works are, in part, also historical fictions; although the plots are invented and the characters are imaginary, the stories play out in contextual perspectives that are very real. It seems that Lebacs was intent on having young adults understand their history in critical ways. This approach reflects her background in education.

Although Lebacs's Leopold works were published in Dutch, that is not to say that she did not produce works in Papiamentu/o. As an artist of the post-1969 uprising era who believed in centering political independence and Afro-Curaçaoan sociocultural and Creole linguistic identity (Broek, "Ideology and Writing" 14), she made efforts to publish in Papiamentu/o as well. Much of her work for children, like the works of Sonia Garmers, the other prominent writer of children's and young adult literature from Curaçao, was published locally and in Papiamentu/o, such as *Buchi wan pia fini* (*Buchi Wan Skinny Legs*; 1974) and *Kompa datu ta konta* (*Uncle Datu Tells Stories*; 1975).

Lebacs also dabbled in young adult literature that was specifically geared toward a Dutch European audience. She understood that to make Euro-Dutch outsiders more culturally sensitive about the Dutch Caribbean, it was necessary to introduce them to the authenticity of Curaçaoan living culture. Furthermore, some Euro-Dutch publishers were eager to introduce the Dutch audience to the culture of their former colonies. And so, we see subsequent children's books by Lebacs such as *De Toembakoning* (*Tumba King*) and *De Spokenband* (*Ghost Bond*), both published in 1985 by Dutch publishers. Both books introduce staple aspects of Curaçaoan traditions, such as the Carnival Tumba King Festival, and the intergenerational link between traditional and contemporary cultural practices. Beyond these early works from the twentieth century, Lebacs has also published in the twenty-first century. Her books continue to be in Papiamentu and Dutch, as she navigated between Dutch European and local Curaçaoan publishers and audiences. Lebacs's ability to successfully produce a staggering amount of work that authenticates the local identity and culture in both the colonial and local Creole language speaks to her thoughtfulness to capture the existentialism of the local and diaspora natives through children's and young adult literature.

Many of the complexities about cultural history, family, identity, and migration or travel that we see in Lebacs's work are also visible in the literary work of the aforementioned Curaçaoan–Sint Maartener, Loekie Morales. She has quickly morphed into a hybrid Dutch Leeward and Windward Island writer of children's literature in the early decades of the twenty-first century. Her recent works embrace the Sint Maarten children's experience. Additionally, her selections bridge the children's and young adult literary connections between the Dutch Leeward and Windward Islands. In order to reach readers across the Dutch Caribbean and beyond, she consciously translates across languages. Her books are produced in Papiamentu/o, Dutch, Spanish, and English.

To maintain authenticity and control of her work, Morales has opted to self-publish many of her books. In a personal interview conducted in 2020, she attributes her choice to proceed independently to a negative experience early in her publishing career. Her first children's book was published in the year 2000. The book, titled *Zonnesproetjes*, fell out of her control after she signed an unfavorable agreement with the publisher. She has since decided to maintain ownership of her stories and publishes under the auspices of her foundation, Beyond Kultura and Beyond Writing. Taking matters into her own hands, she republished *Zonnesproetjes* (*Freckle Bunch*) in both Dutch and English in 2020.

Freckle Bunch is now available along with its sequel, *Tropisch nestje* (*Tropical Shelter*), first published in 2005, also in both Dutch and English. The books consist of a series of forty Caribbean-based stories; both are reflections of Morales's childhood and tell the story of her large family of siblings growing up in Curaçao. According to Morales, "[t]hemes about single motherhood, holding multiple jobs [to sustain a family], siblings as caretakers, and the role of the grandmother as caregiver and matriarch in the extended family are reflected throughout the stories" ("Philosophy of Writing"). The siblings in *Freckle Bunch* are introduced as scoundrels, wandering the streets and exploring their environment throughout the alleys of Willemstad in Curaçao (Morales, "Loekie Morales English"). It is interesting that *Tropisch nestje* was proofread by Jules Marchena and Diana Lebacs (Morales, personal interview), suggesting that Lebacs's skills as a writer have been transferred to Curaçaoan writers of the twenty-first century.

Morales, much like Lebacs, produces stories that educate youth about their history and culture by placing them in the middle of a local town, city, or landscape. Fantasy and magical realism are sometimes introduced to present children with worlds that are different yet still within the realm of a Dutch Caribbean reality. In so doing, Morales takes the speculative fiction stance, presenting and critiquing Dutch Caribbean society, offering alternative pathways to a better existence. In *Mina Marina* (2008), Morales tells a fantasy story about a mermaid, Mina, who lives in Caribbean waters near Curaçao but swims in the deep seas off Venezuela to meet her special Indian merman, Perucho. Together, they agree to keep the sea clean (Morales, "Loekie Morales English"). This fantasy story clearly teaches children about their important role in maintaining a sustainable environment. Considering the proximity between Curaçao and Venezuela, Morales seems to suggest the establishment of a cross-national agreement for keeping the waters between the two countries safe and clean for the people of both lands. Many of Morales's children's and young adult stories follow a similar trend in that they teach youth about their culture and presence in the environment (Morales, "Philosophy of Writing"; personal interview). This approach is similar to what the other Dutch Caribbean writers discussed earlier introduce in their pieces.

Other popular titles by Morales include *Papito en de vertellende boom* published in 2001 and its English translation, *Papito and the Story-Telling Tree*, in 2002; *The Magic Wedding Cake*, published in Dutch, Papiamentu, English, and Spanish in 2011; and *Vrijheids salsa* and its translation, *Freedom Salsa*, both published in 2014. *Papito and the Story-Telling Tree* and *Freedom Salsa* tackle the history of slavery and emancipation, while *The Magic Wedding Cake* explores the history of a Caribbean island (arguably Curaçao) and dissects its "discovery," conquest, and domination by a foreign power (Morales, "Philosophy of Writing"). According to Morales, her intent is to allow children throughout the Caribbean to understand and critically explore the Caribbean story from multiple angles ("Philosophy of Writing"). However, the stories suggest that any angle of exploration should incorporate the agency of citizens. The main characters in all the abovementioned books become a part of the history and culture they explore, whether through a form of magical realism or fantasy, or through genealogical connections to a particular historicity. The characters are thus able to reach back into the past in order to move into the future. It is thus not farfetched to suggest that Morales is embracing a type of Dutch Caribbean futurism in her approach to contemporary children's literature. Most of the writers I discuss in this chapter, in fact, seem to embrace a past or sociological time period to support developing youth in their own process of becoming.

Since Morales is also writing to English-speaking Dutch Caribbean children, many of her books have been translated, as noted above. Morales explains the importance of reaching Dutch Caribbean children in their native language. Furthermore, she sees translation as imperative to expanding one's reading audience (Morales, "Sint Maartener Children's Writer"). Specific to Sint Maarten, Morales published *Bonte boel* (Rainbow Jumble) in 2004, the story of two Sint Maarten girls exploring the island. Later, in 2019, she published *Storm*, which was published in Dutch in 2020 under the title *Monster Storm*. The book narrates the adventures of two Sint Maarten boys after Hurricane Irma. In both *Bonte boel* and *Monster Storm*, Morales tries to maintain an authentic feel to the experiences of the young protagonists. As in the works of Jocelyne Arnell, the character development in Morales's works occurs in the natural habitat of the island. The difference here is that these are human characters with deep environmental sensibilities. It is precisely this aspect that makes Morales's books relatable to older children.

Final Thoughts

Dutch Caribbean children's and young adult literature has undergone multiple evolutions during various key time periods characterized by emancipation, Dutch colonialism, neocolonialism, autonomy, modernization and progress, interregional migration, the struggle for linguistic and cultural self-affirmation, and a shifting and unstable natural and economic environment. All the above factors, and more, continue to influence the themes and stories in this regional literary category. The six islands, regardless of contemporary constitutional differences, have these experiences in common to varying degrees, and island residents relate to each other in the context of these multiple shared realities. The writers discussed in this chapter offer children and young adults expansive insight into their Dutch Caribbean worlds while at the same time allowing them to understand their agency to affect and change their continuously shifting environment and society. Ultimately, youth can value the development of a self-consciousness that is cooperative and in alliance with their local cultures, languages, and historicities. This could strongly contribute to affirming a Dutch Caribbean ontology rooted in local soil, and on local terms.

Notes

1. Although located in the Caribbean Windward Islands region, Curaçao, Aruba, and Bonaire are considered Leeward within the Dutch Antillean constellation of six islands.
2. All translations are mine.
3. Though located in the Caribbean Leeward Islands region, these islands are considered Windward within the Dutch Antillean constellation of six islands.

4. As an example of this resistance, a large group of Sabans moved to Barbados to ensure that their children received an education in English. Rutgers writes of this in *Beneden en boven de wind* (141).

5. Special thanks to the Jubilee Library in Sint Maarten, whose staff went above and beyond in finding the names of a few prominent writers of children's literature from the island.

6. This publishing company was first established in the US in 1982 and later, in 1986, on the island of Sint Maarten. The founder is Lasana Sekou, an Aruban–Sint Maartener.

Works Cited

Alberts-Luijdjens, Monique. "Historical Development of Libraries in the Netherlands Antilles and Aruba." *Caribbean Libraries in the 21st Century: Changes, Challenges, and Choices*, edited by Cheryl Peltier-Davis and Shamin Renwick, Information Today, 2007, pp. 31–40.

Albus, Alida M. G. "From Oral to Written Literature: St. Maarten, Saba, St. Eustatius." *A History of the Literature in the Caribbean*, vol. 2, *English- and Dutch-Speaking Regions*, edited by A. James Arnold, John Benjamins, 2001, pp. 443–49.

Allen, Rose Mary. "Song Texts as Literature of Daily Life in the Netherlands Antilles." *A History of the Literature in the Caribbean*, vol. 2, *English- and Dutch-Speaking Regions*, edited by A. James Arnold, John Benjamins, 2001, pp. 421–30.

Badejo, Fabian A. "Introduction to Literature in English in the Dutch Windward Islands." *Callaloo*, vol. 21, no. 3, Summer 1998, pp. 676–79.

Broek, Aart G. *The Colour of My Island: Ideology and Writing in Papiamentu (Aruba, Bonaire, and Curaçao): A Bird's-Eye View*. In de Knipscheer, 2009.

Broek, Aart G. "Ideological Controversies in Curaçaoan Publishing Strategies (1900–1945)." *A History of the Literature in the Caribbean*, vol. 2, *English- and Dutch-Speaking Regions*, edited by A. James Arnold, John Benjamins, 2001, pp. 375–85.

Broek, Aart G. "Ideology and Writing in Papiamentu: A Bird's Eye View." *Journal of Caribbean Literatures*, vol. 5, no. 1, Summer 2007, pp. 1–20.

Buckley, Olga J. "Bencho Series." https://www.olgajbuckley.com/my-work-books.

Clemencia, Joceline A. "Katibu ta galiña: From Hidden to Open Protest in Curaçao." *A History of the Literature in the Caribbean*, vol. 2, *English- and Dutch-Speaking Regions*, edited by A. James Arnold, John Benjamins, 2001, pp. 433–42.

Cornet, Florencia V. "Dutch Caribbean Women's Literary Thought: Activism through Linguistic and Cosmopolitan Multiplicity." *Wagadu: A Journal of Transnational Women's and Gender Studies*, vol. 18, Winter 2017, pp. 175–202.

Heuvel, Pim, and Freek van Wel. "Jeugdliteratuur." *Met eigen stem: Herkenningspunten in de letterkunde van de Nederlandse Antillen en Aruba*, Koninklijke van Gorcum, 1989, pp. 209–20.

Kock, Anouska. "Literary Critics in Aruba Rave Talent, Mourn Guidance." *Anansesem: News, Ideas, Arts, and Letters from the World of Caribbean Children's & YA Publishing*, September 2, 2010. http://www.anansesem.com/2010/09/literary-critics-in-aruba-rave-talent.html.

LM Publishers. "Cooperation with Editorial Charuba." January 9, 2018. https://lmpublishers.nl/en/editorial-charuba/.

Morales, Loekie. "Loekie Morales English." YouTube, October 30, 2020. https://www.youtube.com/watch?v=9UqDQfUJa7Y.

Morales, Loekie. Personal interview, October 10, 2020.

Morales, Loekie. "Philosophy of Writing for Caribbean Children." Personal correspondence, October 12, 2020.

Morales, Loekie. "Sint Maartener Children's Writer Embraces Self-Publishing: Interview with Loekie Morales." Interview with Summer Edward. *Anansesem: News, Ideas, Arts, and Letters from the World of Caribbean Children's & YA Publishing*, December 23, 2012. http://www.anansesem.com/2012/12/sint-maartener-childrens-writer.html.

Rutgers, Wim. *Beneden en boven de wind: Literatuur van de Nederlandse Antillen en Aruba*. De Bezige Bij, 1996.

Rutgers, Wim. *Bon dia! Met wie schrijf ik? Over Caraïbische jeugdliteratuur*. Charuba, 1988.

Rutgers, Wim. *De Caraïbische jeugdboeken van Miep Diekmann*. Charuba/Leopold, 1984.

Rutgers, Wim. "Diana Lebacs werkt op drie fronten tegelijk." *Ñapa*, May 30, 1986.

Rutgers, Wim. "Olga J. Buckley puliceert vierde deel van haar Bencho serie." Biblioteca Nacional Aruba, July 28, 2020. https://www.bibliotecanacional.aw/pages/olga-j-buckley-publiceert-vierde-deel-van-haar-bencho-serie/.

CHAPTER 2

Children's Literature and the Theme of Childhood in the Francophone Caribbean
An Overview

Louise Hardwick

There is a fascinating slippage in the contemporary Francophone Caribbean between children's literature and literature about childhood. So pronounced is this trend that the significance of childhood as a source of literary inspiration for authors from Martinique, Guadeloupe, and Haiti cannot be underestimated. Remarkably, since the 1990s, almost every prominent Francophone Caribbean novelist has produced childhood memoirs—semiautobiographical accounts of their childhood, known as *récits d'enfance*, as well as children's literature. Because there is often a great deal of contextual and thematic overlap between these two modes of writing childhood, what results is a captivating interplay between the children's literature and the childhood memoirs, forged through deliberate commonalities of theme, character, and language, and a predilection for autobiographical detail.

This chapter opens with a brief analysis of childhood memoirs, outlining in particular the ways in which many of these texts are designated and marketed as young adult literature, and then moves on to consider literature that was specifically written for children. This is followed by a brief discussion of graphic novels, some comments building case studies of centers and cultural initiatives in the Francophone Caribbean that aim to promote children's literature, and reflections on the metaphorical charge of childhood in the Francophone Caribbean.

The time period under examination begins in the 1950s, but the majority of works considered appeared from the 1990s onward. As is relatively common for Francophone literature in general, a significant proportion of the titles were originally published in Paris, but the chapter also maps engagement with other publishing houses located in the Caribbean and Canada. Several texts have been integrated into the metropolitan French education system to some degree, although anecdotal evidence suggests that there is an abiding sense in Martinique and Guadeloupe that "local" works are all too often sidelined in the French national syllabus prescribed by Paris.[1]

This survey is by no means exhaustive, but it attempts to provide a comprehensive synthesis of this important area of Francophone Caribbean literary activity. A strikingly high proportion of the material discussed here has been translated into English—indicative of the broad audience appeal of childhood—with some exceptions, and unless otherwise stated, translations are my own; the original titles have on the whole met with critical acclaim, and works are generally widely available either for purchase (often from major online retailers) or as loans from public or university libraries.

The pronounced Francophone Caribbean preoccupation with childhood can to some extent be attributed to the international success of Joseph Zobel's *La Rue Cases-Nègres* (translated into English in 1980 as *Black Shack Alley*). This pioneering childhood memoir was first published in 1950 and takes the form of a semiautobiographical novel depicting a young boy's experiences growing up on a Martinican plantation and his struggles to obtain an education despite the barriers of race and class. Zobel's novel, influenced by the Négritude Black consciousness movement, was inspired in part by the prose fiction of the Harlem Renaissance, particularly Richard Wright's *Black Boy: A Record of Childhood and Youth* (1945). Looking to the Anglophone Caribbean, comparisons can be drawn between Zobel's childhood memoir and Barbadian author George Lamming's *In the Castle of My Skin* (1953) as well as Trinidadian author Michael Anthony's *The Year in San Fernando* (1965). In further evidence of the pronounced Francophone Caribbean interest in Caribbean childhood, Anthony's novel about childhood and adolescence was translated into French by a Martinican team as *Mon année à San Fernando* in 2008. In the wider Caribbean sphere, comparisons might also be drawn between Zobel's childhood memoir and Colombian author Gabriel

García Márquez's *Vivir para contarla* (2002; translated by Edith Grossman as *Living to Tell the Tale*).

La Rue Cases-Nègres was certainly not an overnight success, and after early print runs in 1950 and 1955 were exhausted, the novel became incredibly difficult to source.[2] However, in 1974, the work was republished by the Franco-African publishing house Présence Africaine. This relaunch led to Keith Q. Warner's seminal 1980 English translation. The canonical status of the novel (in English) was recognized in 2020, when a revised translation was published by Penguin Classics with a new foreword by Patrick Chamoiseau, while in 2018, a new graphic novel adaptation was published by Michel Bagoé and Stéphanie Destin, with particular appeal for younger readers.

The celebrated film adaptation *Rue Cases-Nègres* (1983; released in English as *Sugar Cane Alley*), by the Martinican director Euzhan Palcy, brought Zobel's story to new generations of audiences worldwide. Palcy's *Rue Cases-Nègres* has an established history of being taught in French schools, and the French Centre National du Cinéma et de l'Image Animée (National Center for Cinema and Animation) has produced a dedicated French-language teachers' resource on the film; a wealth of online resources in English are also available. Zobel's novel and Palcy's film adaptation have become staples of Francophone education and culture across the world, and as a direct result, the Francophone Caribbean is approached through the lens of childhood with startling frequency.

In no small part emulating the literary model created by Zobel, the politicized exploration of childhood—with particular attention to the postcolonial specificities of language, race, and schooling—is a recurring theme in more recent Francophone Caribbean childhood memoirs. From the 1990s, several of the most prominent authors from the region turned to the genre of the childhood memoir. In a sense, this significant body of literature could be considered as writing back against what Philip Dine ("The French Colonial Empire"; "Children's Literature") has examined as an existing historical archive of French colonial "juvenile fiction" that promoted a Eurocentric, externalizing colonialist gaze among young French readers.

In 1990, Patrick Chamoiseau's childhood memoir *Antan d'enfance* (*Childhood*, translated by Carol Volk) heralded this new direction and opened the trilogy of texts known as *Une enfance créole* (*A Creole Childhood*), also comprising *Chemin-d'école* (1994; *School Days*, translated by Linda Coverdale) and *À bout d'enfance* (2005; *At Childhood's End*). Other major authors swiftly added to the volume of writing about childhood, producing a substantial corpus that includes Raphaël Confiant's *Ravines du devant-jour* (1994; *Ravines of the Dawn*) and *Le cahier des romances* (2000; *Notebook Romances*); Gisèle Pineau's *L'exil selon Julia* (1996; *Exile: According to Julia*, translated by Betty Wilson); Maryse Condé's *Le cœur à rire et à pleurer* (1999; *Tales from the Heart*, translated by Richard Philcox); and Daniel Maximin's *Tu, c'est l'enfance* (2004; *The You of Childhood*). Both Pineau and Condé expand the genre by focusing on the experience of immigration to France. Many of the authors featured in this chapter have an itinerant lifestyle, living and working between the Caribbean and Europe or North America; indeed, this is a pronounced transnational diasporic phenomenon across Francophone literature and Caribbean literature, more generally. This chapter surveys authors based in the Francophone Caribbean, as well as authors of Francophone Caribbean origin based elsewhere, and for reasons of space will only draw attention to origins and diasporic status when it appears particularly relevant to the texts under discussion.

Also in the 1990s, Haitian childhood came under scrutiny in Dany Laferrière's *L'odeur du café* (1991; *An Aroma of Coffee*, translated by David Homel) and *Le charme des après-midi sans fin* (1997; *The Charm of Afternoons without End*). Further texts, such as Haitian author Émile Ollivier's *Mille eaux* (1999; *One Thousand Waters*) and Guadeloupean Ernest Pépin's *Coulée d'or* (2005; *Golden Ravine*) consolidate childhood's significance in contemporary Francophone Caribbean literature from Martinique and Guadeloupe, as well as from Haiti and its diaspora. Chamoiseau's, Confiant's, and Ollivier's childhood memoirs appeared with the prestigious Parisian publishing house Gallimard in the series *Haute enfance* (literally, "high childhood"). Condé, too, has drawn attention to the *côté exotique* (exotic side) of Caribbean childhood memoirs ("J'ai toujours" 114), and the exoticism of the unknown, coupled with the universal and relatable reference point of childhood, may indeed attract publishers and readers, French and otherwise. In further evidence of childhood's recognized currency in the world of publishing, several of these childhood memoirs were rapidly translated into English, an unusual trend that further suggests the intercultural crossover potential of the genre and its potency as a publishing strategy.

While this is not to say that all Francophone Caribbean literature about childhood is written for children themselves, there is an inherent slippage that sees many of the childhood memoirs designated as young adult fiction:

this is explicit in the marketing of a text such as Pépin's *Coulée d'or*, which appeared with Gallimard's Folio Junior collection and is therefore directly aimed at young adults (texts in this series include an educational dossier with pedagogic activities). Pépin's childhood memoir is also regularly taught in French schools for the *brevet* qualification, a national diploma awarded at the end of *collège* (the French *collège* is the first phase of secondary education, for ages eleven to fifteen).

Important intertextual examples of the reception of Zobel's childhood memoir as children's or young adult literature are written into later childhood memoirs by Maximin and Condé. In Maximin's *Tu, c'est l'enfance*, the narrator recounts how when his parents were attempting to source literature for their children about Francophone Caribbean culture, friends sent the family a rare copy of Zobel's (then out-of-print) *La Rue Cases-Nègres*. These friends, however, also warned his parents to censor passages that they deemed were too risqué for younger eyes (Maximin 26)! In contrast, in *Le cœur à rire et à pleurer*, Condé's childhood memoir, she recalls her discomfort when at school in Paris, a well-meaning teacher instructs her to present a literary work about her country to her classmates. Finally, the young Maryse hits on *La Rue Cases-Nègres* and gives an emotive presentation about plantation culture in the French Caribbean, although internally she recognizes that Zobel's depiction of working-class plantation experiences is far removed from her own comfortable bourgeois upbringing (97–103). Indeed, as Condé's childhood memoir makes clear, her upbringing has included a diet of classic metropolitan French children's fiction such as *Les malheurs de Sophie* (1858; *Sophie's Misfortunes*) by an aristocratic Franco-Russian author, the Countess of Ségur; and *Peau d'âne*, a pan-European fairy tale by Charles Perrault. The narrator emphasizes how her parents ascribed far greater value to metropolitan culture than to the Creole folklore tales of Br'er Rabbit or Zamba the Elephant (29), a decision that stemmed from their bourgeois aspirational values for the family but that also left the young Maryse sensing that she was missing a certain part of her cultural heritage: the very stories that might help her make sense of the Caribbean society around her. From the genre's emergence, then, Francophone Caribbean childhood memoirs have been interpreted as a prime tool for the "initiation" of young readers to Caribbean-centric literature—and moreover, as literature that represents experiences that may be familiar or relatable, and in which readers in the Caribbean and its diaspora have a personal stake.

It is no coincidence that the 1990s Francophone Caribbean revival of the childhood memoir genre directly followed the emergence of the *créolité* movement in the late 1980s. The success of the literary manifesto *Éloge de la créolité* (1989; *In Praise of Creoleness*, translated by Mohamed B. Taleb-Khyar) brought its authors, Jean Bernabé, Chamoiseau, and Confiant, to an international audience of readers and critics. *Éloge* establishes the pivotal role of childhood for analyzing Antillean society anew and asserts the significance of the child's gaze as a literary conceit with political potential. In an important section identifying Antilleans as "fondamentalement frappés d'extériorité" ("fundamentally stricken with exteriority") (14; translation, 76), the manifesto argues that the *regard intérieur* or internal gaze required to counteract this alienation must capture "un peu de ce regard d'enfance, questionneur de tout, qui n'a pas encore ses postulats et qui interroge même les évidences" ("[something of] the child's look, questioning everything, having [as] yet no postulats of its own, and [questioning] even the most obvious facts"; 24; translation 85, with my modifications). The manifesto of *créolité* directly anticipates the post-1990 turn to the childhood memoir and the simultaneous wider outpouring of children's literature. These literary currents are also closely connected to political developments. On May 10, 2001, when the French government promulgated a law known as "la loi Taubira,"[3] France took the unprecedented step of recognizing slavery as a crime against humanity, a decision that was also closely related to the French concept of *le devoir de mémoire* ("the duty of remembrance"), which had become prominent in the 1990s. As a result of this law, the Comité pour la Mémoire de l'Esclavage (CPME), or Committee for the Memory of Slavery, was instated on January 5, 2004. French president Jacques Chirac's decision to invite Condé to serve as the committee's inaugural president highlights the interplay between literature, politics, and public memory. In a newspaper article in *L'Humanité* discussing her role as president of the CPME, Condé directly referenced her childhood memoir, specifically the chapter "Leçon d'histoire" (History Lesson), which focuses on the harmful psychological effects of her parents' enduring discomfort and unwillingness to discuss the slave past when she was a child ("Parce que tu es une négresse").

As a result of the intentional interplay between childhood memoirs and fiction for children and young adults, writing for children is particularly porous in the Francophone Caribbean. The next section of analysis will sketch a survey of children's literature, while remaining attentive to this blurring of generic boundaries. At this juncture, it is also helpful to pause and observe that on both sides of the Atlantic, prominent Black authors, academics, and activists are increasingly turning to children's literature: to take one example, the Black feminist author and academic bell hooks produced a significant volume of books for young children.

One of the earliest texts potentially classifiable in this category is a collection of short stories by Zobel, *Et si la mer n'était pas bleue* (1982; *And What If the Sea Weren't Blue*), which was published by Éditions Caribéennes, a newly established Paris-based publishing house that proclaimed its commitment to raising the profile of Caribbean literature in France.[4] The gentle subject matter, tone, and form make this work of Zobel's particularly suited to younger and adolescent readers. Moreover, the vivid, colorful, and enticing illustrations by Sophie Mondésir on the front cover and in several full-page inserts throughout the text enhance the book's visual appeal and position it as a collection that could be enjoyed by children, young adults, and adults alike.

The leading Guadeloupean author, Maryse Condé, whose work has already been discussed above and whose global reputation was consolidated in 2018 when she was awarded the New Academy Prize in Literature (established as an alternative to the Nobel), is also one of the most prolific authors of texts for children and young adults. Much like her adult literature, in her children's literature Condé tends to tackle prominent social themes. Her works range from a social realist depiction of the plight of Haitian boat people in *Haïti chérie* (1987) and the effects of a particularly devastating hurricane in *Hugo le Terrible* (1991), to a Caribbean foray into sci-fi, *La planète orbis* (2002), the former illustrated by Marcelino Truong and the latter by Letizia Galli. However, the transcultural reception of a text such as *Haïti chérie*, which as Kiera Vaclavik argues represents Haitians "either as villains or victims," has elicited a certain amount of criticism ("Damaging Goods?" 238). Condé is one of the few authors to have reflected on her children's literature praxis in an interview, commenting, "Il y a une forme de plaisir dans les romans pour enfants . . . il y a une sensibilité que vous devez faire intervenir pour intéresser l'enfant. . . . Il faut arriver à trouver le cœur de l'enfant et à le toucher, tout en éveillant sa curiosité." ("There is a certain pleasure in writing for children. . . . [T]o capture the child's interest, you have to write with greater sensitivity. You have to work out what is dear to the child, and manage to stimulate this, while simultaneously awakening their curiosity" [my modified translation]) ("J'ai toujours" 116; translation 120). Nonetheless, despite an increasing number of scholarly monographs dedicated to her oeuvre, Condé's works for children have yet to be discussed at any great length and remain a relatively understudied aspect of her literary output.

A similarly uncompromising approach to challenging adult themes is found in works by Edwidge Danticat, one of the most successful English-language writers to have emerged from the Haitian diaspora and author of several books for children that have attracted critical attention (Vaclavik, "Writing Young"). *Mama's Nightingale* (2015), for example, explores the traumatic separation experienced by a young child after her mother is placed in an immigration detention center. The narrative emphasizes how the child's resilience is forged through a framework of unwavering parental love, and in particular through her mother's oral transmission of Creole folklore. By recording stories and messages onto a cassette tape, her mother can continue to share folklore tales with her daughter throughout their separation, which in turn encourages the young girl to learn to use her imagination to overcome the difficulties of her physical and emotional circumstances. More generally, Haiti is the area most frequently depicted in Anglophone children's literature focusing on Francophone Caribbean culture, and this may in part be explained by the significant and increasing Haitian diasporic population in the US. For instance, the 2020 exhibition Black Voices: Picture Books as Antiracist Resources curated by the Eric Carle Museum of Picture Book Art in Amherst, Massachusetts (with an accompanying online blog post and reading list), featured at least three works published in the US that explore aspects of diasporic Haitian culture: Tami Charles's *Freedom Soup* (2019), LaTisha Redding's *Calling the Water Drum* (2016), and Javaka Steptoe's *Radiant Child: The Story of Young Artist Jean-Michel Basquiat* (2016).

Francophone Caribbean authors are also active in rendering Caribbean children's works written in other languages accessible to French speakers. Most notably, the author and academic Raphaël Confiant has translated two texts by Jamaican authors from English into French. The first is a collection of stories focused on community, James Berry's *Un voleur dans le village* (1993; original title, *A Thief in the Village*), and the second, a sci-fi fantasy by author and screenwriter Evan Jones, *Aventures sur la planète Knos* (1998; original title, *Skylarking*).

Intertextuality between Francophone Caribbean childhood memoirs and children's literature is particularly pronounced in works by Pineau and Laferrière. In *Je suis fou de Vava* (*I'm Crazy about Vava*), a gentle picture book,

Laferrière explores the same childhood crush—a girl in a yellow dress—that runs as a leitmotif through his childhood memoirs, an aspect that has also received critical attention from Vaclavik.[5] For her part, in her tale for children *Un papillon dans la cité* (1992; *A Butterfly in the Projects*), Pineau explores themes of childhood, immigration, social deprivation, and racism in metropolitan France,[6] anticipating her "adult" novel or childhood memoir, *L'exil selon Julia* (1996). Both narratives are set in the department of Sarthe and a Parisian housing project, and both feature a grandmother figure called Julia, who also goes by the name's creolized form, Man Ya.

In *Un papillon dans la cité*, after being raised in Guadeloupe by Man Ya, ten-year-old Félicie, known as Féfé, is sent to France to live with her mother, who emigrated there shortly after her birth. Man Ya has instilled in the young girl such a love for Guadeloupe that this physical separation, although painful, does not shake the child's sense of self, as exemplified when she remains uninterested in the blonde Barbie doll her mother buys for her, and when she proudly describes her Guadeloupean ancestors: "C'était pendant l'esclavage. Ils se révoltaient. Ils brisaient leurs chaînes. . . . Ceux qui s'en sortaient vivaient dans les bois. La nuit, ils attaquaient les plantations pour libérer leurs frères. Ils ont gagné leur liberté" ("It was during slavery. They revolted. They broke their chains. . . . Those who made it went to live in the woods. At night, they attacked the plantations to liberate their brothers. They won their freedom"; 61). It is highly significant that here, the child is proudly demonstrating her knowledge of Caribbean culture and can identify heroic figures of Caribbean history, whose agency in their own liberations is emphasized, and who are unlikely to feature in school history textbooks.[7] Moreover, it is also striking that Pineau's children's book uses Creole language, through dialogue as well as in references to cultural terms—in this respect, the work offers comparative potential with other bilingual Creole (patois) children's texts such as *I Am Dominica / Mwe sé Donmnik* by Mara Etienne-Manley (2013). Pineau includes translations in French in footnotes, a decision that can be interpreted as an educational aspiration to teach children about the significance of Creole in the Caribbean; in a recent study, Natalie Edwards has analyzed this linguistic feature as evidence of Pineau's "evolving translanguaging."[8] *Un papillon dans la cité* has attracted international interest, and the French Ministry for Europe and Foreign Affairs supported the production of a special dossier on the text aimed at schoolteachers by the general consul for France in Boston (Consulat Général de France à Boston).

Four years after *Un papillon dans la cité* was published, Pineau developed the ideas outlined in her children's book into a more complex, adult depiction of diasporic identity in *L'exil selon Julia*. While this text undoubtedly forms part of the 1990s renaissance in Francophone Caribbean childhood memoirs, it is also written in a manner that creates a greater degree of remove between author and child counterpart than is found in other contemporary childhood memoirs, thwarting straightforward identification. Now, the young female narrator (named once as Marie, which is Pineau's middle name) finds solace in the tales recounted by her Guadeloupean grandmother Julia, or Man Ya, while they are both living in metropolitan France. Rather than drawing on lived experience of the Caribbean, as in *Un papillon dans la cité*, here the lead character constructs an imaginary Guadeloupe that functions as a psychological sanctuary from metropolitan racism, but which is then challenged when the family returns to the French Caribbean (first Martinique, then Guadeloupe), and the children must confront the islands' complex modern social realities. From a comparative perspective, Pineau's writing on immigration and intergenerational families could be analyzed alongside the acclaimed BBC TV series *JoJo & Gran Gran* (2020), which was developed from a series of books by Laura Henry and made with guidance from the Saint Lucian High Commissioner and Saint Lucian Tourism Authority.[9] While the works differ markedly in approach and tone, there is significant common ground in the foregrounding of the relationship between a young girl and her grandmother and their shared exploration of immigration and diasporic identities.

From the very beginning of his literary career, the region's most feted living author, Patrick Chamoiseau, has also published literature directly aimed at children. *Au temps de l'antan: Contes du pays Martinique* (*Creole Folktales*, translated by Linda Coverdale) was published in 1988. It was also, significantly, the first of Chamoiseau's works to appear in English. The author's first published works display a pedagogic concern with educating an Antillean public about the history of their islands,[10] a concern similarly demonstrated in his play *Manman Dlo contre la fée Carabosse* (*Water Mama versus Carabosse, the Bad Fairy*), which pits the "baddie" of Antillean fairy tales against Carabosse, a famous malevolent fairy whose tradition is well known in metropolitan France and who has roots in pan-European folklore.[11]

Another important work by Chamoiseau for children, *Émerveilles*, a coproduction with Martinican artist Maure, appeared in 1998. To date, it has not been translated into English, although it has attracted significant critical attention. *Émerveilles* is not a standard French word, but is related to the verb *émerveiller*, which means to amaze or astonish. To the French reader, the term is also connected to the word *merveilles* and thus forges a link with *Alice in Wonderland*, translated into French as *Alice au pays des merveilles*. Indeed, a child might easily mistakenly hear Lewis Carroll's title as *Alice au pays d'émerveilles*. Chamoiseau and Maure are suggesting Martinique as a wonderland, preparing readers for the magical realism and surrealism of the stories that follow.

As I have argued in a previous publication, *Émerveilles* is a "redrawing" of the space of Martinique—the work opens with a mysterious and fantastical map of Martinique, and each story is set in a specific named location on the island ("Childhood Meets the *Tout-Monde*" 53–72). Each story is accompanied by an image that is, more often than not, as challenging as it is enticing. Maure is an established Martinican artist, and her artwork in the collection displays the hybrid influences of Caribbean and continental European children's literature. For example, Maure draws on a more somber color palette than Anglophone readers might expect in a work for children, and frequently uses textured effects and pastels; her whimsical yet sophisticated illustrations are dominated by turquoise, blue, and purple hues. By reading *Émerveilles*, a child learns about the traumatic legacy of slavery and colonialism, how to coexist with this memory, and moreover how to view their home country as a land of wonders through this fantastical text-art collaboration. As a point of comparison, *Émerveilles* is in appearance similar to the surrealist illustrations provided by the Mexican painter Gabriel Pacheco for *12 poemas de Federico García Lorca* (2014), a Spanish poetry collection for children that draws together works by the canonical author. Both books display a similar cross-fertilization between European and American influences and use word and picture collaborations to interest children in prominent authors in a captivating but deliberately challenging and sophisticated manner.

Critic Jill Gaeta argues that *Émerveilles* displays a greater level of innovation in its treatment of gender roles than is typically found in Chamoiseau's "adult" fiction, as she demonstrates in her close reading of the tale "Kosto et ses deux enfants" ("Kosto and His Two Children"). Moreover, the collection is one of the first of Chamoiseau's texts to openly engage with the French Caribbean poetic-philosophical notion of the *tout-monde*, which promotes a philosophy of connectedness: the *tout-monde* is one of the major theoretical concepts generated by the late novelist and philosopher Édouard Glissant, who was Chamoiseau's long-term collaborator and mentor. *Émerveilles* thus represents a remarkable attempt to introduce young readers—and their parents and caregivers—to concepts developed by adult Francophone Caribbean writers.

Chamoiseau has continued to produce works for children and young adults; in 2002, he published *Le commandeur d'une pluie* (*The Rain Maker*), illustrated by William Wilson. And in 2009, *Encyclomerveille d'un tueur 1: L'orphelin de Cocoyer Grands-Bois* (*Encyclo-wonder of a Killer 1: The Orphan of Coco Forest*) appeared, with illustrations by Thierry Ségur, which was intended to be "the first in a proposed series of comic books for children and adolescents" (Knepper 185), although the series was subsequently discontinued. In 2013, Chamoiseau published *Veilles et merveilles créoles: Contes du pays Martinique* (*Creole Marvels: Tales of Martinique*) with illustrations by Giorgia Grippo Belfi, a text that in its preoccupation with folklore is closely aligned with his earliest works for children such as *Au temps de l'antan*.

The concern with the transmission of historical memory—particularly the slave past—is a recurring theme woven across Francophone Caribbean children's literature and childhood memoirs. This results in what Maeve McCusker has identified as a "haunting, primal scene figured in a strikingly similar way" (441). Such scenes recur from text to text and author to author, and I have theorized these moments of tension in a previous study as "the scene of recognition" (*Childhood* 1–23). In the scene of recognition, a child begins to observe inconsistencies in their world and goes on to ask a difficult question of their parents or grandparents that can only be adequately answered with reference to slavery. This answer is almost always deferred or avoided, and instead, the awkward silence of the parent is foregrounded. The dynamics of this scene are also illustrated in a book for young children, *Grand-mère, ça commence où la Route de l'Esclave?* (1998; *Grandmother, Where Does the Slave Route Begin?*) by the Guadeloupean author Dany Bébel-Gisler. According to Bébel-Gisler, the title arises directly from a question posed by her then three-year-old granddaughter; it also makes direct reference to the UNESCO initiative La Route de l'Esclave (the Slave Route) launched in 1994, in which Bébel-Gisler participated until her death in 2003. Bébel-Gisler heightens pathos by focusing on the emotive pull of the child as inquisitive innocent and effectively stages a "scene of recognition" throughout her book. Through this process, she creates a model for the transmission of traumatic knowledge, and this is of importance not only for the identity formation of the youngest members of society but also for the identity formation of wider communities, and indeed for conceptualizations of identity within the dynamics of global society. The book is a large-format, oversize publication that resembles a school history textbook and combines text and illustrations; aesthetically, for example, it resembles the Martinican-produced comparative school history book *Histoire des Antilles françaises des Amérindiens à nos jours* (2012; *History of the French Antilles: From Amerindians to the Present Day*), an outstanding French-language resource for children written by an experienced teacher, Raphaël Nicole, and self-published in Martinique. Bébel-Gisler replicated this format in another book for children (published posthumously) on the subject of Indian immigration to the Caribbean: *Grand-mère, pourquoi Sundari est venue en Guadeloupe? L'arrivée des premiers Indiens en Guadeloupe* (2005; *Grandmother, Why Did Sundari Come to Guadeloupe? The Arrival of the First Indians in Guadeloupe*); here, the marginalized story of Indian indentured labor in the Caribbean forms the subject of the narrative, in a work that once again manages to forge an emotional connection while conveying significant and disturbing historical events.

The genre of the *bande dessinée* or graphic novel is also significant to an exploration of children's literature in the Francophone Caribbean. The *bande dessinée* enjoys great popularity in France, and this cultural tradition also radiates throughout the Francophone world. It has clear crossover appeal for confident readers from around the age of seven to adolescence and adulthood, creating multilayered text and picture narratives that are accessible to all groups but whose nuances may not be fully clear to the youngest readers without appropriate educational intervention (or indeed to readers of any age who are unfamiliar with the Francophone Caribbean context). Key creators working in this genre with Francophone Caribbean origins include Michel Bagoé, whose adaptation of Zobel's *La Rue Cases-Nègres* has already been referenced above, and Roland Monpierre, an author and illustrator who has published about historical figures, producing works such as *Bob Marley: La légende des Wailers* and *La légion Saint-Georges*, about the Black violinist and composer known as Le Chevalier de Saint-Georges. Monpierre has also adapted Zobel's first novel, *Diab'-là* (*Diablo*), as a graphic novel. In addition, he has published his own work for children, *Les rêves de Paris* (*Dreams of Paris*). Another prominent graphic novelist is Jessica Oublié, who, working in collaboration with illustrators, has published *Péyi an nou* (*Our Country*), an award-winning title on Caribbean immigration to France, followed by a dense graphic novel dissecting the French Caribbean chlordecone (Kepone) pollution scandal, *Tropiques toxiques* (*Toxic Tropics*).

While the present analysis has focused on literature by the most prominent authors across the Francophone Caribbean and its diaspora, mention should also be made of the highly trained specialist librarians (*documentalistes*) who work in Martinique and Guadeloupe and who coordinate literacy initiatives between schools and local public multimedia libraries (*médiathèques*). One such example is the Médiathèque de Rivière-Salée, in the south of Martinique, an impressive, vast modern building that boasts world-class holdings of children's literature. In 2015, it was my privilege to work with a team at the Médiathèque, in particular with Raphaëlle Bouville, on a range of cultural initiatives supported by the Town Council of Rivière-Salée to mark the centenary of Joseph Zobel, which included several events held at the Médiathèque and in schools all aimed directly at local schoolchildren at the primary and secondary levels. These activities also complemented and extended existing projects promoting literacy initiatives throughout the community. By including such important cultural centers in the scope of research projects and public engagement activities, scholars are able to gain a more complete picture of contemporary patterns in the consumption of children's literature written in French and in creoles, and to better understand local Caribbean initiatives to promote children's literature and a love of reading more generally. Similarly, the catalogues of independent publishers are an important source for future research into children's literature, particularly Éditions Jasor and Éditions Nestor, which are both based in Guadeloupe, and Éditions Ibis Rouge, originally based in French Guiana but now part of a publishing group based in Réunion, in the Indian Ocean.

This survey would be incomplete without making reference to the way in which the trope of childhood is freighted with its own metaphorical charge in Francophone Caribbean folklore. Under slavery and the plantation system, an unburdened childhood was impossible. Patrick Chamoiseau emphasizes this in *Au temps de l'antan*, his first work aimed at children, which opens with the cautionary message that Creole *contes* are cautionary tales unlikely to furnish a happy ending, and are characterized by "*une dynamique éducative, un mode d'apprentissage de la vie, ou plus exactement de la survie en pays colonisé: le conte créole dit que la peur est là, que chaque brin du monde est terrifiant, et qu'il faut savoir vivre avec*" (10; italics in original; "an educational dynamic, a way of learning about life, or more exactly about survival in a colonized land: the Creole tale states that fear is omnipresent, that each corner of the world is terrifying, and that you have to learn to live with it"). Creole folklore characters are first encountered in childhood stories, and the allegorical function of these tales plays an important role in the transmission of collective history and memory. Chamoiseau's focus on Creole monsters and his exploration of their metaphorical function as a means of conveying the colonial past also nods to a seminal work of Antillean folklore by Thérèse Georgel, *Contes et légendes des Antilles* (1957; *Tales and Legends of the Antilles*), a collection of Creole folklore, which, in its most recent edition, itself appears in a series for young adults.

Finally, it should be noted that in the Francophone Caribbean, childhood has generated its own semantic field through the specific Creole terms *iche/yiche*, which roughly translate as "kid," and *ti-moun(e)*, literally "small people." Moreover, the diminutive prefix *ti-* ("Lil") applies to stock characters from French Caribbean Creole folklore. The most notable example is Ti Jean, a wily, quick-witted hero who is locked in an eternal battle against the slave master, whose stories were collected and reinterpreted by the Guadeloupean author Simone Schwarz-Bart in *Ti Jean l'horizon* (1979; *Between Two Worlds*, translated by Barbara Bray). Another similar folkloric figure is Compère Lapin—the Francophone counterpart to Br'er Rabbit—who is the trickster hero of stories told in plantation societies from the US Deep South to the Caribbean, with origins in West African folklore. Nonetheless, in Francophone Caribbean literature, although monsters abound as residual fragments of a traumatic past, it is equally true that authors and folktales repeatedly emphasize the fact that a diminutive status does not necessarily equal subservience and can become the very position from which resistance—and creative growth—is forged.

In its many iterations and guises, childhood emerges as a complex and rich creative seam in Francophone Caribbean literature. The interplay between children's literature and childhood memoirs is a prominent contemporary literary trend that is remarkable at an aesthetic level for the narrative continuities and intertextual references it generates, and also in terms of reception, due to the connections that are forged with authors' wider "adult" works. Children's literature from the Francophone Caribbean offers the potential to introduce the very youngest readers (and their parents and caregivers) to internationally recognized Francophone Caribbean authors through innovative and dynamic narratives that often include remarkable collaborations with visual artists. The texts attend to how, from the earliest years of life, experiences of place, race, language, and history play an essential role in the construction of identity.

Notes

1. Such comments were made to me by educators in Martinique during our collaborative activities to commemorate the centenary of Joseph Zobel in 2015; these collaborations are discussed in more detail toward the conclusion of this chapter.

2. I explore Zobel's childhood memoir, its major themes, and its complex publication history in detail in *Joseph Zobel: Négritude and the Novel*.

3. French laws often become popularly known by the surnames of the politicians who propose them; in this case, the reference is to the French Guyanese minister, Christiane Taubira.

4. For a fuller discussion of Zobel's involvement with and particular support for Éditions Caribéennes, see Hardwick, *Joseph Zobel: Négritude and the Novel*, 202–3.

5. See Kiera Vaclavik's "More than Mirrors: Dany Laferrière and Frédéric Normandin's *Je suis fou de Vava*" (2011), in addition to her book chapter (in French) offering a discussion of Haitian children's literature more generally, "L'édition de jeunesse en Haïti" (2010).

6. Pineau and other Caribbean children's writers, including Condé and the Haitian author Évelyne Trouillot, are analyzed for their specific insights into globalization in *Mondialisation et littérature de jeunesse*, a major comparative study in French by Jean Perrot, the leading French critic of children's literature.

7. In recent years, the maroons and their ambiguous legacy have been explored by historians and cultural critics; Pineau's account for children is void of the balanced critique that adult studies would typically contain and focuses on presenting positive Caribbean-community role models.

8. For a detailed study of this aspect, see chapter 4 of Edwards's *Multilingual Life Writing by French and Francophone Women: Translingual Selves*: "Gisèle Pineau's Evolving Translanguaging: From *Un papillon dans la cité* to *L'exil selon Julia* to *Mes quatre femmes*."

9. Henry's book series commences with *Jo-Jo and Gran-Gran, All in a Week!* (2016).

10. Chamoiseau is a trained youth worker, a fact emphasized in his novel *Un dimanche au cachot* (A Sunday in the Cells).

11. For an analysis, see chapter 4, "Theatre as Writing and Voice: Patrick Chamoiseau's *Manman Dlo contre la fée Carabosse*," in John Conteh-Morgan and Dominic Thomas's *New Francophone African and Caribbean Theatres*.

Works Cited

Anthony, Michael. *Mon année à San Fernando*. Translated by Monique Zeline, Claire Hanson and Jocelyne Rosette, Association pour la Connaissance des Littératures Antillaises, 2008.

Anthony, Michael. *The Year in San Fernando*. André Deutsch, 1965.

Bébel-Gisler, Dany. *Grand-mère, ça commence où la Route de l'Esclave?* Éditions Jasor, 1998.
Bébel-Gisler, Dany. *Grand-mère, pourquoi Sundari est venue en Guadeloupe? L'arrivée des premiers Indiens en Guadeloupe.* Éditions Jasor, 2005.
Bernabé, Jean, Patrick Chamoiseau, and Raphaël Confiant. *Éloge de la créolité/In Praise of Creoleness,* bilingual edition with translation by Mohamed B. Taleb-Khyar, Éditions Gallimard, 1993.
Centre National du Cinéma et de l'Image Animée. *Rue cases-nègres d'Euzhan Palcy.* 2011. https://www.cnc.fr/cinema/education-a-l-image/college-au-cinema/dossiers-pedagogiques/dossiers-maitre/rue-casesnegres-deuzhan-palcy_209857.
Chamoiseau, Patrick. *Au temps de l'antan: Contes du pays Martinique.* Hatier, 1988.
Chamoiseau, Patrick. *Childhood.* Translated by Carol Volk, U of Nebraska P, 1999.
Chamoiseau, Patrick. *Le commandeur d'une pluie: Suivi de L'accra de la richesse.* Illustrated by William Wilson, Éditions Gallimard/Giboulées, 2002.
Chamoiseau, Patrick. *Creole Folktales.* Translated by Linda Coverdale, New Press, 1994.
Chamoiseau, Patrick. *Un dimanche au cachot.* Éditions Gallimard, 2007.
Chamoiseau, Patrick. *Émerveilles.* Illustrated by Maure, Éditions Gallimard, 1998.
Chamoiseau, Patrick. *Encyclomerveille d'un tueur 1: L'orphelin de Cocoyer Grands-Bois.* Illustrated by Thiery Ségur, Delcourt, 2009.
Chamoiseau, Patrick. *Une enfance créole I: Antan d'enfance.* Éditions Gallimard, 1993.
Chamoiseau, Patrick. *Une enfance créole II: Chemin-d'école.* Éditions Gallimard, 1994.
Chamoiseau, Patrick. *Une enfance créole III: À bout d'enfance.* Éditions Gallimard, 2005.
Chamoiseau, Patrick. *Manman Dlo contre la fée Carabosse.* Éditions Caribéennes, 1982.
Chamoiseau, Patrick. *Veilles et merveilles créoles: Contes du pays Martinique.* Illustrated by Giorgia Grippo Belfi, Le Square, 2013.
Comité pour la Mémoire de l'Esclavage. *Mémoires de la traite négrière, de l'esclavage et de leurs abolitions.* Éditions La Découverte, 2005.
Condé, Maryse. *Le cœur à rire et à pleurer.* Robert Laffont, 1999.
Condé, Maryse. *Haïti chérie.* Illustrated by Marcelino Truong, Bayard Jeunesse, 1987.
Condé, Maryse. *Hugo le Terrible.* Illustrated by Marcelino Truong, Sépia, 1991.
Condé, Maryse. "'J'ai toujours été une personne un peu à part': Questions à Maryse Condé." Interview with Louise Hardwick. *International Journal of Francophone Studies,* vol. 9, no. 1, April 2006, pp. 111–24.
Condé, Maryse. "Parce que tu es une négresse." *L'Humanité,* May 10, 2006.
Condé, Maryse. *La planète orbis.* Illustrated by Letizia Galli, Éditions Jasor, 2002.
Confiant, Raphaël. *Le cahier des romances.* Éditions Gallimard, 2000.
Confiant, Raphaël. *Ravines du devant-jour.* Éditions Gallimard, 1993.
Confiant, Raphaël, translator. *Aventures sur la planète Knos.* By Evan Jones, Dapper, 1998.
Confiant, Raphaël, translator. *Un voleur dans le village.* By James Berry, Éditions Gallimard, 1993.
Consulat Général de France à Boston. "Dossier pédagogique: Gisèle Pineau, *Un papillon dans la cité.*" https://boston.consulfrance.org/un-papillon-dans-la-cite-Gisele-Pineau.
Conteh-Morgan, John, with Dominic Thomas. *New Francophone African and Caribbean Theatres.* Indiana UP, 2010.
Danticat, Edwidge. *Mama's Nightingale: A Story of Immigration and Separation.* Illustrated by Leslie Staub, Dial Books, 2015.
Dine, Philip. "The French Colonial Empire in Juvenile Fiction: From Jules Verne to Tintin." *Historical Reflections/Réflexions Historiques,* vol. 23, no. 2, Spring 1997, pp. 177–203.

Dine, Philip. "Children's Literature." *Postcolonial Realms of Memory: Sites and Symbols in Modern France*, edited by Etienne Achille, Charles Forsdick, and Lydie Moudileno, Liverpool UP, 2021, pp. 343–50.
Edwards, Natalie. *Multilingual Life Writing by French and Francophone Women: Translingual Selves*. Routledge, 2020.
Etienne-Manley, Mara. *I Am Dominica / Mwe sé Donmnik*. Little Bell Caribbean, 2013.
Gaeta, Jill M. "Reevaluating the 'Masculine' and 'Feminine': Patrick Chamoiseau's 'Kosto et ses deux enfants.'" *French Review*, vol. 84, no. 1, October 2010, pp. 140–49.
García Lorca, Federico. *12 poemas de Federico García Lorca*. Illustrated by Gabriel Pacheco, Kalandraka, 2014.
García Márquez, Gabriel. *Vivir para contarla*. Alfred A. Knopf, 2002.
Georgel, Thérèse. *Contes et légendes des Antilles*. 1957. Pocket Jeunesse, 1994.
Hardwick, Louise. *Childhood, Autobiography and the Francophone Caribbean*. Liverpool UP, 2013.
Hardwick, Louise. "Childhood Meets the *Tout-Monde*: *Émerveilles* by Patrick Chamoiseau and Maure." *Francophone Postcolonial Studies*, vol. 7, no. 2, Autumn 2009, pp. 53–72.
Hardwick, Louise. *Joseph Zobel: Négritude and the Novel*. Liverpool UP, 2018.
Henry, Laura. *Jo-Jo and Gran-Gran, All in a Week!* Laura Henry Consultancy, 2016.
Knepper, Wendy. *Patrick Chamoiseau: A Critical Introduction*. UP of Mississippi, 2012.
Laferrière, Dany. *Le charme des après-midi sans fin*. Serpent à Plumes, 1997.
Laferrière, Dany. *Je suis fou de Vava*. Éditions de la Bagnole, 2005.
Laferrière, Dany. *L'odeur du café*. 1991. Serpent à Plumes, 2001.
Lamming, George. *In the Castle of My Skin*. Michael Joseph, 1953.
Maximin, Daniel. *Tu, c'est l'enfance*. Éditions Gallimard, 2004.
McCusker, Maeve. "'Troubler l'ordre de l'oubli': Memory and Forgetting in French Caribbean Autobiography of the 1990s." *Forum for Modern Language Studies*, vol. 40, no. 4, October 2004, pp. 438–50.
Monpierre, Roland. *Bob Marley: La légende des Wailers*. Éditions Albin Michel, 2006.
Monpierre, Roland. *Diab'-là (d'après le roman de Joseph Zobel)*. Nouvelles Éditions Latines, 2015.
Monpierre, Roland. *La légion Saint-Georges*. Caraïbéditions, 2010.
Monpierre, Roland. *Les rêves de Paris*. Tartamudo, 2003.
Nicole, Raphaël. *Histoire des Antilles françaises des Amérindiens à nos jours en parallèle à l'histoire de France et de grands faits de l'histoire de l'humanité*. Éditions de la Frise, 2012.
Ollivier, Émile. *Mille eaux*. Éditions Gallimard, 1999.
Oublié, Jessica. *Péyi an nou*. Illustrated by Marie-Ange Rousseau, Steinkis, 2017.
Oublié, Jessica. *Tropiques toxiques: Le scandale du chlordécone*. Illustrated by Nicola Gobbi, Steinkis/Les Escales, 2020.
Palcy, Euzhan, director. *Rue Cases-Nègres*. NEF Diffusion, Orca Productions, SU.MA.FA., 1983.
Pépin, Ernest. *Coulée d'or*. Éditions Gallimard, 2005.
Perrot, Jean. *Mondialisation et littérature de jeunesse*. Éditions du Cercle de la Librairie, 2008.
Pineau, Gisèle. *L'exil selon Julia*. Stock, 1996.
Pineau, Gisèle. *Un papillon dans la cité*. 1992. Sépia, 1997.
Schwarz-Bart, Simone. *Ti Jean l'horizon*. Éditions du Seuil, 1979.

Vaclavik, Kiera. "Damaging Goods? Francophone Children's Books in a Postcolonial World." *International Research in Children's Literature*, vol. 2, no. 2, December 2009, pp. 228–42.

Vaclavik, Kiera. "L'édition de jeunesse en Haïti." *L'édition de jeunesse francophone face à la mondialisation*, edited by Jean Foucault, Michel Manson, and Luc Pinhas, L'Harmattan, 2010, pp. 137–48.

Vaclavik, Kiera. "More than Mirrors: Dany Laferrière and Frédéric Normandin's *Je suis fou de Vava*." *Contemporary French and Francophone Studies*, vol. 15, no. 1, January 2011, pp. 79–87.

Vaclavik, Kiera. "Writing Young: Edwidge Danticat's Young Adult Fiction." *Edwidge Danticat: A Reader's Guide*, edited by Martin Munro, U of Virginia P, 2010, pp. 86–98.

Zobel, Joseph. *Black Shack Alley*. Translated by Keith Q. Warner, Three Continents Press, 1980.

Zobel, Joseph. *Black Shack Alley*. Translated by Keith Q. Warner, Penguin Classics, 2020.

Zobel, Joseph. *Et si la mer n'était pas bleue*. Éditions Caribéennes, 1982.

Zobel, Joseph. *La Rue Cases-Nègres*. Présence Africaine, 1974.

Zobel, Joseph. *La Rue Cases-Nègres*. Adapted as a graphic novel by Michel Bagoé and Stéphanie Destin, Présence Africaine, 2018.

CHAPTER 3

Anglophone Caribbean Children's Literature
A Snapshot

Betsy Nies

Anglophone Caribbean children's literature finds its beginnings in folklore—whether that be the oral stories of home, the rhymes of the street and school, or the jocularity of Trinidad's talk tents, the provisional pop-up arenas that feature public entertainment at Carnival (James 164). The orality of these typically Creole formations finds itself transformed in print—for the most part, vying with Standard British English in literature written specifically for children. Given the postcolonial interest in preparing students for the global world, Standard English remains a benchmark, but an ambivalent one given the widespread desire to represent for children the language of the familiar—the Creole of the majority. With the influence of Great Britain weighing heavily in the classroom, the 1960s brought change to the newly independent Caribbean nations who sought to embrace a local identity separate from the colonizer. However, structural factors along with an ongoing attachment to the values of the "mother" country produced uneven attempts to celebrate postindependence ideologies. With twelve nations formerly part of the British Empire now independent (gaining independence between 1962 and 1981), and five territories still under British governance, the separation remains incomplete, with strong reliance on publishing companies in the United Kingdom and pedagogical practices influenced by the British model.[1] This chapter will review the transition in children's literature after the 1960s from colonialist to postcolonialist content as a framework for understanding Anglophone Caribbean children's literature.

Beginning as early as the 1930s, Caribbean folklore was making its way into primary classrooms, with the first waves of nationalist sentiment sparking literary output. However, the 1960s—the years leading up to independence—produced far more local publications. Jamaican Sir Philip Sherlock, who in 1964 was serving as a schoolteacher and vice chancellor of the University of the West Indies, committed himself to integrating local folklore into his publications for children: *Anansi the Spider Man* (1954), *West Indian Folktales* (1966), and *Iguana's Tail: Crick, Crack Stories from the Caribbean* (1969). Trinidadian folklorist Al Ramsawack published a series of children's stories influenced by the competing cultural strains of Trinidad and Tobago—Amerindian, French, East Indian, Spanish, and African cultures; he also published *Anansi the Tricky Spider* (1970). Guyanese David Makhanlall contributed to the offerings with an extensive Brer Anansi series, opening with *The Best of Brer Anansi* in 1973. Jamaican Andrew Salkey added to the oral nature of these stories by using both Creole and Standard Jamaican English in his young adult folktale *Anancy's Score* (1973). Many of these texts made their way into the classroom, revised in format for use as readers for young children.

While such books evoked national pride honoring the origins of indigenous and African cultures, they also evoked colonialist sentiments. Jamaican C. Everard Palmer wrote fifteen books for young people, many of which were (and remain) integrated into regional school curricula. He translated folktales into simple didactic stories. While his characters retain some of Anansi's trickster qualities, villagers come across as primitive, conniving creatures or as quaint—stuck in another time and place. For example, in *The Cloud with the Silver Lining* (1966), Palmer features a rural man who is tricked out of his landholdings as a result of his generosity. In *Big Doc Bitterroot* (1968), a charlatan tricks villagers out of their savings through his sale of "medicine." In *The Wooing of Beppo Tate* (1972), the trickster is represented, as Cynthia James notes, as the lower-class "Creole-speaking ne'er-do-well," who tricks the protagonist out of food, a common theme in Anansi's stories. James locates the association of class status and characters' actions as an internalization of negative colonial attitudes toward folk culture and home languages (168). Karen Sands-O'Connor argues that Palmer's books signify a nostalgia for a past featuring rural folk with simple thoughts and simple minds. Palmer positions readers, she notes, as outsiders to this "foreign" culture, for instance describing foods for the benefit of non-Caribbean readers (*Soon Come Home* 148–49). But writers of historical fiction of this same time period embraced postcolonial ideologies that celebrated the fight for freedom, experimenting at times with integrating the vernacular into their children's texts that were disruptive to colonial belief systems.

For example, Jamaican Victor Reid, author of *New Day* (1949), considered the first Caribbean book for adults written in Creole, also wrote historical fiction for school students as a tool for reimaging his nation's new status. Inspirited by the nationalist ideology that first emerged in the 1930s, he published, jointly with the Jamaican Ministry of Education and Longman, his first young adult novel, *Sixty-Five* (1962), set during the Morant Bay Rebellion of 1865, a massive postslavery revolt against the poor economic and political conditions of Black Jamaicans. Reid followed with *The Young Warriors* (1967), about a maroon skirmish with the British, and *Peter of Mount Ephraim: The Daddy Sharpe Rebellion* (1971), a story of the largest slave rebellion in Jamaican history (the Baptist War of 1831–1832); the brutality of the reprisals by the British-led Jamaican government contributed to the abolition of slavery in 1834 throughout the Anglophone Caribbean. Reid reflected on his decision to write children's books in a talk he gave in 1986 at the University of the West Indies, Mona:

> All of us in these English-speaking territories grew up knowing about English life and English countryside much more than about our own. And so I thought that I would try doing some books to be used in schools—local schools. *Sixty-Five* occurred then, or just before that. And then I went into doing another couple of children's books and persuaded the Ministry of Education, or the Department of Education, as it probably was then, to take up these books. ("The Writer and His Work" 7)

These books challenged colonial histories that positioned Black Jamaicans, the majority population, as aggressors instead of leaders. They relied on Jamaican Standard English but included elements of the vernacular in their representations of characters.

While, prior to the 1960s, the use of informal Caribbean Englishes appeared in very limited ways in literature for children, folklorist, poet, and dramatist Louise Bennett, more popularly known as "Miss Lou," brought to the regional forefront orature for children with her public performances and poetry publications. In 1957, she recorded *Children's Jamaican Songs and Games* (1957) for the Smithsonian. Between 1968 and 1980, she hosted a children's show called *Ring Ding* on Jamaica's National Broadcasting Service that provided her young audience with folktales, poems, and other forms of orature in Jamaican patois. Paul Keens-Douglas, a storyteller out of Trinidad and Grenada, similarly published poetry in Creole, and he remains active in public performance venues in Trinidad and internationally. Such poems and stories became popular in school curricula, challenging the hierarchies of race and class so embedded in such material.

The production of Caribbean children's literature was also influenced heavily by the migration of many Anglophone Caribbean writers to Great Britain in what became known as the Windrush generation, named for their first arrival on British shores in 1948 on the vessel HTM *Empire Windrush*. These new immigrants from different islands, meeting for the first time, claimed a West Indian identity that found expression in the development of the Caribbean Arts Movement (CAM), launched in part by children's writer Andrew Salkey. Salkey worked as an interviewer for the BBC radio program *Caribbean Voices* (1943–1958) and developed an extensive network of Anglophone Caribbean writers. In 1966, in London, he founded the CAM with Trinidadian publisher John La Rose and Barbadian poet Kamau Brathwaite to support newly arrived Caribbean visual artists, dramatists, poets, novelists, and musicians (Lloyd). The CAM contributed to the development of several important Black-owned publishing houses including Bogle L'Ouverture and New Beacon Books, both of which played significant roles in the effort to challenge the "whiteness" of British children's literature by providing positive representations of Black children.[2] The CAM also influenced the launch of the first British children's books featuring characters of African descent. Guyanese Beryl Gilroy credits Salkey with encouraging her to write (Fraser); she contributed to Macmillan's Nippers series with stories about Afro-Caribbean immigrant children in the 1970s. Jamaican Errol Lloyd, an artist supported by the CAM, illustrated some early picture books, such as those by Surinamese Petronella Breinburg, known for her Sean series about the daily experiences of a young Black boy, first published in 1973 (Sands-O'Connor, *Soon Come Home*, chap. 6). Salkey communicated the same sense of agency to other artists as he did to his own young readers. In his forays into children's literature, all published by Oxford University Press, he portrays his home country in a way that indicates the importance of surviving, learning, and initiating change. His realistic series for children aged twelve and above—*Hurricane* (1964), *Earthquake* (1965), *Drought* (1966), and *Riot* (1967)—demonstrates, as Sands-O'Connor writes, the importance of remembering colonial history and advocating for social and economic transformation (*Soon Come Home* 147). While Salkey's first three books show the power of community to overcome natural disasters, his final book, *Riot*, suggests that labor unionization might help the disenfranchised gain life-sustaining work (*Soon Come Home* 147). His use of the vernacular deepened as his writing progressed.

Caribbean writers for children and young adults also immigrated to the US and Canada, contributing to an ongoing set of representations of the immigrant experience. Rosa Guy, from Trinidad, made a splash in New York City by participating in the formation of the Harlem Writers Guild in 1950, a collaborative group devoted to supporting the writing practices and publication of those from the African diaspora. Emerging from poverty herself (entering the foster care system at age fourteen with her sister), Guy was not afraid to address the challenges of inner city life in her young adult trilogy: *The Friends* (1973), *Ruby* (1976), and *Edith Jackson* (1978). Guy was one of the first Caribbean writers for young adults to represent a lesbian relationship, in *Ruby*. She portrays the parental struggle that fictionally accompanies immigration—the mother has passed and the father seeks to assert order through authoritarianism. He, however, must also face the racist world and his own economic disempowerment within that world. Such parental rigidity surfaces again in the work of Marlene NourbeSe Philip (Trinidad/Canada), who depicts the drawbacks of authoritarian parenting in her young adult book *Harriet's Daughter* (1988). The protagonist, Harriet, rebels against a Barbadian father (with a submissive Jamaican mother) who wants her to adopt the middle-class mores and manners of racial uplift; she is more interested in Black Power and developing a diasporic consciousness, leading her to Tobago. These young adult books navigate, in a realistic manner, internalized racism, classism, and heterosexism within the Black community and position young adult literature as a force for change.

Contemporary Young Adult Literature

In the twenty-first century, young adult fiction has gained in quality and quantity in the Caribbean region. Young adult literature can help teenagers move beyond the literature of school, which in secondary school features books written primarily for adults, to the literature of recreation. School readers might include selections by Earl Lovelace, Sam Selvon, Erna Brodber, Merle Hodge, and Olive Senior (among others). But school curricula do not typically include young adult literature, a genre written from the perspective of a teen. The launching of the Burt Awards in 2012, funded by the Canadian Organization for Development through Education and awarded at the Bocas Lit Fest in Port of Spain, Trinidad, spurred a host of writers to put pen to paper. The award stimulated the production and publication of realistic, mystery, dystopian, romance, and fantasy novels that directly address issues facing teenagers. Writers use young adult literature as a platform for broad social critique, bringing to light the failures of educational systems and society in their treatment of young people.

Writers of young adult literature often turn to realism to immerse young readers in familiar scenes of everyday life. The narrator's voice mimics the slang and contexts of teenage life, including the use of Creole and other vernaculars. Adults might consider some of the language use and situations inappropriate within instructional settings. Such writing often breaks down the treasured myths of children's literature, drawing attention to societal ills, the irrelevance of school to learning, the failure of parents to parent, and the struggles of the protagonists who are typically on their own even though an adult mentor may be present. Lisa Allen-Agostini's *Home Home* (2018), a 2017 Burt Award finalist, serves as a profound example of this genre. The fourteen-year-old Afro-Caribbean narrator, named Kayla, suffers from test anxiety and scores poorly on the entrance exam for placement in secondary school in Trinidad. She finds herself placed in a school that fails to challenge her intellectually. With a strained relationship with her working-class mother, she falls into depression and attempts suicide. The book opens with her hospitalization and subsequent move to Canada to live with her lesbian aunt and her aunt's partner, who offer her much-needed support. Through the narrator's representation of her home, the book provides a searing critique of homophobia in Trinidad as well as of authoritarian patterns of parenting. It holds up the Canadian-based lesbian relationship as a model family with loving parents who know how to help a depressed teen come into her own. It meaningfully depicts the struggles of mental illness as well as the protagonist's emerging love interest and acceptance of her own beauty. Allen-Agostini's novel stands alongside other realistic novels for teens that capture the anxiety of coming of age, but more importantly, it provides a damning attack on societal norms and educational institutions that fail to support young people.

Colleen Smith-Dennis's *Inner City Girl* (2013), a winner of the 2014 Burt Award, serves as another potent example of the genre with its attention to economic conditions that foster educational inequalities. While the protagonist climbs out of poverty by passing her secondary school exams, she can only do so with the help of her birth father, who shows up in her life at just the right moment to pay the cost of the exams. Otherwise, she is surrounded by prostitution (her mother) and drug dealing (her mother and brother), rape and incest (her half sister's father and her half sister), kidnapping and attempted rape (herself), and food insecurity. Even with its fairy-tale underpinnings—the absent but secretly loving fairy godfather who arrives at just the right moment—the novel depicts the trauma that can accompany poverty. Others in the genre include Joanne Hillhouse's *Musical Youth* (2014), Tamika Gibson's *Off Track* (2020), and Kacen Callender's *Felix Ever After* (2020), featuring a transgender protagonist. Notably, Callender, from the US Virgin Islands, has garnered international recognition by winning the Stonewall Award and the Lambda Literary Award for the middle-grade book *Hurricane Child* (2018), which, set in the Virgin Islands, features the emerging same-sex feelings of the female protagonist. For those interested in locating more titles, the Caribbean Readers' Award, launched in 2020, offer categories in Middle Grade/Tween and Young Adult.

Young adult writers have additionally turned to speculative fiction to draw attention to gender inequality and promote acceptance of neurological or physical difference. In his first award-winning book, *Children of the Spider* (2016), Imam Baksh of Guyana relies on Afro-Caribbean mythology as key to reclaiming gender equality. A female Anansi figure in the form of a successful Afro-Caribbean businesswoman trains the next generation to defeat the patriarchal forces of Western mythology. Arachne, who rules the fantasy world, wants to take over the primary world by teaching its occupants "false history"; as Anansi explains, "Arachne make she people ignorant about them own past" (108). Her protagonist—an indigenous teen named Malayi and her sidekick, Joseph (who lacks hearing and speech)—work together to battle the underlying forces, in part through wit but also with technology. With his computer abilities, Joseph successfully warns the public about the dangers that be, proving that being "disabled" actually might mean "differently abled." Other writers for teens also put forward positive representations of difference. Barbadian author Shakirah Bourne draws on Caribbean folklore to tell a humorous story in the Burt Award finalist *My Fishy Stepmom* (2019). The protagonist, Josephine, must protect her father from a "fishy" girlfriend, a Mami Wata incarnation, who seeks to claim his affections for nefarious gains. Josephine is assisted by her good friend (who has Asperger's syndrome) to solve the mystery of the father's girlfriend's identity. The relationship between the two friends offers readers a model of radical acceptance of neurological diversity. In his most recent book, *The Dark of the Sea* (2019), Baksh addresses learning disabilities through his representation of a protagonist with dyslexia who can cross portals into imaginary worlds to correct power imbalances in the "real" world, but who cannot read. In Tracey Baptiste's Jumbies series, an orphaned boy who rarely speaks helps save the world from the warring battles of Caribbean-based folklore figures. Like Allen-Agostini in *Home Home* and Smith-Dennis in *Inner City Girl*, these authors address themes historically left unaddressed in the public eye or overlooked in literature for young people, opening doors for discussion on gender inequities and difference of many kinds.

The mystery genre has also taken hold with important contributions from Kevin Jared Hosein and Tamika Gibson, both with roots in Trinidad and Tobago. These writers generate readerly interest through an embedded mystery structure, yet offer readers something far richer in terms of cultural milieu. Both writers set their stories in Trinidad, weaving a range of themes that challenge any concept of "innocence" among the young people, who face abusive parents and alcoholism among their siblings; while coming-of-age stories, these contemporary plots weave through the seedy settings of organized crime, drug trafficking, and murder. Hosein emphasizes the lack of any clear division between the world of adults and teens in his novel *The Beast of Kukuyo*, which takes the teen protagonist to a hog farm with dead bodies, a bar with prostitutes, and a shed hiding a brother who cannot stop drinking. Told in Caribbean English, the underlying disorder of the text does not resolve into a tight bundle of meaning (even with the mystery solved), since the harshness of the emotional landscape for the newly orphaned narrator seems pervasive. Similarly, in Gibson's *Dreams beyond the Shore*, winner of the 2016 Burt Award, the protagonist fares better, but only after unpacking the underbelly of her father's political ambitions, which are laced with murder. Both novels show that "growing up" or coming into consciousness, as so often achieved by the narrator and protagonist of the bildungsroman, requires an awareness of the moral ambiguity of the social and economic worlds. Adults no longer exist as a revered category as the cracks in their facades crumble.

Such social critique finds more profound expression in contemporary environmental literature. The failure of the older generation to protect their young finds direct expression in the economic and physical devastation of the physical world. Diana McCaulay of Jamaica, an environmentalist, tells a profoundly difficult story in *Gone to Drift* (2016), which shows the economic effects of overfishing the ocean. The depletion of fish populations leads to desperate measures—such as using dynamite to drive fish up from the bottom of the sea, and capturing and selling dolphins to tourist centers. McCaulay ties the illegal trade in dolphins to the drug trade, betrayal within families, and murder. In her next young adult book, a dystopia, the author tackles global warming. In *Daylight Come* (2020), the unrelenting sun has forced people to live inside, ruined crops, upset rainfall, and left roving gangs of men in charge. A teen protagonist and her mother fight against the odds, finding survival in an isolated communal society, but the coming invasion of North Americans searching for natural resources does not bode well. McCaulay's work complements other books that deal with environmental destruction. Debbie Jacob's *Legend of the St. Ann's Flood* (2004) tackles the topic from a mythological perspective, with humans enraging the folklore protectors of the forest—Mama D'Leau, Papa Bois—who object to the poaching of endangered species. Christine Leo, in *Jessica* (1998), illustrated by Kim Harley, also relies on Caribbean folklore, in particular the mermaid figure, who serves as an activist to prevent the dumping of toxins into the sea by a group of sailors. Other Caribbean speculative texts that draw on Caribbean folklore figures carry underlying environmental messages—such as Tracey Baptiste's *The Jumbie God's Revenge* (2019), in which fierce weather patterns—hurricanes and floods—result from a failure in the community to find balance in their relations with each other, the denizens of the woods, and the environment.

Caribbean literature for children as a whole—including the phalanx of picture books reviewed by Summer Edward in chapter 1 of the second volume of this anthology—has made incredible progress over the past fifty years. Literature for young adults has gained in strength, bringing a self-reflexive edge to the field, voicing concerns about political and social systems that may injure or harm the least powerful members of society—not only children but young adults. Providing venues for exploration, young adult literature speaks in the language of teenagers—in Creole, often with language forbidden but used by adults. The recent interest in young adult literature among Caribbean publishers (in particular Blue Banyan Books of Jamaica, with their young adult imprint, Blouse and Skirt Books), and in Caribbean literature more generally, will hopefully continue to find the resources to support emergent writers with so much to say.

Notes

1. Years of independence in the Anglophone Caribbean are as follows: Jamaica (1962), Trinidad and Tobago (1962), Guyana (1966), Barbados (1966), the Bahamas (1973), Grenada (1974), Dominica (1978), Saint Lucia (1979), Saint Vincent and the Grenadines (1979), Belize (1981), Antigua and Barbuda (1981), and Saint Kitts and Nevis (1983).

2. See Karen Sands-O'Connor's *Children's Publishing and Black Britain, 1965–2015*, for a history of the development of Black-owned publishing houses, some of which specifically targeted children and educational systems in their production of literature.

Works Cited

Allen-Agostini, Lisa. *Home Home*. Delacorte Press, 2018.
Baksh, Imam. *Children of the Spider*. Blue Banyan Books, 2016.
Baksh, Imam. *The Dark of the Sea*. Blouse and Skirt Books, 2019.
Baptiste, Tracey. *The Jumbie God's Revenge*. Algonquin Young Readers, 2019.
Bourne, Shakirah. *My Fishy Stepmom*. Blouse and Skirt Books, 2019.
Callender, Kacen. *Felix Ever After*. Balzer and Bray, 2020.
Callender, Kacen. *Hurricane Child*. Scholastic, 2018.
Fraser, Peter D. "Beryl Gilroy." *The Guardian*, April 18, 2001. https://www.theguardian.com/news /2001/apr/18/guardianobituaries.books.
Gibson, Tamika. *Dreams beyond the Shore*. Blouse and Skirt Books, 2017.
Gibson, Tamika. *Off Track*. Blouse and Skirt Books, 2020.
Guy, Rosa. *Edith Jackson*. 1978. Puffin Books, 1995.
Guy, Rosa. *The Friends*. 1973. Random House, 1995.
Guy, Rosa. *Ruby*. 1976. Just Us Books, 2005.
Hillhouse, Joanne C. *Musical Youth*. CaribbeanReads, 2014.
Hosein, Kevin Jared. *The Beast of Kukuyo*. Blue Banyan Books, 2018.
Jacob, Debbie. *Legend of the St. Ann's Flood*. Macmillan Caribbean, 2005.
James, Cynthia. "From Orature to Literature in Jamaican and Trinidadian Children's Folk Traditions." *Children's Literature Association Quarterly*, vol. 30, no. 2, Summer 2005, pp. 164–78.
Leo, Christine. *Jessica*. Illustrated by Kim Harley, Macmillan Education, 1998.
Lloyd, Errol. "Caribbean Artists Movement (1966–1972)." British Library, October 4, 2018. https://www.bl.uk/windrush/articles/caribbean-artists-movement-1966-1972.

McCaulay, Diane. *Daylight Come*. Peepal Tree Press, 2020.
McCaulay, Diane. *Gone to Drift*. HarperCollins, 2018.
Palmer, C. Everard. *Big Doc Bitterroot*. 1968. Bobbs-Merrill, 1971.
Palmer, C. Everard. *The Cloud with the Silver Lining*. 1966. Macmillan Education, 1987.
Palmer, C. Everard. *The Wooing of Beppo Tate*. 1972. Oxford UP, 2014.
Philip, Marlene NourbeSe. *Harriet's Daughter*. Heinemann, 1988.
Reid, V. S. *New Day*. Alfred A. Knopf, 1949.
Reid, V. S. *Peter of Mount Ephraim: The Daddy Sharpe Rebellion*. 1971. Jamaica Publishing, 1981.
Reid, V. S. *Sixty-Five*. 1962. Longman Caribbean, 2008.
Reid, V. S. "The Writer and His Work." *Journal of West Indian Literature*, vol. 2, no. 1, December 1987, pp. 4–10.
Reid, V. S. *The Young Warriors*. 1967. Hodder Education, 2021.
Sands-O'Connor, Karen. *Children's Publishing and Black Britain, 1965–2015*. Palgrave Macmillan, 2017.
Sands-O'Connor, Karen. *Soon Come Home to This Island: West Indians in British Children's Literature*. Routledge, 2008.
Salkey, Andrew. *Drought*. Oxford UP, 1966.
Salkey, Andrew. *Earthquake*. Oxford UP, 1965.
Salkey, Andrew. *Hurricane*. Oxford UP, 1964.
Salkey, Andrew. *Riot*. Oxford UP, 1967.
Smith-Dennis, Colleen. *Inner City Girl*. LMH Publishing, 2013.

CHAPTER 4

Before and After the Revolution
An Exploration of the Trajectory of Cuban Children's Literature

Zeila Frade

Literary production for children in Cuba reflects the different aesthetic values, genres, and social contexts of each successive historical time period. A colony of Spain until 1898, Cuba achieved independence through the Spanish-American War with the intervention of the US. Expanding from 1902 to 1958, the Cuban republic marks an epoch of nation building. With the triumph of the revolution in 1959, the new system focused on reconsidering educational goals. New structures of power relied on ideology as a pedagogical tool to instill certain sociopolitical values and mold the nation's future citizens. The year 1959 served a fulcrum, highlighting the tremendous contrast between the children's literature written in the pre- and postrevolutionary epochs.

In 1899, the first issue of José Martí's *La Edad de Oro* (*The Gilded Age*[1]) was published in New York; only three issues of this recreational and educational magazine were ever released (July through October 1899). The moral, ethical, and educational values of this landmark work set it apart from others of the time and established a "before and after" in the history of Latin American children's literature. Martí believed in the formative and didactic aspect of a literary work and its ability to not only instruct but also entertain. With each issue, Martí provided explicit instructions for young readers, a dose of medicine with a spoonful of syrup: "Los temas escogidos serán siempre tales que por mucha doctrina que lleven en sí, no parezca que la llevan, ni alarmen al lector de pocos años con el título científico ni con el lenguaje aparatoso" ("The chosen topics will always be such that no matter how much doctrine they carry, they do not seem to carry it, nor do they alarm the young reader") (Martí 1).

With *La Edad de Oro* as a noteworthy literary precedent, the children's literature of the Republic of Cuba (1902–1959) falls into a transition period between the colony and the revolution and has been omitted from the nation's cultural and literary heritage. This work has been labeled as unworthy of scholars' attention because, in accordance with the official political discourse, it is not possible to talk about a literature for children and young adults in Cuba until the triumph of the revolution. The development of children's literature reached its highest point during the revolutionary period, mainly due to the establishment of literary contests that encouraged debutant writers to showcase their work and because publishing houses facilitated and stimulated the production of the genre. A careful look at some of the republic's publications, however, indicates that children's book authors were concerned to nurture young readers with rich knowledge of the natural wonders and beauty of the national landscape, the countryside's customs and traditions, and the importance of social status. Representative works from this period include *El pájaro de lata* (*The Tin Plate Bird*) by Anita Arroyo from 1944, *Cuentos de Apolo* (*Apolo's Stories*) by Hilda Perera in 1947, and *Cuentos de todas las noches* (*Stories for Every Night*) by Emilio Bacardí Moreau from 1950.

Arroyo dedicates *El pájaro de lata* to all Spanish-speaking children, but in particular to Cuban children. The writer wants readers to get to know their homeland, its flora and fauna. She familiarizes the reader with the different landscapes of some of the provinces on the island and alludes to the folklore of the countryside, introducing very young peasants (*guajiritos*) who rely on the colloquial expressions of the time and share the hardships of their everyday lives.

Perera also locates national identity as fundamental to her work. She published *Cuentos de Apolo* at age seventeen, capturing the attention of the public and critics. Through the eyes of Apolo, a seven-year-old boy, the text explores important social and racial differences among people. The rural setting also constitutes a point of reference in this novel, since Apolo lives with his parents and siblings in the countryside, where he spends a happy childhood. Apolo's stories, like Arroyo's, capture the most distinctive features of the country's landscape and the characteristics of the peasantry. The context of the republic also nourishes the narratives of Bacardí Moreau's *Cuentos de todas las noches*. Bacardí Moreau adds an ideological and social dimension to his characters, such that the relationships between them serve as metaphors of power. For example, in "Rafaelilla y Saturnina," a fable, the two title characters are female cats, one representing the noble but oppressed (Rafaelilla) and the other, a politician (Saturnina), symbolizing those driven by corruption and eager to oppress. All of these stories are marked by didacticism and an explicit intention to reaffirm cultural identity; however, the universality of their morals and the seriousness with which they are treated extend their validity and relevance beyond their specific time period. Other publications of the republican era, in the form of textbooks, magazines, and newspapers, provide evidence of a concern to address young readers.

In 1920, the children's magazine *Pulgarcito* began publishing on a monthly basis. It included a fashion and a hobby section as well as a comic strip. *Martí* magazine was a biweekly publication, with its first issue published in 1929 in Havana. Its sections included "pastimes and curiosities," "children's games," "historic figures," "humor," and an honor roll gallery of pictures of outstanding students. Most importantly, it included a section called "Recreo de los Niños" ("Children's Recess") that included texts sent by children. Other magazines of the period were *Ronda* (1941–1943), founded by Herminio Almendros, and *Pinocho* (1941–1942). The former included poems, popular children's songs, pastimes, and calls for contests. *Carteles*, another magazine, was published weekly from 1924 until 1960, featuring a children's section as well.[2]

These works belonging to the republican era have received very limited attention in critical studies, not because of the extent to which they are associated with US influence (US comics were widely available at the time), or because they are unworthy of scholarly research, but because the republic was succeeded by a regime that, due to its revolutionary character, sought to eradicate the past from the collective memory. As a means of validation, by degrading the historical legacy of the republic, the new government was able to highlight its own achievements and create a "New Man" whose historical framework was the revolution and whose national heroes were selected by its leaders. Erasing all possible allusions to the previous period, the revolution began a massive effort to promote and direct the education of its citizens, molding them to follow its ideological platform. Writers and educators were (and remain) stimulated by the official political discourse to develop and create materials for children.

In the second half of the twentieth century, literary production for children became an indispensable vehicle to support the ideological foundation of the government. In 1959, the national printing press was founded, and in 1961 the Organización de Pioneros José Martí (José Martí Organization of Pioneers) emerged, to be followed the next year by the Unión de Jóvenes Comunistas (Union of Communist Youth). With the intention of increasing the number of potential readers, the government launched a literacy campaign in 1961. That same year, a new children's magazine, *Pioneros*, appeared, and one year later the publishing house Editora Juvenil was founded, renamed Gente Nueva (New People) in 1968. Since its foundation, the publishing house, whose name explicitly alludes to the revolutionary project of forming future generations, has stimulated intellectual initiatives targeted to children and teens. Since 1959, the revolution's educational projects for the masses have been ideologically aligned with its politics. Writers of children's books, too, were affected by the sociopolitical changes.

Navidades para un niño cubano (*Christmas for a Cuban Child*) is a collection of fifteen short stories, two plays, and two articles that was published in 1959. Illustrated by René Portocarrero, one of Cuba's most renowned painters, the book includes the work of writers who had already published in the republican period, like Arroyo and Perera. Renée Méndez Capote revisits some of the historic scenarios of colonial and republican Cuba in *Memorias de una cubanita que nació con el siglo* (1963; *Memories of a Cuban Girl Born with the Century*). Very much in tune with the social changes in Cuba in the 1960s, Dora Alonso published *Aventuras de Guille* (*Adventures of Guille*) in 1964. The novel narrates the story of a high school student who embarks on an adventure with his aunt and his science teacher to find a black seagull that lives in Cuba's most remote keys. By emphasizing a sense of adventure and an interest in science, the novel stresses the achievements of the revolution. Following the same line of compromise with the historic framework of pre-revolutionary Cuba, Méndez Capote published *Dos niños en la Cuba colonial* (*Two Children in Colonial Cuba*) in 1966.

Even though the 1970s are marked by a strong didacticism in children's literature, four fundamental works of that decade explore and integrate other routes to develop their aesthetic propositions: Onelio Jorge Cardoso's *Caballito blanco* (*Little White Horse*) in 1974, and *El cochero azul* (*The Blue Coachman*) by Dora Alonso, *Un héroe de once años* (*An Eleven-Year-Old Hero*) by Renée Méndez Capote, and *Cuentos de Guane* (*Stories from Guane*) by Nersys Felipe, all in 1975. The themes of these works align with the national literature of the period, while their discourse and stylistic features are very original.

During this period, two approaches surfaced in literature for children, both in prose and in verse: one continued the tradition of expressing ideological and educational purposes, while the other explored mixed realities, bordering on magical realism, to create a literature with new narrative styles. Alonso's *El cochero azul* is a unique example for appreciating the collision of those two approaches, as it represents a significant innovation in storytelling techniques, aesthetic values, and forms with an ideological nuance that evidences a didactic purpose and a commitment to the tenets of socialist humanism. Three years later, in 1978, Nersys Felipe published *Román Elé*, and in 1984 Onelio Jorge Cardoso published his only novel, *Negrita*.[3] Other relevant works of the period include *Los chichiricú del charco de la jícara*[4] (1985; *The Magical Creatures of the Puddle*) by Julia Calzadilla and *Abuelita Milagro* (1977; *Grandma Milagro*) by Antonio Orlando Rodríguez.

In the first three decades of the revolutionary period, Cuban children's literature focused mainly on educational and ideological purposes, with few exceptions. In the 1990s, however, there was a shift of theme and narrative style toward previously unexplored social problems. National narratives for children and young adults of the late twentieth century began to explore familial and social themes. Divorce, discrimination, generational differences, marginality, disability, and even death highlight these more profound layers of readers' realities.

For the authors of children's literature of this period, the main challenge resided in addressing the imperfections of the world and of particular social contexts. This generation, especially those who began to publish in the late 1990s, are known as *novísimos* ("the newest"). A relevant text from this period is *María Virginia está de vacaciones* (*María Virginia is on Vacation*) by Gumersindo Pacheco, which was awarded the Casa de las Américas distinction in 1994. The second volume of a trilogy, *María Virginia* is a novel of adventure, and a joyful and cunning love story between teenagers. In 1991, Luis Cabrera Delgado published *Pedrín*,[5] introducing in his narrative universe a protagonist with a disability. Five years later, Cabrera Delgado published *Ito*, a short and intense work that explores homosexuality, a theme that continues to be uncomfortable for many in Cuba and sensitive to address. In 1998, Enrique Pérez Díaz published *Inventarse un amigo* (*An Invented*

Friend), in which for the first time a Cuban writer alludes to the theme of the "rafters" through the figure of the protagonist.[6] One text of this period that effectively exemplifies the expansion of themes and issues related to religious syncretism, current social circumstances, racism, and generational and family conflicts is *Cartas al cielo* (published in English as *Letters to My Mother*) by Teresa Cárdenas Angulo (1998). Awarded the David and Hermanos Saínz Association Prize in 1997 and the National Literary Critic Award in 2000, this text, along with most of the writer's other work, represents the contemporary panorama of literature for children and young adults in Cuba.

With unlimited and hyperbolic fantasy, Eric González Conde narrates the adventures of a very peculiar clan in *La familia Tosco* (*The Tosco Family*), published in 2002. Reuniting most of the themes that characterize the children's literature of the 1990s, in 2001 Gumersindo Pacheco published *Las raíces del tamarindo* (*The Roots of the Tamarind*). A finalist for the Premio Edebé de Literatura Juvenil (Edebé Award for Literature for Young Adults), this novel depicts the crises resulting from the divorce of the protagonist's parents and his father's incarceration.

A close look at the works of writers who came of age during the revolution reveals that, in contrast with writers of earlier generations, they project a narrative universe where reality and everyday concerns predominate, showing special interest in shedding light on topics that until then had not been explored in depth. They explore themes of exile, marginality, death, and generational conflict, presenting children themselves as observers of a reality that includes the loss of dear friends or family members and the separation of families due to opposing ideologies.

The historical and cultural contexts of the decades after 1959 are deeply embedded in the plots of the children's books of the era. The contrast between pre- and postrevolutionary literary works for children offers the possibility of establishing connections between the themes and implicit ideologies of the texts and their sociohistorical contexts. While the productions of the colonial and republican eras remained attached to the didactic and conservative aspects of the genre, the publications that followed the triumph of the Cuban Revolution in 1959 highlight the ideological function of children's literature and offer a significant shift in terms of themes, aesthetics, and purposes.[7]

Notes

1. All translations are mine.
2. In 1929, *Carteles*'s children's section was titled "Página Infantil"; from 1932 to 1934, "Felicidad para el Niño"; and from 1952 to 1957, "La Edad de Oro." In 1957, the children's section was no longer included; the rest of the content remained unchanged until the magazine ceased publication.
3. *Negrita* means, in a literal sense, "little Black girl." In this case, it is the name given to the protagonist's dog. It is also often used with an affective connotation when referring to loved ones.
4. *Chichiricús*, also known as *güijes*, are magical creatures or spirits characteristic of Cuban folklore. They tend to be presented as a small, slippery Black children with grotesque facial features and big eyes.
5. Pedrín is the diminutive of Pedro.
6. At the beginning of the 1990s, significant numbers of Cubans left the island on rafts, seeking to cross the Florida Straits in an effort to escape political oppression and gain freedom. They are referred to as *balseros* (rafters).
7. All the works cited in this chapter share the same place of production, Cuba, even if subsequent editions have been published in other countries. The extent of their circulation in Cuba varies. For authors like Hilda Perera, all of whose works were subsequently published outside of Cuba except for her first one, *Cuentos de Apolo*, circulation inside Cuba is very limited or almost nonexistent. If a copy is available on the island, it is because it has been brought there, not because it was printed there. For authors like Antonio Orlando Rodríguez and Gumersindo Pacheco, who emigrated from Cuba, their books' circulation in Cuba is also limited, but they continue to publish in other Latin American countries. It is mainly those writers who live in Cuba and have published all or most of their works there who have the most significant circulation on the island. Primary sources are available via used book markets, special collections such as the Cuban Heritage Collection at the University of Miami, and via broader Latin American networks.

Works Cited

Alonso, Dora. *Aventuras de Guille*. 1964. Gente Nueva, 1969.
Alonso, Dora. *El cochero azul*. Gente Nueva, 1975.
Arroyo, Anita. *El pájaro de lata*. Editorial San Juan, 1973.
Bacardí Moreau, Emilio. *Cuentos de todas las noches*. 1950. Playor, 1972.
Cabrera Delgado, Luis. *Ito*. Casa Editora Abril, 1996.
Cabrera Delgado, Luis. *Pedrín*. Ediciones Capiro, 1991.
Calzadilla, Julia. *Los chichiricú del charco de la jícara*. 1985. Ediciones Colihue, 2008.
Cárdenas Angulo, Teresa. *Cartas al cielo*. 1998. Gente Nueva, 2013.
Cardoso, Onelio Jorge. *Caballito blanco*. Gente Nueva, 1974.
Cardoso, Onelio Jorge. *Negrita*. Gente Nueva, 1984.
Felipe, Nersys. *Cuentos de Guane*. Casa de las Américas, 1975.
Felipe, Nersys. *Román Elé*. Casa de las Américas, 1978.

González Conde, Eric. *La familia Tosco*. Gente Nueva, 2002.
Martí, José. *La Edad de Oro*. Pueblo y Educación, 1995.
Méndez Capote, Renée. *Dos niños en la Cuba colonial*. 1966. Gente Nueva, 2002.
Méndez Capote, Renée. *Memorias de una cubanita que nació con el siglo*. Universidad Central de las Villas, 1963.
Méndez Capote, Renée. *Un héroe de once años*. 1975. Gente Nueva, 2002.
Pacheco, Gumersindo. *María Virginia está de vacaciones*. 1993. Editorial Plaza Mayor, 2003.
Pacheco, Gumersindo. *Las raíces del tamarindo*. Grupo Edebé, 2001.
Perera, Hilda. *Cuentos de Apolo*. Franhil Enterprises, 1975.
Pérez Díaz, Enrique. *Inventarse un amigo*. Gente Nueva, 1998.
Rodríguez, Antonio Orlando. *Abuelita Milagro*. Gente Nueva, 1977.

CHAPTER 5

Puerto Rican Children's Literature on the Archipelago

María V. Acevedo-Aquino

Situating Puerto Rico

Children's literature is situated in sociopolitical and sociocultural contexts (Botelho and Rudman 71). In the case of Puerto Rico, these contexts have historically been shaped by years of Spanish dominion, US coloniality, natural disasters, and acts of resistance. Puerto Rico is an archipelago located in the Caribbean, between the Dominican Republic and the US Virgin Islands. Originally inhabited by the indigenous Taíno, Puerto Rico became a Spanish possession in 1493 and underwent over four centuries of slavery, exploitation of local resources, and imperialism, which led to unequal power structures that are still visible today. In 1898, the group of islands became a US nonincorporated territory as a result of the Spanish-American War. Some significant events that have exemplified Puerto Rico's colonial status include numerous attempts to establish English as the official language; multiple military occupations across the archipelago; and, more recently, the imposition of US federal law in 2016—the Puerto Rico Oversight, Management, and Economic Stability Act—which allows a US-appointed Fiscal Oversight and Management Board to make all financial decisions for Puerto Rico (Medina and Soto-Santiago). This complex sociopolitical context brings years of oppression but also creates spaces for constant resistance, particularly in the field of children's literature. Books can serve as vehicles for resistance by making visible the stories of individuals and communities whose experiences and identities have been historically misrepresented or underrepresented while privileging, in the case of Puerto Rico, colonial voices.

Resisting Colonial Discourses and Invisibility

Historically, the field of Puerto Rican children's literature on the archipelago has been characterized by a lack of careful documentation and scholarship (Piñeiro de Rivera 2; Maisonet-Quiñonez 134; Torres-Rivera, "Publishing Perspectives"; Ayes Santiago; Jiménez-García). Flor Piñeiro de Rivera attributes the first Puerto Rican literary works published for a young audience to writers and activists Lola Rodríguez de Tió and Eugenio María de Hostos in collaboration with Cuban poet José Martí (8). Their work was characterized by a strong interest in supporting the educational level of people across Latin American countries (17). For example, Rodríguez de Tió's prologue for *Mis cantares* (*My Songs*,)[1] published in 1876, advocates literature, libraries, literary circles, and theaters as vehicles for intellectual motivation and social change (i–vi).

In the years following the 1898 US military invasion, a strong discourse of assimilation or "Americanization" emerged. This discourse was promoted by the local Department of Education, established in 1900 based upon the US educational model. Consequently, the department declared English as the language of instruction. This language policy was strongly challenged by educators and politicians across Puerto Rico (Kerkhof 261). In order to provide textbooks that would promote the native language, leaders in Puerto Rico such as Manuel Fernández Juncos translated books into Spanish, including *Libro cuarto de lectura* (*Fourth Book of Reading*; 1944), written by Sarah Louise Arnold under the title *Stepping Stones to Literature: A Second Reader* (1897). He also published Spanish textbooks on Puerto Rican history, such as *Antología puertorriqueña: Prosa y verso para lectura escolar* (*Puerto Rican Anthology: Prose and Verse for School Reading*; 1907). An emphasis on folklore and landscapes emerged as authors attempted to develop a curriculum reflecting the local culture. Titles celebrating Puerto Rican folklore include Carmelina Vizcarrondo's *Poemas para mi niño* (*Poems for My Child*; 1938), María Cadilla de Martínez's *Juegos y canciones infantiles de Puerto Rico* (*Puerto Rican Children's Games and Songs*; 1940), Abelardo Díaz Alfaro's short story collection *Terrazo* (1947), Ricardo Alegría's *La historia de nuestros indios: Una versión elemental* (*The History of Our Indigenous Peoples: An Elementary Level*; 1950), Monserrate Deliz's *Renadío del cantar folklórico de Puerto Rico* (*Aftermath of Puerto Rican Folklore*; 1951), and Rubén del Rosario, Isabel Freire de Matos, and Antonio Martorell's *ABC de Puerto Rico* (1968). The iconic latter title, the first alphabet book to be published in Puerto Rico, acknowledged by Piñeiro de Rivera for "the quality of the poetic language and the authenticity of its Puerto Rican illustrations" (38), was removed from classrooms and libraries in the same year it was published by a pro-statehood administration after being considered "anti-American" (Lugo; Jiménez).

Contributing to an awareness of environmental issues, Ester Feliciano Mendoza highlights Puerto Rican traditional stories *Juegos y canciones infantiles de Puerto Rico Sinfonía de Puerto Rico: Mitos y legendas* (*Symphony of Puerto Rico: Myths and Legends*; 1979). She also encourages young readers to learn about Puerto Rico's fauna and flora through her poems in *Ronda del mar* (*Nursery Rhymes from the Sea*; 1981) and *Ilán ilán* (1985). Author and storyteller Tere Marichal-Lugo has also shared stories about environmental conservation as well as Puerto Rico's culture, folklore, and politics since 1975. Although she has published more than forty books, such as *Pancha la planchadora* (*Pancha the Ironer*; 2013), about global warming, and *Carla feliz* (*Happy Carla*), addressing gender identity, most of her stories remain unpublished. Her goal of reaching people through oral literature has prompted her to open several workshops on art, puppet making, and the Japanese street theater technique of Kamishibai for children, families, and educators (Kortright Roig 358). Her work positions oral, written, and artifactual stories as equally valuable in the lives of young children as well as adults. Storytelling conducted in Puerto Rico and beyond has served as an act of subversion and cultural preservation.[2]

However, folklore, while often employed as a means for resisting first Spanish imperialism and then Americanization, was also grounded on fixed identities, patriarchy, and colonial ideologies. Authors like Rosario Ferré created texts that talked back. Ferré's *El medio pollito* (*Half Chick*; 1977) challenged androcentric views and conventions of class, and advocated a national identity through a collection of *cuentos* inspired by the Puerto Rican oral tradition (Fernández Olmos 45). These fixed identities and colonial ideologies also contributed to a lack of racial diversity in children's literature in Puerto Rico (Torres-Rivera, "Puerto Rican Children's Literature" 81), for instance through an emphasis on the *jíbaro*, a white Puerto Rican man living in the mountains. Ana Lydia Vega has consistently explored racial diversity as the cultural connection between Puerto Rico and the Caribbean. Titles like *Otra maldad de Pateco* (*Another Evil by Pateco*; 1987) explore the need to acknowledge and value the Afro–Puerto Rican identity. Her texts challenge racism, human exploitation, and the subordination of peoples (Falcón 43). Torres-Rivera notes that the following titles that validate the experiences of Afro–Puerto Ricans are out of print: María Rijos Guzmán's bilingual *Y llegaron los esclavos/So the Slaves Came* (1993), Fernando Picó's *The Red Comb* (1994), Carmen Bernier-Grand's *In the Shade of the Níspero Tree* (2001), and Vega's *En la bahía de Jobos: Celita y el Mangle Zapatero* (*At Jobos Bay: Celita and the Zapatero Mangrove*; 2004). This situation creates an issue of access to this important literature.

Contemporary efforts that challenge the invisibility of Afro–Puerto Rican characters and experiences in Puerto Rican children's literature include the project Cátedra de Mujeres Negras Ancestrales, directed by author Yolanda Arroyo Pizarro, which encourages the production and sharing of literature that celebrates the lives of historical Black females in Puerto Rico (Kortright Roig 342). Arroyo Pizarro's work explores the intersection of race, Afro-identity, and colonialism through titles like *Pelo bueno* (*Good Hair*; 2018) and *Mejorar la raza* (*Improving the Race*; 2019). Additional initiatives like Isar Godreau and colleagues' *Arrancando mitos de raíz: Guía para una enseñanza antirracista de la herencia africana en Puerto Rico* (*Unraveling Myths by the Root: A Guide to an Anti-Racist Teaching of African Heritage in Puerto Rico*; 2014) help educators integrate Afro–Puerto Rican voices in their curricula.

Resistance after September 2017

Hurricanes Irma and María hit the archipelago in September 2017. While Puerto Rico's political and economic crisis preceded the hurricanes (Ficek 102), their aftermath magnified the situation and created an urge to question, resist, and change. Authors in Puerto Rico have supported children coping with the traumatic experience through titles published in 2018 like Laura Rexach Olivencia's *Por ahí viene el huracán* (*The Hurricane Is Coming*), Yolanda Arroyo Pizarro's *Thiago y la aventura del huracán* (*Thiago and the Hurricane Adventure*), Tere Marichal-Lugo's *La cucarachita Martina y el huracán* (*Martina, the Cockroach, and the Hurricane*), and Isset Pastrana Andino's *Mi isla bella/Mi isla hermosa* (*My Pretty Island/My Beautiful Island*). These titles explore individual resilience, agency, and communal activism (Torres and Medina). Authors and illustrators in Puerto Rico and from the diaspora also created collaborations like *Puerto Rico Strong* (2018), a graphic novel anthology edited by Marco Lopez and colleagues that explores the complexities of being Puerto Rican before, during, and after Hurricane María. In an attempt to connect the diaspora with Puerto Rican children's literature on the archipelago, Carlos Goyco and others developed Libros787, an online bookstore that provides international visibility to local authors. Only a handful of Puerto Rican authors on the archipelago, like Georgina Lázaro, are known internationally.

Puerto Rico's infrastructure collapsed after Hurricane María (Ficek 2). To better understand the experiences of Puerto Ricans with the hurricane's aftermath, Ricia Anne Chansky and her collaborators implemented an initiative through the University of Puerto Rico, Mayagüez Campus, titled *Mi María: Puerto Rico after the Hurricane*, which focuses on collecting oral stories from Puerto Rican youth in an attempt to create a collective memory. The project also helps teachers to integrate issues of climate change and environmental justice into the curriculum through a special collection of thirty bilingual children's books geared toward the "María Generation." With a similar goal of collecting and elevating unheard Puerto Rican voices, *Anansesem*, an online Caribbean children's and young adult literature magazine, published a special issue on Puerto Rican children's literature to capture the work of resistance, transformation, and empowerment of Puerto Rican literacy, literature, and storytelling projects by scholars, authors, illustrators, librarians, and educators on the archipelago after the hurricane (Lugo Vázquez).

Hurricanes, government corruption, earthquakes, and the COVID-19 pandemic perpetuate the need to recover, resist, and protest. Some recent initiatives address the availability of stories. Publishing in Puerto Rico is a complex endeavor, forcing many authors to self-publish. While not sustainable, self-publishing has produced titles like *La gran Victoria* (*The Great Victoria*; 2020), written by Verónica de la Cruz and illustrated by Jonathan A. Vega. The story, inspired by the events of summer 2019 that led to the impeachment of Governor Ricardo Rosselló, narrates how two sisters protested against an unfair leader. During the summer of 2020, the University of Sagrado Corazón, in collaboration with Lilac Publishing, launched the Incubadora de Literatura Infantil y Juvenil de Puerto Rico, an intensive ten-week series of workshops and seminars to support authors and illustrators in creating and publishing their work.

Other initiatives focus on access to literature. Rossana Barrios Llorens's advocacy project Puerto Rico Necesita Bibliotecas creates awareness of the importance of public libraries as spaces for the development of cultural and social capital, intellectual growth, and educational transformation. Also addressing access, storytellers like Tere Marichal-Lugo and the storytellers' community organization Los Cuentacuentos de Puerto Rico have supported displaced children and families living in shelters after the hurricanes. The theater company Y No Había Luz facilitated sing-along plena (a genre of music and dance that originated in Puerto Rico in the late nineteenth century) and performed their show, *El centinela de mangó* (*The Mango Sentinel*), in shelters, schools, and hospitals (Bayne). Other authors like Laura Rexach Olivencia, Wanda De Jesus, and Ada Haiman have organized book sharing activities and transportable libraries in shelters and beaches, and at the front lines of the summer 2019 protests (Jiménez). In January 2020, Ita Venegas Pérez, in collaboration with the theater company Jóvenes del 98, shared titles like *Yo opino* (*I Think*; 2019) in communities affected by the earthquakes that impacted Puerto Rico during that month. Their work served as a vehicle to restore hope and encourage unity and action.

Further Considerations

This chapter provides a window into the history of children's literature in Puerto Rico, with a focus on selected examples of authors and stories that serve as vehicles for resistance to the dominant discourses that have shaped and continue to shape what it means to be Puerto Rican. Further accounts of children's literature on the archipelago can be found in Piñeiro de Rivera's *Un siglo de literatura infantil puertorriqueña/A Century of Puerto Rican Children's Literature* (1987), the most cited reference on the history of children's literature in Puerto Rico. *Anuario iberoamericano sobre el libro infantil y juvenil* (*Iberoamerican Journal of Children's and Adolescent Literature*) has documented the history of this body of work since 2004. El Centro para el Estudio de la Lectura, la Escritura y la Literatura Infantil (CELELI), established in 2006 at the University of Puerto Rico, with more than six thousand books available to students and the general public, encourages access to the literature as well as documentation, research, and integration of children's literature into the classroom.[3] Authors like Lulu Delacre, Esmeralda Santiago, Judith Ortiz Cofer, Nicholasa Mohr, Carmen Bernier-Grand, and Eric Velasquez, and scholars such as Sonia Nieto, Carmen L. Medina, Marilisa Jiménez, and Carmen Martínez-Roldán, all from the diaspora, continue to expand what it means to be Puerto Rican through their complex, authentic, and critical approaches. Together, the voices showcased in this chapter rewrite and rebuild the history of Puerto Rican children's literature.

Notes

1. All translations are my own.
2. From the 1920s to the 1940s, Pura Belpré, the first Afro–Puerto Rican librarian to work in New York's library system, used storytelling to support the development of the Puerto Rican community in the US. Books like *Pérez and Martina: A Puerto Rican Folktale* (1932), published in Spanish in 1966, offered Puerto Ricans in the diaspora an opportunity to connect to Puerto Rican folklore and created a space for Puerto Rican voices to be heard in the context of the US. According to Marilisa Jiménez-García, "Belpré's 'archive of repertoire' opened up spaces within the community in which children and young adults could act out constructs of cultural memory" (118). Her multimodal, performance-based storytelling of published and unpublished narratives, using puppets and other physical props, contested deficit views of Puerto Rican children and families who had recently immigrated to the US as exotic and without culture (114). She further contested the format and content of children's literature in the US.
3. Educators, researchers, caregivers, and readers can find children's and young adult literature in Puerto Rico in libraries dedicated to young audiences, like Aparicio, founded in 1998, and Leo Leo Libros, operating since 2014. Some publishing houses of books for children and adolescents in Puerto Rico not mentioned elsewhere in this chapter include Editorial EDP University, Editorial de la Universidad de Puerto Rico, Ediciones SM, Ediciones Huracán, Editorial Instituto de Cultura Puertorriqueña, and Editorial Destellos.

Works Cited

Ayes Santiago, Zulma. "Literatura infantil y juvenil en Puerto Rico: Trayectoria, legado y retos presentes." Zoom, uploaded by Instituto de Cultura Puertorriqueña, May 19, 2020. www.facebook.com/watch/live/?v=241628210598990&ref=watch_permalink.

Barrios Llorens, Rossana I. "Puerto Rico Necesita Bibliotecas (Puerto Rico Needs Libraries)." *Anansesem: News, Ideas, Arts, and Letters from the World of Caribbean Children's & YA Publishing*, May 2019, pp. 63–66.

Bayne, Martha. "Y No Había Luz Brings the Voices of Post-Maria Puerto Rico to Chicago." *Chicago Reader*, July 9, 2018. www.chicagoreader.com/Bleader/archives/2018/07/09/y-no-habia-luz-brings-the-voices-of-post-maria-puerto-rico-to-chicago.

Botelho, Maria José, and Masha Kabakow Rudman. *Critical Multicultural Analysis of Children's Literature: Mirrors, Windows, and Doors*. Routledge, 2009.

Chansky, Ricia Anne. "Exhibit to Use Books to Help Children Make Sense of Hurricane María, Climate Change." *Anansesem: News, Ideas, Arts, and Letters from the World of Caribbean Children's & YA Publishing*, June 5, 2019. www.anansesem.com/2019/06/mimariaproject.html

Falcón, Rafael. "Aleluya a la caribeñidad: Los cuentos negristas de Ana Lydia Vega." *Afro-Hispanic Review*, vol. 13, no. 2, Fall 1994, pp. 40–44.

Fernández Olmos, Margarite. "Los cuentos infantiles de Rosario Ferré, o la fantasía emancipadora." *Revista del Instituto de Cultura Puertorriqueña*, no. 99, 1992, pp. 42–52.

Ficek, Rosa E. "Infrastructure and Colonial Difference in Puerto Rico after Hurricane María." *Transforming Anthropology*, vol. 26, no. 2, October 2018, pp. 102–17.

Hernández, Carmen Dolores. "La LIJ en Puerto Rico en el año 2011." *Anuario iberoamericano sobre el libro infantil y juvenil*, Fundación SM, 2012, pp. 207–16.

Jiménez, Marilisa. "How to Survive the End of the World: Youth Literature at Puerto Rico's Front Lines." The Latinx Project, April 14, 2020. www.latinxproject.nyu.edu/intervenxions/how-to-survive-the-end-of-the-world-youth-literature-at-puerto-ricos-front-lines.

Jiménez-García, Marilisa. "Pura Belpré Lights the Storyteller's Candle: Reframing the Legacy of a Legend and What It Means for the Fields of Latino/a Studies and Children's Literature." *Centro Journal*, vol. 26, no. 1, 2014, pp. 110–47.

Kerkhof, Erna. "The Myth of the Dumb Puerto Rican: Circular Migration and Language Struggle in Puerto Rico." *New West Indian Guide/Nieuwe West-Indische Gids*, vol. 75, nos. 3–4, 2001, pp. 257–88.

Kortright Roig, Dinah. "La literatura infantil y juvenil en Puerto Rico: En clave de viento y marea." *Anuario iberoamericano sobre el libro infantil y juvenil*, Fundación SM, 2019, pp. 337–67.

Lopez, Marco, Desiree Rodriguez, Hazel Newlevant, Derek Ruiz, and Neil Schwartz, editors. *Puerto Rico Strong: A Comics Anthology Supporting Puerto Rico Disaster Relief and Recovery*. Lion Forge, 2018.

Lugo, Sujei. "Enhancing Children's ABCs and Vocabulary through 9 Alphabet Books." Latinxs in Kid Lit, September 22, 2014. latinosinkidlit.com/2014/09/22/enhancing-childrens-abcs-and-vocabulary-through-9-alphabet-books/.

Lugo Vázquez, Sujei. "Y este cuento (no) ha terminado: Rebuilding, Rewriting and Resisting in Puerto Rico." *Anansesem: News, Ideas, Arts, and Letters from the World of Caribbean Children's & YA Publishing*, May 2019. www.anansesem.com/2019/05/y-este-cuento-no-ha-terminado.html.

Maisonet-Quiñonez, Ivette. "Actividad editorial en Puerto Rico." *Anuario iberoamericano sobre el libro infantil y juvenil*, Fundación SM, 2010, pp. 133–46.

Medina, Carmen Liliana, and Sandra L. Soto-Santiago. "Critical Literacy in Puerto Rico: Mapping Trajectories of Anticolonial Reaffirmations and Resistance." *Handbook of Critical Literacies*, edited by Jessica Zacher Pandya, Raúl Alberto Mora, Jennifer Helen Alford, Noah Asher Golden, and Roberto Santiago de Roock, Routledge, 2021.

Piñeiro de Rivera, Flor. *Un siglo de literatura infantil puertorriqueña/A Century of Puerto Rican Children's Literature*. U of Puerto Rico P, 1987.

Rodríguez de Tió, Lola. *Mis cantares: Libro poético*. Imp. de M. Fernandez, 1876.

Torres, Francisco L., and Carmen Liliana Medina. "Cuentos combativos: Decolonialities in Puerto Rican Books about María." *Journal of Literacy Research*, vol. 53, no. 2, June 2021, pp. 242–64.

Torres-Rivera, Carmen Milagros. "Publishing Perspectives: Interview with Carmen Milagros Torres, Puerto Rican Children's Literature Scholar." Interview with Summer Edward, October 14, 2014. www.summeredward.com/2014/10/publishing-perspectives-interview-with.html.

Torres-Rivera, Carmen Milagros. "Puerto Rican Children's Literature and the Need for Afro–Puerto Rican Stories." *Bookbird: A Journal of International Children's Literature*, vol. 52, no. 3, July 2014, pp. 81–85.

CHAPTER 6

Blackness, Imperialism, and Nationalism in Dominican Children's Literature

Stacy Ann Creech

The history of the Spanish-speaking Caribbean, much like that of the rest of Latin America, is a history of imperialism, domestic and foreign conflict, and the effacement of national identity. Nationhood in Caribbean locales is complicated by the region's cultural and racial diversity, which results largely from its colonial and imperial history. The sociopolitical and cultural spheres of countries like the Dominican Republic, for example, have always been under threat from outside imperial influences, contributing to the (re)production of narrowly focused cultural narratives that place white roots and a particular construction of indigeneity in higher esteem than Black African heritage. A look at children's literature in the Dominican Republic illustrates the ways that foreign and domestic material designed for the instruction and enjoyment of young people has relied on distorted representations of race that are neither accurate nor affirming.

The convoluted history of the Dominican nation reveals ongoing racial anxieties tied to empire and colonialism; the way this history has shaped concepts of nationhood in the Dominican Republic becomes more overt when examined alongside the development of the reading material that has been available to children. By contextualizing instructional literature for Dominican children and young adults from the pre-Columbian, Spanish colonial, Haitian, American occupation, and Trujillo dictatorship eras, I show that the nation has traditionally identified itself in opposition to the African components of its culture and history, and that artists and educators in the Dominican Republic have traditionally promoted a lineage that gestures almost exclusively toward Indigenous, European, and Anglo-American roots. This tendency increased after the island of Hispaniola divided into two nations: the Republic of Haiti to the west and the Dominican Republic to the east. Ongoing conflicts with Haiti, dating back to the early nineteenth century, augmented and reinforced a concept of Dominican nationhood that has historically rejected Blackness. Since the 1990s, however, national debates about national identity and cultural representations have prompted a series of education reforms, and the advent of the twenty-first century has seen an upsurge in Dominican authors writing stories for children that endeavor to be more racially inclusive. These changes have resulted in a literature that foregrounds the country's diverse ancestry, including its Indigenous, European, and African heredity, opening up an instructional and analytical area through which the previously reigning racial imaginary can be challenged and subverted.

The Legacy of Colonial and Postrevolutionary Views in Dominican Children's Literature

The Dominican Republic's anti-Blackness has its roots in its colonial and imperial history. These systems of oppression have both threatened and produced Dominican identity, based on racial, social, and religious inequality (Galtung 81), and have prompted Dominican artists and educators to promote a lineage that gestures almost exclusively toward explicit constructions of indigeneity and whiteness, favoring representations that efface Blackness.[1] During the pre-Columbian period, prior to initial contact with European colonizers in 1492, the island now known as Hispaniola was predominantly inhabited by the Indigenous Arawak Taíno tribe that had migrated there from South America.[2] These peoples had a rich cultural tradition attached to a set of religious beliefs passed down from one generation to the next by means of storytelling, recounting stories of both the real and the fantastic through a religious ceremony called Areíto, in which certain members of the tribe danced and sang about physical migration, polytheistic beliefs, the significance and conferral of honor, and natural phenomena (Rouse 15). By the 1530s, the Taíno were mostly extinct, having been greatly affected by European diseases, physical exploitation, and enslavement.[3] Access to their oral traditions, however, had enabled members of the Spanish clergy, as well as royal chroniclers, to record their culture as literature.

Donald Thompson has identified people like Ramón Pané and Bartolomé de Las Casas as some of the most prominent chroniclers of Taíno cultural traditions (183). Their oral history has survived in books recounting the origins and subsequent development of the Dominican nation and has been notably featured in literature for Dominican children and young adults written up to the present day. Novels like Manuel de Jesús Galván's *Enriquillo* (1882), for instance, are still in circulation and included in elementary school syllabi, so that Dominican children can learn about the Taíno chieftain who rebelled against Spanish colonizers. It is significant that *Enriquillo*, a postindependence novel, shows how the Taíno are being used to construct a postcolonial national identity that is palatable in the wake of colonialism and that holds at bay some of the more complex implications of the Black populations.

The way in which representations of Taíno peoples have contributed to a discourse of anti-Blackness is rooted in the country's colonial history. In the fifteenth century, Hispaniola became an early contact zone, to borrow a phrase from Mary Louise Pratt, between European colonizers representing the Spanish Crown and the Arawak Taíno peoples who inhabited it in the fifteenth century. Europeans chronicled aspects of the Native culture in Spanish-language tracts and documents, resulting in histories shaped by colonialist forces and designed to instill in readers a sense of both admiration and grief for the exterminated Indigenous population. Additionally, by idealizing certain physical characteristics, such as straight black hair and olive complexions, these texts set in place a racial imaginary that continued to be promoted through the twentieth century, despite not corresponding to the majority Dominican population. Two of the most widely consumed historical texts written by Dominican authors are devoted to the histories of these peoples: Frank Moya Pons's *The Dominican Republic: A National History*, for instance, dedicates its first two chapters to describing these "lost" Natives, their traditions, and their beliefs. One of the preeminent historians of the Dominican Republic, Moya Pons imbues the text with words like "violent" (30) and "terrorized" (31) to decry the extermination of the Indigenous population at the hands of Spanish conquerors, but unwittingly becomes part of a national discourse produced by colonizing efforts that position the Taíno as being more worthy of attention and compassion than the enslaved Africans who were later brought to the island. Ultimately, the history text adds to the construction of a postcolonial narrative that contributes to the establishment of a social hierarchy in which the Indigenous population and even European settlers are regarded above Africans, since the book condemns slavery while also lauding the progress brought to the island by the colonizing machine.

Another text traditionally employed in school settings to teach Dominican children and young adults about the Taíno is Roberto Cassá's *Los Taínos de la Española* (*The Taínos of Hispaniola*; 1974), which aims primarily to "englobar las particularidades de la explotación de la mano de obra aborigen, base de la economía colonial de la primera época" ("cover particulars of the exploitation of the aboriginal workforce, which was the basis of the colonial economy of the first era"; 9).[4] Both of these texts establish Indigenous peoples as noble in nature, though naïve and childlike in their disposition, which creates a dual definition that continues to resonate in perceptions of race today, as it reinforces racialized constructions of social hierarchies in the Dominican Republic. The phenotypical descriptions of the Taíno taken from early accounts and reproduced in these didactic texts depict them as having light brown skin, straight raven-black hair, and brown eyes—traits that have been repeatedly used by illustrators of children's books recounting the histories of these peoples. Some examples of these kinds of texts include the Puerto Rican editions *Tai: El pequeño Tayno* (*Tai: The Little Taíno*; 2008, no author mentioned) and *Mitos del pueblo Taíno: Libro de colorear* (*Myths about the Taíno Peoples: A Coloring Book*; 2011, by Mercedes López-Baralt), both heavily circulated in the Dominican Republic.

These recurrent physical descriptions have transcended the pages of children's books, allowing Dominican authorities to use the descriptor "Indio/a" ("Indian") as a widely accepted category of racial distinction used in officially issued identity documents such as photo cards and passports to classify mixed-race Dominican citizens who phenotypically appear to have a lighter complexion than Black Dominicans, regardless of their genetic constitution. Elizabeth DeLoughrey notes that "in parts of the Spanish-speaking Caribbean, especially the Dominican Republic, . . . national discourse celebrates Taíno figures such as Enriquillo . . . over the perceived Africanism of Haiti" (237–38). This selective national discourse persists in literature, with Dominican historical and didactic textbooks repeatedly highlighting the history of Indigenous Taíno communities while failing to include African history. In doing so, even inadvertently, textbooks further efface the country's African ancestry in favor of the romanticized Native past. Indigenous scholarship detailing the history of the Caribbean region prior to contact with the European colonizing machine is necessary and significant, but without a concomitant effort to promote Dominicans' African heritage, children's literature encourages nonwhite children and young adults to seek their likeness exclusively in these Native figures. Consequently, generations of sociopolitical circumstances have shaped a Dominican educational system that propagates literature in which dark-skinned children cannot see "their physical likeness, beliefs, and immediate everyday experiences reflected" (Edward 21), even though they constitute a large part of the population. As a result, the Dominican history of the enslaved Africans brought by the Spanish to replace the labor of these Indigenous peoples, their oral histories and traditions, has been at best ignored and at worst completely lost. The success of rebellions by enslaved Africans against European enslavers—in processes called Marronage—only added to the European desire to erase Afro-Dominican history.[5] Owing to this, and later to sociopolitical tensions with the neighboring Haitian Republic, African heritage was positioned in imperial and colonial history as undesirable. As a consequence, inherited attitudes against Blackness have produced an unequal and misrepresentative children's literature in the Dominican Republic.

Dominican children's literature did not emerge as a recognized genre until the nineteenth century, partly as an attempt to define a postcolonial national identity. Miguel Collado singles out author Virginia Elena Ortea as a pioneering writer in the field in a national context. Her publications for children include a collection of short stories entitled *Risas y lágrimas* (*Laughter and Tears*; 1899), in which tales like "Los diamantes de Plutón" (Pluto's Diamonds) and "La mala madrastra" (The Evil Stepmother) offer reimagined versions of European classical mythology and fairy tales. Herself a product of a system dating back to colonial times that presented misleading racial and cultural representations to Dominican children, Ortea reinforced representations favoring white characters in European or Anglo-American settings, that carried through to the end of the twentieth century. Having been brought up in an affluent Spanish household, Ortea is complicit in creating a Dominican literary tradition that draws on foreign sources but fails to remake them to better suit a national context.

The construction of nationhood based on imperial ideology in the Dominican Republic thus consciously and unconsciously promoted the erasure of Blackness. A racial imaginary that began with what Spanish colonizers perceived as insurrection by the enslaved Africans who in colonial times defied oppression was reinforced by a long period between those times and the nineteenth century marked by racial violence and political instability. The Africans' revolts began the process of division of the island, as Spanish and French colonial powers fought to maintain dominion over the territory. By the nineteenth century, then, the new generation of nationals on the island was torn between the Africans who had settled in the west, and who had waged the revolutionary war that established Haiti as an independent republic, and the easterners, who were mostly descendants of Spaniards and whose hold on the territory had become tenuous at best. After an extended period of racial, cultural, and sociopolitical tensions between the two sides of Hispaniola, the Dominican Republic's inception as a nation occurred in 1844, in a revolutionary war of independence that overthrew twenty-two years of Haitian rule. The concerted effort by "nationalists" and "patriots" is described in history books available to Dominican schoolchildren as being a war waged against vilified Black peoples who had taken control of the island, as is the case with Moya Pons's text.

José Luis Escalante notes that instruction of children in the Dominican Republic, including reading comprehension and writing skills, was confined to school settings rather than at-home learning and remarks that by 1844 the national curriculum focused on pedagogy favoring "la lectura, escritura, cálculo y cuentas, bordado y oración a coro" ("reading, writing, calculus and accounting, embroidery, and choral prayer"; "La educación dominicana"), since the Roman Catholic Church was largely tasked with Dominican children's education. The books to which children were exposed in the eastern part of the island followed strict Catholic doctrine; Spanish-language editions of the Bible were extensively used, especially in the eighteenth and nineteenth centuries, to impart catechism to children. The most popular editions imported to the Dominican Republic include Pedro Lozano's text (1786), as well as the *Sagrada Biblia de Torres Amat* (*Torres Amat Holy Bible*; 1890) edition of the text (Yebra Rovira 16). Conventionally, education of Dominican children and young adults was geared "hacia la formación de personas obedientes al gobierno, a las leyes y a Dios, con una actitud conformista" ("toward the formation of people who were obedient to the government, to the laws and to God, with a conformist attitude"; Escalante, "La educación dominicana" 6). Traditionally, educational access in the Dominican Republic has been reserved for light-skinned people of a high social class and Spanish ancestry, while the vast majority of the population has been kept in the dark.

Tracing the subsequent evolution of the Dominican educational system and the reading patterns created thereby, Escalante writes that in the decades following the declaration of independence and well into the twentieth century, school curricula were modified and expanded around European values, "introduciendo la enseñanza de la gramática Castellana; aritmética y teneduría de libros" ("introducing the teaching of Castilian Spanish grammar, arithmetic, and bookkeeping"; "La educación dominicana"). It is imperative to note that this turn follows twenty-two years of Haitian rule in the eastern part of the island, during which laws instituted against people of Spanish descent included land expropriations, forced military service, and restricted use of the Spanish language in public spaces. Moya Pons notes as well that, in addition to these restrictive laws, the Haitian government also banned the practice of European cultural traditions and deported the majority of clergy from the island, since the young republic wanted nothing to do with European Catholicism (124–25). All of this legislation forcibly enacted by the Haitian government augmented proto-nationalist sentiments in what would later become the Dominican Republic and reinforced racial, cultural, and religious hierarchies. Humberto García Muñiz and Jorge L. Giovannetti outline this period in Dominican history as being the direct antecedent of a culture that still "rejects blackness and favors the 'whitening' of the society" (139). In this sense, it is unsurprising that the national ideologies of the Dominican Republic, which in many ways shaped children's literature, are based on principles that deny African heritage, and that by the twentieth century, racial tensions reached a crucial point of contestation.

Postindependence Dominican governments launched what seemed to be explicit campaigns to erase all visible traces of Blackness from the nation, reaching a critical point during the dictatorship of Rafael Leónidas Trujillo from 1930 to 1961.[6] As the dictator's government controlled all aspects of social and cultural production, and as he was determined to *limpiar la raza* ("cleanse the race"), school curricula soon contained only textbooks and literature that depicted his racial and historical bias.[7] Under Trujillo's regime, an entire generation of children and young adults was exposed to racially prejudiced state-mandated social and educational discourse and thereby further indoctrinated to negate its African ancestry, as Trujillo intensified already existing attitudes and discrimination. Ana Gallego Cuiñas recounts the development of Dominican literature and posits that, just as other Latin American writers did, Dominican authors and educators sought to build a sense of national identity with their works. Such texts elucidate

> los problemas de la construcción de la nación y de la construcción de imágenes de lo popular. . . . Es decir, se pretende la construcción de lo nacional como colectividad unida por lazos históricos—y de lo popular como un espacio compatible de identidad . . . que crea un ambiente propio mirando hacia atrás y reproduciendo el período colonial y el precolombiano. (20–21)

> (the problems of nation building and of the construction of images of the popular. . . . That is to say, they imagine the construction of "the national sphere" as a collective bound together by historical links—and the popular as a shareable space of identity . . . which creates a specific backward-glancing environment that reproduces the colonial and pre-Columbian periods.)

In this sense, written works produced and circulated in the Dominican Republic for children and young adults, including short stories, textbooks, and poetry from the nineteenth century through to the latter half of the twentieth century, created a sense of nationhood that was as foreign as it was long deceased, within a field created by the narrowly focused works of the previously mentioned Ortea. The early twentieth century in the Dominican Republic was marked by sociopolitical upheavals, civil wars, and economic decay, prompting the US to invade the eastern part of the island in 1916. Escalante estimates that at the time of the American occupation, more than 90 percent of the Dominican population was illiterate; a first educational reform took place during occupation, promoting the construction of schools primarily for the education of young children aged seven to fourteen. The school curriculum was designed by Dominican educators who had studied in the US (Escalante, "La educación en la era de Trujillo" 3). Writing about this period, Richard A. Haggerty observes that "the continued violence and instability prompted the administration of President William H. Taft to dispatch a commission to Santo Domingo" ("Occupation by the United States"). That commission would later lead the US Marine Corps to proclaim a military government, which maintained rule for eight years. Haggerty goes on to enumerate the immediate and enduring aftermath of this seizure:

> The surface effects of the occupation were largely positive. The Marines restored order throughout most of the republic (with the exception of the eastern region); the country's budget was balanced, its debt was diminished, and economic growth resumed; infrastructure projects produced new roads that linked all the country's regions for the first time in its history; a professional military organization, the Dominican Constabulary Guard, replaced the partisan forces that had waged a seemingly endless struggle for power. Most Dominicans, however, greatly resented the loss of their sovereignty to foreigners, few of whom spoke Spanish or displayed much real concern for the welfare of the republic. ("Occupation by the United States")

The passage above alludes to the resentment felt by Dominican citizens at having their freedom taken away once again by an imperialist nation. The inevitable consequences of entering into contact with the English language and American customs have been extensive and thorough. Even today, more than a century after this first invasion took place, the Dominican Republic is one of the most "Americanized" countries in Latin America, and English is spoken throughout. Certainly, the Castilian Spanish spoken in the eastern part of the island was transformed, metamorphosing into a mixture of both languages.[8] Since then, the school curriculum has reflected these changes by including instruction in English as a key aspect in all schools. During the US occupation, new books began to circulate for children and young adults, which now included Anglo-American stories, characters, and settings. It is important to note that the American intervention exploited racial tensions on the island, as Karen Sands-O'Connor and Caroline Hagood observe, and American children's literature about the Dominican Republic during this period suggests that keeping the African influence out allowed the nation "to be 'one of the showplaces of the West Indies,' free from the 'stain' of the 'wrong' color of blood" (131). Furthermore, American occupation of the territory had greater far-reaching effects, since Trujillo's contact with the US military during his formative years had been a precursor to his rule and part of what began shaping the tyrant's sociopolitical ideologies. Haggerty explicates that, during the occupation, a young Trujillo enjoyed a position of power, having enlisted in the National Police in 1918, a time when the upper-class Dominicans, who had formerly filled the officer corps, largely refused to collaborate with the occupying forces. Trujillo harbored no such scruples. He rose quickly in the officer corps, while at the same time he built a network of allies and supporters. . . . Trujillo saw the armed force not for what it should have been—an apolitical domestic security force—but for what it was: the main source of concentrated power in the republic. ("The Era of Trujillo" 3)

Once his dictatorship was established, the leader of the republic maintained control that historians such as Howard J. Wiarda describe as "probably the strongest and most absolute ever to be established in Latin America," since he "maintained all authority in his own hands" (551). Trujillo's government, beyond its control over state policy and civic policing, was also responsible for policing the sociopolitical and cultural spheres, including media and artistic productions. As part of totalitarian rule, Trujillo's ministry of education was directed to maintain and improve the educational laws that had been implemented in the Dominican Republic by the US government during the occupation. The educational system under Trujillo's regime borrowed from the American one but established its own set of reforms with the goal of enabling "que la escuela dominicana evolucionara hacia modalidades más amplias y sistemas más acordes con el espíritu científico, también, la tendencia experimental de las prácticas pedagógicas modernas" ("Dominican schools to evolve toward broader forms and systems more in keeping with the scientific spirit, and also attending to the experimental nature of modern pedagogical practices"; Escalante, "La educación en la era de Trujillo"). Even though this was the purported goal, and texts that were available to children in the Dominican Republic included both European and American stories, access to education, opened and encouraged during the American occupation, was limited once again during the dictatorship: "[P]ocos dominicanos tenían oportunidad de asistir a la escuela, las pocas que había, funcionaban por estar localizadas en las zonas urbanas, cuando la mayoría de la población residía en el campo" ("Few Dominicans had the opportunity to attend schools, and the few that existed were located in urban zones, while the majority of the population resided in the countryside").

Educational materials at this time were also heavily censored by the government, and while children's books containing stories featuring Spain and the US and some from other Latin American countries were available, they had to undergo a preapproval process, especially in the later years of Trujillo's dictatorship when he did not allow the public circulation of material that would endanger his authority. Some examples of textbooks and literary works that were introduced and are still in circulation today include the Spanish didactic collection entitled *El sembrador: Libro de lectura* (*The Sower: A Student Reader*), and the Dominican issue of *Nacho: Libro inicial de lectura* (*Nacho: A Beginner's Reader*). Created to instruct children in Spanish-language grammar, critical thinking skills, and moral values, these texts advance visual representations of characters with white European or American phenotypes and exclude Black African or mixed-race characters with dark complexions.

An early Argentinian edition of *El sembrador*, for instance, written by Héctor Pedro Blomberg in 1925, shows on its cover a white, redheaded man who is farming the land with his white children. This particular issue of the collection, widely distributed in the Dominican Republic, is suffused with instructional stories about familial bonds in a rural setting, its content mostly preoccupied with depicting life in the countryside. It is essential to recall Escalante's observations that children living in Dominican rural areas had no access to education and were most likely illiterate. If these children, who constituted the majority of the population, were to have access to this publication, would they have recognized themselves in the stories contained in the text? As for children in urban areas like Santo Domingo and Santiago who would have had the privilege of accessing this reading material, perhaps learning about white farming families in Argentina was not conducive to building a true sense of Dominican identity. Governments allowed these misleading narratives to circulate because they upheld an idealized national imaginary. In an equally insensitive and culturally damaging manner, the *Nacho* anthology illustrates ways that Dominican authors writing for children were themselves a product of the racially exclusionary ideologies so ubiquitous in the formation of a Dominican canon, since authors and illustrators like Melanio Hernández allowed their efforts to be used in the production of texts that displayed blatantly false images of Dominican society. Hernández's text, published in the 1970s and widely regarded as having instructed generations of Dominicans how to read and write, contains various scenarios in which white parents are teaching their children Spanish-language grammar, phonetics, and phonology. Employing alliterative phrases in a system of rote memorization, the text ingrained in the collective psyche of the Dominican nation the belief that only light-skinned people are capable of imparting and receiving this linguistic knowledge learned from Spanish colonialism. Some of these repetitive phrases include "Mi mamá me mima" ("My mother pampers me") and "Mi papa fuma pipa" ("My father smokes a pipe"). Additional content and illustrations in this text reinforce very narrow representations of Dominican phenotypes and necessarily raise questions about the kinds of people who were perceived as being authoritative enough to teach Dominican children and young adults. These observations are in direct accordance with the colonialist and imperialist mindset that formed and underpinned the sense of nationhood taught to generations of children and, in many ways, still prevails in the Dominican Republic today.

Current Trends in Dominican Children's Literature: From 1993 to the Present

The extant educational curriculum in the Dominican Republic, spanning kindergarten to grade 12, reflects years of thought and scrutiny, as well as deliberation about national identity, multiculturalism, and visual representations of "real Dominicans." Owing its foundations to the 1993 Educational Reform Act, current legislation mandates inclusivity in Dominican culture and seeks to incorporate textbooks and literary works that showcase the diverse ethnicities that compose Dominican society. According to legislation viewable on the Dominican Republic's government website, the reform that gave birth to the new curriculum was a result of "el inicio de un nuevo período social y político consecuencia de los cambios estructurales producidos por el agotamiendo del modelo de desarrollo vigente hasta ese momento" ("the beginning of a new sociopolitical period resulting from structural changes produced by the exhaustion of the extant model of development in place up to that time"; Secretaría de Estado de Educación y Cultura 11). The moment of national crisis that engendered this call for more inclusive classroom material is explicitly stated in the legislation, since its chief aim is to "crear y fortalecer una conciencia de identidad y de valoración e integración nacional, en un marco de Convivencia" ("create and strengthen a consciousness of national appreciation and integration, in a framework of coexistence"; 26). This subtle use of language carries with it questions about racial representations that drove Dominican educators to challenge the texts being used to instruct and entertain children until then.

A general sense of indignation permeates the document, as its designers note that the Spanish-speaking Caribbean region is one of the most racially and culturally diverse in the Western Hemisphere and that the exclusion of Blackness in all social and cultural productions until that point was something to be decried. The field of children's literature since then has been increasingly dominated not by stories and didactic materials with European and Anglo-American origins, but instead by native Dominican folktales, short stories, and novellas that include diverse representations of the nation's African ancestry.

Rufina Báez Zabala notes that, in the twenty-first century, Dominican literature for children and young adults has sought to strengthen areas perceived by educators and students as deficient and has focused on presenting texts that include "fiestas patronales, religiosas, y temáticas culturales" ("patron saint celebrations, religious festivities, and cultural subject matters"). Understanding the various levels of interconnectedness between sociopolitical and cultural categories becomes an exercise not only in identifying but also in rooting out colonialist and imperialist imperatives that informed national identity and patriotism in the Dominican Republic. For children and young adults in the nation, the changes in the 1993 reform improved the long tradition that favored whiteness in children's books and excluded many readers from identifying with the books they read. But this legislation did not end this tradition completely, as a recent scandal over a history textbook shows. The text in question, *Ciencias Sociales 6* (*Social Sciences*), was published in 2014 by Editorial Actualidad and was approved by the Dominican Ministry of Education to be employed as an official textbook for grade 6, across national school curricula. Historian Manuel Núñez raised concerns about the book in 2015, since it "encierra una distorsión de la verdad histórica, lagunas imperdonables e inducir a los alumnus a creer que RD es un país racista" (Pantaleón; "contains distorted historical truth and unforgivable gaps, and prompts students to believe that the Dominican Republic is a racist country"). To be clear, Núñez's concern stemmed from the fact that the book devoted too much effort to explaining the African ancestry of the Dominican Republic, making explicit the years that the nation had been part of Haiti and referring to a construction of nationhood that depicted Dominican "nationalists" as having problematic racial attitudes. The book sparked national controversy following Núñez's comments, and was pulled from schools and replaced with another text, further revealing that national definition is a constant debate and that children's literature provides a platform on which that debate can take place.

By borrowing from early traditions of children's books like those published by Ortea, who seems to be merely reproducing the conventions she inherited, many Dominican authors for children are presently engaged in remaking these traditions in reparative ways, as their works seek to break historical (mis)representations of race. One such author is Leibi Ng, a mixed-race Dominican of Chinese descent, whose career started in the 1980s as a contributor to *Revista Infantil Tobogán*. Her publications include *Huellas de la leyenda* (*Traces of the Legend*; 1999), *Tragaluz* (*Light-Swallower*; 2008), and *Salto a las estrellas* (*Jump to the Stars*; 2016), stories and poetry that deal directly with Dominican settings and characters.[9] Particularly relevant is her *Secreto de monte* (*Secret of the Mountain*; 2000), in which she remakes the Dominican myth of the Ciguapa, a female creature who lives in the wilderness and whose feet point backward.[10] Ann González posits that Ng's reimagining of the traditional tale of the reclusive entity who dies when men imprison her carries new sociopolitical implications that make it culturally relevant today. While the traditional Ciguapa story adheres to violent phallogocentric gender roles and representations inherited from imperial and colonial systems, Ng's version (re)imagines the entity marrying a man of Spanish descent and having a female child with him; the story then revolves around the mother's fear that her child will look like her, with dark skin, black hair, and brown eyes, and that she will inherit the same unnatural feet. The story's ending finds the Ciguapa feeling relieved once she realizes that her daughter is "normal" after all, and that she looks like her father. It is easy to interpret this as a deliberate authorial move to show that even this mythical creature inhabiting the Dominican wilderness is not untouched by racist views, as her satisfaction only comes once she has made sure that her child is white and "normal." However, González writes that the ending of Ng's version of the folktale carries an ambivalent message, since "the mother wants the little girl to look like everyone else, but the little girl longs for her roots and the fundamental difference that would define her" (145). This signals a change in the literature written for Dominican children, as it shows that authors are now exploring deeper cultural struggles and are implicitly promoting conversations about these themes of difference, acceptance, and belonging.

The long list of contemporary Dominican authors writing for children and young adults includes authors Margarita Luciano López, Eleanor Grimaldi

Silié, and Rafael Peralta Romero, who explore racial relationships and carry messages of inclusion while encouraging children to build self-esteem. Luciano López's book ¿Quién se robó el verde? (*Who Stole the Green?*; 2000), for example, features a woman remembering her youth and describing the lush Dominican landscapes, asking the children around her if they know who has taken the color green away. The message behind the text is multifaceted, since it serves to highlight the island's natural beauty and resources, motivating readers to care for nature, but it also laments the industrialization and urbanization of the country, indicating perhaps all the skyscrapers and modernized constructions that have been built in recent years by owners from Europe or the US. Grimaldi Silié's contributions to the field of Dominican children's literature have centered around issues of racial bias and racial relations in different ways, as demonstrated in her collection of poems and short stories *El sueño de Penélope* (*Penelope's Dream*; 2010). The anthology includes eight short stories and thirty-seven poems, all dealing with crucial thematic concerns such as biodiversity, familial bonds, and Dominican cultural traditions, depicting ethnically diverse characters who wonder aloud why they look different from one another. The text is richly illustrated by Teresa Jiménez, Julio César Martínez, and Werner Olmos, all of whose artistic drawings present diversity in order to "embellecer y estimular a la creatividad, favorecer la comprensión del texto y promover el interés hacia su lectura" (Luciano López, "El sueño de Penélope"; "embellish and stimulate creativity, encourage the comprehension of the text, and promote interest in reading").

Another interesting example of the type of literature being written for Dominican children now is the work of Rafael Peralta Romero, whose collection of short stories *A la orilla de la mar* (*By the Seashore*; 2012), features ten tales addressing cultural traditions inherited from Africa. One of the tales features a young Black character named Mediopeje, who is concerned because he has not been able to find himself in any of the stories that he reads; another one tells the story of a teenaged mixed-race boy named Boquita, who is wondering what he will do when he becomes an adult. It is promising to discover that the field of Dominican children's literature is now populated with writers and illustrators who are operating against colonialism and whose work depicts characters representative of the population. Recent examples of Dominican children's literature depart from the emphasis on Taíno and European identity to address the nation's more complex racial history, resulting in insightful and nuanced texts. Undoubtedly, this signals the country's reckoning with its actual history and the diverse identities of its population.

From the pre-Columbian period through to the twentieth century, Dominican children's literature has struggled to define itself due to pressures from outside—imperialist, colonizing forces. A combination of Spanish imperialism, Haitian domination, and American intervention meant that until fairly recently Dominican children and young adults were exposed almost exclusively to stories in which African roots were absent, signaling an effacement of Blackness. As this chapter has illustrated, racial relations on the island of Hispaniola are more than a little complex, and, as Summer Edward has noted, "[W]hat this can mean for children's books is that still, and all too often, others are telling our stories at the expense of authenticity and 'own voices,' leading to the perpetuation of a North American/European outsider view of our cultures" (22). However, recent publications for Dominican children and young adults, produced since the 1993 Educational Reform Act, work against the legacy of historical contexts that shaped this literary field around racially exclusionary colonial systems. If previous centuries popularized works that favored one kind of ethnicity and culture over another, then the texts being produced presently suggest reparative, restorative ways of enabling Dominican children to recognize and understand themselves.

Notes

1. According to the Oficina Nacional de Estadística (National Statistics Office), in the 2017 DR census, 49 percent of the population is of African descent, 39 percent of European descent, and 4 percent of pre-Columbian peoples' descent. See www.one.gob.do; see also the findings of the 2016 genetic study conducted by the University of Pennsylvania, available in the e-journal *Acento*: www.acento.dom.do.

2. See Irving Rouse's *The Taínos: Rise and Decline of the People Who Greeted Columbus* for more detailed information.

3. See the 1992 Penguin Classics edition of Bartolomé de Las Casas's *A Short Account of the Destruction of the Indies*, in which the colonist and social reformer recounts the extermination of the Indigenous tribes that first inhabited the Caribbean region. Forced to engage in arduous physical labor including mining for gold and other precious stones of value to Europeans, thousands of Taíno lost their lives, as their physical constitution could not withstand enslavement and hard labor.

4. Unless otherwise stated, all translations are mine.

5. See Filiberto Cruz Sánchez, *Historia de República Dominicana*, and Wenceslao Vega Boyrie, "El cimarronaje y la manumisión en el Santo Domingo colonial," for historical accounts detailing enslaved Africans' revolts against Spanish colonizers.

6. See Lauren Derby, "Haitians, Magic, and Money," and Richard Lee Turits, *Foundations of Despotism*, for details of Trujillo's dictatorship.

7. See Wendy Carrasco, "La prensa en la dictadura de Trujillo," for information on the kinds of books that were preapproved by Trujillo's government and the limited newspaper publications that were allowed during his dictatorship.

8. Some popular Anglicized terms borrowed from the English language used in the Dominican Republic include *suape* (from "swap") instead of the Spanish word *fregona*; *computadora* (from "computer") instead of the Spanish word *ordenador*; and *yipeta* (from "jeep") instead of the Spanish word *todoterreno*.

9. For a complete list of Leibi Ng's publications and editorial information, visit the author's partner websites: www.loqueleo.com/do/, www.leibyng.blogspot.com, and www.nidoderatones.com.

10. The Dominican folklore creature is reminiscent of the *douen* mythological creatures from Trinidad and Tobago folklore, showing the interconnectedness between Anglo-Creole Caribbean stories and those originating from the Spanish-speaking Caribbean (see Hill).

Works Cited

Báez Zabala, Rufina. "Enseñanza del eje transversal." Base de Dato Referencial de Investigaciones Educativas de la República Dominicana, n.d. www.ideice.gob.do/inered/.

Blomberg, Héctor Pedro. *El sembrador: Libro de lectura*. Ángel Estrada, 1925.

Carrasco, Wendy. "La prensa en la dictadura de Trujillo: Censura, manipulación y distorsión de la verdad." *Hoy*, May 29, 2013. http://hoy.com.do/la-prensa-en-la-dictadura-de-trujillo-censura-manipulacion-y-distorsion-de-la-verdad/.

Cassá, Roberto. *Los Taínos de la Española*. Editora de la Universidad Autónoma de Santo Domingo, 1974.

Collado, Miguel. *Historia bibliográfica de la literatura infantil dominicana (1821–2002)*. Banco de Reservas de la República Dominicana, 2003.

Cruz Sánchez, Filiberto. *Historia de República Dominicana*. Editora El Nuevo Diario, 2003.

DeLoughrey, Elizabeth M. *Routes and Roots: Navigating Caribbean and Pacific Island Literatures*. U of Hawai'i P, 2007.

Derby, Lauren. "Haitians, Magic, and Money: Raza and Society in the Haitian-Dominican Borderlands, 1900 to 1937." *Comparative Studies in Society and History*, vol. 36, no. 3, July 1994, pp. 488–526.

Edward, Summer. "Beyond the 'Four Fs': Caribbean Own Voices." *Horn Book Magazine*, vol. 93, no. 6, November–December 2017, pp. 21–26.

Escalante, José Luis. "La educación dominicana desde la independencia hasta la restauración." Trayectoria por la Educación, n.d. sites.google.com/site/trayectoriaporlaeducacion/proceso/actividad-4.

Escalante, José Luis. "La educación en la era de Trujillo, 1930–1961." Trayectoria por la Educación, n.d. sites.google.com/site/trayectoriaporlaeducacion/proceso/actividad-8.

Gallego Cuiñas, Ana. *Trujillo: El fantasma y sus escritores (Análisis y sistematización de la novela del trujillato)*. 2005. Universidad de Granada, PhD dissertation.

Galtung, Johan. "A Structural Theory of Imperialism." *Journal of Peace Research*, vol. 8, no. 2, June 1971, pp. 81–117. www.jstor.org/stable/422946.

Galván, Manuel de Jesús. *Enriquillo*. Casa de las Américas, 1977.

García Muñiz, Humberto, and Jorge L. Giovannetti. "Garveyismo y racismo en el Caribe: El caso de la población cocola en la República Dominicana." *Caribbean Studies*, vol. 31, no. 1, January–June 2003, pp. 139–211. www.jstor.org/stable/25613393.

González, Ann. *Resistance and Survival: Children's Narrative from Central America and the Caribbean*. U of Arizona P, 2009.
Grimaldi Silié, Eleanor. *El sueño de Penélope*. Editorial Santuario, 2010.
Haggerty, Richard A. "The Era of Trujillo." US Library of Congress, n.d. http://countrystudies.us/dominican-republic/11.htm.
Haggerty, Richard A. "Occupation by the United States, 1916–24." US Library of Congress, n.d. http://countrystudies.us/dominican-republic/10.htm.
Hernández, Melanio. *Nacho: Libro inicial de lectura*. Ediciones Susaeta, 1974.
Hill, Donald R. *Caribbean Folklore: A Handbook*. Greenwood Press, 2007.
Las Casas, Bartolomé de. *A Short Account of the Destruction of the Indies*. Translated by Nigel Griffin, Penguin, 1992.
López-Baralt, Mercedes. *Mitos del pueblo Taíno: Libro de colorear*. Editorial Instituto de Cultura Puertorriqueña, 2011.
Luciano López, Margarita. *¿Quién se robó el verde?* Editorial Letra Gráfica, 2000.
Luciano López, Margarita. "El sueño de Penélope." *Listín Diario*, June 26, 2010. www.listindiario.com/ventana/2010/06/26/147849/el-sueno-de-penelope.
Moya Pons, Frank. *The Dominican Republic: A National History*. Markus Wiener, 2010.
Pantaleón, Doris. "Educación retirará de las aulas libro de historia de sexto grado." *Listín Diario*, September 7, 2015. www.listindiario.com/la-republica/2015/09/07/387167/educacion-retirara-de-las-aulas-libro-de-historia-de-sexto-grado.
Peralta Romero, Rafael. *A la orilla de la mar*. Editorial Santuario, 2012.
Pratt, Mary Louise. *Imperial Eyes: Travel Writing and Transculturation*. Routledge, 2010.
Rouse, Irving. *The Tainos: Rise and Decline of the People Who Greeted Columbus*. Yale UP, 1992.
Sands-O'Connor, Karen, and Caroline Hagood. "Good Neighbors, Bad Magic: Reading American Policy in the Caribbean through Popular Literature." *Critical Perspectives on Caribbean Literature and Culture*, edited by Dorsía Smith, Tatiana Tagirova, and Suzanna Engman, Cambridge Scholars Publishing, 2010, pp. 121–40.
Secretaría de Estado de Educación y Cultura. "Fundamentos del Currículum." 1993. www.educando.edu.do/UserFiles/P0001/File/Curriculo/Fundamentos delcurriculo1.pdf.
Tai: El pequeño Tayno. Editorial El Antillano, 2008.
Thompson, Donald. "The *Cronistas de Indias* Revisited: Historical Reports, Archeological Evidence, and Literary and Artistic Traces of Indigenous Music and Dance in the Greater Antilles at the Time of the *Conquista*." *Latin American Music Review/Revista de Música Latinoamericana*, vol. 14, no. 2, Autumn–Winter 1993, pp. 181–201. www.jstor.org/stable/780174.
Turits, Richard Lee. *Foundations of Despotism: Peasants, the Trujillo Regime, and Modernity in Dominican History*. Stanford UP, 2004.
Vega Boyrie, Wenceslao. "El cimarronaje y la manumisión en el Santo Domingo colonial." *Clío*, vol. 74, no. 170, July–December 2005, pp. 65–102. https://en.calameo.com/books/000530775b10e014b0d0d.
Wiarda, Howard J. "Dictatorship and Development: The Trujillo Regime and Its Implications." *Southwestern Social Science Quarterly*, vol. 48, no. 4, March 1968, pp. 548–57. www.jstor.org/stable/42867911.
Yebra Rovira, Carmen. *Las biblias ilustradas en España en el siglo XIX*. Institución San Jerónimo, n.d. http://www.verbodivino.es/hojear/4412/las-biblias-ilustradas-en-espa%C3%B1a-en-el-siglo-xix.pdf.

CHAPTER 7

A Brief History of Costa Rican Children's Literature

Ann González

In 1917, a good half century before courses on children's literature began to appear in the Western academy, Costa Rican scholar Joaquín García Monge, director of the famous *Repertorio Americano*, which promoted and published young writers from all over Latin America, and Carmen Lyra, one of his former students and by all accounts the founder of children's literature in Costa Rica, established the first Cátedra de Literatura Infantil (Children's Literature Department and Professorship) in the Escuela Normal de Heredia in Costa Rica. This academic interest in children's literature predated Costa Rica's own production in the field. Carmen Lyra, a pseudonym for María Isabel Carvajal Quesada, did not publish her groundbreaking collection of children's stories *Cuentos de mi tía Panchita* for another three years (1920), and Joaquín Gutiérrez, distinguished writer and named by Costa Rican newspaper *La Nación* as the most important national literary figure of the twentieth century, did not publish his foundational children's novel *Cocorí* for another thirty years (1947).

As in the rest of Central America, writing intended specifically for children was slow to take off in Costa Rica despite the early academic interest in the topic; in the first part of the twentieth century, parents and teachers depended mostly on European classics, myths, and folktales. Part of the impetus encouraging local writing for children throughout the region emerged from a nationalistic desire to form future citizens who would distinguish themselves from other Latin Americans based on their regional identity, marked most clearly by vernacular speech patterns. By imitating popular speech, which contrasted notably from elite, cultured Spanish, early Costa Rican children's writers, particularly Lyra, merged the dual purposes of children's literature outlined by José Martí in 1889, to educate and entertain. By entertaining her young audiences with characters whose speech was distinctly Costa Rican, she ultimately taught them a great deal about who they were or who she thought they should be.

National identity, then, has been the underlying motif running through children's literature in Costa Rica for the past one hundred years. In general, Costa Ricans have promoted themselves, and to some extent still do, as the words of their national anthem describe them, as simple working folk, mostly descended from Europeans, who farm the Central Valley. Despite radical changes to the national economy, modernization, and technology, they still claim to be campesinos (simple country people) at heart. The small indigenous populations living in the mountains and the Jamaican Blacks brought to Costa Rica to work on the railroads in the nineteenth century have largely been ignored in this ideological construction of national identity, yet not so in Costa Rican children's literature. Both Lyra and Gutiérrez go out of their way to include the Atlantic coast in their portrayal of what it means to be Tico (Costa Ricans' name for themselves, derived from their tendency to use diminutives). Lyra's most famous story, "La cucarachita Mandinga," is a Costa Rican adaptation of a Caribbean fable originally about the marriage of a tiny ant named Martina to Pérez the rat. In the Costa Rican version, the female protagonist morphs into a tiny cockroach named Mandinga (echoing the name of an African tribe) who marries the debonaire "ratón Pérez." Mandinga is clearly modeled after the stereotypical erotic Black woman from Costa Rica's Atlantic coast. Most of the characters in Lyra's other stories, even those that include kings and queens, sound like stereotypical Costa Rican campesinos. While at first Lyra was criticized for teaching children to speak improperly, Costa Ricans soon realized the benefits of her work toward furthering the ideological construction of national identity. Thus, her stories have remained immensely popular.

Gutiérrez's famous children's novel *Cocorí* goes even further by creating a heroic Black child protagonist named after a famous indigenous chieftain. The action takes place entirely on the Atlantic coast, and despite a number of contemporary criticisms pointing to racist and Eurocentric stereotypes in the novel, the work is groundbreaking for its inclusion of a brave little Black boy as a model for Costa Rican identity. When the Ministry of Education responded to racist criticisms by removing *Cocorí* from the required reading list for elementary schools in the country in 2003, there was such a public outcry that the president at the time, Abel Pacheco, became involved in defending the book. He ultimately worked out a compromise in which required reading lists were abolished and substituted with lists of suggested titles.

Writing for children really took off in the second half of the twentieth century. The annual Carmen Lyra Prize for the best work of children's literature was established in 1975. Quince Duncan, Costa Rica's most notable Afro-Caribbean writer, published a collection of stories for children, *Los cuentos de Jack Mantorra*, in 1977, featuring a Black storyteller from the Atlantic coast whose tales are an interesting blend of African, Jamaican, and European elements. More recently, the market has been flooded with children's works of all kinds, from indigenous stories to eco-conscious appeals. The two most notable contemporary writers for children in Costa Rica today are Lara Ríos (a pseudonym for Marilyn Echeverría Zürcher) and Carlos Rubio, both of whom have taken pains to emphasize diversity and inclusion in their work. Ríos made her name in children's literature through a series of short humorous books for children based on a male child protagonist clearly suffering from attention-deficit/hyperactivity disorder in *Pantalones cortos* (1982) and two sequels. Later in her career, she published a novel that centered on the Cabécar tribe in Costa Rica with a female indigenous teenager as protagonist, *Mo* (2006). While she has suffered some criticism for appropriating an indigenous culture, she did base the story on her own experiences and research living with the tribe for a time. In addition, the book made a statement about the value of indigenous cultures and the need to incorporate them into the national identity.

Carlos Rubio has also gone out of his way to include marginalized characters as protagonists of his stories. In *La mujer que se sabía todos los cuentos* (2003), he emphasizes the foundational role of women in the formation of Latin America. What is more, his novel *Papá es un campeón* (2006) as well as some of his short stories feature artistic, subtly effeminate boy protagonists who find themselves at odds with the dominant macho sports culture of Costa Rica.

This unusual trend over the past century to include and promote characters who are typically ignored or suppressed in other regional literatures has offered a subtle, yet consistent, counternarrative to Costa Rica's dominant views of national identity. While it has not completely undermined the notion of Costa Ricans as simple farmers, it has clearly opened the doors to include more ethnic and racial minorities in the national imagination.

Works Cited

Amoretti, María. *Debajo del canto: Un análisis del himno nacional de Costa Rica*. Editorial de la Universidad de Costa Rica, 1987.
Duncan, Quince. *Los cuentos de Jack Mantorra*. Editorial Nueva Década. 1977.
González, Ann. *Resistance and Survival: Children's Narrative from Central America and the Caribbean*. U of Arizona P, 2009.
Gutiérrez, Joaquín. *Cocorí*. Editorial Rapa-Nui, 1947.
Lyra, Carmen [María Isabel Carvajal Quesada]. *Cuentos de mi tía Panchita*. 1920. Legado, 2005.
Quesada Villalobos, Patricia, and Magdalena Vásquez Vargas. "La literatura infantil en Costa Rica: Aportes y ausencias desde la historiografía literaria." *Revista Comunicación*, vol. 20, no. 1, January–June 2011, pp. 32–38.
Ríos, Lara [Marilyn Echeverría Zürcher de Sauter]. *Mo*. Farben Grupo Editorial Norma, 2005.
Ríos, Lara [Marilyn Echeverría Zürcher de Sauter]. *Pantalones cortos*. 1982. Farben Grupo Editorial Norma, 1995.
Rubio, Carlos. *La mujer que se sabía todos los cuentos*. Farben Grupo Editorial Norma, 2003.
Rubio, Carlos. *Papá es un campeón*. Farben Grupo Editorial Norma, 2006.

PART 2

DECOLONIZING CHILDREN'S LITERATURE IN THE ANGLOPHONE CARIBBEAN AND ITS DIASPORA

CHAPTER 8

Back to *Backfire*
The Pedagogical Impact of the Giuseppis' Caribbean Short Story Collection in the Secondary School System of Trinidad and Tobago from the 1970s to the Present

Geraldine Elizabeth Skeete

Background

Published in the early 1970s after the independence movements in the 1960s and within the context of a legacy of colonial education, Neville and Undine Giuseppi's short story collection *Backfire* epitomizes a time in the Caribbean's sociocultural, political, and literary history when Caribbean writers and writing were beginning to be taught more often in educational institutions including secondary schools and the University of the West Indies. While scholar Supriya M. Nair, for example, has cast doubt on the canonicity of Caribbean literature because of its instability as well as its "insubordinate status" within the US academy (8, 10), *Backfire* nonetheless played an important role in paving the way for young readers who were later introduced to the popular and classic Caribbean literature for which the canonization process had begun.

Its publication offers additional local and regional content in Caribbean storytelling for teenage readers besides folkloric literature, which is associated mainly with the oral tradition. Writing in 1990, Trinidadian Merle

Hodge, author of two young adult novels, lamented the dearth of Caribbean literature in the school curriculum due to an insufficient quantity of good fictional material suitable for every age group; secondary school teachers were teaching Caribbean literature written for adult readers, and primary school teachers depended greatly on folktales in their effort to include Caribbean literature ("Challenges of the Struggle" 207–8). It is well established that during the British colonial era, the reading and literature syllabi used in Caribbean schools were chiefly of content alien to students' day-to-day realities and lacked diversity in regard to racial, ethnic, religious, and sociocultural representations otherwise typical of the Caribbean region. British characters, language, philosophical outlook, landscape, climate, cuisine, and flora and fauna, for example, were as a whole presented, both overtly and subtly, to Caribbean children as components of an ideal world—resulting in both the advertent and inadvertent derogation of their own real environment, language, and way of life. English-born educators, and Caribbean-born ones who acceded to that world view, through their attitudinal, behavioral, and pedagogical practices also played a significant role in this indoctrination. Caribbean authors, poets, and calypsonians who grew up and were therefore schooled during that time period are among those who have addressed the subliminal and obvious impacts left by such curricula.

For example, C. L. R. James (1901–1989), acknowledged as one of the foremost intellectuals of the twentieth century, discusses in *Beyond a Boundary* (first published in 1963) his academic study of Latin, Greek, French, and English languages and literatures, as well as the history of Britain and other European countries, at the prestigious all-boys' secondary school Queen's Royal College in the Trinidadian capital, Port of Spain, which he attended from age ten to eighteen. He engaged in avid reading of the English literary masters, enabled by his home, college, and public libraries, and tells of his two obsessions, cricket and English literature, particularly his obsessive rereading of William Makepeace Thackeray's *Vanity Fair*. He mentions, too, the influence of his school principal, an "Englishman of the nineteenth century" (38). James does not disavow the benefits of his colonial education but later in life reflects on his realization of its drawbacks:

> But this school was in a colony ruled autocratically by Englishmen.... It was only long years after that I understood the limitation on spirit, vision and self-respect which was imposed on us by the fact that our masters, our cur-

riculum, our code of morals, *everything* began from the basis that Britain was the source of all light and leading, and our business was to admire, wonder, imitate, learn; our criterion of success was to have succeeded in approaching that distant ideal—to attain it was, of course, impossible. Both masters and boys accepted it as in the very nature of things. (38–39)

Austin Clarke, originally from Barbados, befittingly nicknamed "Little England," became a successful writer of the Caribbean Canadian literary tradition and also writes of his colonial secondary school education in the 1940s at Barbados's prestigious Combermere School in his memoir *Growing Up Stupid under the Union Jack* (1980). Jamaican Olive Senior is another literary stalwart, and like Clarke a multiple-award-winning writer, whose poetry has been studied in Caribbean secondary schools for several years including the popular "Colonial Girls' School" from her collection *Talking of Trees* (1985), which encapsulates the foreignness, irrelevance, and constraints of colonial education—"nothing about us at all" is one repetitive phrase in the poem. Hodge, an educator and author, does the same on this topic in her classic Caribbean bildungsroman *Crick Crack, Monkey* (1970), as does Grenadian-born Trinidadian calypsonian Slinger Francisco (sobriquet, Mighty Sparrow) in his calypso "Dan Is the Man (in the Van)" (1965). At the tertiary level, as John T. Gilmore points out in his review of the revised 2004 edition of *The West Indian Novel and Its Background*, Kenneth Ramchand, professor emeritus of literature and author of this seminal text (first published in 1970), can be credited for introducing full courses in West Indian literature on all the campuses of the University of the West Indies and shifting the central focus in teaching and research from English literature to literatures in English. *Backfire* serves as one outstanding example of how these gaps and imbalances began to be redressed pedagogically as well as literarily.

Joan B. Elliott and Mary M. Dupuis, editors of *Young Adult Literature in the Classroom*, observe regarding choice of reading material that "[y]oung adults are interested in books with main characters they can relate to—people of similar ages, facing similar problems" (3). They note,

> A few topics that attract YA readers focus on individual issues in growing up, such as potential career choices, parents and their expectations, relations with siblings, and sex and developing sexual attractions. Other popular topics focus on the reality of adult life: death and dying; drugs, alcohol, and sub-

stance abuse; divorce; spousal and child abuse; race and class discrimination. The list could go on. All of these issues are full of moral and ethical questions. As adolescents struggle to understand how different people and cultures deal with the issues that are important to each of us, they can explore a range of options through YA literature. (2)

Backfire typifies this kind of literature, albeit not all the types of preoccupations listed. The collection does not address sex, although its intended readers are at the cusp of or already at an age interested in the subject because of their physiological changes. The short stories variously explore relationships among family and friends, moral and ethical choices, fear and the supernatural, and tragic and comic circumstances, to name a few, and feature both child and adult protagonists.

Backfire includes both republished and original stories, the former from publications such as Undine Giuseppi's edited anthology *Writing Is Fun* (Joy Moore's "Mama's Theme Song," and Ida Ramesar's "Paradise Lost" and "Ramgoat Salvation"), the Jamaican literary magazine *Focus* (Robert Henry's "Give and Take"), and the London radio broadcast *Caribbean Voices* (Barnabas J. Ramon-Fortuné's "The Kite"). Notably, the author of "The New Teacher" was eighteen-year-old Ninnie Seereeram, a Trinidadian who, at the time of *Backfire*'s publication, had recently graduated from high school; as her first published story, it originally appeared in *Writing Is Fun*. Here a young adult writes for young adult readers; since YA literature typically targets twelve- to twenty-year-olds, teenagers preparing for examinations and adjusting to the different personality and teaching style of a new teacher are certainly issues with which many young readers can identify.

As a school text, *Backfire* serves a similar function to Cecil Gray's compiled 1982 publications *Wavelengths* and *Perspectives*, both subtitled *A Course in Narrative Comprehension and Composition for Caribbean Secondary Schools*, which include short stories by well-known writers from throughout the English-speaking Caribbean and follow-up exercises. Both were republished by Oxford University Press in 2014. These follow his similarly named *Response: A Course in Narrative Comprehension and Composition for Caribbean Secondary Schools* (1969). In his prefatory statements titled "To the Teacher," found in both *Wavelengths* and *Perspectives*, Gray observes what can also be applied to the reasoning behind the Giuseppis' publication of *Backfire*. While *Response* was geared toward secondary school students possessing language attainment levels for a "normal" course of study, a very substantial widening in the range of those levels occurred when other types of schools—the junior secondary among them—were established. This situation required the provision of one or more texts that could replace *Response* in order to satisfy "very low initial needs while helping the pupils to make progress towards the recognised goals of secondary schooling."

The junior secondary school was a primary focus of attention in the implementation of Trinidad and Tobago's 1968–1983 educational development plan; "[f]or the people of a society that was just emerging from colonialism, the expansion of secondary education through the creation of Junior Secondary Schools promoted the social and economic upward mobility that they were denied during the colonial era" ("Planning the Growth"). Although the shift system generated criticism and controversy, the junior secondary school was especially welcomed by working-class parents, who saw it as an opportunity that was more beneficial to their children than a postprimary class in a primary school or a substandard education at a private secondary school for which they would have to pay ("Planning the Growth"). The junior secondary system accommodated first to third form students, ranging from ages eleven to fourteen, before they graduated to the senior comprehensive school level after sitting for what was called the fourteen-plus examination. This was not an entry examination, because the senior comprehensive school into which each student matriculated was based largely on zoning. Instead, students' performance in this examination was a determinant of the area of study—sciences, language arts, business studies, and so on—for which they would focus in preparation for the ordinary level examinations.

Many primary school–aged students who passed their common entrance examination for a junior secondary school were more deficient in reading and literacy skills, and less inclined to be leisure readers of literature, than their five- and seven-year school counterparts. Most of them were products of homes with working-class parents who could ill afford the purchase of books and for whom reading was not a regular pastime. The reading ability and interests for this age group within the system would straddle both children's and young adult literature, the latter because, as noted by Elliott and Dupuis, it "is written for readers whose reading interests and skills are not yet mature but who are themselves maturing" (1). The Giuseppis' *Backfire* was included in the 1975 junior secondary syllabus for English along with, for example, Kenneth Ramchand's *West Indian Narrative*, Jan Carew's

Black Midas, Vic Reid's *Peter of Mt. Ephraim*, John Steinbeck's *The Pearl*, and Cecil Gray's *Language for Living* (1 and 2), *Bite In* (1, 2, and 3), and *Response*. *Backfire* was listed only for first form students, together with Reid's *Peter of Mt. Ephraim* and Gray's Book 1 for *Bite In* and *Language for Living*.

The author of this chapter was a student at the Marabella Junior Secondary School from 1977 to 1980, now renamed Marabella South Secondary School, located in the southern part of Trinidad, as the name implies. So indelible was the personal experience of *Backfire: A Collection of Caribbean Short Stories* (1973) in cultivating my love for reading, literature, and the short story, particularly the Caribbean short story, and in pursuing the discipline of literature all the way to the doctoral level, that I felt obliged to pay homage by penning this essay on the pedagogical significance of its publication. Declarations from peers and teachers also testify to the text's abiding effect.

A Brief Backstory on the Giuseppis

Neville and Undine Giuseppi were short story writers, poets, and educators, born in Trinidad and Barbados, respectively. Neville published the poetry collections *The Light of Thought* (1943) and *Selected Poems* (1972), and his work was also included in school textbooks, the BBC program *Calling the West Indies*, and early anthologies of short stories and poems such as *Papa Bois* (1947). Contributors to these anthologies included members of a group who in the 1940s met at the home of Judge Hallinan and included Giuseppi, Ernest A. Carr, Errol Hill, Barnabas J. Ramon-Fortuné, Edgar Mittelholzer, Seepersad Naipaul, and C. A. Thomasos (King 46–47). Neville Giuseppi's other writings are also dated from the 1930s to the 1950s, which attest to the longevity of his career as "free-lance writer, poet and essayist" even before his retirement from the Civil Service in 1969 (*Backfire* 112). Both Giuseppis contributed stories to *Backfire*, two by Undine ("Chung Lee" and "Journey by Night") and one by Neville ("Horace's Luck"). For the titular story of the collection, they chose Trinidadian Shirley Tappin's "Backfire," which had won a local television short story competition following her participation in "a short course on 'The Art of Writing' which was conducted by Mrs. Undine Giuseppi in 1971" (*Backfire* 114).

She came face to face with a tall, dark man.

Figure 8.1. *She came face to face with a tall, dark man*. From Shirley Tappin's "Backfire," *Backfire: A Collection of Caribbean Short Stories*, p. 4. Springer Nature Limited. Reproduced with permission of the Licensor through PLSclear.

Neville and Undine, as husband and wife, founded the Giuseppi Preparatory School in Arima, Trinidad, in 1982; Undine had previously been principal of the University School, the preparatory school affiliated with the University of the West Indies, St. Augustine, Trinidad. Prior to this, she had also taught and was vice principal at St. Augustine Girls' High School (SAGHS), which is still considered one of the "prestige" schools in Trinidad and Tobago. In celebration of the school's sixty-fifth anniversary in 2015, the *Broadcast* newsletter, a twice-yearly publication by the Naparima Alumni Association of Canada (founded in 1978 in Toronto by and for graduates of secondary- and tertiary-level educational institutions run by the Presbyterian Board, of which SAGHS is one), carried a piece by alumna Celia Kalloo-Borges, who had begun her first term on September 19, 1950. She writes of Undine Giuseppi, whom she encountered that day for the opening ceremony and who has left an indelible impression upon her, that she "taught Language, Literature and Latin . . . [and her] . . . impeccable use of the English language was impressive, her vocabulary, precise, her pronunciation correct." This account epitomizes Giuseppi's commitment to the word. Having begun writing as an eight-year-old, she was known throughout her life as a "prolific writer and lover of the English language" who "built up a veritable library of literary work some of which is still used in Caribbean schools" (*Trinidad and Tobago Newsday*). For her work in education, she was awarded the Humming Bird Gold Medal by the government of Trinidad and Tobago in 2001. She penned a newspaper column titled *Do You Know* for fourteen years in the *Sunday Newsday* and seven years in the *Sunday Guardian* that addressed matters of grammar and usage. She coauthored books with her husband including short story collections and authored others such as an autobiography, biographies, books on the English language titled *Caught in the Slips*, *Developing Word Power*, *Writing Is Fun*, and *Writing Is Still Fun*, a poetry anthology for Caribbean primary schools, and the *Nelson's New West Indian Readers* series, published in the 1970s, which was a staple text throughout primary schools in Trinidad and Tobago.

Note on Interviewees

The concluding section of this chapter provides a sampling of responses solicited on the impact *Backfire* has had on adults who studied the collection as youths and/or now teach it. While some could not recall exact memories of the stories from so many years ago in the 1970s and therefore could not be included in this assessment, other respondents have retained vivid and positive impressions of how *Backfire* affected them as teenage readers or how teaching it in the twenty-first century also reaps these same effects for their learners. Selected email interviews with four individuals—two former students from junior secondary schools in southern Trinidad who are now adults in their early fifties, and two teachers (current and retired) at a high school in the central region of Trinidad—demonstrate the outcomes of teaching and learning experiences with the Giuseppis' text. This section presents much of these interviewees' recollections in their own voices to distinctly capture the extent of *Backfire*'s enduring influence.

An Analysis of *Backfire*

A common observation among the interviewees is that young readers are able to identify with many narratives in *Backfire* because details in the story elements (such as theme, setting, characterization, and plot) mirror their own sociocultural realities. In addition, as borne out by some of the testimonials, readers learn how to develop understanding and empathy for others not like them and awareness of situations unlike their own past or present experience. Hence, cognitive and affective responses to both least and most favorite stories in the collection are related to the extent to which adolescents are able to imaginatively immerse themselves in the story worlds constructed by each writer, critically evaluate stylistic and narratological elements commensurate with expectations for that age group, and uncover subtextual meaning.

In the literature classroom, the teacher strives to guide the student through the process of developing from a novice to a professional reader. Susanne Reichl describes professional literary reading, in part, as "a nexus of awareness, knowledge and strategies that the reader draws on actively to engage successfully in complex reading tasks" (140). Hence, as with instructors in other subject areas, the literature teacher takes into consideration and helps to develop students' learning styles, whether they are defined by David Kolb's model (of divergers, assimilators, convergers, and accommodators), Howard Gardner's theory of multiple intelligences (particularly the linguistic, interpersonal, and intrapersonal intelligence types as pertain to the study of literature), or the VARK (visual, auditory, read-write, and kinetic) learning style model. Learning styles can also be classified, according to Joy M. Reid, as cognitive, sensory (perceptual, environmental, and sociological), and temperament or affective styles (Reichl 135–37). At the secondary school level, the beginning stages of these processes of teaching and learning are evident, and in the junior secondary system, this, too, was possible even if in Lilliputian scale compared to what occurred in five- and seven-year secondary schools where the cohort of students possessed more advanced reading proficiencies. *Backfire* assisted in these efforts of honing learning styles and literary reading skills with its talking and writing response exercises, its short narratives, and the Giuseppis' varied story selections.

Rebecca J. Lukens, in *A Critical Handbook of Children's Literature*, discusses the various functions, experiences, and rewards of literature such as experiencing pleasure and understanding; showing human motives; providing vicarious experiences, and forms for experience; revealing life's fragmentation, the institutions of society, and nature as a force; helping us focus on essentials; and meeting a writer-creator (3–9). Lukens alludes to the seminal text *Literature as Exploration* by citing the belief of its author, Louise Rosenblatt, celebrated scholar on the teaching of literature and a pioneer of reader-response theory, that "reading is a transaction and that the aesthetic—thinking, feeling, and experiencing—of reading literature must be recognized" (Lukens xvii). *Backfire*, through both its stories and its exercises, fulfills the tenets of Rosenblatt's transactional theory and provides opportunities for what she calls efferent and aesthetic reading. Wayne Booth, in his foreword to the 1995 edition of Rosenblatt's text, notes how "[g]enuine responses to literature always entail a meeting of the 'cultural environment' of the reader with that of the text," and he reiterates Rosenblatt's plea to "treat reading as a transaction between two great kinds of stuff—literary works and living persons" (viii, ix).

Storytelling is an ingrained part of Trinidad and Tobago culture—in the home, at informal community gatherings, in the calypso tent, and in many other contexts in which there are at least two interlocutors. Trinidad-born, UK-based award-winning writer Monique Roffey has referred to Trinidadians as "linguistic acrobats" because of their word smithery. Lucy Evans, in her introduction to *The Caribbean Short Story: Critical Perspectives*, notes how Amerindian, African, and Indian cultural practices in oral storytelling have been a fundamental aspect of the development of the twentieth-century Caribbean literary tradition, and therefore how within such a context, the short story genre comprises in a very integral way both oral and written modes of storytelling (17).

In the foreword to the same text, Emma Smith observes how the short story is "an effective route into literature, both for new writers and as a learning aid for young readers" (8). This statement epitomizes the Giuseppis' *Backfire*. The brevity of the form aids in sustaining adolescent students' attention and memory, and this along with narratives within a single collection allows for a range of both commonalities and differences in thematic focuses to be presented for enjoyment and didactic purposes. Author William Marx expresses concern in his monograph *The Hatred of Literature* about the internet's impact: "[T]he very proliferation of screens and the ubiquity of social networks make it very difficult, especially for young generations, to find the mental concentration that is required to read literature" (qtd. in Day). Within the contemporary context of such competing online distractions, more so than in the 1970s when *Backfire* was published, the short story form can offer the reduced concentration level of which Marx speaks; for example, the length of most stories in the Giuseppi collection classify them as short-short stories.

The account later in this chapter from teacher Lorna Thompson of students' reactions to the stories indicates, in part, Reichl's observation that "[i]t is characters that readers depend on most when they construct a text-world, and it is characters they remember best long after they have read the book" (108). Most of *Backfire*'s exercises in the "Time for Talking and Writing" sections prepared by Joy Ackbarali, a Trinidadian teacher who also taught at SAGHS and holds undergraduate degrees in English and education, require students to identify, explain, and relate to the fictional characters' motivations, feelings, and behavior. Bearing in mind, too, that varied learning styles are found within a classroom, *Backfire* provides opportunities for diverse activities involving reading silently and aloud as well as talking and writing individually and in groups. This is reminiscent, therefore, of Reichl's explanation that good learners are not necessarily the extroverted ones, and "given that the actual reading process is dependent on a degree of introversion and reflection, whereas participating in a discussion requires some degree of extroversion" (138), *Backfire*'s goals and objectives cater to both the introverted and extroverted young reader.

In addition to learning about the use, meaning, and significance of story titles and literary tropes, student readers are exposed, for example, to how writers employ the discursive strategies of free direct thought (FDT) and free indirect discourse (FID), and particularly free indirect thought (FIT), to give deeper insight into characters' inscape/mindscape—their feelings and motivations—in *Backfire*'s third-person narratives. Readers also learn about the distinction between closed- and open-ended stories and the possibilities for implicature and inference in the latter, as well as how, according to Janet Burroway, the form of short narratives can resemble a check mark whereby "the falling action is likely to be very brief or non-existent, and often the crisis action itself implies the resolution, which is not necessarily stated but exists as an idea established in the reader's mind" (40).

Since this is a collection of prose fiction, it is unsurprising that students are asked questions related to its form and elements, but they are also invited to engage in thinking about cross-genre considerations. Hence, a holistic appreciation of both literary reading and analysis applicable to prose, poetry, and drama—ergo, of the English syllabus as a whole—is encouraged. For example, as it pertains to story endings as well as to story titles, students are asked in "Time for Talking and Writing" to contemplate the following: "Very often a good short story has an unexpected ending. In this story what makes the end unexpected?" (*Backfire* 67) and "Why do you think the writer of the story chose that particular title for the story instead of a title like '*Chester*'?" (77) for Undine Giuseppi's "Journey by Night" and Ian Robertson's "Up the Wind Laka Notoo-Boy," respectively. But they are also invited to see how writers experiment with form and therefore to discern parallels and contrasts among literary genres. For example, students are asked the following after Joy Clarke's "De Trip": "This is a story which resembles a play with several scenes. In each scene of the story there are silent listeners. See if you can guess to whom the speaker is talking in each of these scenes" (57). This is an obvious and apt student activity, since "De Trip" (52–56) comprises solely an unnamed narrator's monologic and dialogic expressions—the latter with other characters whom readers do not see or hear and instead must determine what they asked and said based on the narrator's utterances. Additionally, readers rely on the narrator's remarks, queries, and responses to be informed where the plot action is taking place—be it on the way to the airport, at the airport, on the airplane, or arriving in the country of destination. There is no narration akin to stage directions in a play. The narrator's voice, and so the entire story—including its title—is relayed in the Creole dialect, making it one of only two narratives in *Backfire* (the other being Robert Henry's "Give

Back to *Backfire*: Giuseppis' Caribbean Short Story Collection in Trinidad and Tobago 137

No tanks, none a dem dry-up tarts fuh me.

Figure 8.2. *No tanks, none a dem dry-up tarts fuh me.* From Joy Clark's "De Trip," *Backfire: A Collection of Caribbean Short Stories*, p. 55. Springer Nature Limited. Reproduced with permission of the Licensor through PLSclear.

and Take") to be thus presented, lending to the authenticity of its characterization and plot, which deal with a Caribbean woman's experiences (both serious and comic) as she travels abroad. Therefore, "De Trip" requires that students imagine and infer to fill in gaps deliberately left by the writer, and it is one among many stories of travel and migration (including Ida Ramesar's "Paradise Lost" in this collection), a characteristic theme of Caribbean literature that reflects the region's—and the students' and those whom they know—economic, historical, and sociocultural realities.

As a literature student in the Marabella Junior Secondary School classroom, *Backfire* was my first exposure to Trinidadian Creole in written form. While Creole is the first language of most Trinidadians, Standard English is the country's official language and, hence, the language of instruction in schools. The junior secondary school syllabus of English, therefore, in its suggestions for a methodological approach by teachers, took account of this language situation and the common problem of Creole interference in students' learning of Standard English (Ministry of Education 2). In addition, as Hodge has indicated, there is no standardized orthography for Caribbean creoles, and the transcription of Creole phonology, lexicon, and grammar is challenging for fiction writers ("The Writer" 144). Regardless, she notes, "[m]ost West Indian writers of fiction have found it necessary to engage in one way or another with the first language of their community, so that the appearance of Creole on the page is a long-standing Caribbean tradition"; as she also reminds us about this geolinguistic bloc of the Caribbean region, "writers have [always] taken on board the fact of language variety as a feature of the society" (144). Former Caribbean professors of language and literature, like Barbara Lalla, Jean D'Costa, and Velma Pollard—all also creative writers—in their collaborative work *Caribbean Literary Discourse*, have also written extensively about the legitimization of Creole representation in Caribbean literature.

In spite of Undine Giuseppi being renowned for her pedantic insistence on the use of correct Standard English grammar, *Backfire* encourages students at an early age to embrace Creole as a legitimate means of expression. As Lawrence Carrington and Clive Borely's 1977 report documents—with its inclusion of letters to the editors of daily newspapers as well as commentary from the authors themselves who were professors of linguistics—following the publication of the 1975 English syllabus for primary schools, controversy and debate ensued in Trinidad and Tobago among the general populace about the syllabus's thrust for the legitimacy of Creole and the appropriateness of teachers using it as a means of instruction. In his introduction to dialect poet and storyteller Paul Keens-Douglas's 1976 collection *Tim Tim*, Carrington references that controversy and, as a linguist, provides explanations in narrative style of the terms "dialect" and "standard language" for readers' edification. Hence, in the 1970s—as opposed to the 2000s, characterized by a wider range of tolerance, acceptance, and destigmatization—there was still a strong degree of stigmatization of Creole as an inferior language and resistance to its assignation as a teaching/learning medium and tool.

Within such a context, *Backfire* as a prescribed text on the secondary school syllabus can be deemed as part of a concerted effort by consultants, policy makers, and educators to acknowledge the worth of incorporating the native language of Creole-speaking students in honing their literary and linguistic competence and performance. Notably, Ackbarali's "Time for Talking and Writing" encourages students to engage in metalinguistic activity by asking them to consider some of these issues. For Henry's story, the questions include the following: "This story has the dialect or local language of a particular West Indian island. Can you suggest to which West Indian island it belongs? Pick out any of those expressions which helped you decide on the island" and "Why do you think the local dialect is very suitable for this story?" (22); and for Seereeram's, "The writer of this story feels that if we learnt only our local dialect as 'English' we might face a problem. What problem is that?" and "How can the use of our local dialect in the classroom help students? Be specific" (72). With respect to the titular story of the collection, students are asked to draw on their knowledge and familiarity of the Creole lexicon: "There is a local expression which you can put in place of the title *Backfire*. Can you say what that expression is?" (6).

The vernacular of the majority of students was and is Creole, and it was a novelty experience as a junior secondary school student, not having used books in the primary school that included it, to see and read Creole words off the page—and it would be more difficult to attempt to write it. Yet, it was a thrilling and welcoming encounter seeing one's everyday language in writing (whether conveyed as the medium of an entire story or in part within dialogue only), in narratives that were enjoyable and imbued with familiarity, relevance, and authenticity. Therefore, *Backfire*, for me, planted the seed of appreciation for writings in Creole—both for dialogue and narration—later encountered in the works of Earl Lovelace, Samuel Selvon, V. S. Naipaul,

Olive Senior, Louise Bennett, Paul Keens-Douglas, and many other authors in the Caribbean canon.

One stark feature of *Backfire* that helps to fictionally convey the realities aforementioned, augment readers' imaginative impulses, and diagrammatize story elements is the inclusion of black-and-white illustrations, one for each narrative. In a paradoxical sense, these drawings lend realism to each story, allowing *Backfire*'s young Caribbean readers to see characters who look like them and settings familiar to their everyday world. Lukens outlines, among other reasons, that growing awareness of the significance of childhood, as well as awards for, critical evaluation of, and courses on children's literature, have resulted in "children seem[ing] to be continuously blessed with well-illustrated literature" (39). With respect to Carol J. Fuhler's definitions of the picture book, picture storybook, and illustrated book, about which experts sometimes differ, the latter's "illustrations merely function to decorate the story but do not extend the text in some important way" (173). *Backfire* can be categorized as an illustrated book in Fuhler's definition, which specifies that "the story can clearly stand alone, and the reader imaginatively supplies the majority of the pictures. The few illustrations that are available may help set the scene or highlight particular points in the story, but their primary role is to be aesthetically pleasing rather than to help tell the tale" (173). However, for some junior secondary school students for whom *Backfire* was geared and whose reading age was lower than their chronological age, the illustrations would indeed, to a limited extent, provide assistance in telling the story. This type of visual communication also helps young readers at the upper primary school level and others at the primary or secondary level who are given remedial instruction.

Lukens observes that in the past illustration was deemed "a lesser art" because of its connection to text, but this is now no longer the case with the improvement of printing presses, publishers employing art editors, and reputable artists illustrating and collaborating on children's books (39). Therefore in children's—as well as in YA—literature, including what is evident in *Backfire*, the literary stories are complemented by these visual stories with their "visual signifiers like lines, dots, light and dark, and composition" (Bal 163). Lukens also addresses how in illustration, for example, symbolic language is used for communication, as is the case with other art forms; visual and verbal symbols create content and meaning; and a distinct reality is constructed and a vision is facilitated that are, respectively, illusory and imaginary (40).

Each full-page illustration in *Backfire* either conveys a peak scene or moment of tension, or encapsulates the defining theme, in the narrative, and is accompanied by a caption in italics comprising an identifying short sentence or phrase from the story. The latter provide a gateway toward identifying the gist and underlying message of each story.

Story Messages: A Synopsis

The following brief outlines of each narrative in *Backfire* show how they create opportunities for young Caribbean readers to make direct connections with their own observations, experiences, and feelings, or vicariously offer those that are unknown to them. Synopses of the messages garnered from the seventeen stories give a sweeping overview of how *Backfire* affords the teaching and learning of myriad lessons in the classroom.

Ramesar's "Paradise Lost" teaches readers that as citizens they each have a role to play in fixing their country's deficiencies while appreciating its positive features. Relevant aspects of Clarke's "De Trip" have already been discussed, but readers can compare this story with "Paradise Lost," noting the "hows" and "whys" of how two writers treat the purposes of overseas travel and Caribbean nationals arriving in foreign lands. Additionally, "De Trip" exemplifies for readers the ways in which serious matters can be couched in humor to create satire.

Undine Giuseppi's "Chung Lee" conveys the close-knit relationships within the Chinese diasporic community in Caribbean society with the story being set, realistically, in the 1940s during World War II when food and other necessities were scarce. Young readers of all ethnic and racial backgrounds would be aware of the Chinese presence in Trinidad and Tobago. They are a minority group comprising both immigrants from China who still speak their native language and descendants born in the Caribbean. Their ubiquitous involvement in business and enterprise—many own shops, groceries, laundries, and restaurants, for instance, across cities, towns, and villages—make the Chinese shopkeeper in this story a familiar trope to readers. "Chung Lee" also stands out as one of the few fictional depictions of the Chinese in Caribbean literature. Giuseppi includes another aspect of realism with her representation of the first-generation Chinese's articulation of the English language.

Ninnie Seereeram's narrative "The New Teacher," as noted earlier, can resonate with young readers who encounter a teacher for the first time and worry about new expectations. This story focuses specifically on students' surprise and concern in having an English teacher, Mr. Singh, who speaks in Trinidadian Creole—especially because their former but now retired teacher was a stickler for adherence to proper Standard English speech. However, Mr. Singh's proficiency in written Standard English is also evident even as he encourages students to orally convey their ideas in "we mudder-tongue" (70). This character's viewpoint harkens back to the earlier discussion on the acceptance and appreciation of Creole as a valid medium of expression and instruction in the classroom. The narrator-protagonist also presents the familiar dilemma for the Creole speaker having to do academic writing and examinations in Standard English and being "forced to wonder which posed the greater problem—translating 'English-as-written' into the 'mudder tongue' for purposes of speech, or translating the 'mudder-tongue' into 'English-as-written' for exams and communicating with the rest of the English-speaking world?" (71). Mr. Singh also impresses upon the class to remain in the country, a lesson similar to that depicted in "Paradise Lost" of the value of patriotism and good citizenship.

In Henry's "Give and Take," the shortest story in the collection, the reader is faced with the reality of death, specifically a parent's loss of a child. It touches on the parent-child relationship, like other narratives in *Backfire*, particularly "The Kite," "Mama's Theme Song," and "After the Game," which focus on fathers and sons. Henry's story highlights the oral tradition of information passing on via word of mouth as well as the practices of hearsay, rumor, and gossip—all prevalent in Caribbean society. "The Teddy Bear" by C. Arnold Thomasos includes a devoted, single, and childless female teacher and a gentleman grieving the loss of his daughter; the latter thus resembles the father in "Give and Take," who has suffered the death of a child. Thomasos's story reveals how adults who have never had or have lost offspring compensate in their dedication to children not their own. In "The Hustlers," Barbadian writer Flora Spencer employs punning, most evidently as it applies to the importance of naming in furthering characterization, plot, and theme, since the two major characters, both undertakers, are called "Mr. Grasper" and "Mr. Grabbit." Like "Give and Take" and "The Teddy Bear," Spencer's story deals with the taboo subject of death; whereas the other two stories depict death poignantly, here the author includes an element of humor. Notably, too, the dialogue is conveyed in Barbadian Creole, an example of *Backfire* exposing students to other English-lexicon Caribbean creoles besides their own.

"Mama's Theme Song" by Joy Moore can resonate with adolescent readers who face confrontations with as well as disciplinary actions and perceived nagging from their parents—particularly mothers. Issues with which readers, especially those belonging to the working class, can identify pervade this story's plot, which treats a family's financial insecurity, the threat of the father losing his breadwinning role because of unhealthy employer-employee relations, fears about bearing more children compounding economic hardship, flaunting by more well-to-do neighbors, and the importance of education in overcoming poverty. "Tantie Gertrude" by Oliver Flax is yet another narrative about irony and mother-child conflict. Ending at its peak, this narrative typifies the check-mark structure expounded by Burroway. Since it is open-ended, readers can infer lessons not only about the obvious struggles of single motherhood and the absence of a father who has migrated but also about the taboo and shame surrounding illegitimate pregnancy and offspring, despite the prevalence of this social issue in the Caribbean.

"Up the Wind Laka Notoo-Boy," written by Guyanese Ian Robertson, is set in Guyana. Even if the title is confusing to non-Guyanese readers, the story's resonance would rest on young readers' awareness of how group dynamics influence and embolden peers to do things they otherwise would not attempt individually. Additionally, they would be familiar with the issue of vagrancy as well as the fear and myths surrounding outcasts in their own communities. "Ramgoat Salvation," another story by Ramesar, emphasizes homosociality and peer pressure, with irony and humor used to undercut the males' bravado. The construction of setting as well as plot, character, and thematic development is underscored by the binary oppositions of urban/rural, natural/supernatural, fantasy/reality, humor/suspense, and secular/religious as six young men are converted from, in Trinidadian terms, "limers" and "badjohns"—loafers and miscreants—into roadside itinerant preachers. Readers learn about the capacity for and sources of redemption. Barnabas J. Ramon-Fortuné's "After the Game" depicts not only the conflicts but also the friendship bonds among males, and highlights filial affection and duty. It provides lessons to the young reader about the importance of resolving problems with others through conciliation and not violence, and that there are ups and downs even among friends.

The last story of the collection, "The Cousins," another written by Moore, focuses on delinquency, peer pressure, and adult-child relationships, this time the daughter-father/daughter-mother interaction and fosterage, a common practice in the Caribbean in which people welcome into their homes and care for less fortunate or needy friends, acquaintances, or relatives. This story also encourages discussion on the controversial issue of the (de)merits of corporal punishment, and on adolescents accepting the serious and far-reaching consequences of rule-breaking and disruptive behavior. The collection's first and title story, Shirley Tappin's "Backfire," is a morality tale about retribution and irony, teaching a lesson on how one can be punished for unethical deeds when they backfire. Even though the denouement makes it seem as though pickpocketry is rewarded without any punitive consequences, the story indirectly conveys a message to the young reader about the dangers of crookedness and thievery.

Among the very short narratives in *Backfire* is Neville Giuseppi's "Horace's Luck." In the Caribbean, young readers would be aware of the lottery and other games of chance played by adult family members, neighbors, and other acquaintances, and so this story teaches them that some of life's happenings can embody uncertainties, coincidences, and mysteries. A second story by Undine Giuseppi, "Journey by Night," another of the shorter stories in the collection, reminds readers of the potential fears and dangers involved in being a solitary traveler and reinforces the lesson we are taught as young children to mistrust strangers.

Richard Skeete, a teacher and interviewee in the next section, purposefully reads "The Kite"—another contribution by Ramon-Fortuné—to his primary school students during the kite-flying season. This story teaches the lesson of the importance of perseverance and fighting for a cause. Because it presents a father's viewpoint relayed to his son as being gender-specific—"Stay there and fight. This is a man's world" (29)—it raises the opportunity for important discussion and debate in the classroom about gender (in)equality in the Caribbean region as well as globally, an issue not included in the "Time for Talking and Writing" section.

Backfire Then and Now: Testimonials

Louise Rosenblatt testifies in *Literature as Exploration* that for her, the formal elements in works of literature function as only one component of the entire literary experience. She affirms that for most readers "the human experience that literature presents is primary" (8). Additionally, she outlines how attaining knowledge of the world, understanding the resourcefulness of the human spirit, and gaining insight that helps bring more comprehension to one's life are benefits of the vicarious participation in someone else's vision. Hence, the "teacher of adolescents, in high school or in college, knows to what a heightened degree they share this personal approach to literature" (8).

This approach is borne out in the student-teacher engagement with *Backfire* in the classroom, especially with regard to "Talking" exercises provided in the text. In their introductory remarks, the Giuseppis advise that "[s]ubjects of a controversial nature arising out of some of the stories should be used for class discussion or debate" and that "[s]tudents are never too young to learn to comment logically on their environment" (*Backfire*, vi). A recently retired teacher at a five-year secondary school in central Trinidad, who preferred to remain anonymous (the school is situated in a high-risk area, and the student population includes individuals with disciplinary and behavioral problems) illustrates this point. She comments on the reaction of first form students to "The Hustlers":

> The titles elicit much discussion prior to the actual reading of the stories. The titles provoke thought and allow the students to express their deep and innermost feelings. They speak openly about their environment. It has therefore been a task to steer the discussion skillfully away from information that one would not want to discuss, yet at the same time remembering that literature helps us to be more humane.

Such information that made the teacher uncomfortable entails real-life instances of criminal activities by persons known to her students. That is, the title would evoke for students other kinds of "hustling" of a more illegal nature besides what is portrayed in Spencer's story. The students' reaction to the semantics of the title is reminiscent of this retiree's own experience as a youth studying *Backfire* in the year of its publication in another high school in central Trinidad, but one that is a prestigious seven-year, all-girls school. It is noteworthy, therefore, that the text had a reach beyond the junior secondary level. Just like primary school teacher Richard Skeete, this former teacher has engaged with the text as a student and as an educator.

For her, the most memorable story is the titular one, and she recounts how her teacher, an expatriate, misunderstood the meaning of a local phrase that conveys the idea of when men admire women, in the narrative's second, single-sentence paragraph: "The limers were in their usual places—at the corners and in front of the stores—observing the hustle and bustle, digging the chicks, heckling and ole-talking" (1):

> The first story we read in class was "Backfire." My classmate from Marabella explained "digging the chicks" to our teacher Sr. Magdalena from Ireland. She thought the chickens were scratching the dirt. We were the teachers and she was our student. That always reminds me as a teacher that I can learn from my students. A sense of humility. I remember there was always a volunteer to read the stories. We were the experts in the vernacular and she was the expert in Standard English. We understood some of the social situations. We learned what we did not know.

Unlike what pertained in the three-year junior secondary system, in literature classes of the seven-year school a wider range of authors and texts were on the syllabus. Hence, in addition to Caribbean oral literatures like the calypso and Caribbean texts like *Backfire* and *Bite In*, a three-series poetry collection for secondary schools edited by Cecil Gray, she also read and studied Chaucer, Shakespeare's plays, Charles Dickens's *David Copperfield*, Joseph Conrad's *Heart of Darkness*, and other fictional texts like Alan Paton's *Cry, the Beloved Country* from South Africa. Therefore, she declares, "Literature had a significant impact on my life. As I reflect, it was an enjoyable, pleasurable and diverse experience. More importantly, literature class helped me understand the gamut of human emotions. I learned about our society and the wider world. It helped to shape my thinking and actions."

The same teacher further recollects her experiences studying the Giuseppis' short story collection:

> I did *Backfire* in 1973 as a Form 3 student. I was very conscious that we were reading and discussing a collection of stories that dealt with the multicultural and multiethnic society of Trinidad. The stories were written partly in Standard English and the characters' speeches were in vernacular. I learned about peoples' emotions—their actions and responses to social situations. It helped me to understand life: behavior, attitudes, choices, and consequences.

> We had to eventually write answers to the questions in Standard English. The vocabulary in the stor[ies] enabled better writing and expression.

She avers that the collection contributed to her love for reading and literature. Additionally, as a teenager coming of age in the 1970s, she became more aware of her physical and cultural environment, with its watershed movements and sociopolitical upheavals. *Backfire* was imbued with a level of familiarity that resonated with her in a way that differed from what the fictional texts from outside the region were able to do:

> *Backfire* stories were short. They dealt with social issues and events pertaining to the Trinidadian society. There were some situations, names that appeared familiar. I often went into Port of Spain and I remember my observations of the street. I knew some of the places or of them. The country at that time had just experienced the Black Power revolution in 1970. I read the *Trinidad Guardian* and *Evening News* on a daily basis. And so *Backfire* stories spoke to the changes that were taking place and continue to speak to current situations. That's the difference.

Therefore, taught at a single-sex secondary school by some foreign-born teachers—like C. L. R. James many decades earlier, but at a time when the literature syllabus was less Eurocentric—this respondent's sentiments underpin the puissance of the Caribbean short story and of *Backfire*.

Echoing this definitive and ongoing impact on *Backfire*'s readers is Lorna Thompson, another teacher at the same five-year high school in central Trinidad, who also comments on her experience teaching the collection to students and their most and least favorite stories:

> The children always seem to connect with the world of text—"After the Game," "Tantie Gertrude," "Journey by Night," "Horace's Luck," "Backfire." They are always ready to relate to you their experiences especially in those stories mentioned. Also, through some of the stories I noticed how mature the students are in the way they discuss the themes, and talk about the characters and judge their actions in the text. The stories are also memorable—students are able to recall events long after reading the text, especially in an informal situation. Favorite stories are "Backfire," "Chung Lee," "The Kite," "Horace's Luck," "Journey by Night," "After the Game," "Tantie Gertrude," "Ramgoat

Salvation." Except [for] "Ramgoat Salvation," many students can easily connect their world with those of the world of the characters in the short stories above. They talk about their experiences and the way their situation[s] are dealt with. They sometimes say how they would have dealt with the situation in their own way different from the characters.

For instance, in "Tantie Gertrude," many students are of the opinion that Tantie was too strict with Annetta and Dalma and adults like to quarrel too much. However, when Edwin and Steve fought in "After the Game," they appreciate their reconciliation and the resolving of the [two] families' dispute. Depending on the present situation around them or in a class discussion, sometimes the students make references to a character, the story, or theme from the short stories in *Backfire*. Students always seem to be sad and sympathetic for Horace in "Horace's Luck." Many students see it as just bad luck and move on to the next story. In other words, they don't pay much attention to the story.

Over several years, *Backfire* has been included on the selected reading list for class study and library reading on the Caribbean Secondary Education Certificate (CSEC) literature syllabus used by all types of schools in Trinidad and Tobago. Thompson has been using *Backfire* voluntarily in her classroom for more than ten years as a supplementary text whenever her school has selected other core material to prepare students for the English A and English B examinations—language and literature, respectively. As a literature teacher, she says that it is a primary text of choice for her "because the stories are easy to read and understand on a level of characterization, setting, plot, resolution, and conflict. Also, themes are easily recognizable and appreciated." Furthermore, she shares how she chooses the short stories from the collection for teaching purposes in her English language classes to assist with exercises in the conversion of Creole dialect to Standard English, for writing direct speech, for reading comprehension in which students write their own questions, and just for entertainment. Unlike the other three interviewees, Thompson had not studied the Giuseppis' text at secondary school, but she nonetheless knew of its existence from other family members: "Although I . . . never used *Backfire* in school my siblings did so; the book was always familiar to me. Therefore, my experience with the stories was reading for entertainment and very enjoyable." This is identical to a nugget of information that cropped up in another anecdote told to me by a university instructor and published poet who did not study the text in school, but whose brother did; and having read it herself for pleasure, "Ramgoat Salvation" is her favorite story, and most impactful.

Although *Backfire* was initially geared to secondary school students in the lower forms, it has also been used successfully at the primary school, as attested to by Richard Skeete, a teacher at this level who had also studied the text from 1977 to 1980 when he was a junior secondary school student:

> There are a number of stories contained in *Backfire* that I enjoy reading to my students. Even though the compilation of short stories was intended for secondary students, my pupils have no difficulty relating their own experiences with the characters, setting, and plot of the stories because of the local content. The three most favorite and memorable stories have been "Ramgoat Salvation," "The Kite," and "Backfire," in that order. I would recommend that these stories be read to children from nine years up.

As a reader, he therefore has experience as both a young student and an adult teacher of the text, with the former influencing the latter in terms of pedagogical and literary choices while also exemplifying the long-lasting impact of the short narratives.

Another former junior secondary school student from the 1970s to the 1980s, Agnes Stafford, indicated that literature classes paved the way for her to appreciate the subject, especially Caribbean literature; the short stories also contributed to her love of reading novels. She, too, professed to enjoying *Backfire*'s "Ramgoat Salvation" the most; it reminded her of the times her siblings and cousins would share stories at night, attempting to scare one another. She cites a particular story that made her always afraid of the dark, yet it also reinforced the notion of camaraderie and support among friends even though they may prank each other. While she does not name this latter story, with the reference to pranking it bears resemblance to the hide-and-seek game in "The Cousins." As a grown-up, Agnes observes that *Backfire* has been different from other fictional texts she has read because of how it draws connections to many aspects of her childhood and "touches on so many related topics in our lives."

These responses are a testament to *Backfire*'s fifty-year period of sustained relevance and significance in shaping the literary and linguistic competence of young minds at the same time that it shapes their appreciation for the study of Caribbean literature, in particular of the short narrative. The story elements and discursive strategies employed in these narratives have helped to solidify *Backfire*'s legacy and longevity as both a literary and a resource text in the classroom. From tragedy to comedy, an array of life topics are presented in these stories rooted mainly in realism—none belong to the genre of science fiction and only one has elements of fantasy literature also popular among young readers. While its title page says *Backfire: A Collection of Short Stories from the Caribbean for Use in Secondary Schools*, the text has also proven to appeal to elementary school students and adult readers. For many, the quality and range of *Backfire*'s content—both literary and academic—instill a steadfast appreciation for literature and the short story form inside and outside of the classroom.

Works Cited

Anonymous. Personal interview, December 17, 2017.
Bal, Mieke. *Narratology: Introduction to the Theory of Narrative*. 2nd ed., U of Toronto P, 2004.
Booth, Wayne. Foreword. *Literature as Exploration*, by Louise M. Rosenblatt, 5th ed., Modern Language Association of America, 1995, pp. vii–ix.
Burroway, Janet. *Writing Fiction: A Guide to Narrative Craft*. 6th ed., Longman, 2003.
Carrington, Lawrence D. Introduction. *"Tim Tim": The Dialect Poetry of Paul Keens-Douglas*, Keensdee Productions, 1976, pp. 5–7.
Carrington, Lawrence D., and Clive B. Borely. *The Language Arts Syllabus 1975: Comment and Counter-Comment*. School of Education, U of the West Indies, 1977.
Clarke, Austin. *Growing Up Stupid under the Union Jack: A Memoir*. 1980. Ian Randle Publishers, 2003.
Clarke, Joy. "De Trip." *Backfire: A Collection of Caribbean Short Stories*, edited by Neville Giuseppi and Undine Giuseppi, Macmillan Caribbean, 1973, pp. 52–57.
Day, Gary. Review of *The Hatred of Literature*, by William Marx. *Times Higher Education*, February 1, 2018. https://www.timeshighereducation.com/books/review-the-hatred-of-literature-william-marx-harvard-university-press.
Elliott, Joan B., and Mary M. Dupuis. Introduction. *Young Adult Literature in the Classroom: Reading It, Teaching It, Loving It*, edited by Joan B. Elliott and Mary M. Dupuis, International Reading Association, 2002, pp. 1–7.
Evans, Lucy. Introduction. *The Caribbean Short Story: Critical Perspectives*, edited by Lucy Evans, Mark McWatt, and Emma Smith, Peepal Tree Press, 2011, pp. 11–28.
Flax, Oliver. "Tantie Gertrude." *Backfire: A Collection of Caribbean Short Stories*, edited by Neville Giuseppi and Undine Giuseppi, Macmillan Caribbean, 1973, pp. 92–97.
Francisco, Slinger. "Dan Is the Man (in the Van)." Bandcamp. https://mightysparrow.bandcamp.com/track/dan-is-the-man-in-the-van.
Fuhler, Carol J. "Picture Books for Older Readers: Passports for Teaching and Learning across the Curriculum." *Young Adult Literature in the Classroom: Reading It, Teaching It, Loving It*, edited by Joan B. Elliott and Mary M. Dupuis, International Reading Association, 2002, pp. 170–93.

Gilmore, John T. "A Literature of Our Own." *Caribbean Review of Books*, February 2005. http://caribbeanreviewofbooks.com/crb-archive/3-february-2005/a-literature-of-our-own/.
Giuseppi, Neville, and Undine Giuseppi, editors. *Backfire: A Collection of Caribbean Short Stories*. Macmillan Caribbean, 1973.
Giuseppi, Neville. "Horace's Luck." *Backfire: A Collection of Caribbean Short Stories*, edited by Neville Giuseppi and Undine Giuseppi, Macmillan Caribbean, 1973, pp. 34–37.
Giuseppi, Undine. "Chung Lee." *Backfire: A Collection of Caribbean Short Stories*, edited by Neville Giuseppi and Undine Giuseppi, Macmillan Caribbean, 1973, pp. 14–19.
Giuseppi, Undine. "Journey by Night." *Backfire: A Collection of Caribbean Short Stories*, edited by Neville Giuseppi and Undine Giuseppi, Macmillan Caribbean, 1973, pp. 64–67.
Gray, Cecil. *Perspectives: A Course in Narrative Comprehension and Composition for Caribbean Secondary Schools*. Nelson Caribbean, 1982.
Gray, Cecil. *Response: A Course in Narrative Comprehension and Composition for Caribbean Secondary Schools*. Thomas Nelson and Sons, 1969.
Gray, Cecil. *Wavelengths: A Course in Narrative Comprehension and Composition for Caribbean Secondary Schools*. Nelson Caribbean, 1982.
Henry, Robert. "Give and Take." *Backfire: A Collection of Caribbean Short Stories*, edited by Neville Giuseppi and Undine Giuseppi, Macmillan Caribbean, 1973, pp. 20–23.
Hodge, Merle. "Challenges of the Struggle for Sovereignty: Changing the World versus Writing Stories." *Caribbean Women Writers: Essays from the First International Conference*, edited by Selwyn Reginald Cudjoe, Calaloux, 1990, pp. 202–8.
Hodge, Merle. *Crick Crack, Monkey*. Heinemann, 1970.
Hodge, Merle. "The Writer in the Caribbean Language Situation." *Writing Life: Reflections by West Indian Writers*, edited by Mervyn Morris and Carolyn Allen, Ian Randle Publishers, 2007, pp. 144–54.
James, C. L. R. *Beyond a Boundary*. 1963. Yellow Jersey Press, 2005.
Kalloo-Borges, Celia. "Memories of the First Term at SAGHS." *Broadcast*, vol. 39, no. 1, Fall 2015, p. 15. http://www.naactoronto.ca/documents/broadcast_Oct15.pdf.
King, Bruce, editor. *West Indian Literature*. 2nd ed., Macmillan, 1995.
Lalla, Barbara, Jean D'Costa, and Velma Pollard. *Caribbean Literary Discourse: Voice and Cultural Identity in the Anglophone Caribbean*. U of Alabama P, 2014.
Lukens, Rebecca J. *A Critical Handbook of Children's Literature*. 8th ed., Pearson Allyn and Bacon, 2007.
Ministry of Education, Government of the Republic of Trinidad and Tobago. "Syllabus of English: The Junior Secondary School." 1975.
Moore, Joy. "The Cousins." *Backfire: A Collection of Caribbean Short Stories*, edited by Neville Giuseppi and Undine Giuseppi, Macmillan Caribbean, 1973, pp. 98–110.
Moore, Joy. "Mama's Theme Song." *Backfire: A Collection of Caribbean Short Stories*, edited by Neville Giuseppi and Undine Giuseppi, Macmillan Caribbean, 1973, pp. 38–45.
Nair, Supriya M. "Introduction: Caribbean Groundings and Limbo Gateways." *Teaching Anglophone Caribbean Literature*, edited by Supriya M. Nair, Modern Language Association of America, 2012, pp. 1–26.
"Planning the Growth of Secondary Education." Educational Portal of the Americas, Organization of American States. http://www.educoas.org/Portal/bdigital/contenido/interamer/BkIACD/Interamer/Interamerhtml/Alleynehtml/AllCh6.htm.
Ramesar, Ida. "Paradise Lost." *Backfire: A Collection of Caribbean Short Stories*, edited by Neville Giuseppi and Undine Giuseppi, Macmillan Caribbean, 1973, pp. 7–13.

Ramesar, Ida. "Ramgoat Salvation." *Backfire: A Collection of Caribbean Short Stories*, edited by Neville Giuseppi and Undine Giuseppi, Macmillan Caribbean, 1973, pp. 85–91.

Ramon-Fortuné, Barnabas J. "After the Game." *Backfire: A Collection of Caribbean Short Stories*, edited by Neville Giuseppi and Undine Giuseppi, Macmillan Caribbean, 1973, pp. 78–84.

Ramon-Fortuné, Barnabas J. "The Kite." *Backfire: A Collection of Caribbean Short Stories*, edited by Neville Giuseppi and Undine Giuseppi, Macmillan Caribbean, 1973, pp. 24–33.

Reichl, Susanne. *Cognitive Principles, Critical Practice: Reading Literature at University*. Vienna UP, 2009.

Robertson, Ian. "Up the Wind Laka Notoo-Boy." *Backfire: A Collection of Caribbean Short Stories*, edited by Neville Giuseppi and Undine Giuseppi, Macmillan Caribbean, 1973, pp. 73–77.

Roffey, Monique. Interview by Geraldine Skeete. Podcast 31, The Spaces between Words: Conversations with Writers, University of the West Indies, St. Augustine, March 11, 2013. https://libraries.sta.uwi.edu/podcasts/.

Rosenblatt, Louise M. *Literature as Exploration*. 5th ed., Modern Language Association of America, 1995.

Seereeram, Ninnie. "The New Teacher." *Backfire: A Collection of Caribbean Short Stories*, edited by Neville Giuseppi and Undine Giuseppi, Macmillan Caribbean, 1973, pp. 68–72.

Senior, Olive. "Colonial Girls' School." Poetry Archive. https://poetryarchive.org/poem/colonial-girls-school/.

Skeete, Richard. Email interview by Geraldine Skeete, February 17, 2018.

Smith, Emma. Foreword. *The Caribbean Short Story: Critical Perspectives*, edited by Lucy Evans, Mark McWatt, and Emma Smith, Peepal Tree Press, 2011, pp. 7–10.

Spencer, Flora. "The Hustlers." *Backfire: A Collection of Caribbean Short Stories*, edited by Neville Giuseppi and Undine Giuseppi, Macmillan Caribbean, 1973, pp. 58–63.

Stafford, Agnes. Email interview by Geraldine Skeete, December 4, 2017.

Tappin, Shirley. "Backfire." *Backfire: A Collection of Caribbean Short Stories*, edited by Neville Giuseppi and Undine Giuseppi, Macmillan Caribbean, 1973, pp. 1–6.

Thomasos, C. Arnold. "The Teddy Bear." *Backfire: A Collection of Caribbean Short Stories*, edited by Neville Giuseppi and Undine Giuseppi, Macmillan Caribbean, 1973, pp. 46–51.

Thompson, Lorna. Email interview by Geraldine Skeete, December 8, 2017.

Trinidad and Tobago Newsday. "Undine Giuseppi Is Dead." November 25, 2006. http://archives.newsday.co.tt/2006/11/25/undine-giuseppi-is-dead/.

CHAPTER 9

Creole vs. Standard English
Negotiating Voice in Caribbean Children's Literature

Karen Sanderson-Cole and Barbara Lalla

The issues that surround negotiating voice in Caribbean children's literature require the establishment of a context. We must consider, first, the impact of the varied geography of the region in which works for children have been produced, and second, the variety of settings in which the speakers find themselves within the fiction. Additionally, the position of the child as protagonist or as a reader governs choices between systems of expression such as Standard English and Creole. Other questions impact the very definition of children's literature itself: Is children's literature written about children? Or is it literature for children? Peter Hunt argues, "If the word 'literature' presents obvious problems, the word 'children' proves to be equally slippery. The notion of childhood changes from place to place, from time to time, and the history, definition and study of childhood as a concept has burgeoned in recent years" (3). Still, there are brave attempts by critics to continue to define "children's literature." David Rudd offers the following:

> Children's literature consists of texts that consciously or unconsciously address particular constructions of the child or metaphorical equivalents in terms of character or situation (for example, animals, puppets, undersized or underprivileged grownups), the commonality being that such texts display an awareness of children's disempowered status (whether containing or control-

ling it, questioning or overturning it).... But it is how these texts are read and used that will determine their success as "children's literature." (26)

Rudd links ideas about the definition of the child to that of the status of the child as crucial to the success of a text as children's literature. Notions of power also influence the status of children in a society since they seldom have the right to exclusively determine what they read and at what age. These issues affect discursive constructions that reflect the distribution of power in a society.[1] What is conveyed to the reader depends on point of view—how the narrator is positioned in terms of physical space to the events narrated (perceptual)—and also on the attitude or orientation of the narrator to the events described (conceptual).

In selecting specific literary works for this study, we have chosen works that contribute to a general understanding of approaches to Caribbean language in the crafting of children's literature within the region. We specifically look at the representation of voice. Voice here is taken to mean mimetic voice—following Stephen Ross, who points to the verbal imitation and representation of speech within the narrative text—as distinct from textual voice, which refers to the written discourse exclusive of represented speech or speaker (300). We consider mimetic voice to be important within the ambit of children's literature, taking into account the history of the Caribbean region. Clare Bradford reminds us that it has traditionally been the case that mainstream writing tends not to scrutinize "cultural difference" in meaningful ways when presenting characters from different ethnic groups (49). Certainly, one of the challenges for Caribbean writers has been how to represent the Caribbean space while balancing their need for authentic representation against marketability on an international scale.

What is considered to be children's literature in the former British West Indian islands has been impacted by contesting and contrasting issues of context, marketability, and ethnicity, as well as the history of the issue of representation and the role of Standard versus Creole. As Bradford points out, the colonial who is writing about unfamiliar settings, ethnographies, and folklores tends to alter the narratives of indigenous peoples "to accord with European narrative practices" and to publish them "as children's stories":

> Detached from the cultures from which they originated, such stories were incorporated into western frames of reference. Indeed, such stories con-

tinue to appear as "West Indian," "Native American," or "African" stories in anthologies, where readers can have little or no understanding of how these stories are woven into the values and beliefs of the cultures from which they were derived. (44)

The association of what was *Native* or *indigenous* with the *childlike*, through traditional stereotyping, may similarly account for tendencies in the Caribbean to identify folk material as children's literature.

Addressing the issue of what constitutes children's literature within a Caribbean context also involves addressing the language choices implicated. Do the texts attempt to reinterpret, perpetuate, or critique the colonial past through a reverence for colonial languages such as Standard English? What are the implications of the writing styles and word choices, for example, used to orient children to society? Are the child readers to be indoctrinated into the values of the society through the language of the former colonizer or offered the indigenous creoles that have been developed over time? Are dichotomies of language use and attitude established between home and school, work and play, personal exchange and interaction in the wider society?

We found it impossible within the space of one chapter to pursue a discussion of such issues in literature that extends beyond the novel form so as to take in verse, drama, oral performance, nonfictional prose, or even short stories. We felt, too, that the novel form allows extended and varied portrayals of settings. In our selection, we sought to be representative, to maintain some balance between male and female protagonists of varied ethnic backgrounds and from different territories in the Caribbean, as well as to allow some latitude for differences in genre. We attempt roughly a sixty-five-year spread to enable any historical developments to emerge, and we approach the books chronologically—the first group published in (or slightly before) the 1960s and 1970s, the second in the 1980s and 1990s, and the third since 2000.

Some well-known favorites like Sam Selvon's *A Brighter Sun* (first published in 1952) and Olive Senior's *Summer Lightning* (1986) do not appear in this study because they seem to address more mature audiences, whereas Zee Edgell's *Beka Lamb* (1982) is included, since it popularly appears on secondary school syllabi for twelve- to sixteen-year-olds. Also, some obvious possibilities like Andrew Salkey's *Hurricane* (published originally in 1964) are left out—*Hurricane* being only one of many Jamaican-authored books in the study. We endeavored to represent writing from across the Caribbean in an effort to explore a wide range of settings—school and home, rural and urban—and characters, including boys and girls. We narrowed the study to readers mainly between ages nine to sixteen—although this demarcation is difficult to maintain.

Creole vs. Standard English in Setting and Voice

In the early history of Caribbean children's fiction, writers faced a variety of challenges in projecting the voices of their region. Early novels include some dialogue in Creole but maintain Standard English in the narrative. In this section, we examine ways in which a distinctly Creole sensibility is incorporated within the text. In *Christopher* (1959) by Geoffrey Drayton, a white Barbadian author, the male protagonist is a child in a young planter family. European outlooks and interests are clear in recent family memory: his uncle hunted lions in Kenya. Like his parents, the central consciousness speaks and thinks in Standard English ("of course they didn't smell like that"; 14) but his most intimate acquaintance, his nurse, Gip, is a Creole speaker: "I'se not to tell you nothing" (12). Other servants, like Jo and Cinder, speak Creole as well, and the child obviously has passive competence in the language.

How comfortable the author might be in Creole remains unclear. As noted by Thomas Armstrong, Drayton himself, the offspring of a planter family, often made reference to the autobiographical influences in his work. His writing perhaps reflects the historically limited interaction the white privileged class would have had with the Black laboring class. Interestingly, characteristics of Creole speech, as rendered in the novel, overlap with Black American structures: "The master and mistress ain't even had their tea yet" (36); "they's good signs" (44); "Mr. Chris been breaking off fern-shoots" (20); "what you doing outside" (33); "they don't have no closets . . . and that ain't all either" (152). This resemblance perhaps widens the common ground for audience comprehension. In any case, the writer focuses on grammatical structures rather than manipulating spelling to reflect characteristics of sound, an approach that makes the dialogue widely accessible to readers with or without competence in Creole.

Michael Anthony's *The Year in San Fernando* (1965) adopts a similar strategy to Drayton's in conveying the voice of the young protagonist (Francis) with predominantly Standard English, while using Creole to typify other characters. Unlike Christopher, though, Francis is probably a Creole speaker for the most part. How the Standard English is used for this protagonist is of some interest. Long run-on sentences characterize an immature consciousness:

> I tried to keep out the lonely feeling because it was no good now and I walked close to Mr. Chandles and I watched the brighter parts of the street where the street-lamps hung and I noticed how most of the houses were fenced round and some were open to the street without any hedge or fencing and how the steps from some of them came almost right on to the pavement of the street. (11)

Creole structures are deftly avoided through the use of reported rather than direct speech. Repetition also suggests the youth of the speaker: "I sat waiting. I could not remember sitting on any chair quite so soft as this one. I could not remember being in any place so grand and rich-looking. I had always looked upon the Forestry Office as a house of grandeur, but there was so much more grandeur here" (13). Interestingly, when Francis is frightened, Creole structures emerge, underlying the extent of his unease. When, for example, Mr. Chandles finds him idling under the house instead of working, Francis responds, "I does do work sometimes, . . . I doesn't always come under here" (33).

The prose of the text subtly inserts a Creole sensibility. A Creole voice surfaces in the exasperation of Mr. Chandles when his mother opens the door and says, "Oh, it's you," to which he responds, "Who you thought it was!" (12). To a Creole speaker, the preceding sentences would be read "Oh is you," to which the reply would be, "who you thought [pronounced *taught*] it was." Creole-type structures also characterize certain people who come into the protagonist's life, like Brinetta, Mrs. Chandles's former helper: "All the big bands does come and practice here" (25). The Indian women whom Francis meets in the market also use Creole: "That bwoy, eh! I don't know! Every marning!" The author foregrounds Creole orality through orthography in the spelling of both "boy" and "morning." In the mid-1960s, therefore, a general reluctance to employ Creole more obtrusively in the protagonist's speech implies the author's need for a wide audience to accept and empathize with the main character.

Jean D'Costa's *Voice in the Wind* (1978) presents far more Creole in the dialogue, including some carefully limited representation of sound, while projecting Jamaican diction in the narrative, for example by reference to local foods such as "bullah" (44). Essentially, Creole is the code natural to characters like Maud, who works for the family in a long-standing and intimate relationship. An extensive stretch of Creole sets forth Maud's sustained account of loss in the 1907 earthquake:

> Is de work of de Devil pure and simple. . . . All him good for is to do Satanwork. . . . All de h'ashes blow pan de floor an' dutty de place! Fram me born me never see big man gwaan like pickney so much! Savior give me patience! . . . Is dat mek no woman want fi married to you! Tek clappers an' throw in de fireplace like pickney; ef Captain did de ya, unnu woulda behave unnu self an' don' come trouble poor ol' lady kitchen! (53)

The text indicates Creole at the level of sound—for example, through reduction of consonant clusters (*nex'*) and hypercorrection by an initial [h] (*h'eart'quake*)—and at the level of sentence structure: "Nex' day when de h'eart'quake come, she know what 'appen, an' same day she leave go search fi dem . . . She beg 'Im fi go wid 'ar" (71). But here again the author places greater dependence on the grammar for conveying the Jamaican voice as well as non-English words like *unnu*, the second person plural pronoun, a Twi borrowing.

In addition to the kitchen, the schoolyard provides a crucial setting for Creole. A boy at school harasses the lighter-skinned sibling in the family about what would happen if Hitler won:

> "Im will take you brother an' sister first t'ing," said his tormentor matter-of-factly, "an' all like you will 'ave to clean 'im shoes an' carry 'im top-hat an' cane while dem chain up in de cellar under de 'ouse like dog. You lucky you so white. 'Im 'ave puss-eye same like you." (44)

In addition to other structures already cited above, the schoolboy's speech includes Jamaican grammatical structures like "dem chain up" (where the pronoun "dem" is the patient of the action) along with specifically Creole vocabulary such as "puss-eye."

D'Costa has explained that her earliest novel, *Sprat Morrison* (1972), was cleaned of all local expressions by officers of the Ministry of Education in Jamaica before the manuscript reached its publishers. Jamaican Creole dialogue was possible in subsequent novels like *Voice in the Wind* because of the interest in local culture shown by a member of the publication team for Longman. Subsequent discussion with a different publisher regarding another book resulted in the local voice being crushed out of the work and that manuscript stalling for good.[2]

Nevertheless, the earliest Caribbean novels for children establish the role of language as a crucial dimension of Caribbean setting, indicative of both location and identity. In writing for all ages, Creole is the language of folk material and oral lore, and functions as the indispensable medium for the informal transfer of information about the personal past as well as a natural channel for fictional characters in lower social strata—not, normally, the child protagonists or their parents. Moving on to the late twentieth century, we see an expansion of the roles within which a Creole voice is articulated.

Expansion of the Creole Voice

During the 1980s and 1990s, the use of Creole in Caribbean's children's literature shifted away from indicating a lack of education to becoming a vehicle for expressing sudden and intense emotion, for those speakers who are at home along a wide range of the language continuum. This movement to a wider use of Creole was no doubt influenced by an increasing sense of the language as a symbol of burgeoning national (versus colonial) identity in the Anglophone Caribbean. We see, then, the appearance of a central consciousness who speaks Standard English but may easily shift to Creole. Zee Edgell's *Beka Lamb* (1982), a popular choice in secondary school curricula in the Caribbean, is set in Belize and employs Creole in the grandmother's speech: "Befo' time . . . Beka would never have won that contest, and but things can change fi true" (1). However, the central consciousness, a girl of fourteen, reflects: "Her mother watched her of late, Beka felt, like a john crow watching dead crab" (5). Not only do Creole elements emerge in her thoughts, but in speech Beka switches to Creole in moments of extreme grief: "Toycie gone and dead, Granny Ivy, Toycie gone and dead on us!" (158). In this novel in which education is an explicit theme, however, Beka resumes Standard English when she pulls herself together: "I have no objection to that, Miss Boysie" (159). The code switch expresses a move toward self-control and the achievement of dignity, and thus reflects governing attitudes to language choice.

The novel reflects other aspects of the Caribbean language situation, such as attitudes to race in language and gesture, and Beka clearly observes social strata and relations between races, reinforcing this awareness with odd expressions in the usual way, like the use of a proper name or the name of a food. Throughout, the dialogue demonstrates contrasts in expression appropriate to age differences between speakers. At the larger level of discourse, the novel projects the strong oral culture in which the events unfold, not only by representing the importance of anecdote but, at the end of the novel, by displaying the lack of facility that some characters have in written language. This discomfort with the written language is strongly projected in the abruptness of the letter that brings news of Toycie's death.

Comparison across the novels remains difficult, however, because of the variation in both competence and maturity to be expected in an audience of child readers. *Beka Lamb* addresses issues for a more mature reading audience than, say, *Voice in the Wind* or perhaps even *Christopher*, and might be considered a young adult novel. Yet the coming-of-age theme, in relation to an experience of death, is common to all three. The lines between reader age groups are difficult to draw not only in relation to suitability of topic but in reader sensitivity to issues such as ethnicity, gender, and class stereotyping. Child readers' exposure to, say, the gulf between wealth and poverty, or ability and inability, is variable and unpredictable. On the other hand, circumstances like an encompassing colonial ideology as conveyed through education are ubiquitous, and general changes in these circumstances can be more easily tracked chronologically over decades.

Both subject matter and setting—teen suicide and the secondary school environment—allow Merle Hodge in *For the Life of Laetitia* (1993) to explore a range of voices so as to give a fairly representative sample of variations between Creole and Trinidad Standard English. The narrating voice of the protagonist Laetitia, more commonly known as Lacey, is conveyed in Standard English, but as a participant in the action of the novel, she also transmits the voices of those around her in a variety of ways. In her function as the narrating voice, she uses Standard English. In her function as participant, she interacts with her friends in Creole. When she talks with Anjanee, her best friend, Creole figures prominently: "I only making joke, Anjanee. . . . I know it was because you didn't have money. But I don't see why you shame for that. We ain't have no money neither, and I ain't shame" (63).

Vocabulary choices can also indicate an indigenous voice in the text. Laetitia's father bursts with pride because his daughter (whom he had earlier financially and paternally ignored) has passed the national exam, which entitles her to placement in a secondary school: "I wasn't so bright as you—I didn't get pick to go to secondary school. I only make it to seventh standard" (4). Here, "so bright," "pick," and "make it" distinguish the register that differs from more formal English ("intelligent," "selected," "achieved") in the same context. In the school setting, the language usage of some teachers such as Mrs. Lopez, also known as the "Circus Horse," is the vehicle for the pain, embarrassment, and anger inflicted on the protagonist. Yet Standard English use is not always associated with oppression. Lacey is quick to point out that "not all of our teachers were foolish people.... We did have some sensible ones" (52).

Individual speakers in the fictional setting shift between codes as do speakers in the real world. A sentence can begin in Standard and then end in Creole—especially when the speaker becomes angry. Creole in the texts of the 1980s and 1990s is the language of intimacy, of friendship, of belonging, of claiming one's identity—reflective of the wider changes in society following the acquisition of national independence and the affirmation of a distinctive national identity as symbolized by language.

Contemporary Approaches to Creole Usage

Novels that have appeared subsequent to 2000 are even freer in their use of Creole, although they are perhaps more difficult to place in terms of target audience age. Material for younger readers, often heavily illustrated, includes less prose and relies heavily on Standard English. In any case, fiction for younger children does not characteristically fall within the novel form. Nevertheless, a brief consideration of material for younger children (age eight and younger) offers a useful introduction to fiction for those in the older group.

An excellent example is a collection for children "by" children, the 2011 edition children's stories from the Bocas Lit Fest, compiled by Marina Salandy-Brown. Salandy-Brown revealed that the team driving the project prompted the children with questions so that they might develop characters, and create plots and settings. They lay no strictures on the children regarding their own use of language because the idea was to demystify books, to encourage them to participate in the creation of a narrative, and to present this creative process and the book evolving from it as fun. The collection falls into two parts, addressing younger and slightly older children. The adults took notes, trying to capture the children's voices as they built their composite tales. The children were encouraged to talk freely in Standard English or Creole, but the adults made notes in Standard English with a view to introducing children to a wide range of books, most of which would be in the official language.

The Bocas Lit Fest collection was published in Standard English, the official language, rather than in Creole. Trinidad Standard English shows up in occasional preferences of diction, like "I was practically bawling" (87). However, Creole speech appears in the taunting song of Santana, the school bully: "I is a bully. / You eh 'fraid me or what? / I is Santana" (37). His brave opponent, Terry, speaks Standard English: "You're just a big bully! Take this!" (42). Nevertheless, throughout, the language of the stories projects the children's interest in their surroundings and their attention to the world in which they find themselves. Local voice is conveyed in place names like Lambeau Beach (17), Chaguanas (65), and Devil's Woodyard (73); in animal names like "corbeau" (12, 53, 74); in names for plants like "fatpork" and "chenette" (47); and in food names like "curry channa" (39). While the adult insertion of language might be off-putting to some, it is this interplay between the children's use of language and the adults' adjustments that point to some of the challenges in creating literature for children in the context of a Creole and a standard language.

In contrast, texts with full adult authorship are marked by mature observation of local expression conveyed in Standard English, with Creole expressions in play to evoke the local setting. A beautifully illustrated story by Trish Cooke and Caroline Binch, *Look Back!* (2013), presents female and male characters of four to six years old. French terms like *bonsoir* (3), and a French Creole name, Ti Bolom (the name of a folk character), reinforce the sense of place—set in the formerly French-colonized Commonwealth of Dominica. The traditional marker "Eh Kwik, Eh Kwak" signals the introduction of folk material. The authors associate Creole with older and rural speakers. Grannie, who tells the tale, shifts between Standard English and Creole: "One time, down the way from us" (2); "I reach by Ma Constance" (3). Characteristics of sound are only lightly indicated ("'fraid"; 2), but Creole grammar, which relies on an unmarked past tense (unlike Standard English), is more frequently used ("when I reach"; "my mummy send me"; 3).

Look Back! is unusual for the amount of language variation in fiction for this time period, and the significant presence of Creole speech may well be related to its inclusion of folk material. Grannie shifts freely, including or dispensing with the copula "when you walking," followed directly by "she's gone" (1). Grannie relives talking in Creole as a child to an older woman—"Is me, Cristophine" (3)—but she addresses the child character, her grandson, mainly in Standard English, slipping in the direction of Creole as excitement mounts with onomatopoeic expressions such as "bladdaps! I fall down" (4). When the child narratee, Christopher, breaks in "full of fear" (9), he speaks Standard English, only mimicking onomatopoeic words: "'Bladdaps!' laughed Christopher. 'You caught Ti Bolom!'" (14). Later, Granny assures him, "Yes, but I didn't give up. No sah. I make a plan" (16). Then, the omniscient narrator takes over and remains in Standard English. So does Christopher as Ti Bolom recedes into a dream. Only while the folk character is treated as real is there significant Creole narration.

Readers within this younger age group are still engaged in learning to negotiate English orthography and, usually, children's fiction for young readers maintains Standard English throughout narrative and dialogue. Diane Browne's Jamaican picture book *Abigail's Glorious Hair* (2015) presents a young girl having her hair washed, combed, and plaited in a gathering of women of all ages who are exchanging memories—but never in Creole. Similarly, books in English set in non-Anglophone territories barely hint at the language of their settings, and the issue of Creole versus Standard is less evident. The child trapped in the earthquake in Edwidge Danticat's *Eight Days: A Story of Haiti* (2010) governs his thoughts by reflecting intimately on all that is central to his life, using only one non-English term, *Mamam*. The same is true of such fiction for older children. Julia Alvarez, in *Before We Were Free* (2002), projects her female protagonist's awareness of an American frame of thought as alien and includes a few proper nouns as Spanish-language indicators, like Señor, Tomasito, and Policiasecreta. It would be outside the scope of this study to consider how Creole has evolved in Spanish and French, but no doubt it would be difficult to reflect in English the social variations relevant to non-Anglophone territories. Generally, though, we see Standard English, the official language, associated with formality and introducing children to the language patterns of the wider society, and Creole being used to create a sense of place through setting, animal names, food, self-assertiveness, endearments, and the age of characters. Creole can also be "hidden" in unmarked forms such as the past tense.

Contemporary books for young adults written by local authors play more completely with language structures as they seek to speak to their audience. Colleen Smith-Dennis's *Inner City Girl* (2009) includes all levels of Jamaican language structure. More clearly aimed at a *tween* audience (roughly ages eleven to thirteen), this text takes the child reader into the consciousness of Martina, a growing girl, from her entry to high school to her Caribbean Examinations Council (CXC) graduation. As a reader, Martina is steeped in literary English, so well-read that other children call her "bookhead" or "reada," though she dislikes the latter because she associates it with the word "obeah." But her family has established Creole as her mother tongue. Her mother's complaint opens the novel: "But Miss Turner, mi nuh understand why Martina go behind mi back an' choose school inna big claas people area when so much school down ya so." Marina's mother, Miss Fuller, reveals her social circumstances: "Is only me one. Mi nuh have nobody fi help mi an' the other two haffi go a school to. Mi ca spen' out all a wha mi no have pon her" (chap. 1). The Jamaican perspective emerges not only through linguistic details but also through folk references that make use of local terms. When the mother tries to heal Yvette by recourse to obeah, the narrator informs us, "The mother woman had confirmed that she was beset by a ghost and an East Indian one called coolie duppy" (chap. 12).

In contrast to the substantial dialogue in Creole, Standard English serves generally as the language of narration, but draws on local sayings like "puss bruk coconut in her eye." Along the way there are some errors in the Standard English of the book itself, quite distinct from code switching. For example, "He was a man who height had snubbed" (chap. 3) may constitute a grammatical or a typographical error, but is certainly an oversight in editing, since "whom" would not be used in Creole and the context is clearly Standard English. Language awareness or variation in the novel is nevertheless very strong. The author clearly allocates codes to speakers from different social and educational strata, just as she distinguishes active and passive competence. The school principal speaks Standard English but understands Creole, and students who might otherwise use Standard English choose Creole for insult even in writing: "TIEFING GHETTO GAL" (chap. 11). Jamaican Creole is naturally employed for oral material, for example in taunting expressions that may be formulaic: "Straw eye jump through needle, hide backa thread, and one little ants come pull her out" (chap.13). However, Martina's friend Andre, from a quite different social class and a speaker of Standard, relaxes in her company into informal Jamaican English: "I know that was going to happen, I saw it long time" (chap. 17). Such language shift indicates comfort, trust, and a relinquishing of self-consciousness, but it can also be a projection of a sense of self—of self-awareness, selfhood, perhaps disobedient self-assertion. In children's literature, as in other discourse, language conveys a sense of power, powerlessness, empowerment, and assertions of independence.

A-dZiko Gegele's *All Over Again* (2013) is included for consideration of language in a different Jamaican setting. Gegele presents a twelve-year-old boy, about the same age as Martina at the beginning of *Inner City Girl*, but he talks to himself in an informal Jamaican register. Local expressions abound: a "bull-cow" (4), "more unreasonableness" (5), "wet down" (8), "rockstone" (16), "makka" (17), "too nuff" (23), and "Gweh" (25). But the boy narrator moves steadily in the direction of Standard Jamaican English by the end of the book, where only occasional Creole is injected to invoke local voice: "That's what happen" (144); "like you did fight and overcome" (148).

The writer clearly projects multivocality in the rural community and code shifting by individuals, along with a sense of language changes as the narrator matures. Throughout, we encounter significant Creole dialogue from the narrator's father: "[Y]ou a tell me wafi do now?" (4), and his sister, Mary Janga: "me sorry mi mash up yu plane" (7); "mi trow it because mi waan see how it fly" (8). In between, his mother speaks informal Jamaican English: "[T]omorrow we going to keep a party for Grandpa" (9). Along the way, quite complex shifts between voices occur, such as when the narrator visualizes his father comforting his mother: "No gwaan so Patrice, dem a go find him" (20).

A Guyanese fantasy by Imam Baksh, *Children of the Spider* (2016), seems more clearly directed to a young adult rather than a child audience than Gegele's novel. But this novel is worth touching on for the sake of including a wider range of genres as well as considering writing from another territory, and the novel is interesting, as is *Beka Lamb*, in its sensitivity to language attitudes and the social significance of variation. Indeed, language is a crucial topic in the novel. One can infer the age level from its mild sexual references and descriptions of incidents such as the injury and death of a dog—a portrayal that might well be troubling to a younger child (97–98). In addition, some conversations occur in a register that may not widely be considered appropriate for younger readers:

"Fed up with damn Spider."

"It real though," Mayali told her [Tara]. "The whole story true."

"I know is true." Tara picked up the remote and switched channels. "I still fed up with it backside." (147)

In this universe of discourse, the world of the spider gods is a web of lies, as Anansi explains to the main characters, Mayali and Joseph. Anansi, who is female, appears to be the most trusted servant of Arachne in an apparently male-oriented world that is actually run by women. Anansi speaks Creole (81) as well as educated Standard English (84).

Here, as in *Voice in the Wind*, *Beka Lamb*, and *Inner City Girl*, language choices connect with affective states such as excitement, fear, shock, and disgust. The narrative is Standard English, and one of the central characters, Joseph, maintains Standard English as his language for broadcasts. He switches voices using some form of technology, but "Joseph never used Creole. People had trouble understanding it with the accents the computer programme provided. Besides, he needed to practice his English. The priest had told Joseph he could get a job operating equipment at a real radio station if he kept learning" (13). Joseph himself is deaf and mute but conveys his voice on the broadcast through technology. However, a threatening shadow presence speaks directly to Joseph's brain, in Standard English:

"Are you in compliance with the law?"

For the first time he could remember, Joseph heard words. But not with his ears. Those words went directly into his thoughts. They felt like talons clawing at his brain. (13)

Mayali, who is trying to escape these presences from another world, also speaks to Joseph's brain in Standard English. However, Mayali has learned to speak Creole like a native speaker, and she addresses the police in Creole in such a way that Joseph is able to hear her (20): "They does thief people from over there. They using them as slave. I get away and come here" (21). Similarly, the police, Lieutenant Dasrath in particular, respond to her in Creole: "You telling people about how I'se a drunkard" (22). Baksh manipulates language as supportive to genre, for example, to signal interfaces with the unfamiliar, to highlight mystery, or to underscore discovery or adventure in this fantasy novel.

The novels that employ more extended and precise representations of code shifting between Caribbean Standard English and Creole most vividly emphasize setting and characterization and most poignantly convey their protagonists' inner struggles. At the same time, this precision unavoidably produces the Creole of a particular territory and makes the speech more Jamaican, for example, rather than broadly Caribbean. The level of familiarity of the particular Creole in turn affects the degree to which the language of the text is widely comprehensible. When the narrative (in addition to the dialogue) includes the accurately rendered Creole of a specific territory, even Caribbean readers of other territories may flounder. Representing characteristics of Creole sound structure intensifies the potential for alienating readers, especially since the orthography learned in school is essentially an already contradictory English orthography.

Final Considerations

The roughly sixty-five-year span attempted in this brief overview of the issue of negotiating voice in Caribbean children's literature draws attention to a number of key issues involved in forging an identity out of a historical past that has traditionally disregarded/misrepresented the voice of indigenous peoples. Early narratives provide examples of techniques that weigh heavily in the direction of Standard English, with Creole used to introduce the child target audience to characters who exist outside the conventions of mainstream society—either through age, location, or occupation. The Creole child's consciousness can be represented through repetition or reported speech rather than through the use of Creole structures. Types of narrators (grandmother, nanny, cook) affect code choice. Language variety is also impacted by the specific age group that the writing is done for—with less use of Creole for an audience of eight and under, and more variety in the narratives that target the nine-to-thirteen age group. Writers from the 1970s onward introduce more Creole into the narrative through dialogue and characterization—as far as publishing censorship allows. At the same time, reader recognition of and identification with Caribbean voices in the text evoke immeasurable reader satisfaction.

Evidence over the time space teases the potential of writers to challenge the notion of what constitutes Caribbean children's literature and to interrogate notions of who sees, who speaks, and what is considered appropriate for children. The issues of language representation in literary material for Caribbean children are thus manifold and complex, especially for literature that projects a Caribbean setting in the fiction and reflects the Caribbean context of the work as a whole. A major challenge to the writer remains achieving that balance in which representation evokes a glow of identification without sacrificing immediate comprehension and so distancing young readers from the text.

Notes

1. For more extended discussion, see Barbara Lalla, "Possible Caribbeans: Assembling the Fictional Voice."
2. Jean D'Costa, personal communication, April 30, 2019.

Works Cited

Alvarez, Julia. *Before We Were Free*. 2002. Random House, 2004.
Anthony, Michael. *The Year in San Fernando*. Heinemann, 1965.
Armstrong, Thomas. "Lifting the Lid on Geoffrey Drayton and His Outsider Role in Barbadian Literature." Arts Etc, last modified May 2, 2022. http://www.artsetcbarbados.com/feature/lifting-lid-geoffrey-drayton-and-his-outsider-role-barbadian-literature.
Baksh, Imam. *Children of the Spider*. Blouse and Skirt Books, 2016.
Bradford, Clare. "Race, Ethnicity and Colonialism." *The Routledge Companion to Children's Literature*, edited by David Rudd, Routledge, 2010, pp. 39–50.
Browne, Diane. *Abigail's Glorious Hair*. N.p., 2015.
Cooke, Trish. *Look Back!* Illustrated by Caroline Binch, Papillote Press, 2013.
Danticat, Edwidge. *Eight Days: A Story of Haiti*. Orchard Books, 2010.
D'Costa, Jean. *Sprat Morrison*. Jamaica Ministry of Education; William Collins and Sangster, 1972.
D'Costa, Jean. *Voice in the Wind*. Longman Caribbean, 1978.
Drayton, Geoffrey. *Christopher*. Heinemann, 1959.
Edgell, Zee. *Beka Lamb*. Heinemann, 1982.
Gegele, A-dZiko. *All Over Again: A Novel*. Blouse and Skirt Books, 2013.
Hodge, Merle. *For the Life of Laetitia*. Farrar, Straus and Giroux, 1993.
Hunt, Peter. "Introduction: The World of Children's Literature Studies." *Understanding Children's Literature*, edited by Peter Hunt, Routledge, 1999, pp. 1–14.
Lalla, Barbara. "Possible Caribbeans: Assembling the Fictional Voice." *Reassembling the Fragments: Voice and Identity in Caribbean Discourse*, edited by Paula Morgan and Valerie Youssef, U of the West Indies P, 2013, pp. 94–113.
Ross, Stephen M. "'Voice' in Narrative Texts: The Example of *As I Lay Dying*." *PMLA*, vol. 94, no. 2, March 1979, pp. 300–310.

Rudd, David. "Theorising and Theories: How Does Children's Literature Exist?" *Understanding Children's Literature*, 2nd ed., edited by Peter Hunt, Routledge, 2005, pp. 15–29.

Salandy-Brown, Marina. *Children's Stories for the Bocas Lit Fest*. Bocas Lit Fest, 2011.

Salkey, Andrew. *Hurricane*. 1964. Peepal Tree Press, 2011.

Selvon, Samuel. *A Brighter Sun*. 1952. Longman, 1987.

Senior, Olive. *Summer Lightning*. Longman, 1986.

Smith-Dennis, Colleen. *Inner City Girl*. LMH Publishing, 2009.

CHAPTER 10

Tradition and Modernity
Grace Hallworth and a Vision of the Caribbean for British Readers

Karen Sands-O'Connor

Traditional literary forms are often used to embrace a nostalgic, or "once upon a time" view of a place; this is particularly true in children's literature about the Caribbean, where folklore, nursery rhymes, and singing games tend, intentionally or unintentionally, to fix Caribbean people in a subjected, rural past. Grace Hallworth is known for retelling traditional forms of literature for children from various parts of the Caribbean. But although her work focuses on traditional literature, tradition does not, for Hallworth, trap the region or its people in the past. Instead, heritage becomes an anchor for identity as well as a site for growth and dialogue, not only for Caribbean children but more particularly for children of Caribbean descent living in Great Britain. Her collecting and retelling of folktales and nursery rhymes, and her authorship of picture books detailing everyday life in the Caribbean, allow British child readers to see a modern, vibrant Caribbean that connects in multiple ways with their own lives in Britain.

Hallworth's concern with blending the modern and the traditional is unsurprising given her background. Born in 1929 in Trinidad, Hallworth grew up "listening to and reading stories, especially those of the islands' folklore" (*Cric Crac* back matter). Folklore in Trinidad is complex, as the island's population came from Africa, Asia, and Europe. Trinidad was colonized by Spain and England, and its culture and economic history were influenced by French planters; enslaved Africans and indentured Indian and Chinese populations all brought their cultural and linguistic heritages as well, making for a rich mix of storytelling traditions. But folklore was not considered "proper" *reading* material; by the time an elementary education act was passed in the late nineteenth century, parents with middle-class aspirations knew that the key to class mobility was a very British education. Valerie Joseph points out that this link between economic improvement and an acceptance of the British education system tended to "create British subjects who . . . were trained in an imperial consciousness" (146). Folklore was the provenance of the oral storyteller, usually an older female figure, and was not considered a school subject. As Cynthia James writes, "[E]ven in the old days this treasured folk tradition was a hidden curriculum, saddled with the stigma of inferiority" (164). Hallworth makes this distinction herself when she writes in the introduction to her first published collection of stories, "One could read stories about giants and ogres, about dragons breathing fire and smoke . . . and all the enchantments of fairy land" (*Listen to This Story* 7), but "[t]he West Indian folk tale comes from a people with a long tradition of oral storytelling" (9). In that sense, the stories of the vast majority of Trinidadians were considered fit only for the uneducated, the poor, and the very young. Books were the ultimate goal, and books for children at that time did not typically contain the folklore of the West Indies.

Although Trinidadians valued the British education system, they did not necessarily feel the same way about British colonial government. The 1930s, when Hallworth was a child, was a time of great political upheaval in Trinidad as attempts were made to upend the British Crown Colony system on the island and move toward independence. Eric Williams notes, "The Crown Colony system was based on sugar workers and needed only sugar workers. It did not need citizens. If Trinidad aspired to citizens instead of sugar workers, it necessarily had to achieve the destruction of the Crown Colony system" (214). This meant uniting Afro- and Indo-Trinidadians, who had been largely segregated through religion, language, and specific Crown Colony policies (toilet facilities were often separate for Afro- and Indo-Caribbeans on sugar plantations, for example). Education was one of the key reforms that Trinidadians put in place, initially through nongovernmental schools that offered more opportunity for the nonwhite population. As Halima-sa'Adia Kassim writes, "By the 1940s, education had replaced land as the status for mobility" (119) and "education meant some measure of socialization" (120). Among these newly opened secondary schools were coeducational secondary schools aimed at Afro-Trinidadians (Nakhid, Barrow, and Broomes) and single-sex Muslim schools for girls (Kassim). Hallworth herself went to a high school where she "had the opportunity to meet children from many different backgrounds. We were a fantastic mix—Chinese, African, Asian, Portuguese, Spanish, English, Dutch, Jewish, French Creole, Syrian and others. Although we represented so many races, our culture was the same—Trinidadian" (*Down by the River* n.p.). The generation of Trinidadians born in the 1930s were educated into a different vision than that of previous generations: they looked forward to a modern nation that at the same time embraced its multicultural traditions.

Economic advancement in Trinidad, however, still depended on a connection to the metropole. Hallworth grew up in a Trinidad that put an emphasis on the value of a British education, even while beginning to reject the supremacy of white British government over an Afro- and Indo-Trinidadian population. The cultural values of Trinidadians had currency outside the school setting—particularly during Carnival and in the calypso tent, as well as in individual homes—but education for all Trinidadians continued to be dominated by the literary traditions of Shakespeare, Wordsworth, and other writers in the "Mother Country." Hallworth's parents were both teachers, and both Afro-Trinidadian—and thus, Hallworth from an early age experienced both British and Trinidadian cultures as valuable. This dual nature—British tradition in schools and Afro- and Indo-Trinidadian traditions outside of it—would be reflected in Hallworth's literary output.

However, before she became an author, Hallworth trained as a librarian in Trinidad, having a deep love of books from childhood. In the early 1950s, when she was in her early twenties, Hallworth set up the children's library service for Trinidad and Tobago. Although she claimed it was "a thriving time for children's books in the West Indies" (Carey), the books available were largely British or American. The publishing houses that did exist in the West Indies during the period were either connected to the local newspapers (the *Jamaica Gleaner*, for example, published geography and history texts used in Jamaican schools) or were branches of British publishers, such as Macmillan Caribbean, which also concentrated largely on school texts in terms of children's literature. The Caribbean bookstores and libraries would stock these books and a selection of "classics" from the US and Britain; most

Caribbean islands did not have any publishers producing books specifically for the Caribbean population. Children might have had access to a London- or New York-published edition of white Jamaican educator Philip Sherlock's *Anansi the Spider-Man* (1956) with its illustrations by American artist Marcia Brown late in Hallworth's tenure as a librarian, but children's books authored by Afro- or Indo-Caribbean people, or published by Caribbean publishers, were next to nonexistent. The available books for children tended to reinforce what the colonial education system taught: that literature was the province of white authors, publishers, and educators, and the stories of the Afro- and Indo-Trinidadians were not as valuable.

In 1956, after studying in Canada and the US, Hallworth left for Britain, becoming part of the Windrush generation who reinvigorated the postwar UK through the labor, but also the culture, that they brought with them to the "Mother Country." Working for the Hertfordshire Library Service, Hallworth encountered the gifted British children's librarian Eileen Colwell, who mentored and encouraged Hallworth. Colwell, who was instrumental in creating the idea of the professional children's librarian in Britain, knew that a library was more than books; she developed storytelling sessions at her own children's libraries and encouraged Hallworth to do the same. Just as Colwell told stories that came from her own childhood, she encouraged Hallworth to tap into her Trinidadian past and tell the stories that mattered to her. This was not difficult for Hallworth, who enjoyed her work as a librarian and storyteller in her new British home, but never lost her love for her old Trinidadian one. Telling stories to children in the UK was revelatory for Hallworth; she not only realized that her listeners were fascinated by them, but was surprised to find that many of the rhymes she had learned as a child had parallels in other parts of the world. In one of the collections she published later, *Buy a Penny Ginger* (1994), she would write in the introduction, "I played many of these games and chanted the taunts when I was a child. In those days I believed that they belonged only to us—the children of Trinidad and Tobago. Now I know that isn't true. Children all over the world play the same kind of games and say the same kind of things." British literature in the 1950s included many collections of such rhymes and games, including Iona and Peter Opie's pioneering collections such as *The Oxford Dictionary of Nursery Rhymes* (1951) and *The Lore and Language of Schoolchildren* (1959), which considered children's nursery rhymes in their sociological, historical, and cultural contexts. In

Britain, the playground rhymes of children had intellectual, academic value—at least those of white British children did.

Hallworth valued the storytelling tradition in Britain, both oral and written. As a librarian, she compiled (with fellow librarian Julia Marriage) *Stories to Read and to Tell* (1978) for the Youth Libraries Group in the UK: "The purpose of this short guide is to introduce . . . librarians and teachers . . . [to] the wealth of material available for storytelling purposes" (1). What is included—and what is left out—is instructive. The pamphlet is split into two sections: "Picture Storybooks" and "Anthologies." All the selections in both sections have white European or American authors and illustrators, even those about African, African American, or Caribbean characters. This may seem surprising, given that Hallworth had already published her own first collection of West Indian stories, *Listen to This Story* (1977). But in addition to any strictures she may have had through coauthorship, Hallworth was aware that her audience—British teachers and librarians—was almost exclusively white, and the British education system gave preference to literature written in standard British versions of English. It is unlikely that most of those potential storytellers that Hallworth was targeting would choose to tell a story that included, for example, patois (so Hallworth's collection includes white British Jamaican educator Philip Sherlock's edition of Anansi stories rather than one with patois by a Black Jamaican author such as Louise Bennett).

That it was the teller of stories who was being targeted in Hallworth and Marriage's choices is underscored when they write, "The editors have not aimed to provide practical hints on techniques to adopt when telling each story since such techniques are usually a matter for personal preference" (1). Their "Anthologies" section includes both collections of folktales retold by British or American authors, and original stories that follow folktale conventions, including selections from Ted Hughes's *How the Whale Became* and Rudyard Kipling's *Just So Stories*. For Hallworth, folktales were just that: stories told (or written down but meant to be told) by people. Folktales did not belong only to the past but were a living, changing part of the present, a true literary heritage. While her pamphlet for the Youth Libraries Group focused on white storytellers, the principles behind the choices she made for the pamphlet informed her own work for children. Use of language, an emphasis on the creative ability of storytellers, and the belief that stories constitute a living, changing tradition are all hallmarks of Hallworth's literary output, and each of these elements played a vital role in connecting Black British readers with their Caribbean heritage.

Hallworth began publishing at a critical moment in Black British history. Her earliest books were published in the late 1970s and early 1980s, when for the first time, thanks to restrictive immigration laws, more children with Caribbean ancestry were being born in Britain than were coming from the Caribbean directly. The 1971 Immigration Act, according to Peter Fryer in *Staying Power*, "virtually ended all primary immigration" (385); he goes on to report, "By the mid-1970s, two out of every five black people in Britain were born here" (387). This generation, born Black and British, nonetheless faced discrimination and, often, a crisis of identity as they felt neither connected to their origins as their parents had been, nor accepted as British by the dominant white society. They not only felt disconnected from their Caribbean heritage; they were considered by white Britons as being, as John Solomos and colleagues comment, "in Britain but not of Britain" (30). Hallworth's early work provides readers with an introduction to Caribbean heritage, but of a very specific type. Rather than replicating an image of the Caribbean that was popular and propagated by imperial Britain—one of palm trees, market women carrying fruit on their heads, and tin-roofed poverty—her books demonstrate a new, modern, multiracial Caribbean that embraces tradition without looking backward.

The Caribbean immigrants who came to Britain were seen by white Britons, including educational experts, as having no literature of their own. Most British school anthologies ignored Caribbean folktales, short fiction, and poetry. Well-meaning white educators saw a need to create reading material for Black Britons. Government education reports such as the Rampton Report (1981) noted the poor school reading ability of West Indian immigrants, but recommended creating and adopting new material for them (largely written by white authors) that would "reflect the cultural background of all children" (21) rather than suggesting using material already in existence. The report recommended particularly the "Breakthrough to Literacy" reading scheme, which, as I have noted elsewhere, "suggests a strong desire to assimilate the New Commonwealth immigrant" through its reading texts, but "raises doubts about the ultimate success of the integration process" (Sands-O'Connor, *Children's Publishing* 40). By having assimilation as a goal, British educators discounted the value of Black Britons' literary traditions.

Hallworth approached literature for Black Britons very differently, and her earliest publication for children, *Listen to This Story* (1977), makes clear her priorities for British children's books. The introduction states that "these stories have been written down and published not only so that a wider audience might enjoy them, but also because this is one way of preserving the stories for West Indian children at home and abroad" (9). In "preserving" these stories for West Indian children, Hallworth is giving child readers a sense of tradition, a tradition that is as old as European fairy tales, and possibly older. Her introduction to *Listen to This Story* puts the folktales of the West Indies on par with European stories through direct comparison, for example when she writes, "In West Indian folklore, as in the folklore of many other countries, midnight is often a magic hour when anything can happen" (8). Hallworth connects West Indian folklore to its global counterparts to ensure that readers see its value.

In retelling Caribbean folktales, Hallworth also makes deliberate choices about the way she presents the tales to her audience, particularly in terms of language. As a librarian, she places the story first; while Hallworth felt that language was important to a story, her stories include patois sparingly: "I have attempted to use these speech patterns or dialect where they add colour and humour to the story without making it too difficult for everybody to understand" (*Listen to This Story* 9–10). Her decision to use language, and particularly patois, in this way relates directly to attitudes in Britain at the time. Patois was seen, especially by white educators, as a barrier to learning. One report, from the National Association of Schoolmasters, suggested, "The West Indian child usually arrives speaking a kind of 'plantation English' which is socially unacceptable and inadequate for communication" (5). At the time of *Listen to This Story*'s publication, many Afro-Caribbeans had been placed in "educationally subnormal" (ESN) classrooms, often (at least ostensibly) due to their "inadequate" English. Bernard Coard, in *How the West Indian Child Is Made Educationally Sub-Normal in the British School System* (1971), wrote that "over 28 per cent of all the pupils [in ESN classrooms] are immigrants, *compared with only 15 per cent immigrants in the ordinary schools*" (5). Most of these students, according to Paul Warmington, "found themselves *permanently* placed in special schools that were not equipped to support mainstream academic achievement" (59). The idea that the language that West Indians spoke at home was "inadequate for communication," though illogical, affected the way that Black British children were seen and the way they saw themselves.

In her early books, including *Listen to This Story*, Hallworth acknowledges the standard British view of patois, at one point even seeming to accept this view uncritically by labeling patois as a "not very good" (*Listen to This Story* 45) version of the dominant language. Yet she does not abandon patois entirely, even in her early work. Hallworth's *Listen to This Story* begins with "How Agouti Lost His Tail," which contains no patois at all and only slight use of nonstandard English: "How d'ye do?" (11) and "Mornin'" (11). The sentences follow English grammatical patterns, even in dialect, as when Brer Dog says to Anansi, "Mornin', Brer Anansi. What are you doing up so early?" (11). Later stories in the collection slowly increase their use of nonstandard English and patois. Thus, while "Compère Anansi and the Pig" has Anansi stating, "The doctor says that I must take a white pig up the hill, kill it and eat it all by myself, otherwise I may die" (18), "The Courting of Miss Annie" several stories later has Anansi declare, "A-i-ee, a-i-ee, I mus' die if I mus'" (54). The only real use of the grammatical patterns of patois comes in one of the rhymes included in the penultimate story, "Brer Anansi and Brer Snake," in which Anansi chants, "*Snake swift and he strong, / Snake soft and he long, / But today we go prove who right and who wrong*" (67). Rather than tell her stories in the patois of the original storytellers from whom she heard the tales, Hallworth uses standard British English in the narrative and nonstandard English in the less formal dialogue, including grammar patterns of patois only near the end of her collection.

Like the trickster figure Anansi, the main character in the majority of the tales in *Listen to this Story*, Hallworth uses verbal gymnastics (or, in Jean-François Lyotard's term, language games)—appearing to agree with the official view of patois while inserting it in increasing amounts through the book—to give value to the language that many West Indian immigrants and their children spoke. She introduces the stories to British children—Black or white—without connecting the Caribbean to what many white British teachers saw as an inability to speak properly. She thus ensures, through her use of language, that child readers in Britain will indeed "listen to this story." Later collections by Hallworth, such as *Cric Crac* (1990), make no apology for their use of patois; but by this time, as Gillian Klein writes in *Reading into Racism*, a shift in attitudes had taken place: "English is just one of a myriad of equally effective languages, and 'standard' only one of a considerable number of dialects" (102). British English was still the lingua franca of the classroom, but patois had become another common version of English, heard as frequently as Cockney or Yorkshire in the public arena.

In addition to her strategic use of patois, Hallworth credits storytellers with and calls attention to their ability to use language to tell a better story. This point may seem self-evident, but in a culture that, at the time, demeaned West Indian linguistic ability, it is in fact crucial to Hallworth's project of valuing West Indian stories in Britain. She does this in two ways. First, she highlights the artifice of story. In *Mouth Open, Story Jump Out* (1984), she argues, "Supernatural beings still have a strong hold on our imaginations if not our actual lives, and among a group of West Indians in a relaxed atmosphere it is not difficult to start a chain of stories which . . . have the power to thrill and entertain" (10). Just as she uses the stories to prove West Indians' linguistic acumen, she also "modernizes" the Caribbean by putting superstitions in the past; ghost stories were valued for their entertainment, not for their reality, just as in British literature. West Indian writers, Hallworth posited, have the power to create new stories from traditional folkloric material. In a Britain that valorized the postwar writing of J. R. R. Tolkien, C. S. Lewis, and Susan Cooper, all of whom used British folklore to create new worlds, this is a powerful message.

Second, Hallworth indicates through her collections, just as she did in her earlier publications for librarians and teachers, that new stories are always possible—even in folklore. In *Cric Crac*, Hallworth stresses the notion that child readers can create as well as adult authors: "You too can make each of these stories your own tale by telling it in your own way" (5), she writes in the introduction. *Listen to This Story* includes a tale "The Kiskadee" that Hallworth herself made up "as a possible explanation of why the bird so called cries 'Qu'est-ce qu'il dit?' from dawn till dusk" (10). She uses traditional folktale patterns in her story, including an emphasis on the number three that would be familiar to readers of European folktales as well, but she creates her own unique story. In essence, Hallworth modernizes the traditional folktale by indicating to her readers that new stories can be written in traditional styles.

The animals in "The Kiskadee" sometimes speak in French, which Hallworth does not translate, again highlighting the importance of language and Hallworth's expectation that readers will master more than just English. The use of French-speaking animals also, however, connects Trinidad with its colonial past. Although France did not colonize Trinidad, the 1783 Cedula of Population issued by the Spanish government offered land grants to Roman Catholics, most of these being French planters from nearby islands.

Hallworth's casual inclusion of French phrases, which would have been familiar to Trinidadians, challenges the notion that Caribbean people not only have no language and no literature, but also have no history.

The Windrush generation, of which Hallworth was a part, came to Britain well schooled in both British and Caribbean history. When the children of Windrush went to school, however, the only history that was taught to them was British history; and it was a history that almost entirely, even in its discussion of Empire, left out the Caribbean and particularly the British involvement in slavery there. Even when slavery was mentioned, the British were credited with ending it, and then the Caribbean conveniently disappears from British history books.[1] In Hallworth's own childhood education, the history taught was that of Britain as well; there were few textbooks that taught the history of Trinidad. Any picture that British children received of the Caribbean was likely to be full of stereotyped images (women walking to market with baskets on their head, rural poverty, coconuts and beaches), if they weren't the caricatures of golliwogs and people of color found in the comics pages.

While Hallworth did not write history books or historical fiction for children, she did write about her own childhood in books for the Cambridge Reading series such as *Going to School* (1996). In so doing, she offered an alternative portrayal of what the Caribbean and Caribbean people looked like in the past. *Going to School*, which is illustrated by Patrice Aggs and coauthored with Hallworth by Richard Brown, has on the cover a picture of a girl in a dress sitting on the floor reading a book. The dress is nice but not fancy, and the flowers in the background, though tropical, are in flowerpots. The illustration could be of a modern-day child in Britain. The text suggests that this is not the case, because the opening line is, "When I was little, I lived with my Aunt Daisy" (2). It is set in the past, and a careful reader might surmise from the tram on the next page and the hats that people are wearing that it is in the somewhat distant past—but not the past that many Britons associate with the Caribbean. The people in the story are clearly not slaves, nor are they visibly under imperial rule. Aunt Daisy is a teacher, and her house has middle-class attributes such as a piano. They live in a bungalow in a town big enough to have a tram and traffic. Grace has several dolls, and the bookshelves are full of books. The story itself is slight—Grace is too young to go to school but sets out one day on her own only to be stymied by a busy road and the fact that it is Saturday—but the story and its illustrations take the Caribbean out of the realm of the stereotyped poor, rural, and uneducated Third World. Hallworth challenges stereotypes about the Caribbean and offers her readers an alternative version of history.

The vision of the Caribbean provided by Hallworth comes largely from her books' illustrations rather than the text. This is true in books such as *Going to School* but in her nursery rhyme books as well. Hallworth never illustrated any of her books, but she did, unusually, have considerable influence over the choice of illustrators, particularly in her later books. As a librarian, Hallworth had spoken out about the need to depict all kinds of children in books: "Children have a natural curiosity about people who appear to be different whether the difference is one of colour of skin, race, speech, costume or of physical form and features" (*My Mind Is Not in a Wheelchair*). She felt that curiosity should be satisfied by quality text and illustrations. Hallworth's editors at Longmans and at Heinemann routinely sent her illustration samples for her comments; their letters are preserved in the archive at Seven Stories, the National Centre for Children's Books, in the UK. Sarah Wallis, at Longmans, wrote up the following artist's brief, which she sent to Hallworth for her approval:

> We would like lots of life and vigour in this book where the children are the important thing. The children are outdoors for all the rhymes, wearing summer T-shirts, jeans, skirts (not uniform). Please see photos supplied by Grace Hallworth and her letter about the representation of Trinidadian people.

This representation is key; especially in her nursery rhyme books, Hallworth wanted contemporary children playing, from all the ethnic groups in Trinidad. Such a depiction would demonstrate to readers that Trinidad was not stuck in the past, but was a modern place that has a history. Although *Down by the River* is subtitled *Afro-Caribbean Rhymes, Games, and Songs for Children* and Hallworth herself is Afro-Caribbean, she was especially keen to highlight Indo-Caribbeans, whose history and presence were (and are) often left out of Caribbean literature. Hallworth wrote to Jane Fior, her editor at Heinemann, "My sister who was here during the summer holidays, tells me that it is now believed that the East Indians are in the majority, therefore it is all the more important that illustrations are not found to be misrepresentative." She was pleased that the illustrator they eventually selected for *Down by the River*, white Briton

Caroline Binch, traveled to Trinidad and Tobago to sketch children, praising "Caroline's sensitivity" in the same letter to Fior.

Throughout her career, Hallworth remained committed to this nuanced presentation of the Caribbean, one that "reflects the cross-cultural aspect" of the region (Letter to Jane Fior). But Hallworth was also concerned with the cross-cultural background of Black Britons in the UK. While most of her books, whether folktales, rhymes, or stories, were set in the Caribbean, she wrote for a British audience primarily. And while she wanted Black British children to be aware of their literary heritage and history, she also wanted them to feel at home anywhere in the world. Many of her nursery rhyme books, such as *Buy a Penny Ginger*, *Rhythm and Rhyme*, and *Down by the River*, contain global rhymes in local variants. Rhymes such as "Here we go gathering nuts and may" (*Rhythm and Rhyme* 16–17) and "I saw Esau" (*Buy a Penny Ginger* 12) are included, in versions similar or the same as those known in Britain (both rhymes, in fact, originated there, and one formed the title for one of the Opies' collections). Others, such as "Miss Lucy had a baby" (*Rhythm and Rhyme* 35), are also known in Britain but are introduced by Hallworth in a specifically Caribbean form; Miss Lucy pours "rum with mustard" (35) over her baby Tiny Tim. *Down by the River* includes three "Rainy Day Rhymes," one that specifically mentions Trinidad and one that chronicles the months of the rainy season in the Caribbean flanking the rain rhyme best known in Britain, "Rain, rain / Go away." Hallworth included this variety because the "more I share these games and rhymes[,] the more clearly I see that we share many things and that our differences lie in the expression of what is shared" (*Buy a Penny Ginger*, introduction). Her nursery rhyme books use a traditional form to emphasize commonalities among all children, but they also put Caribbean literature on par with the literature of other countries, including Britain.

Hallworth's earliest introduction to literature was through the storytelling tradition and playground rhymes of Trinidad. Unlike many colonial subjects, who were trained to devalue this oral tradition by a British colonial education, Hallworth used her knowledge of British literature to point out the similarities between Caribbean oral tradition and that of other places. In her work as a librarian, she encountered students unaware of their histories and cultures, and her collections of folktales, nursery rhymes, and singing games aim to introduce that tradition to her readers. However, as she introduced them to the past, she also connected them with a present-day and modern

Caribbean, and with a way of influencing their own and others' future by telling their own versions of old stories. Hallworth's books embrace past, present, and future, creating "a living example of the interrelationship of different cultures" (*Down by the River*, introduction) for all her readers—Black or white, Caribbean, British, or citizen of the world.

Note

1. See Sands-O'Connor, *Soon Come Home to This Island: West Indians in British Children's Literature*, 71–80, for a more detailed discussion of British versions of Caribbean history.

Works Cited

Carey, Joanna. "Spinner of Yarns under the Palms." *The Guardian*, April 22, 1997, B5.
Coard, Bernard. *How the West Indian Child Is Made Educationally Sub-Normal in the British School System*. New Beacon Books, 1971.
Fryer, Peter. *Staying Power: The History of Black People in Britain*. Pluto Press, 1984.
Hallworth, Grace. *Buy a Penny Ginger and Other Rhymes*. Pearson Education, 1994.
Hallworth, Grace. *Cric Crac: A Collection of West Indian Stories*. Heinemann, 1990.
Hallworth, Grace. *Down by the River: Afro-Caribbean Rhymes, Games, and Songs for Children*. Scholastic, 1996.
Hallworth, Grace. Letter to Jane Fior, November 18, 1994. Seven Stories Archive GH/09.
Hallworth, Grace. *Listen to This Story: Tales from the West Indies*. Methuen, 1977.
Hallworth, Grace. *Mouth Open, Story Jump Out: Spellbinding Stories from the Caribbean*. Methuen, 1984.
Hallworth, Grace. *My Mind Is Not in a Wheelchair: Books and the Handicapped Child*. Hertfordshire Library Service, 1982.
Hallworth, Grace. *Rhythm and Rhyme: Songs, Rhymes and Games*. Addison-Wesley, 1995.
Hallworth, Grace, and Richard Brown. *Going to School*. Cambridge UP, 1996.
Hallworth, Grace, and Julia Marriage. *Stories to Read and to Tell*. Pamphlet no. 13, Youth Libraries Group, 1978.
James, Cynthia. "From Orature to Literature in Jamaican and Trinidadian Folk Traditions." *Children's Literature Association Quarterly*, vol. 30, no. 2, Summer 2005, pp. 164–78.
Joseph, Valerie. "How Thomas Nelson and Sons' *Royal Readers* Textbooks Helped Instill the Standards of Whiteness into Colonized Black Caribbean Subjects and Their Descendants." *Transforming Anthropology*, vol. 20, no. 2, October 2012, pp. 146–58.
Kassim, Halima-sa'Adia. "Education and Socialization among the Indo-Muslims of Trinidad, 1917–1969." *Journal of Caribbean History*, vol. 36, no.1, 2002, pp. 100–126.
Klein, Gillian. *Reading into Racism: Bias in Children's Literature and Learning Materials*. Routledge and Kegan Paul, 1985.
Nakhid, Camille, Dorian Barrow, and Orlena Broomes. "Situating the Education of African Trinidadians within the Social and Historical Context of Trinidad and Tobago: Implications for Social Justice." *Education, Citizenship, and Social Justice*, vol. 9, no. 2, July 2014, pp. 171–87.

National Association of Schoolmasters. *Education and the Immigrants*. Educare, 1969.
Rampton, Anthony. *West Indian Children in Our Schools*. Her Majesty's Stationery Office, 1981.
Sands-O'Connor, Karen. *Children's Publishing and Black Britain, 1965–2015*. Palgrave Macmillan, 2017.
Sands-O'Connor, Karen. *Soon Come Home to This Island: West Indians in British Children's Literature*. Routledge, 2008.
Solomos, John, Bob Findlay, Simon Jones, and Paul Gilroy. "The Organic Crisis of British Capitalism and Race: The Experience of the Seventies." *The Empire Strikes Back: Race and Racism in 70s Britain*, edited by the Centre for Contemporary Cultural Studies, Routledge, 1982, pp. 9–46.
Wallis, Sarah. Letter to Grace Hallworth, March 24, 1993. Seven Stories Archive GH/04/02/15.
Warmington, Paul. *Black British Intellectuals and Education: Multiculturalism's Hidden History*. Routledge, 2014.
Williams, Eric. *History of the People of Trinidad and Tobago*. André Deutsch, 1962.

CHAPTER 11

Reading Words, Reading Worlds
Understanding the Value of the Literary Experience in the Process of Reading Caribbean Children's Books in the Jamaican Primary School System

Aisha T. Spencer

Reading in a Postcolonial Space

Our perceptions of and approaches to reading significantly influence the kind of literary experience teachers and students will have both in and outside of the classroom. The situation of reading in Caribbean countries with a British colonial past produces an even deeper layer of complexity. Within the Caribbean context, literacy is intricately connected to the social identity of Caribbean children, as their ability to read and respond to texts—through their knowledge and use of Standard English—becomes, for many, an indicator of their competence and their potential for access to higher rungs of the economic and social ladder. Language remains a central marker of an already complex set of factors constituting a Caribbean individual's identity, often determining their ability to function in different social spaces.

In many Caribbean countries, many regard the mother tongue as inferior to the official language (in this case, Standard English), with the latter being a signifier of acceptance and worth. Many theoretical discussions on language use in Jamaica provide evidence of the stereotypical labels used to frame the classroom experiences of predominantly Creole-speaking children who lack fluency in Standard English (Devonish; Craig; Bryan). Traditional Western perspectives have influenced the educational structures in place for decades, affecting the way we perceive and treat various subject areas. This includes the traditionally limited outlook that has continued to shape the way we engage in processes of reading, interpreting, and responding to children's literature. Although more Caribbean-language textbooks are being published, featuring distinctly Caribbean contexts in their focus, the use of literature in these textbooks is predominantly language-based, centered on the use and acquisition of English, with little or no use or mention of Caribbean children's literature in ways that promote literary engagement and competence. Subsequently, many students feel alienated by educational practices that encourage regurgitation and surface-level engagement, and that fail to allow students to "meet" themselves and the world(s) in which they will participate. Not only are they alienated from the deeper layers of meaning in the text, but they are also not sufficiently provided with the opportunity to build the literary skills they will need to evolve, particularly in the areas of critical thinking, analysis, and problem solving.

Teachers of language arts in primary and lower secondary schools are scarcely aware of Caribbean children's literature books and their authors. Such texts remain either unknown or undervalued. This is largely because of the limited knowledge of and minimal exposure to literary studies and literary pedagogy in the subject areas of language arts and English language and literacy by pretrained teachers at the tertiary level. The teachers who are more conversant with and confident in literary studies are often those who have been specifically trained in literature or literacy studies, and so tend to be more aware of what is happening in the literature arena culturally. Additionally, because literature is placed as a kind of appendage in the language arts curriculum framework, teachers are often not encouraged to discover Caribbean children's books and are usually not aware of the vast literary strategies that can be used to engage children with these books, other than read aloud moments, having students read quietly, or allowing whole class discussions that are centered on students responding to dozens of questions about the text.

Many of our primary and lower secondary school teachers who specialize in language and literacy have not received sufficient training in literature in ways that would enable them to build literary competencies and skills. They are therefore unaware of how to help students read, interpret, and respond to literary texts, and this reduces their feelings of confidence about teaching the subject. Many teachers are therefore unfamiliar with experiencing literature and learning how to read, interpret, and respond to literary content, style, and structure in distinctive and strategic ways. Instead of being introduced to literary texts as offering several worlds of possibility, those without this experience may avoid encounters with such texts.

The marginal place of the literary text in early childhood, primary, and lower secondary Jamaican classrooms minimalizes the literary experience for both teachers and students. The primary or elementary school system rarely locates literature as a distinct subject area, even though it plays a crucial role in enabling access to the world of language. Literature is often treated as a tool for learning various elements of written language instead of as an opportunity for content analysis and connection between texts and experience. Conceptual and pedagogical fissures often occur when the school curriculum does not reflect the complementary relationship between language and literature. This in turn problematizes the understanding and treatment of critical literacy by teachers in the school system.

This chapter will examine the current reality concerning reading and Caribbean children's books in Jamaican classrooms, where both teachers and students continue to be confined to colonial ways of reading and teaching, even after more than sixty years of independence. It will examine how reading is theorized, approached, and taught. It will look at how reading has primarily been situated and how, by operating in a particularly restrictive space, reading in a Jamaican classroom context has become a problematic process. Additionally, it will demonstrate ways in which the marginal positioning of Caribbean children's literature has contributed to limiting reading experiences for both Jamaican teachers and students. The chapter will also explore ways for students to encounter Caribbean children's literature within an active-learning, response-oriented context. Doing so can allow students to "engage the world within its complexity and fullness, [and] . . . reveal the possibilities of new ways of constructing thought and action" (Darder, Baltodano, and Torres 11). Additionally, a section of the chapter will present the views of three primary school teachers as well as my own observations of the place and function of children's books in primary or preparatory classrooms across the island of Jamaica. Finally, the chapter will demonstrate the value of the literary experience in a postcolonial context through analyses of specific Caribbean children's books with examples of possible ways to read and respond to literary texts in the Jamaican classroom.

Unfortunately, outside the realm of higher education, literacy in the Caribbean has tended to be more connected to a set of basic skills with a binary thinking process associating literacy with education and social and economic success, and illiteracy with educational failure and subsequent social and economic restrictions. These oppositions were created by and perpetuated through colonial precepts built on classist notions of superiority and inferiority. Within this mindset, reading becomes a mere skill associated with literacy, academic achievement, and eventually elevated social standing, rather than a process that liberates, helps us to construct our identities, and allows us to imagine and create individual and collective goals that can influence future realities.

Recognizing how deeply the roots of colonialism are embedded within Jamaica's educational system is crucial to addressing the matter of developing children from all walks of life with the creative mindset, behaviors, and tools needed to truly ensure higher and more sustainable levels of literacy. Creating a people who are literate cannot solely be about the pronunciation and recognition of words on a page. Neither can it be simply about a child's ability to spell words and read and write sentences. Such views of literacy continue to perpetuate a cycle of superficial knowledge acquisition disconnected from the sociocultural realities of many Caribbean children. Consequently, such a limited approach to and understanding of literacy also produces thousands of children who enter our secondary school system without the ability to meaningfully comprehend and respond to the literary texts they encounter at this stage because they lack important foundational experiences with books in the early childhood and primary periods of schooling.

Additionally, this narrow approach to the teaching and use of literary texts in the classroom sustains a set of educational policies, curricula, and pedagogies that stifle both teachers and students and limit their experiences in the classroom. For students in early childhood through grades K–7, classroom reading practices are predominantly characterized (at different points in time based on the grade level) by "picture reading," read aloud moments, phonemic awareness, vocabulary items, and sets of comprehension questions. These views and practices of literacy are generally formulated and performed through knowledge of traditionally based conceptualizations of reading that situate reading as occurring through the acquisition of a set of "'separately defined' comprehension skills" (Sheridan 66). Consequently, classroom reading practices for children between the ages of one and twelve have largely occurred without due attention to the significant role of the literary experience in the development of children's linguistic and literary competencies when responding to children's books of all kinds.

Reading functions as a major part of the model of a literate society. In fact, very often the term "literacy" in a Caribbean context is used synonymously with the term "reading," although both words tend to be much wider in their characterization than the meanings they are ascribed by parents, teachers, and students. Therefore, we must provide meaningful and practical definitions, because how we perceive each of these processes or experiences depends greatly on how we define them. In order to help both teachers and students in educational contexts to understand and appreciate the value of engaging with children's literature, both inside and outside of classroom spaces, we must carefully examine the definitions of literacy that have remained at the center of our educational curricula. Understanding what literacy involves is essential, because our perceptions and beliefs deeply influence and shape our approaches to teaching in the language classroom. This includes the teaching and use of children's literature. UNESCO's 2018 definition of literacy provides one of the most practical and relevant characterizations of the term: "Literacy is the ability to identify, understand, interpret, create, communicate and compute, using printed and written materials associated with varying contexts" (Montoya). This expanded definition enables a holistic frame through which to position literature as an integral part of literacy acquisition and use in the language arts classroom.

When only perceived as vehicles for language learning, literary texts become mere objects used to introduce students to vocabulary items, sentences, paragraphs, rhythmic sounds, and linguistic patterns. Yet the process of reading automatically creates a fusion between language and literature that insists on an in-depth knowledge and understanding of both areas and an appreciation for the levels of critical awareness this fusion enables. A lack of understanding of the conventions and elements connected to both these areas limits the way teachers and students engage with them through the process of reading. Furthermore, knowledge of these will not encourage academic or personal growth if students are not able to actively engage with the meanings constructed through these conventions and elements. For example, a grade 4 student could be taught the importance of themes in stories—and may be able to fully comprehend the concept of a theme—yet, he or she may find access to the theme's meaning challenging. The practice of reading and interpreting a literary text involves the set of processes and methodologies teachers use to help to build students' literary knowledge and skills in their effort to understand and respond to the stories they read.

To focus on one key aspect of the process of reading and ignore or pay scant attention to the other is bound to, in Paulo Freire's term, *dehumanize* the process of teaching and learning for both teachers and students. Children's books were not written for words and sentences to be dissected or for portions of texts to be pulled out and used without an understanding of the full frame surrounding the content. The process of reading involves much more than vocabulary items, rhythmic patterns, and knowledge of the basic story line. It requires much deeper levels of participation from the reader. To remove the reader from the integral process of seeing, interpreting, and responding to the thoughts and ideas in a text is to destroy the essence of the reading process for the participant. As Louise Rosenblatt explains in her discussions of the reading process, the reader ought to be allowed to give his or her "selective attention" to the text ("The Literary Transaction" 270). This selective attention occurs based on whatever lens the reader has chosen to help him or her to understand or experience the text, or whatever way a student chooses to focus on a text to derive meaning from it. For this to happen, the reader needs to be an integral part of the reading process. Reading, therefore, becomes a practical and attainable transactional experience between reader and text. The text cannot be perceived as the container of meanings. It is the reader who, through interaction with the text, will create meaning (Rosenblatt, "The Literary Transaction" 272). Reading ought not to be characterized by passivity or attention solely to technicality. Although students need to learn the features that define a story or poem or play, they can only minimally appreciate a text's structural importance if it is not connected to meanings in that text. How we read texts (the lenses through which we read, the perceptions framing our reading of texts, and so on) should significantly influence how we teach students to read, interpret, and respond to the texts they encounter.

Reading in the classroom is not solely about the student; it also heavily involves the teacher. Teachers should not simply seek to help their students pronounce words, read aloud in class, or identify the setting in a story; they can help students access diverse experiences through the connections established among text, context, and students' personal experiences, emotions, and imagination. What teachers are unable to feel or access, based on their level of engagement with a text, is likely to have an impact on the feelings and access of students to a text. The deeper the experience the teacher has with the meanings embedded in that text, the more meaningful and authentic the experience of the text will be for the students. As Donna E. Norton states in *Through the Eyes of a Child*, "[T]he extent to which books play a significant role in the lives of young children depends on adults" (2). A restricted view of reading and an approach to literacy that privileges the use of teaching principles and activities that simply borrow from British and American contexts and guides (although an awareness and use of international best practices is undoubtedly valuable and necessary) will only serve to encourage the prevalence of past colonial thinking and practices, and twenty-first-century imperialist notions, regardless of how discreetly these are inserted into the national curricula.

The importance of sociocultural contexts as part of a frame for the process of reading has been discussed by many writers in the fields of language and literature education, yet many Caribbean primary school classrooms continue to engage in practices that are void of these contexts. School systems continue to introduce students to texts and tasks that lack relevance, purposefulness, and appropriate contexts based on the historical and socioeconomic background of many students in the Caribbean primary and lower secondary school classrooms. Caribbean children's literature is marginally read, analyzed, and explored in Jamaican classrooms, despite the realistic and relevant contexts it provides for students. When it is present, it is usually restricted to popular cultural folklore traditions celebrated at various times during the year. Anansi stories and Jamaican Creole poems by Miss Lou (Louise Bennett) are quite often the types of Caribbean children's literature texts Jamaican children are exposed to on a regular basis in the classroom. Often, however, they are read or performed with only a slight glance at their literary content and with few opportunities for students to interpret and respond to the various meanings in the text and manner of presentation. Additionally, children are more likely to be introduced to basal readers or readers' series; these are, in most cases, viewed as technical texts used to support a language and literacy focus and a set of curriculum objectives, without meaningful consideration given to their literary qualities and the aesthetic experience they can provide.

The value of reading in a Caribbean postcolonial context cannot be fully appreciated until we tap into a deeper understanding of what it means to be able to read and why it is important to be discriminating about what we read. The situation of reading in classrooms becomes even more relevant when we recognize that how we perceive the process of reading shapes the literacy and literary journeys both teachers and students will experience. Additionally, how we approach reading in the classroom can either cause us to lose sight of ourselves or to gain further insight into our identities and the places we might occupy in the world based on who we are, individually and collectively.

As Freire explains in his renowned book *Pedagogy of the Oppressed,* for education to become valuable to students, they must be able to establish connections between what they are being taught and how they can use that knowledge to navigate the world in which they live (32). To see reading as "an end product of decoding" (Kravis 14), emphasizing only the technical aspects of the reading process without helping readers connect with and gain access to the different levels of meaning embedded within the text, is to allow students' experiences in the classroom space to become oppressive rather than transformative. Furthermore, we need the students "doing" more with books and participating in critical tasks that establish a purpose for reading rather than encouraging practices that limit the reading process to simple verbalization of content. As Janice Bland reminds us, "When reading or listening to stories, children should be allowed to guess at meanings and to make informed predictions about what the writer or storyteller will say next. They should not be encouraged to expect to understand every single word, leading to risk avoiding rather than risk taking" (8).

Caribbean Children's Literature

While the presence of Caribbean children's literature texts in the primary classroom has grown since the early twenty-first century, predominantly through their promotion across social media and through publishers like Macmillan Caribbean, most primary teachers are unaware of what Bland terms "the literary potential" (2) of these children's books. Bland argues that this situation, as it occurs globally, reveals a kind of "resistance towards employing children's literature in language teaching" (1). Readers need to be provided with opportunities for holistic, dynamic, and contextual dimensions of engagement with the books they read.

Caribbean children's literature formally emerged in the late 1960s, after the historical year of independence in 1962. In the introduction of her thesis, Sujin Huggins examines the contemporary children's literature collection in the National Library of Trinidad and Tobago. She explains how the popular focus on the emerging corpus of Caribbean literature during the late 1950s and into the period of independence for the different Caribbean territories led to a situation in which the "drive and urgency" surrounding the construction of "new cultural identities . . . occurred outside of existing patterns of literacy and available literature at the time" (8). She argues that "[a]ttention was duly paid to the genesis of this new body of literature, which did not directly consider children as its audience" (8). Caribbean children's literature authors who published titles from the 1960s through the 1980s were therefore not acknowledged for their contribution to Caribbean children's literature as a genre in and of itself, because their texts were already subsumed within the category of the newly emerging body of Caribbean literature texts. Most of these authors were male and positioned the Caribbean child in the literary text largely within the national discourse of the times. By the 1980s, Caribbean female writers (such as Olive Senior, Erna Brodber, and Lorna Goodison) had emerged on the literary scene, and the short story genre had begun to showcase the female child figure in a consistent manner, exploring aspects of the childhood experience (the impact of migration, the influence of social class on Caribbean childhood identity, and so on). Poems for children by Caribbean writers such as Louise Bennett, John Agard, Grace Nichols, and Mervyn Morris were also published but not treated as part of the body of Caribbean children's literature nor given the kind of critical attention they deserve. Their use in the Jamaican classroom was minimal; teachers lacked the kind of response-orientation training needed to promote meaningful engagement and analysis.

Authors such as Andrew Salkey, Jean D'Costa, Michael Anthony, C. Everard Palmer, Rosa Guy, George Lamming, and Therese Mills, to name a few, have published Caribbean children's books and contributed significantly to the collection of texts now being characterized as Caribbean children's literature. Cynthia James argues that during the period from independence to the early 1990s, "literacy and documentation were the main elements propelling the use of folk materials in West Indian children's literature—a literature that began in textbooks. The main thrust was didactic—both to promote literacy and moral rectitude" (167). In my chapter in *The Routledge Companion to International Children's Literature* (2018), I note that this marginalized posture of Caribbean children's literature continued through the creation and use of "folk tales of West Indian cultures written by 'foreigners' over a century ago," which led to "the consequence that the Caribbean children's books that tend to be more commonly discussed both locally and internationally are those that present Caribbean folklore, . . . rather than the more contemporary and recent books written for children" (115).

Although multicultural children's literature has steadily grown in popularity on the international scene since around 2010, tackling taboo subjects and interrogating status quos and stereotypes, Caribbean children's literature remains largely underrepresented both internationally and in local spaces. Subsequently, theoretical discussions on the distinctive Caribbean textual features in and the unique literary experience of Caribbean children's literature continue to be insufficient. This reality seriously weakens the knowledge and awareness of teachers and educational administrators on the teaching and use of Caribbean children's literature, particularly with respect to the situation of reading for Jamaican students engaged in primary and early high school education.

Teachers' Accounts of Reading in Jamaican Primary Classrooms

As was discussed at the start of the chapter, the typically marginal historical characterization of children's literature has deeply influenced the way the genre is seen and taught in Caribbean educational systems. The impact of colonialism has played and continues to play a major role in the construction and use of Caribbean educational curricula at all levels of education. The context within which Caribbean children's literature is introduced to both teachers and students greatly impacts the place this genre is given regionally and the role it will play as part of a greater and broader category of works in the diasporic space through multicultural literature. Caribbean children's literature writers have complained over and again about being left off booklists or remaining unnoticed because their works do not fit the stereotypical and traditional labels of what constitutes a book appropriate for learning to read. These labels may stem from the skewed perception of reading many of our own national literacy specialists hold. These perceptions are grounded in beliefs about reading that minimize the value of the literary aspect of the process, as a result of lack of knowledge or awareness. James points to the marginal treatment and use of literature in Trinidad's primary schools. She quotes Eunice Patrick's unpublished dissertation on the topic: although "teachers felt the teaching of literature should be central to the child's entire primary education," the subject continued to be placed on "the periphery" and was only "minimally taught" (6).

Since this chapter focuses on literature as both a subject and a tool in the classroom, the voices of those who play a fundamental role in shaping this process deserve attention. I interviewed three Jamaican primary school teachers who held posts at different schools across the island. Although each teacher gave consent to have her opinions published, their real names will not be disclosed for ethical reasons. At the time of the interview, each of these teachers possessed a teachers' college diploma in language education and English and was awaiting their graduation exercise as in-service teachers who had recently completed their two-year Bachelor of Education degree from a university. Each of these three teachers had entered their two-year in-service teaching program with high hopes of learning how to handle the "matter of reading and writing" so they could go back to their classrooms feeling more qualified and prepared to teach reading to their students. Ms. Cherwood was in her late twenties and had taught for three years, Ms. Gordon was in her late forties and had been teaching for over twelve years, and Ms. Brissett was in her late fifties and had been teaching for approximately twenty years. Although each of these teachers had different personalities and levels of teaching and classroom experience, each faced common challenges surrounding the teaching of reading in their primary classrooms. Three dominant themes surrounding the place of the literary text in the classroom surfaced from the teachers' responses: (1) a focus on the technical aspects of the text dominated the teaching of the reading experience, (2) few or no opportunities existed for in-depth engagement and interaction between the text and the student, and (3) text selection was highly problematic.

Joseph Milner and Lucy Milner outline four principles that characterize "traditional learning": (1) acquiring "discrete pieces of information," (2) transferring the knowledge of teachers to students who in turn "store" and regurgitate this information, (3) testing "students' mastery of knowledge and skills," and (4) focusing on the interaction between the teacher and student

(8). These traditional learning principles are all present in the classrooms the three teachers describe, even at a time when student-centeredness, "constructivism," and "critical thinking skills" have become buzzwords promoted by the Ministry of Education and throughout teacher training institutions across Jamaica. Many principals and teachers would not characterize the way reading is taught in their schools as being highly traditional, yet the practices seem to suggest that this description is in fact applicable. In the guidelines of the Jamaican primary school curriculum document, the term "Literature" is subsumed within the umbrella term of "the Arts" and is spoken of in very broad ways, such that its use is designated "as a vehicle to encourage independent thinking, creative and learning skills and holistic learning" (Ministry of Education 24). In the case of the lower secondary school curriculum (grades 7–9), the purpose of literature is only addressed in two of fourteen objectives written on the mode of reading in the language arts classroom. The teacher, therefore, is left to navigate his or her way through these indistinct aims and descriptions surrounding the place and use of the literary text in the classroom space. Each of the teachers in their interviews spoke candidly about the difficulties they experienced when approaching the concept of teaching the literary text in their classrooms.

A common approach to the teaching of literature in primary and early secondary educational institutions in Jamaica is to treat the text the way Ciaran Cosgrove describes in his contribution in Judy Kravis's *Teaching Literature* (1995), as though it "already has its meaning which one has to retrieve and, if one is assiduous enough, one will find it" (83). This "pedestal-like" posturing of literature merely serves to perpetuate the kind of pedagogical approach that causes student readers to feel isolated from the text and to see the author and teacher as superior and themselves as inferior. As Cosgrove notes, "You do whatever you can to make literature something that belongs to students rather than something that is distant, remote" (qtd. in Kravis 59). Yet, during my interview with the teachers, Ms. Gordon expressed her frustration with respect to the administrative guidelines that demanded that she "stick to the text." She felt that this approach caused more harm than good to the children, as "our children are very imaginative, and we must be able to appeal to their imagination when we give them things." Ms. Cherwood, too, explained that she always felt that if she did not "stick to the text," she would not be "teaching reading properly," as she was told "not to go outside of the text"; her experience of both the internal and external structuring of test papers on reading comprehension made her recognize that "questions were always set . . . on the same types of focus on aspects in the text." What became immediately recognizable was that all the teachers interviewed were at some point teaching in constant fear about their thoughts and actions in the classroom. It was not that they were afraid of not having the ability to provide students with the best possible experience of reading, but instead that they did not want their children to fail internal and external tests and therefore be stamped with the label "illiterate." This crucial issue cannot be taken lightly. The action of focusing on the technical aspects of the text is directly connected to the presence of a standardized testing practice.

Additionally, many who manage our educational system believe that failing students suggests a failing teacher. Each of the teachers interviewed was very aware that both the internal and external grades of students would be viewed as evidence of their own performance as teachers. Ms. Cherwood, who taught at the grades 2 and 3 levels, explained that whatever she taught about reading in the classroom was always "focused on whatever the text is," because she felt that both herself and her colleagues were schooled to understand that "whatever was written in the text was to determine whatever the teachers would teach and the students would learn." Ms. Cherwood noted that this practice reflected that internal and external examinations focused on student recall of specific details of a story with limited attention to inferencing or deeper levels of interpretation and response. The other teachers immediately agreed. Ms. Gordon added that there was "no way she was going to end up being the teacher that would have to get the bad name if her children did not pass the tests set by the school and the Ministry." Ms. Brissett also chimed into the discussion, explaining that "at the end of the day everybody is focused on the literacy results, so you have to make sure the students can answer those questions they set." This is not a new phenomenon. Standardized tests across the Caribbean region and in American and British school systems are often heavily criticized for their restrictive focus and the way they are used to determine levels of knowledge and intelligence.

The focus here is not to prolong discussions on the restrictive nature of these forms of testing and their role in perpetuating superficial ways of teaching and learning. Instead, we need to explore how we, as language and literature educators, can create spaces and opportunities in classrooms at all levels, where Caribbean students can perform well on standardized tests and at the same time become active learners, rather than robots—learners who are able to demonstrate high levels of critical thinking and analytical skills and possess an in-depth awareness of self that will build their self-confidence and empower them to respond freely and responsibly.

The presence of a text is not the totality of one's reading experience. As Caribbean educators, it is important that we understand the multiple paradigms that inform the way we see both the content and pedagogy of whatever subject matter we teach. In her book *Literature as Exploration*, Rosenblatt describes two different postures of reading important to this discussion: the efferent stance and the aesthetic stance. She explains that the efferent stance focuses on the information the student will "carry away" (32) from the text. It is concerned with gaining information. The aesthetic stance, however, causes readers to engage on deeper levels, where they "'live through' what is being created during the reading" (33). Meaning-making becomes more integrated and complete when we understand the difference in these stances. We will then shift the way we teach and the kinds of tasks we set for students as we engage them in the process of reading and learning to respond to texts. We must begin to understand that the "capacities and readiness" (33) of the reader are fundamental to the process of teaching literature, and students ought to be centrally positioned to be active participants who are given the opportunity to engage not simply in "reading" experiences but also "literary" experiences.

An important point of consideration for Caribbean language and literature educators is the history influencing our educational systems and curriculum decisions. If we are to contribute meaningfully to the lives of both our teachers and our students in the area of language and literature education, then we must understand that when participating in the teaching and learning processes involving language, literacy, and literature, we are also engaging with colonial perceptions from which we must untangle ourselves; colonial ways of seeing and experiencing education need to be interrogated and reconceptualized. For anything with an "English" mark on it, we must be especially careful because the English language and the literatures associated with it immediately invoke a sense of "otherness," of something we must strive to acquire to help situate us as being literate or educated. Language, literacy, and literature have therefore become qualifying terms used to characterize the written and spoken aspects of the English language and English literature subject areas, which, if regurgitated and used competently, will determine the kind of worth or value attached to the student and teacher.

Additionally, lack of awareness and understanding of the literary features and functions of a text and limited exposure to literary experiences will create a situation that stifles the processes of teaching and learning literature for both teacher and student. Ms. Gordon, one of the three teachers, had an engaging and dynamic experience of literature during her college years of training, and this zest spilled over into the way she now approaches the teaching of texts in her classroom. Despite this, she still feels that her ability to zoom in on some of the literary qualities of the text is insufficient, and it affects her level of confidence when teaching stories and poetry to her grade 3 students. Ms. Gordon questions her ability to make the content relatable and comprehensible to students. She admits that many times she has asked herself, "How can I put this in a way that my children can get something from it?" Many teachers have not had the opportunity to "experience" literature. Their exposure to literature, as is the case with their exposure to language and literacy, has predominantly, though not completely for some, been based on acquiring knowledge solely on the technical aspects of the subject area. Their ideas of competence in the area are based, therefore, on the literary terms and elements of literature they know that can boost the language awareness, knowledge, and competence of the students they teach. The interesting reality is, however, that many teachers, despite the attainment of their diplomas and their degrees, are fully aware that there are gaps based on how they feel in the classroom space and the kinds of responses they receive from their students. Many tend to ignore these feelings and to dismiss what they see as inadequacies, but their dismissal of the situation does not prevent the reality from emerging. Meaning-making occurs through the transaction between the reader and the text. As Rosenblatt reminds us, "meaning is not 'in' the text or 'in' the reader" (*Literature as Exploration*, 27). For teachers to meaningfully engage students in the reading process, they must first have that experience for themselves. Teachers need to be taught how to make meaning and, by extension, how to help others engage in meaning-making when engaging with the text.

The issue of text selection also serves as a fundamental part of any discussion on the experience of reading in the Caribbean. Educators must consider two main points when examining text selection: (1) promoting the use of texts that are culturally relevant and age appropriate, and (2) selecting texts that encourage diverse types of responses on varying levels (personal, academic, social, etc.) from students. The tendency is to consider these two strands only at the secondary level (and this still occurs to a minimal extent in secondary institutions), but this should be done with children as early as two years old. Often, the texts students are exposed to in the Jamaican classroom are framed within a foreign context, in which characters, settings, and situations are unfamiliar to both teachers and students. Ms. Gordon spoke of this issue when she described the problem of her children using books that they "would not be able to grasp based on their background knowledge and where they are coming from." She lamented that "the words were not relatable. The language was not relatable."

When the texts selected are based on the Caribbean, then they are usually proverbial and folkloric texts. Ms. Cherwood said that using these texts as primary texts was problematic. She explained that "in the school that I was at, the reading book that was from the Ministry . . . had Anansi stories. The students used these books up to grade 6, and those were the only reading books students would use in the classroom." For Ms. Cherwood, this created a limited experience of reading for students, and she explained that she was unable to do many of the things she wanted to do with the students because of the insistence that these texts be used as the main texts by the administrative leaders of her institution.

Additionally, many of the texts selected for use in the Jamaican primary classroom are categorized as basal readers. Basal readers are written with the purpose of reading instruction instead of storytelling and build reading skills in a specific way. Importantly, basal readers are often used as textbooks rather than as trade books, and so students utilize them as texts written with the specific purpose of conveying information. These texts have their place and can be used for specific circumstances, but they should not be the *primary* type of texts used during the process of reading. Very often, they fail to provide students with the kind of connection essential for meaningful comprehension to take place, and this is crucial if students are going to learn critical thinking skills through their reading of and response to the texts. If basal readers are being used, they ought to be used in conjunction with other texts or stories, or they ought to be accompanied by response-oriented tasks that focus on the readers of the text, providing them with avenues for deeper levels of engagement with content.

The continued practice of reading based on Rosenblatt's "efferent stance" only and not activating the "aesthetic" stance also creates a serious challenge for the teacher and the student engaged in the process of reading. Unless the teacher makes the texts relatable, students will merely be encountering and responding to the words on a page. Their moments of reading are likely, therefore, to be restricted and based solely on the literal, with very limited access to the varied levels of meaning existing within the text. Ms. Gordon and Ms. Brissett spoke of the process of reading often being confined to occurring only during the "Drop Everything and Read" (D.E.A.R) hour that forms a part of the school's timetable. Ms. Gordon recalled

> being frustrated, and my frustration was largely because I, myself, didn't understand what was required. Like when it was quiet time for reading, everyone takes up a book and goes and sits down to read. There are very few children when you look at them who are genuinely reading. Whether or not they can read, . . . they are mostly looking at the pictures or scribbling in the books . . . and the truth is if they have the option, most of them would not take up the book.

Ironically, those who support the use of a traditional approach to the process of reading fail to recognize that the wide range of students' comprehension skills will not be accessed through this kind of approach. The focus on comprehension of which the teachers speak in the interview is extremely traditional and offers a limited experience of the meanings in a text for both teacher and student.

Most students will only be able to utilize comprehension skills that limit them to identifying, recalling, and regurgitating or restating information. It is not that comprehension questions have no value. It is that they should not be asked until the student has had an in-depth experience of the text. Furthermore, the kinds of comprehension questions assigned to a text also reflect the philosophy the entity has of the reading process. If the teacher has little or no knowledge or experience of the literary dimensions of the text, the situation worsens. This is the mode of learning initially described by Ms. Cherwood. The content focus here is primarily on information. Literary texts are not textbooks, however, written with the intention of merely presenting information. They were written for pleasure and entertainment and possess solid textual moments that provide avenues through which students can escape the boundaries of time and connect deeply with characters, situations, and geographical spaces. Children learn more when they are able to engage with the kind of "worlds" that literature offers, particularly

Caribbean children's literature, since they are easily able to identify with the characters, thematic concerns, and settings in these texts. Furthermore, there are actually textual elements in Caribbean children's literature that will resonate with young readers because they tend to be culturally specific and socially constructed.

It is not the presence of information that enables students to connect with texts. It is how students are introduced and empowered to interact with the texts. How we read, interpret, and respond to these texts form a significant part of the process needed to acquire meaning and to a great extent also determine the levels and kinds of meanings we discover. Children's responses to texts should be a major part of the process of teaching reading. In fact, meaning-making depends on the child's ability to make sense of and engage with the text. It is through their responses to the text that, as teachers, we can determine what they have acquired and understood about what they have read. It is also through the various ways they respond to any given text that the multiple layers of the text begin to surface. How we teach students to read will greatly influence how they in turn respond to the text during the process of reading. This will be discussed in the final section of this chapter.

Many teachers are completely unaware of the large number of Caribbean children's literature texts that exist. Caribbean children's texts are only minimally present in the primary classroom, and when they are present, they are predominantly used for the purposes of teaching and learning structural aspects of language, and for having students respond to comprehension-type questions.

Transforming the Reading Process through Caribbean Children's Literature in Jamaican Primary Schools

It is not that Caribbean children should only read Caribbean children's literature texts and avoid exposure to US and British texts. Caribbean children are more likely, however, to read and respond positively to texts that reflect their identity and culture. Interaction with these texts will enable them to produce scribal utterings and textual patterns that reflect the way they think, act, and communicate. It is key for educators to understand the way meaning is acquired. Meaning does not reside within the texts themselves but instead occurs through the transactional process outlined by Rosenblatt in

"The Literary Transaction," in which the reader comprehends the ideas in the text through his or her own personal experiences, contexts, and academic background. If we grasp what Rosenblatt argues, then we will understand why a focus on the mechanics of language and the ability of students to decode words and sentences will not bring about sustained, meaningful comprehension of any given text. It is not that we should skip over helping students pronounce letters and understand phonemic and syntactical patterns. This is necessary. It is problematic, however, when we leave out the literary dimension of the reading process and focus solely on these technical and structural elements. Centering the teaching and learning processes around "acts" of reading through time allotted for silent reading, read alouds, and answering a set number of "recall" comprehension questions will not be sufficient for helping students to acquire literacy and literary skills in a sustainable way, and will definitely not promote critical literacy or the building of analytical skills.

Internationally, advocates of the "Read Naturally" strategy and other educators consider five main factors as necessary for reading instruction to be considered effective and valuable: phonemic awareness, phonics, text comprehension, fluency, and vocabulary (Read Naturally). These can all be accomplished by actively engaging the child through a focus not solely on reading words, but also on reading about and responding to the worlds presented in texts. As Arda Arkian reminds us, when "students read for comprehension, they do not only comprehend the linguistic forms but they grab the facts, thoughts, and values implicitly as well as explicitly" (75). For the remainder of this chapter, I will focus on three possible "readings" of three Caribbean children's literature texts and demonstrate how engagement with these texts might enable students to experience reading, rather than robotically participate in "acts" of reading. The aim is to demonstrate the need for a balanced approach that fuses the literary and literacy spheres.

In *A Long Way from Home* (2014), Janet Plummer presents the experience of migration through the eyes of a child. Migration, a reality for many children in the Caribbean, plays a significant role in the formation of identity, the perception of the world the child has or will have, and the psychological and emotional realities the child will face when parents or families migrate. The text describes the fear a child experiences as her family separates in order to attain a better standard of living. At the beginning of the story, the child narrator states in a somewhat subdued tone: "We're leaving today. For good" (2). The jarring two-word sentence infuses a creolized way of speaking into the poetic narrative through the oral rhythmic pattern it establishes, and at the same time it immediately enables the child reader to access the depth of the emotional pain the narrator experiences. The narrator tries to remain strong despite the whirlwind of emotions brewing inside her, producing an opportunity for connection with the child reader. Teachers might ask students to highlight the words in the text that convey the idea that the child is feeling pain, and elements such as tone and mood (which play a crucial role in helping readers to interpret and comprehend the ideas present in a text) automatically become a part of this discussion or focus.

The syntax in this poetic narrative reflects a child's thought processes, and the sentence structures align with the child's feelings. The text is presented as a long narrative poem, enabling the reader to experience rhythm and rhyme, and a variety of textual language patterns and structures. Literary elements also help convey the feelings of the narrator as she moves from the "home" world she has known to a new world where there are "so many people, moving so fast!" (11). The presence of similes, metaphors, and onomatopoeic sentences in the text are couched within a context and so are easy to retain and reuse in other contexts. They are much better understood than if they were merely offered as a part of a word-recognition exercise. "We land with a thud!" (11) the narrator says when she uses onomatopoeia to describe the arrival of herself, her mother, and her sibling to the new country that they will now learn to call home. This drives home the harshness of the moment for the narrator, which can be used to help students understand the various ways in which the theme of departure or leaving home is being presented through the writer's style. And as the plane slows down, the narrator explains that her "legs feel like rubber" (11). She has already described the "large bundles of cotton wool" (9) she saw as they flew through the sky. Not only does this description produce a vicarious experience for the child, it also engages the reader with letter sounds, new vocabulary, and metaphoric uses of language and imagery in one brief moment of the reading process. This combination of factors makes the use of Caribbean children's literature in the Jamaican classroom such a powerful experience. By merging literacy with the literary, the child becomes a part of a reading experience that helps to build reading and comprehension skills not merely through reading instruction, but through natural ways of interacting with relatable textual content anchored in sociocultural events and realities.

When the child narrator feels anxious, the sentences become short—sometimes only a single word. This informs the reader's understanding of the process of "storying." The child reader can begin to absorb information about both reading and writing by seeing how the words and sentences on the page produce meanings through reading and interpretation. The teacher might provide students with an opportunity to put together their own words and place these in lines of different length to produce the kind of emotional response that occurs when the child reads the text. Reading at this point becomes an active experience that promotes the use of other skills while at the same time enabling the development of knowledge and abilities needed to demonstrate competence in the reading process. When conveying a mood of deep sadness, Plummer uses run-on sentences, and such sentences become long, drawn-out sets of lines. The effect, of course, is to powerfully convey the intensity of the sorrow experienced by the child narrator; the speech patterns embedded in the text directly connect to the Jamaican child's experience.

By engaging with both the literacy and the literary aspects of a text, students will not simply be able to recognize words and gain access to how they function in different types of sentences, but they will also be able to feel the kinds of emotions these words evoke. This allows students to engage fully in an experience rather than encountering reading as just an act. By facilitating opportunities for student responses to a text, the situation of reading becomes more purposeful and dynamic and less "boring"—no longer just a "text-focused" act—for both teachers and students. The more a child responds to a text, the more that child will gain from the text and the more he or she will comprehend, not only about the specific text in question but about other texts and how they function.

Diane Browne's children's story *Abigail's Glorious Hair* (2018), illustrated by Rachel H. Moss, also allows us to see the value of fusing literacy with the literary. The story celebrates the natural hair of a Black female Jamaican girl, who proclaims: "My hair is soft like my baby blanket and looks like hummocky clouds" (1). Abigail's little brother uses the word "poufy" to describe her hair. The book highlights the theme of identity, encouraging readers to interrogate stereotypical and European concepts of beauty and appearance imposed on Caribbean Black female children. Browne subverts these standards through her symbolic focus on Abigail's hair, and also through the characterization of a Caribbean family and their culturally motivated action. The ritual of a daughter retrieving a comb and brush and some hair oil, and sitting between her mother's knees awaiting the combing of her hair, is well known to Black female children in the Caribbean and the diaspora, as well as to Caribbean boys who observe this daily or weekly action. Abigail relates, "Mum sits on the big chair and I sit on the stool between her knees, snug and safe," (3) then pulling her brother into the moment, too, by declaring, "And my brother Jason, sits on the verandah steps.... I know it's to watch the combing of the glorious, poufy hair" (4). The Creole-influenced dialogue and tone play a significant role in engaging the child reader with varying uses of the language. For the Jamaican child, who lives in a bilingual culture and who struggles with thinking in Creole while being asked to respond in Standard English, the target language, this feature may be especially important. The linguistic patterns Browne inserts into the text allow different characters to express similar thoughts in different ways, thereby providing an opportunity for the child to realistically observe the translation of a Creole phrase or statement into a Standard English phrase or statement. For example, when Abigail recounts a situation in which her mother is combing her hair, Grandma says, "What a way this child has a lot of hair, eh. Just like me when I was little. You don't want to give me some, Abigail?" (5). This phrasing, though it contains Standard English structures, is creolized. Abigail's thoughts in response to her grandmother are represented in Standard English: "I grin. Grandma does not have a lot of hair anymore" (5). This tiny statement has two main functions: (1) it translates what the grandmother is asking her granddaughter, and (2) through Abigail's physical response—her grin—it offers the child reader the opportunity to understand the difference between literal meaning and a deeper meaning that lies behind the actual statement of the character (the grandmother does not actually want some of Abigail's hair; she is simply expressing the desire to be at a stage in life when she still had a lot of hair). Accessing meaning that goes beyond the literal is a major challenge for young readers at all levels, and so a text that provides the opportunity to help students both encounter and possibly resolve this comprehension challenge deserves serious consideration. This might sound like a minor factor, but it is quite significant when exploring the experience rather than the act of reading for a Caribbean child or a child from the Caribbean diaspora who thinks in two different languages, sometimes resulting in confusion when reading and responding to written texts.

Finally, Olive Senior's *Birthday Suit* (2012), illustrated by Eugenie Fernandes, serves as an example of a Caribbean children's literature text that can help to boost children's reading experiences by fusing together both literacy and the literary. This picture storybook tells the story of a little boy who loves running around naked but whose parents want him to wear clothes in public, as he is now growing up and is therefore "too old" for "running around with no clothes on." The theme of freedom and the right to access this freedom pervades the entire text, creatively connecting with the innocence of childhood and the power that resides in that innocence through Senior's presentation of the main character, four-year-old Johnny.

The story also highlights the importance of showing respect for children. This is especially important in Caribbean societies where often children are taught that they should be "seen and not heard." Although Johnny's mother explains that, because he is now four years old, he cannot go around without clothes, she can't seem to get through to him. He still desires and continues to play naked on the beach. His father, however, uses a somewhat different approach from merely insisting that he change his behavior because of his new age. He does not command Johnny but instead tactfully presents him with a proposition: "Come here, Son. Let's have a talk man to man. One fact of life is, big kids wear clothes when they're out in the great wide world. Do you want to be big like Dad?" This approach works not simply because it is his father who has spoken, but more because of what Johnny is able to imagine through how his father has engaged him in conversation. The idea of negotiation as a part of parenting in the Caribbean household is a novel but relevant one. As Caribbean societies begin to address the treatment of children in a more serious manner due to occurrences of abusive behavior in the region, Senior's picture book raises our level of consciousness on the topic and provides a possible way forward through conversation that causes the child to feel empowered while simultaneously offering guidance and protection from parents. In Senior's book, the mother is not at all being abusive, but her method of instruction is simply not effective. Instead of continuing with what is clearly not working, the father provides an alternative and effective approach to solving the problem. The question the father poses gives the child a chance to decide for himself and to see his father's position alongside his own feelings and thoughts as a child. Whereas his mother's approach caused him to feel suffocated and oppressed by the thought of being restricted by clothing, his father's approach offers him a whole different world where he can see clothes in a way that creates a new role and identity for him, one that he relishes: "Johnny looks way, way, way up at his dad, and thinks that almost touching the ceiling isn't such a bad thing. For if he grew that tall he'd be able to pick the ripest mangoes at the top of the tree without ever using a stick." The third-person omniscient narrator allows the reader access to the mind of the child, so we recognize the moment Johnny begins to change his mind about wearing clothes. By allowing Johnny to conceptualize the positive aspects of growing older, his father has allowed him to shift his perspective and strike a balance. Teachers could develop literary competence through this book in a variety of ways. For example, the teacher could promote visual literacy, and literary analysis and interpretation, through this picture book by allowing children to identify and explain the facial expressions and images that are associated with the different emotions of the main character. This can be done through the use of a collage, a chart, or a graphic organizer. The teacher could also place a copy of a facial expression on the board and have each student affix a happy, sad, or angry face on the image to help them identify and talk about the emotions of the characters. Students could also examine pictures of different symbols in the book that help readers understand when Johnny feels free or when he feels trapped. Discussions or small talking moments could easily occur through these tasks to help students understand things they might look for when they open a picture book. Here, the teacher develops a sense of literariness in the students based on what he or she requires them to do. The students will learn not simply through what they are hearing but through what they are doing. Different activities could be appropriated for different levels of learners, but the focus would remain the same.

Plummer's narrative in *A Long Way from Home* utilizes long sentences (through the use of short, line-after-line visual presentations of words) that reflect the way a child thinks and speaks. The rhythm is fast paced but slow enough to capture and showcase an enormous amount of emotions and ideas all at once. This stylistic feature reflects the child's consciousness as thoughts float in and out quickly. The use of this feature by certain Jamaican children's literature writers extends the usual use of orality by international writers of picture books by also including one of the characteristics of Kamau Brathwaite's "nation language," in which the orality of the text enables the fusion of Standard English and Jamaican Creole in the narrative. Because Jamaica predominantly uses basal readers or texts from Great Britain and the US, we have become accustomed to a specific type of text that utilizes Standard English in a particular way. Most Jamaican children do not speak Standard English only, however, and so both word recognition and fluency, when reading texts that utilize Standard English (possessing tone, intonation, vocabulary, and accented patterns of speech associated with a "foreign" culture), are more difficult to retain and comprehend, especially for struggling readers. In *A Long Way from Home*, a Jamaican-creolized way of speaking merges with a voice that also utilizes Standard English vocabulary, syntax, and phonemes. Plummer thus allows Jamaican children to hear their mother tongue merge with the target language in a way other "foreign" texts are unable to do. Plummer's narrative presents the story line through distinct cadences aligned with the Jamaican storytelling experience.

A Long Way from Home does not only offer the visual script on the page; it also provides textual patterns of language that appeal to the auditory senses, helping to create familiarity with the varieties of sound connected to the words on the page. When the child narrator becomes submerged in the anxiety of leaving all that is familiar to her, the narrative introduces us to this Standard English–Jamaican Creole fusion: "The ground falls away," she expresses through her thoughts, "*like when* Junior drives really fast downhill" (15; italics added). It is a simple insertion that one might miss, but it is a common Jamaican Creole phrase used to indicate that what will follow is an example of what was stated previously. This language situation subtly presents itself again as the child considers whether her mother could fly a plane: "*Wonder* if she could drive a plane . . . *I mean* fly a plane" (8; italics added). Although Plummer has used English spelling to present the word "Wonder" and the phrase "I mean," the Caribbean child who is familiar with the sound of their Creole tongue would easily recognize the syntactical patterns here as reflective of typical and simple ways of speaking using the Creole language. The omission of the pronoun "I" is a common characteristic of the start of a Jamaican Creole sentence. Similarly, although the words "I mean" seem to be a simple use of Standard English, a Jamaican child would pick up on those two words as forming part of a popular Jamaican Creole phrase used to indicate the speaker's intention of clarifying what has been said or is being stated. These seemingly simple stylistic features provide important opportunities for both teachers and students in the Caribbean classroom. Through a dual focus on both literacy and the literary in the primary classroom, therefore, Caribbean children's literature texts enable a powerful and dynamic experience of reading for children that will help motivate them to read and introduce them to various avenues through which to encounter, engage with, and respond to reading.

It is important that we help children not simply to read words, but to be better able to interpret and respond to the thoughts and ideas being conveyed by words through the meaningful connections they will make in the process of reading. As teachers and educators, we must approach the teaching and use of literary texts in ways that enable this dynamic experience, in which children meet the worlds inside of and around them, as they establish connection with the words they read. By utilizing a response-oriented, active learning approach to reading and by utilizing Caribbean children's literature texts in Caribbean classrooms, both teachers and students will be able to access greater and more in-depth dimensions connected with the process of reading. To be literate will no longer simply refer to the ability to read words and sentences fluently, and will no longer be tied to classist and racist ideas that use acts of reading as indicators of a certain kind of colonial identity and as the premise on which acceptance and status are handed out. Instead, the blending of the literary experience with literacy through Caribbean children's literature will help to create child readers who celebrate their Afro-Caribbean identity and heritage, and who are profoundly transformed by each experience they have with a children's book, not simply because the book exists but because both the pedagogical approach to reading and the text selection are centered on enabling moments of connection that will then be used to construct competent, skilled readers, whatever their age or circumstances.

Works Cited

Arkian, Arda. "Topics of Reading Passages in ELT Coursebooks: What Do Our Students Really Read?" *Reading Matrix*, vol. 8, no. 2, September 2008, pp. 70–85.

Bland, Janice. *Children's Literature and Learner Empowerment: Children and Teenagers in English Language Education*. Bloomsbury Academic, 2013.

Brathwaite, Edward Kamau. *History of the Voice: The Development of Nation Language in Anglophone Caribbean Poetry*. New Beacon Books, 1984.

Browne, Diane. *Abigail's Glorious Hair*. Illustrated by Rachel H. Moss, Blue Banyan Books, 2018.

Bryan, Beverley. *Between Two Grammars: Research and Practice for Language Learning and Teaching in a Creole-Speaking Environment*. Ian Randle Publishers, 2010.

Cambridge Assessment. "What Is Literacy? An Investigation into Definitions of English as a Subject and the Relationship between English, Literacy and 'Being Literate.'" January 2013. https://www.cambridgeassessment.org.uk/Images/130433-what-is-literacy-an-investigation-into-definitions-of-english-as-a-subject-and-the-relationship-between-english-literacy-and-being-literate-.pdf.

Craig, Dennis R. *Teaching Language and Literacy to Caribbean Students: From Vernacular to Standard English*. Ian Randle Publishers, 2006.

Darder, Antonia, Marta P. Baltodano, and Rodolfo D. Torres. "Critical Pedagogy: An Introduction." *The Critical Pedagogy Reader*, 2nd ed., edited by Antonia Darder, Marta P. Baltodano, and Rodolfo D. Torres, Routledge, 2008, pp. 1–21.

Devonish, Hubert. *Language and Liberation: Creole Language Politics in the Caribbean*. Karia Press, 1986.

Freire, Paulo. *Pedagogy of the Oppressed*. Continuum, 2007.

Huggins, Sujin. *How Did We Get Here? An Examination of the Collection of Contemporary Caribbean Juvenile Literature in the Children's Library of the National Library of Trinidad and Tobago and Trinidadian Children's Responses to Selected Titles*. 2012. U of Illinois, PhD dissertation.

James, Cynthia. "The Status of Literature in Six Types of Trinidad Secondary Schools: Issues, Implications, and Recommendations." *Caribbean Curriculum*, vol. 10, 2003, pp. 1–36.

Kravis, Judy. *Teaching Literature: Writers and Teachers Talking*. Cork UP, 1995.

Milner, Joseph O'Beirne, and Lucy Floyd Morcock Milner. *Bridging English*. Pearson Education, 2008.

Ministry of Education, Youth, and Information, Government of Jamaica. "Grade 3: National Standards Curriculum Guide; Integrated Science/Language Arts/Mathematics." 2018. https://pep.moey.gov.jm/grade-3-national-standards-curriculum-guide-integrated-science-language-arts-mathematics/.

Montoya, Silvia. "Defining Literacy." UNESCO Institute for Statistics, October 17–18, 2018. http://gaml.uis.unesco.org/wp-content/uploads/sites/2/2018/12/4.6.1_07_4.6-defining-literacy.pdf.

Natov, Roni. *The Poetics of Childhood*. Routledge, 2003.

Norton, Donna E. *Through the Eyes of a Child: An Introduction to Children's Literature*. 8th ed., Pearson Education, 2010.

Plummer, Janet. *A Long Way from Home*. WestBow Press, 2014.

Read Naturally. "Essential Components of Reading." https://www.readnaturally.com/research/5-components-of-reading.

Rosenblatt, Louise M. "The Literary Transaction: Evocation and Response." *Theory into Practice*, vol. 21, no. 4, Autumn 1982, pp. 268–77.

Rosenblatt, Louise M. *Literature as Exploration*. 5th ed., Modern Language Association of America, 1995.

Senior, Olive. *Birthday Suit*. Illustrated by Eugenie Fernandes, Annick Press, 2012.

Sheridan, E. Marcia. "Theories of Reading and Implications for Teachers." *Reading Horizons*, vol. 22, no. 1, October 1981, pp. 66–71.

Spencer, Aisha. "'Breaking the Mirror': Reshaping Perceptions of National Progress through the Representation of Marginalized Cultural Realities in Caribbean Children's Stories." *The Routledge Companion to International Children's Literature*, edited by John Stephens with Celia Abicalil Belmiro, Alice Curry, Li Lifang, and Yasmine S. Motawy, Routledge, 2018, pp. 114–22.

CHAPTER 12

Seriously!

Reading and Righting Images of the Caribbean in the American Classroom

Consuella Bennett

Statistics from the US-based Migration Policy Institute indicate that in 2017, of the 44.5 million immigrants who resided in the US, approximately 4.4 million or 10 percent were from the Caribbean. This heavy presence also makes the US the top destination for Caribbean migrants (Zong and Batalova). But outside of being the number one destination of choice for Caribbean migrants, the US has had a strong presence in the Caribbean region since the nineteenth century. In the decades subsequent to implementing the Monroe Doctrine in 1823, the US was successful in controlling islands such as Cuba, Haiti, the Dominican Republic, Puerto Rico, and the US Virgin Islands, making them into protectorates (Cwik). In fact, except for Jamaica, all major Caribbean nations were once under direct US political control (Zong and Batalova). Generally regarded as a subregion of North America, the Caribbean should carry much significance for the US; yet, despite this proximity and the heavy presence of Caribbean immigrants in the US, little, if anything, is taught about the Caribbean (or the rest of the world) in US schools. David Rutherford, a specialist in geography education at the National Geographic Society, comments, "Young Americans just don't seem to have much interest in the world outside of the U.S." (qtd. in Roach). In fact, most states do not require geography courses in schools, according to a *US News & World Report* article on US students' performance in geography (Camera).

Americans who know about the Caribbean usually gain their knowledge through their experiences as tourists, and even then, fewer use the toponym *Caribbean*, referring instead to the geographical area as "the islands." In fact, most Americans associate the Caribbean with only a few islands, with stereotypical representations—Jamaica (reggae, Bob Marley, and beaches), the Bahamas (beaches and casinos), Cuba (communism), Haiti (poverty and natural disasters), the Dominican Republic (beaches and baseball), the Cayman Islands (beaches). Given Americans' limited knowledge of the region, often they mistakenly identify other Caribbean islanders as Jamaicans because of either their appearance or their accent. While people from the Caribbean, especially those from the Lesser Antilles, find this ignorance of Caribbean geography and linguistics mildly irritating (Inniss; Jones), we resent more the stereotypes and myths that so readily reduce us to sea, sun, and service. One myth widely held of the Caribbean purports that the "natives" do not work but enjoy incessant fun and frolic—what Bahamian author and scholar Ian Strachan describes as "accumulated leisure, [and] excessive freedom from toil" (83). These assumptions beg the question: who or what is responsible for this reductive concept of Caribbean life?

Many Americans form images of the Caribbean during childhood through children's programs such as *Sesame Street*. The children's classic "Caribbean Amphibian" sung by the character Kermit the Frog (Saltzman), for example, embodies in general terms an outsider's view of the Caribbean—a region of exotic islands. Kermit's cousin, according to the song, lives on a tropical island that has a "mango moon," "banana sunshine," and "soft Caribbean sand." Sometimes the "Caribbean Amphibian" climbs a coconut tree, or sometimes he island-hops from Jamaica to Haiti and finally to "a warm Puerto Rico beach." The lyrics of this song conjure images of a Caribbean topography that is inaccurately and unattainably idyllic. Good intentions aside, Kermit's song embodies the skewed information fed to American children. They thus begin to formulate idealistic (and therefore misleading) concepts of the Caribbean even before they begin formal education, since parents and teachers often use *Sesame Street* to stimulate preschoolers' learning. *Sesame Street* markets itself as "bridg[ing] many cultural and educational gaps with a fun program," and we applaud them for this effort, but no country or region, not the least the Caribbean, can live up to the paradisiacal ideals described in this song.

In the classic 1989 children's animated film *The Little Mermaid* (Musker and Clements), Sebastian, supposedly a Jamaican crab, sings "Under the Sea" (more like "unda da sea") to a calypso beat (Ashman and Menken). The song, performed by Samuel E. Wright, won an Academy Award for Best Original Song in 1989 and a Grammy Award for Best Song Written for Visual Media in 1991. Both the song and the character, Sebastian, however, convey stock representations of the Caribbean as a place where music and jollity are the order of the day, absent of sadness even in the face of impending adversity and doom. While others work hard all day, those under the sea are "devotin' full time to floatin'," and "all the fish is happy" because they "got no troubles." Children may view this film as a true representation of Caribbean culture and people.

Launched in 2003, the very popular *Pirates of the Caribbean* film series, watched by older children and adults, further represents warped images of the Caribbean, though at a more mature level. Despite being set in the Caribbean for the most part, the series includes no significant Caribbean characters—except for Tia Dalma in *Pirates of the Caribbean: Dead Man's Chest* (2006) and *Pirates of the Caribbean: At World's End* (2007). Sly and chameleonesque, Tia Dalma, played by the British actor Naomie Harris, speaks with an acquired Jamaican accent and practices obeah and voodoo. Likened to the goddess Calypso, she is elusive and inviting, enchanting and devious, while being beautiful and hideous all at once, no doubt designed to mirror another perception of the Caribbean as a place of grace and beauty, as well as a place of charming mysticism. Combining all these descriptors, the media often repackages the Caribbean region as "paradise," a word associated with, according to Strachan, primitivism, innocence, and perpetual sunshine and leisure (5). Without a doubt, the media often presents images of the Caribbean that are selectively homogeneous and deceptively inauthentic.

We must admit, however, that the outsider's perception of the Caribbean is partly shaped by the region's desperation to market and sell itself. The outside world—mainly tourists and investors in tourism—always demand what they imagine of the Caribbean. And those at the political and economic helm, in their urgency for economic gains, have expanded and marketed this Caribbean "paradise" as a place where untold experiences can be had by foreign bodies who come bearing cash. Strachan contends that advertisements promise "[b]acchic release . . . eternal youth, sexual adventurism . . . and partying" (1). He adds that these advertisements often contain scenes that middle-class Americans and Europeans want to see of "the islands" (1). These images of the Caribbean repetitively surface on television and the internet, in brochures and posters. Nobel laureate Derek Walcott, in his Nobel acceptance speech, describes the relationship between visitor and islander in more scathing terms:

> This is how the islands from the shame of necessity sell themselves; this is the seasonal erosion of their identity, that high-pitched repetition of the same images of service that cannot distinguish one island from the other, with a future of polluted marinas, land deals negotiated by ministers, and all of this conducted to the music of Happy Hour and the rictus of a smile. What is this earthly paradise for our visitors? Two weeks without rain and a mahogany tan, and at sunset, local troubadours in straw hats and floral shirts beating "Yellow Bird" and "Banana Boat Song" to death.

Caribbean hosts have not simply offered the islands in exchange for their economic survival, but historically they have taught the region the art of pandering for pennies. Rendered negotiable, Caribbean cultures can be easily adjusted, reshaped, or even sold to the highest bidder. For example, in his research on the history of the Jamaican tourist industry, historian Frank Fonda Taylor describes the "gigolo psyche" (172) in which there is always the hint of sexual exchange as a reciprocal act for tourist dollars, in language such as "Love Bird," the nickname of Air Jamaica, the former national carrier. Advertisers have also described the island as a "virginal *je ne sais quoi*" (Taylor 172), a combination of an English word with a French phrase suggestive of unknown allure, an unsullied and indescribable experience for visitors. Often, visitors do not care to know that "paradise" experiences poverty, political upheaval, and natural disasters. No, they will not pay for abject reality. So the Caribbean, aiming to please, sells itself through "brilliant vacuity" (Walcott). Paradise, then, is a myth designed "to cloud a . . . painful reality often mythologized" (Strachan 3). Certainly, a culture pliable and malleable for the convenience of the outsider will continue to be an experience on demand for a price. The image of the Caribbean, then, has resulted in part from the transactional encounters of the region with outsiders who are willing and able to pay for the fantasies they themselves create.

How, then, do we change or repair this view of the Caribbean as an exotic but primitive paradise, these images that have been etched in the American psyche? What is more, given the significant presence of Caribbean immigrants in the US, and given the proximity of the two geographic regions and the technological advancement that has created an increasingly interconnected global community, what can and should be done to present more culturally accurate images of the Caribbean in the US? This chapter posits that positive and accurate images of the Caribbean in the US can be achieved through education—focusing on instructional practices that address diversity in cultures and, through democratization, provide relevant materials to facilitate growth in literacy and cultural awareness.

The Case for Presenting Accurate Images of the Caribbean in American Schools

The Nigerian novelist Chimamanda Ngozi Adichie captures the effects of a monolithic, univocal approach to literature in her 2009 TED Talk entitled "The Danger of a Single Story." In this presentation, Adichie uses her early relationship with books while growing up in Nigeria to illustrate her point. At the age of four, when she started reading, all the storybooks available to her were authored by British or American writers who (understandably) wrote about their local culture and landscape. When Adichie started writing at age seven, she wrote exactly the kinds of stories that she had read—about characters playing in the snow, eating apples, and talking a lot about the weather. Seeing no reflection of herself in books, she had formulated a "single story" of herself and her people and culture; hence, she did not know that people who look like her could be characters in literature. Adichie emphasizes how impressionable and vulnerable we are, especially as children influenced by the stories we read.

Educational researchers Jocelyn Glazier and Jung-A Seo observe that the curricula in American schools tend to "privilege students from the dominant culture while excluding and often disconfirming the experiences of subordinate groups" (687). Therefore, our schools, by their very design, have been facilitating and promoting the "single story." For a student of a minority group, such as those from the Caribbean, the single story affects identity formation. In the absence of written texts from one's culture, one generally resorts to embracing and celebrating the dominant culture, and by the same process diminishing and discounting one's own cultural heritage. But the single story also affects those in the dominant American culture, creating cultural myopia and robbing them of exposure to a world broader than the one their own culture frames them in. The answer to the problem of insularity and exclusiveness in schools therefore lies in making important and necessary adjustments to curriculum content and teaching practice.

Our first step is to see and treat the classroom as a democratic space. Writer and educator bell hooks observes that "no education is politically neutral" (37). Our teaching philosophy and methodology, for example, invariably reflect our politics of race and culture. Any attempt to be inclusive and accurately represent different cultures must be achieved through deliberate efforts to challenge cultural hegemony that privileges certain cultures above others. Noted professor and author Steven Wolk emphasizes the importance of stories in the middle-grade and young adult classrooms to teach what he calls a "caring and critical democracy" (45). The democratic classroom prepares students beyond reading or passing tests to molding them into responsible citizens who "understand the global diversity of people and cultures" (49–50). More specifically, Wolk contends that the American school should have the primary aim of educating children and young adults to "participate in the ongoing pursuit of a more caring and thoughtful society and a more harmonious world" (45). In essence, students in the democratic classroom use books as modes of inquiry into concerns beyond their personal lives to interrogate their society and the world. The democratic classroom, therefore, is all-inclusive and explorative, allowing all students to feel included and important, and seeking to present unbiased and accurate representations of diverse cultures.

A democratic classroom will invariably be a multicultural classroom. This space nourishes, sensitizes, and educates students of all backgrounds. Susan Landt, a teacher and specialist in adolescent and children's literature, adds that multicultural literature gives students a broader view of the world by serving as a bridge to other cultures. Diverse literatures also serve to interrupt prejudice and misunderstanding, helping students to see themselves reflected in the books that they read ("Multicultural Literature" 691–95). As with all other cultures, students of Caribbean backgrounds, particularly those newly immigrated to the US and in cultural transition, need to see themselves represented in their reading materials (Malcolm and Lowery 46). The answer, therefore, lies in using culturally diverse or multicultural literature, which helps children become aware of their own cultures and those of others. Susan Colby and Anna Lyon posit that not only do literatures of diverse cultures motivate students to read, but also they "help students better understand the principles of tolerance, inclusiveness, diversity, and respect for all" (27). A school that intentionally selects literary texts that appeal to diverse cultures has taken a bold step to reduce stereotypes and misleading ideas of said cultures.

If students' ability to become proficient readers impinges on their making connections with what they read, then, clearly white children are positioned at an advantage to be better readers, since, generally, the books they read disproportionately represent their culture(s). Literacy expert Jane Gangi clarifies that white children can make many more "text-to-self, text-to-text, and text-to-world" (30) connections through the texts that the teacher or school often chooses. While students need a variety of literature that will stimulate their imagination and improve their knowledge of the world, they also need to see themselves as part of human experiences and possibilities. Renowned multicultural educator Rudine Sims Bishop employs the metaphors of "mirror" and "window" books to explain the effects of literature on the student. According to Bishop, "Books are sometimes windows, offering views of worlds that may be real or imagined, familiar, or strange." These windows "can also be . . . mirror[s]" in that "[l]iterature transforms human experiences and reflects it back to us, and in that reflection, we can see our own lives and experiences as part of the larger human experience. Reading, then, becomes a means of self-affirmation, and readers often seek their mirrors in books." Gangi reinforces that whereas both "mirror" and "window" books produce well-rounded readers, it is in reading the "mirror" books that proficient reading starts (30). The problem generally faced by students of a minority group, especially lesser-known ones like those from the Caribbean, is that books chosen by teachers seldom mirror their experiences and cultures; hence they often grapple with contents that alienate them and, by the same process, diminish the importance of their culture.

For students from the Caribbean, the dilemma of exclusion lies deeper than for other students of color. Examining book lists that purport to support diversity, one often sees lists arranged in the following categories: African American, Latino/Latina, Asian and Pacific Island American, Native American, and Arab American.[1] Often, no mention is made of Caribbean writers, and we cannot address and cater to those whom we fail to acknowledge. This, therefore, means that teachers of Caribbean students must work doubly hard to integrate these students into the American classroom. And those who simply want to diversify the literature read in the classroom by presenting authentic Caribbean texts must be aware that if Caribbean texts are rarely highlighted as genres of children's and young adult literature, then as a corollary, authentic, well-written texts will be more challenging to find.

The Teacher's Task: The Culturally Responsive Approach

Much of the responsibility for creating positive and accurate images of the Caribbean rests with the classroom teacher, who must employ the cultural-response approach to avoid implementing a pedagogy of exclusion. The culturally responsive approach is based on the premise that "race and class matter, and . . . some schools fail to send diverse students signals that they belong," according to Sophie Quinton of the *Atlantic*. To ensure that all students feel valued, teachers need to examine their own biases, work intentionally to understand their students as individuals, find ways to incorporate students' culture and community into the classroom, and hold all students to a high academic standard (Quinton). One of the first challenges the teacher faces lies with getting to know the sociocultural background of Caribbean students; with islands as diverse as their cultures, this background must include knowledge of the geography of the Caribbean region. We cannot fully engage our students when we homogenize their backgrounds, which often results in our creating social mythologies about them that can never accommodate their needs. Apart from the teacher's own research in the geography, history, and culture of their students' home countries, education writer Nick Woolf suggests the "Two-by-Ten strategy," in which the teacher takes two minutes out of the day for ten consecutive days to simply sit, talk to, and learn about a student. This approach creates an atmosphere of comfort and acceptance for students from minority cultures such as those from the Caribbean.

Teachers should also know the linguistic background of their students. I must underscore here that language awareness is inexorably linked to cultural awareness and to a culturally responsive classroom. The philosopher and educator Paulo Freire and his coauthor, linguist Donaldo Macedo, posit that "language is culture" (5), that is, the concrete entity that conveys knowledge into what we express as words. In essence, our students' language conveys who they are more than does any other aspect of their persona. For the multicultural classroom to be effective and democratic, students must be able to engage in both oral and written discourse. Students from the

English-speaking Caribbean islands, for example, generally migrate from countries with widely spoken English-based creoles. Quinton reminds us that while "[t]eachers need to help students speak and write in Standard English . . . they'll be more successful in that effort if they begin by respecting the way a student and his family speak at home." Too often, teachers perceive students from the Caribbean as severely deficient and having diminished learning capacities because they bring with them dialectal differences. Teachers must therefore cultivate positive language attitudes that embrace students' diverse languages; this includes English-based creoles. I am using this language group as an example, because at least eighteen countries in the Caribbean (of twenty-six total) employ English as their official language, and the same number use English-based creoles as home codes. Teachers should use culturally responsive language, that is, incorporate their students' language, where possible, to foster inclusiveness and acceptance of the students' cultures and, when culturally relevant texts are being discussed, create a greater depth of understanding and appreciation of the text.

One must applaud the New York State Education Department, for example, for producing the *Resource Guide for the Education of New York State Students from Caribbean Countries Where English Is the Medium of Instruction*. This document provides an "overview of the cultural and linguistic background of Caribbean English Creole-speaking (CEC) students" (Ruiz, Latortue, and Rosefort v). It also identifies linguistic features of Creole languages that can affect these students' learning American English. The document further provides information on the social history of the Caribbean countries, along with "contemporary considerations" impacting Caribbean English Creole-speaking students and their parents (v).

Apart from the creoles spoken as home codes, teachers must begin to understand the issue of dialectal differences or language variation as it pertains to the different Englishes spoken by students from the different Caribbean countries. Often, teachers become purveyors of what linguist Paul Kei Matsuda calls the "myth of linguistic homogeneity" in insisting that students speak in the American dialect of English with the assumption that standard Jamaican English, for example, is inferior to Standard American English. Noted scholars in education Jacqueline Jordan Irvine and Willis D. Hawley emphasize the importance of teachers' use of students' differences in race, ethnicity, culture, and language to enrich their teaching to facilitate learning in the multicultural classroom (1). Knowledge of and exposure to the linguistic backgrounds of students from the Caribbean will no doubt help teachers to better understand, appreciate, and teach Caribbean texts, and provide some theoretical framework from which to adequately engage all students in the multicultural classroom.

Once teachers begin to understand their students' backgrounds, they can proceed to appropriately and effectively address what is read and discussed in class. While one school of thought contends that the teacher should discuss literature that features diverse cultures only if the class includes students matching the cultures that the text features, I agree with Landt's position that all students benefit when literature "represents the range of individuals both in and outside of our classrooms" ("Children's Literature" 21). Reading and "righting" images of the Caribbean, then, should not be left solely to the schools or classrooms with Caribbean students. Yu Ren Dong suggests using the text as "a cultural artifact" (56) through which students who are inside or outside the culture represented can learn of and appreciate its diverse features. The teacher, however, with careful preparation, will find additional resources in journals, magazines, videos, and other works to complement the text, thus facilitating greater depth of critical access. Where possible, the teacher should utilize what are called "cultural insiders"—students (or guest speakers) from the culture under study—who act as resources, and from whom the class can gain other perspectives on issues raised in the text (Dong 57). The culturally responsive classroom facilitates open and healthy discussions on racial and cultural differences implied or stated in the text. With knowledge of Caribbean cultures, for example, the practitioner can direct the class in critical reading that will eventually challenge stereotypes held of the minority group.

The challenge therefore lies not only in recognizing the need for culturally diverse literature but also in choosing texts. The questions below, condensed from Landt's larger list, have proven helpful as guidelines for choosing culturally diverse literature:

- What are the author's qualifications to write about the culture?
- From whose perspective is the story told?
- What connections might the students make to this story?
- Are the characters part of society and not depicted as outsiders?
- Are the characters portrayed as individuals, not generic representations of culture?

- Are the situations realistic and not perpetuating stereotypes?
- Are problems and conflicts solved by individuals from within the culture rather than by individuals from outside it?
- Is the plot respectful of all cultures involved? ("Children's Literature" 23–24)

The following books written by Caribbean authors, given the use of cultural-response techniques in the classroom, will convey positive images of the Caribbean, make Caribbean students feel more included in the American educational system, and make all other students—and teachers—more culturally aware of the Caribbean region. In evaluating each text below, I have condensed Landt's criteria above into seven categories: author's qualification, point of view, students' connection to the story, authenticity of action and characters, absence of stereotypes, problems solved by individuals within the culture, and whether the plot is respectful of all cultures involved.

Evaluation of Andrew Salkey's *Hurricane* (1964)

(Ages Twelve and Up)[2]

When asked about her favorite overlooked or underheralded writer, British writer Zadie Smith (of Jamaican ancestry) mentioned the Jamaican author Andrew Salkey, who wrote the young adult book *Hurricane*, which sparked her interest in writing. Few readers outside of the Caribbean know about Salkey. His novel *Hurricane* is even less known outside of the region, but it embodies, nevertheless, one of the best Caribbean narratives written for the adolescent and early teen. Born in Panama to Jamaican parents, Salkey (1928–1995) spent his early years in Jamaica but later moved to England before finally settling in the US. He authored more than thirty books, including novels for adults and children. While in England, Salkey, as Karen Sands-O'Connor notes, formed part of "the Windrush generation of writers who began producing literature for the children of immigrants struggling to fit into and make sense of British society." Hailed as a pioneer in the establishment of West Indian children's literature, Salkey has the distinction of being the first West Indian to publish children's books with a major British publisher; his disaster novels (*Hurricane*, *Earthquake* [1965], *Drought* [1966], and *Riot* [1967]) were all published by Oxford University Press (Sands-O'Connor).

Hurricane captures the characters' range of emotions during a hurricane—from skepticism to preparation, from fear and suspense to disaster. Using Landt's list of evaluation criteria as a (condensed) guide, the teacher can effectively and comfortably teach this text in the American classroom.

a) Author's qualification: Salkey, a Jamaican who lived and taught in Britain, also taught in the US from 1976 until his death in 1995. This indicates that, although Salkey grew up in the Caribbean, he also had a world view that adds international appeal to his work.

b) Point of view: Thirteen-year-old Joe (Joseph Nathaniel Brown) narrates the story with all the range of emotions and naïveté of a boy living in Kingston, Jamaica.

c) Students' connection to the story: Most students in the US may not have direct experience with a hurricane, but they would have heard about it as a phenomenon recurring in southern US states, especially Florida, Texas, and Louisiana. Many can also compare a hurricane experience to being in tornadoes and severe storms. With its dominant themes of fear, change, and uncertainty, the text enables students, especially immigrants, to explore their fear about sudden changes of physical environment due to natural disasters or displacement. The story, ending with the almost complete destruction of the protagonist's family's new house in Harbour View, Kingston, represents an objective reality for life in the Caribbean. American students can relate to the changes that a hurricane brings, but Caribbean students can add the dimension of teaching students of other cultures about the role of the community in rebuilding an area damaged by a natural disaster. Typically, in the US, when buildings sustain damage during a natural event, most homeowners can petition their insurance companies to pay for the restoration and/or repair of the building/property. In the Caribbean, many householders do not have homeowner's insurance. In most cases, owners must finance repairs or rely on relatives abroad to help. Through differences such as these, Caribbean students can feel empowered as cultural insiders to teach the rest of the class.

d) Authenticity of action and characters: The members of the Brown family (Joe, his sister, and their parents) and friends all display behavior typical of Jamaican middle-class families living in Kingston. Children look forward to visiting relatives in rural areas, teenagers visit the movie theater for entertainment, and the threat of natural disaster often interrupts the calm of family life. Folk elements, additionally, add to the authenticity of the work. Amid the narration in Standard English, Salkey inserts elements of Jamaican Creole speech such as "cho" (slang used to express disgust, frustration, or annoyance, or to entice a desired reaction) and "bangarangs" (confusion and conflict resulting in an uproar, fight, or disturbance) to create distinct linguistic features of the work. The text also features Jamaican cuisine: ackee and saltfish, rice and peas, and mangoes. *Hurricane* additionally highlights the ubiquitous prophetess of doom, in this case Mother Samuel, who portends nothing but damnation for unrepentant evildoers. The "Mother" or "Madda" in common parlance, a quasi-spiritual being, figures prominently in Jamaican culture. She often speaks of her ability to evoke the wrath of supernatural forces, thus inducing at once fear and mockery from her audience.

e) Absence of stereotypes: Countering popular beliefs that most Jamaican households are headed by a female, Salkey chooses to create a Jamaican middle-class nuclear family in which the father heads the household. The text also excludes the preoccupation with eking out an existence, a theme often seen in the literature of the Caribbean. Rather, Salkey presents conflicts with external forces—the family versus nature.

f) Problems solved by individuals within the culture: The hurricane is forecast by the local meteorology office, and the intermittent updates and preparations are all done by locals, who will later face the responsibility of repairing the damage done.

g) Plot respectful of all cultures involved: The plot highlights one cultural group—Black Jamaicans. Salkey mentions subgroups such as relatives in rural Jamaica who often display some difference in cultural habits in contrast to city dwellers such as the Brown family. Mother Samuel belongs to another subgroup of local spiritualists. In all cases, the writer depicts all groups with respect and authenticity.

Evaluation of Tracey Baptiste's *The Jumbies* (2015)

(Ages Nine and Up)

Tracey Baptiste, author of *The Jumbies*, was born and raised in Trinidad but now lives in the US. A former elementary school teacher, Baptiste now teaches at Lesley University, Cambridge, Massachusetts, in the MFA in Creative Writing program. The text, though contemporary, identifies with the genre of fantasy fiction deeply rooted in the culture of Trinidad. The main character, eleven-year-old Corinne La Mer, fearless and tomboyish, must call on her hidden powers when she discovers a plot by the jumbies to destroy the islanders or to control and convert them into jumbies. Baptiste describes a jumbie as "the name of every bad-thinking, sneaky, trick-loving creature that comes out at night with the purpose of causing trouble" (232).

a) Author's qualification: The dedication page of *The Jumbies* reads in part: "And to all the children of the Caribbean (no matter your age). See, you have fairy tales too." This indicates Baptiste's mission to showcase Trinidadian folktales, thus legitimizing and chronicling them for posterity. In an address entitled "Telling the Untold Stories" given at Lesley University, Baptiste expresses concern that only one-fifth of children's books feature characters of color, and among those books, less than half are written by authors of that race or culture. Baptiste concludes that "every storyteller may have the power to affect a universal consciousness, but not everyone gets to tell their story."

b) Point of view: The third-person narration develops the character of Corinne, who gains strength and overcomes her opponents because of her tenacity and willingness to tap into the resources available to her as a half-jumbie. Students can relate to this story as they see similarities with sci-fi heroes such as Thor and Superman who live as "normal" human beings but do, in fact, possess superpowers, based on their lineage.

c) Students' connection to the story: *The Jumbies* depicts universal themes that appeal to all audiences—the importance of courage, the triumph of good over evil, concern for others, and family bonds. While this story enriches the culture of the Caribbean student, it also broadens the perspectives of all students, teaching them that the Caribbean is more than sun and fun; each island has a rich heritage. In an interview with Gwendolyn Hooks for Brown Bookshelf, Baptiste comments,

> Princes, princesses, helpful fairies, vindictive witches, magical mishaps, and cleverly hatched plans that led to happy endings were all I dreamt of all day long as I flipped through the pages of my beautifully illustrated Grimms' fairytales. . . . But fairytales were something that happened in places far away from my native Trinidad. . . . But on warm island nights when the books were closed, and the ships at port bellowed out mournful horns, the stories were different. They came with warnings from the adults in my life such as "Never answer if you hear your name called at night. That is how the douens [a kind of evil jumbie] will get you."

Baptiste laments that as a child, she was living her Trinidadian fairy tales, but they were not in books. She questions, "Why didn't the children who looked like me have their own fairytales? We were just as clever. We had to be just as brave. Our foes were just as treacherous. Didn't our stories deserve to be written down?" *The Jumbies*, then, offers teachers a chance to harness and share a Caribbean fairy tale with students from all backgrounds in the American classroom.

d) Authenticity of action and characters: All characters represent the Trinidadian sensibility, using local mores such as visiting the graves of loved ones, believing in spirits that will either harm or hurt, and engaging the local flora and fauna that form the landscape of the text. Caribbean children's literature scholar Cynthia James comments that "in the old days [the] treasured folk tradition was a hidden curriculum, saddled with the stigma of inferiority" (164). Thankfully, now the folk tradition has entered what James calls its third and present phase, "marked by a fusion of oral and literary agendas—a fusion propelled by changing concepts of education and literacy" (165). *The Jumbies*, then, exemplifies the fusion of the oral and the scribal or literary, in which the author incorporates elements of local tales into the novel. The story is designed to be a fantasy fiction to which most, if not all, students can relate. All cultural groups preserve folktales that they often recount, especially to children.

e) Absence of stereotypes: Baptiste creates characters and action with a complexity that renders them free of stereotypes. Corinne and the other children represented, while courageous, face the vicissitudes of challenges so that, although they ultimately conquer their archrivals, they become aware that not all problems can be solved—sometimes one must make peace with challenges. Readers will also notice that the text excludes the subject of calypso and the revelry typically associated with Trinidadian life.

f) Problems solved by individuals within the culture: The plot consists of Trinidadian characters who both create and unravel the conflicts.

g) Plot respectful of all cultures involved: The plot focuses on a single culture with elements of the supernatural infused in the story. All are authentically represented and respected.

Evaluation of Julia Alvarez's *Before We Were Free* (2002)

(Ages Twelve and Up)

Described as "one of the most respected voices in America today" (Alvarez, "Profile"), Julia Alvarez won the 2002 Américas Award for Children's and Young Adult Literature, sponsored by the Consortium of Latin American Studies Programs, and the American Library Association's Pura Belpré Medal for Narrative in 2004 for an outstanding work of literature for children and youth that "portrays, affirms, and celebrates the Latino cultural experience" (Alvarez, "Vita"). Alvarez has authored numerous books for children and young adults, most, if not all, about Dominicans and their experiences as migrants in the US. Although she was born in New York, she went with her parents to the Dominican Republic when she was three months old. She later returned to the US when she was ten. Among other challenges, Alvarez faced prejudice in the US, as she recounts, "I did pick up enough English to understand that some classmates were not very welcoming" ("Vita").

Before We Were Free draws from real-life experiences of a tense and turbulent time in the history of the Dominican Republic under the brutal dictatorship of Rafael Leónidas Trujillo Molina (El Jefe), who ruled from 1930 until his assassination in 1961. The young adult novel employs the first-person narrative of twelve-year-old Anita de la Torre, who lives through an attempted overthrow of the dictator before fleeing to the US. The story embodies her fears as she is forced to grow up too fast amid the tensions of seeing her family disperse to escape the secret police of El Jefe. Anita's experience then expands to include a combination of frightening events that threaten the lives of her family and her own complex period of adolescence. The story spans the tensions in the Dominican Republic and later the US, where she must face a new and alien physical and relational environment and the loss of her father and uncle. The book qualifies as a great read for the diverse classroom in the following ways:

a) Author's qualification: Alvarez, as mentioned above, moved to the US at age ten during the time of Trujillo's dictatorship. On her website, she notes that while her family lived in the Dominican Republic, her father "got involved in the underground, and soon [her] family was in deep trouble. [They] left hurriedly in 1960" ("Vita"). For Alvarez, then, not only did she experience the political tensions in the Dominican Republic but she also endured abject hostility toward Dominicans in the US. She would have heard the stories of torture and near escape from the Dominican Republic that would later inform her narrative.

b) Point of view: The first-person narration heightens the story's appeal to children and young adults. Anita also invites readers into her personal space by recording some of the events in her diary. Although the text embodies pain and devastation, the narration ends on a positive note, but not an unrealistic one. Anita simply promises her father that she will try to "fly"; this tone at the end can serve to encourage all students, especially immigrants who still miss home and who feel alienated, despite the many promises of a blissful life in the US. Students can conclude from the text that the present circumstances may be bleak, but they can, through perseverance, overcome.

c) Students' connection to the story: Adolescents reading *Before We Were Free* will learn not to take for granted the freedom that they experience in the US. As a story that draws from history, the text engages readers' emotions when they realize that Dominicans were jailed, tortured, and killed if they opposed Trujillo. The themes range from naïveté to fast maturation, from love and family to fear and betrayal—all relatable to young readers. Readers can also look at the fight for freedom in the Dominican Republic and compare it to the fight that the founding fathers encountered in each country represented in the classroom. Indeed, the Caribbean has had its fair share of internal struggles and insurrections, many to create and/or maintain a democratic system. Cindy L. Rodriguez, in her spotlight of Alvarez for the Pura Belpré award for *Before We Were Free*, observes that "Alvarez makes a complex political situation accessible to younger readers through Anita, who faces political drama alongside normal twelve-year-old milestones, like getting her period and having a first crush." Other concerns in the novel involve Anita being placed in a lower grade level in the US than is commensurate with her age and ability. Unfortunately, for the Caribbean student in American schools, the experience of being placed one grade below is all too familiar. The novel also addresses issues of mental health or instability (for example, Anita's mother takes tranquilizers to calm her nerves) as an outgrowth of the trauma, fear, alienation, and displacement that are all part of the immigrant experience. Many students from war-torn countries and students from the inner cities where violence is rife can easily see themselves in this story. The theme of alienation—both from the Dominican Republic and from the US—will resonate with all immigrant students who must maneuver between their old culture and the new culture. In an interview with Elizabeth Huergo following her receipt of the F. Scott Fitzgerald Literary Award, Alvarez remarked that before she had published any of her stories, she thought that they did not belong in the field of US literature because she had not seen or read books like the ones that were inside her. So many students from the Caribbean will see their own experiences reflected in this text.

d) Authenticity of action and characters: The story captures the trauma experienced by a twelve-year-old girl in Trujillo's Dominican Republic, and later, the experience of the immigrant child in the face of alienation through linguistic, ethnic, and cultural differences. The text presents an excellent model for reading, class discussion, and group projects. Students can compare the main character's life in the Dominican Republic with life in the US. Other areas of interest include the role of the family and the compound that includes the extended family as a cultural element in the Dominican Republic. Immigrant students in the classroom will also relate to the double consciousness of embracing the past while both fearing and desiring their current existence.

e) Absence of stereotypes: The story presents in realistic terms a period that documents the sordid history of the Dominican Republic, and although the narrative is at times moving and disturbing, the reader cannot help but note the freshness and specificity with which the author treats each character and action.

f) Problems solved by individuals within the culture: Although *Before We Were Free* relates that the problems of dictatorship and human rights violations are confronted by some US diplomats living in the Dominican Republic, none can solve the persistent violations. Trujillo's death results ultimately from the sacrifices made by local characters. The challenges of isolation and alienation that Anita and her family face in the US are not solved; realistically, they will have to devise ways of combating and enduring these challenges.

g) Plot respectful of all cultures involved: With the inclusion of both Dominican and American cultures, Alvarez is careful to depict all with respect.

Choices: Interrogating the Canon

No one expects that including more multicultural books (and by specificity, more Caribbean books) in a curriculum for children's and young adult literature will be an easy task. For one thing, many parents and other members of the public often question why certain books are chosen, even when the motive is to create inclusiveness and educate students about the experiences of others, especially those who represent minority groups with different and often more nuanced and negative experiences than those of the mainstream groups. A classic example is the case of a South Carolina police union that objected to a high school reading list that included Angie

Thomas's *The Hate U Give* (2017) and Jason Reynolds and Brendan Kiely's *All American Boys* (2015) because, the union claimed, the books promote distrust of the police (Flood). But we cannot address racial and cultural stereotypes and other inaccuracies and inequities without incorporating the lived experiences of those who represent these cultures and without creating an atmosphere where all become stakeholders in the most basic democratic process—education.

It therefore stands that "righting" images of the Caribbean in the American classroom must also entail "righting" how teachers and students read Caribbean texts, and also how educators determine which books should be included in the canon. Journalist Wesley Morris comments, "On its face, canon-making is a fairly human impulse" that assumes that everyone should love what we love. Morris continues that "over time a single book becomes a library; the library becomes a school of thought; the school of thought becomes a prism through which the world is supposed to see itself." Thus, a canon becomes by nature value-determining in that it privileges one set of books—representing a class or culture—above others. One approach to changing the canon requires the teacher to replace some of the current texts, according to high school educator Tricia Ebarvia, to create space for the "literary and intellectual history of people of color." Ebarvia suggests asking if all the texts that form the so-called literary canon are essential, especially if they reinforce the same voices. Another strategy suggests examining whose voice is not being reflected in the literature and choosing texts that present these points of view. Both approaches require the teacher to be observant of students' needs and decisive and intentional about building a bridge between students and diverse cultures. In addressing the issue of the canon, Landt takes a more direct approach by eliminating separate groupings or multicultural units in favor of incorporating multicultural literature as we do any other literature, thus making it mainstream ("Weaving Multicultural Literature" 20). Using Landt's method, the teacher would naturally include Caribbean literature on the list of books to be read and discussed in the class, instead of classifying it in a separate group labeled "diverse" or "multicultural" literature.

At the same time, educators Tonya Perry and B. Joyce Stallworth contend that "*how* we teach students to read text is more the issue than just *what* they are reading" (17). Rather than focusing on the "selection of quality canonical or noncanonical literature to teach students," our emphasis should be on "how we ask students to examine different types of texts as independent thinkers" (17). One method is "the selection of texts as complementary elements," or "clustering" texts, which enables teachers to use a variety of readings to engage and challenge students (17). In the case of Caribbean literature, one cluster might entail pairing Julia Alvarez's *Before We Were Free* with *The Diary of Anne Frank* (first published in Dutch in 1947). Both texts depict a tense political situation that requires each protagonist to go into hiding. Both also use the technique of journaling to add to the authenticity of the story and to invite the reader into the characters' experiences. The point of departure would entail examining the cultural markers in each text. Below are suggested clusters for Andrew Salkey's *Hurricane*, Tracey Baptiste's *The Jumbies*, and Julia Alvarez's *Before We Were Free.*

Texts That Can Be Clustered with *Hurricane*

Drowned City: Hurricane Katrina and New Orleans (2015) by Don Brown (for ages twelve and up)

Drowned City captures the tragedies and triumphs that resulted from Hurricane Katrina's devastating effects on New Orleans in August 2005.

Orleans (2013) by Sherri L. Smith (for ages twelve and up)

The Gulf Coast has been separated from the US mainland since 2025 after a series of hurricanes resulted in a deadly plague. This text addresses issues of global warming, racism, political corruption, and human resilience. A fantasy novel.

No Safe Haven (2018) by Kyla Stone (for ages thirteen and up)

A young girl on a wildlife refuge in northern Georgia must use her survival skills to protect her family and animals against a potentially devastating disease and the anarchy of the outside world. A fantasy novel.

Texts That Can Be Clustered with *The Jumbies*

The Dreamer (2010) by Pam Muñoz Ryan (for ages nine and up)

This text combines poetry, literary fiction, and magical realism with biography to tell the inspiring story of the early life of the great Chilean poet Pablo Neruda.

Monstrous (2016) by MarcyKate Connolly (for ages eight and up)
   The city of Bryne suffers under the rule of an evil wizard whose curse causes girls to sicken and disappear. Kymera comes to the city to rescue the girls, but doing this cautiously and secretly will not be easy.

Serafina and the Black Cloak (2015) by Robert Beatty (for ages nine and up)
   When children at the Biltmore Estate start disappearing, Serafina must use her knowledge of the estate and its secret corridors before any more children are lost.

Texts That Can Be Clustered with *Before We Were Free*

The Diary of a Young Girl (reprint 1993) by Anne Frank (for ages twelve and up)
   Anne Frank and her family endure the horrors of the Nazi occupation of Amsterdam while hiding in a warehouse. This true story enables the reader to peer into Anne Frank's diary, which chronicles her preoccupations with teenage angst even as she faces impending doom.

Never Fall Down (2013) by Patricia McCormick (for ages twelve and up)
   Arn, a young Cambodian, is separated from his family and sent to a Khmer Rouge labor camp. In this true story, the young protagonist must master the art of survival to save himself and others, who will die without his help.

Habibi (1997) by Naomi Shihab Nye (for ages twelve and up)
   A young American girl is taken to Palestine, the home of her father. She feels lost and alienated in this strange country until she finds hope in a forbidden friendship with someone who is Jewish.

Run, Boy, Run (2011) by Uri Orlev (for ages twelve and up)
   Srulik, a young Jewish boy, endures harsh conditions to survive in Nazi Germany. Based on the true-life experiences of an eight-year-old forced on the run to escape the Holocaust, *Run, Boy, Run* is a story of resilience, courage, generosity, and loss.

With the availability of methods and means, reading and "righting" images of the Caribbean in the American academy must begin with practitioners taking an interest in the region—getting to know as much as possible about place and people. Teachers and practitioners must take more than a cursory interest in their Caribbean students, for whom coming to America often engenders a confluence of fear and excitement. Parties to their parents' quest for a better life, these students often come with an expectancy that surpasses what becomes their reality after they have settled in the US. Once they are here, multiple alienating forces intersect—new housing and neighborhoods, new weather patterns, new schools and educational systems, new foods, new attitudes, and new language(s)—resulting in Caribbean students being uncomfortably aware of their differences from mainstream America. Imagine, then, the added disadvantage of their being in classrooms where the literature simply flattens identities or propagates stereotypes of Caribbean culture(s). Susan Landt reinforces that "[n]ot seeing oneself, or representations of one's culture, in literature can activate feelings of marginalization and cause students to question their place in society" ("Multicultural Literature" 694). Teachers must therefore choose books that accurately present images of the Caribbean, books that enable Caribbean students to embrace and celebrate their differences while respecting representations of other cultures in the classroom.

But even without a single Caribbean student in the classroom, teachers must prepare their students to be global thinkers by creating an interest in the literature of the Caribbean. Our students' world is increasingly global, yet our curriculum is often insular, focusing only on works written by authors who form a select reading list, or on authors in and from the US. While we do not anticipate that a more inclusive curriculum will erase all negative or reductive images of the Caribbean (nor of any place or culture for that matter), we must remember that our education system is an integral part of our democracy, and thus must recognize the needs of all.

Notes

1. See, for example, Fenice Boyd, Lauren Causey, and Lee Galda's list in "Culturally Diverse Literature: Enriching Variety in an Era of Common Core State Standards," 383.

2. Age levels are taken from Amazon.com. See product details for each book. Sources referenced in this chapter range from books (fiction and nonfiction) to journals, newspapers, songs, movies, television series, and nonprofit organizations. These are written, produced, or published by writers and creators, mainly from the US and the Caribbean. All sources are available in print and/or electronic formats, and dates of publication range from the 1964 to 2018.

Works Cited

Adichie, Chimamanda Ngozi. "The Danger of a Single Story." TED Talks, 2009. https://www.ted.com/talks/chimamanda_ngozi_adichie_the_danger_of_a_single_story?language=en.

Alvarez, Julia. *Before We Were Free*. Alfred A. Knopf, 2002.

Alvarez, Julia. "Profile: Julia Alvarez." PBS, aired May 18, 2002. www.pbs.org/video/profile-julia-alvarez.

Alvarez, Julia. "Vita." January 17, 2018, www.juliaalvarez.com/about/vita/php.

Ashman, Howard, and Alan Menken. "Under the Sea." *The Little Mermaid: An Original Walt Disney Records Soundtrack*, 1989.

Baptiste, Tracey. *The Jumbies*. Scholastic, 2015.

Baptiste, Tracey. "Telling the Untold Stories." Lesley University, Stories, 2017. https://lesley.edu/stories/tracey-baptiste.

Baptiste, Tracey. "Tracey Baptiste and the Story behind *The Jumbies*." Interview with Gwendolyn Hooks, the Brown Bookshelf, United in Story, April 28, 2015. https://thebrownbookshelf.com/2015/04/28/tracey-baptiste-and-the-story-behind-the-jumbies/.

Beatty, Robert. *Serafina and the Black Cloak*. Disney-Hyperion, 2015.

Bishop, Rudine Sims. "Multicultural Literacy: Mirrors, Windows, and Sliding Glass Doors." Reading Is Fundamental, January 3, 2015. https://scenicregional.org/wp-content/uploads/2017/08/Mirrors-Windows-and-Sliding-Glass-Doors.pdf.

Boyd, Fenice B., Lauren L. Causey, and Lee Galda. "Culturally Diverse Literature: Enriching Variety in an Era of Common Core State Standards." *Reading Teacher*, vol. 68, no. 5, February 2015, pp. 378–87.

Brown, Don. *Drowned City: Hurricane Katrina and New Orleans*. Houghton Mifflin Harcourt, 2017.

Camera, Lauren. "U.S. Students Are Really Bad at Geography." *U.S. News & World Report*, October 16, 2015. https://www.usnews.com/news/articles/2015/10/16/us-students-are-terrible-at-geography.

Colby, Susan A., and Anna F. Lyon. "Heightening Awareness about the Importance of Using Multicultural Literature." *Multicultural Education*, vol. 11, no. 3, Spring 2004, pp. 24–28.

Connolly, MarcyKate. *Monstrous*. HarperCollins, 2016.

Cwik, Christian. "U.S. Intervention in the Caribbean." 1914–1918 Online, *International Encyclopedia of the First World War*, edited by Ute Daniel et al., October 8, 2014. https://encyclopedia.1914-1918-online.net/article/us_intervention_in_the_caribbean.

Dong, Yu Ren. "Taking a Cultural-Response Approach to Teaching Multicultural Literature." *English Journal*, vol. 94, no. 3, January 2005, pp. 55–60.

Ebarvia, Tricia. "Disrupting Texts as Restorative Practice." *Council Chronicle*, vol. 28, no. 2, December 2018. https://triciaebarvia.org/2018/07/11/disrupting-texts-as-a-restorative-practice/.

Flood, Alison. "South Carolina Police Object to High-School Reading List." *The Guardan*, July 3, 2018. https://www.theguardian.com/books/2018/jul/03/south-carolina-police-object-to-high-school-reading-list.

Frank, Anne. *The Diary of a Young Girl*. 1952. Translated by Barbara M. Mooyaart, Bantam, 1993.

Freire, Paulo, and Donaldo Macedo. *Literacy: Reading the Word and the World*. Bergin and Garvey, 1987.

Gangi, Jane M. "The Unbearable Whiteness of Literacy Instruction: Realizing the Implications of the Proficient Reader Research." *Multicultural Review*, vol. 17, no. 1, Spring 2008, pp. 30–35.

Glazier, Jocelyn, and Jung-A Seo. "Multicultural Literature and Discussion as Mirror and Window?" *Journal of Adolescent and Adult Literacy*, vol. 48, no. 8, May 2005, pp. 686–700.

hooks, bell. *Teaching to Transgress: Education as the Practice of Freedom*. Routledge, 1994.

Huergo, Elizabeth. "Interview with Julia Alvarez, 2009 F. Scott Fitzgerald Award Honoree." YouTube. www.youtube.com/watch?v=HZ2xe2OFTX8.

Inniss, Kaiomi. "9 Caribbean Countries That Are NOT Jamaica." *Odyssey*, May 31, 2016. https://www.theodysseyonline.com/8-caribbean-countries-that-are-not-jamaica.

Irvine, Jacqueline Jordan, and Willis D. Hawley. "Culturally Responsive Pedagogy: An Overview of Research on Student Outcomes." Prepared for Teaching Tolerance, Southern Poverty Law Center. https://silo.tips/download/culturally-responsive-teaching-awards-celebration.

James, Cynthia. "From Orature to Literature in Jamaican and Trinidadian Children's Folk Traditions." *Children's Literature Association Quarterly*, vol. 30, no. 2, Summer 2005, pp. 164–78.

Jones, Trent. "The 7 Most Common Caribbean Myths and Stereotypes." *The Root*, June 23, 2015. www.theroot.com/the-7-most-common-caribbean-myths-and-stereotypes-1790860296.

Landt, Susan M. "Children's Literature with Diverse Perspectives: Reflecting All Students." *Dragon Lode*, vol. 32, no. 1, 2013, pp. 21–31.

Landt, Susan M. "Multicultural Literature and Young Adolescents: A Kaleidoscope of Opportunity." *Journal of Adolescent and Adult Literacy*, vol. 49, no. 8, May 2006, pp. 690–97.

Landt, Susan M. "Weaving Multicultural Literature into Middle School Curricula." *Middle School Journal*, vol. 39, no. 2, November 2007, pp. 19–24.

Malcolm, Zaria T., and Ruth McKoy Lowery. "Reflections of the Caribbean's Picture Books: A Critical Multicultural Analysis." *Multicultural Education*, vol. 19, no. 1, Fall 2011, pp. 46–50.

Matsuda, Paul Kei. "The Myth of Linguistic Homogeneity in U.S. College Composition." *College English*, vol. 68, no. 6, July 2006, pp. 637–51.

McCormick, Patricia. *Never Fall Down*. HarperCollins, 2013.

Morris, Wesley. "Who Gets to Decide What Belongs in the 'Canon'?" *New York Times Magazine*, May 30, 2018. https://www.nytimes.com/2018/05/30/magazine/who-gets-to-decide-what-belongs-in-the-canon.html.

Musker, John, and Ron Clements, directors. *The Little Mermaid*. Walt Disney Pictures, 1989.

Nye, Naomi Shihab. *Habibi*. Simon and Schuster, 1997.

Orlev, Uri. *Run, Boy, Run*. Translated by Hillel Halkin, Houghton Mifflin Harcourt, 2003.

Perry, Tonya B., and B. Joyce Stallworth. "21st-Century Students Demand a Balanced, More Inclusive Canon." *Voices in the Middle*, vol. 21, no. 1, September 2013, pp. 15–18.

Quinton, Sophie. "Good Teachers Embrace Their Students' Cultural Backgrounds." *Atlantic*, November 11, 2013. https://www.theatlantic.com/education/archive/2013/11/good-teachers-embrace-their-students-cultural-backgrounds/281337/.

Roach, John. "Young Americans Geographically Illiterate, Survey Suggests." *National Geographic News*, May 2, 2006. http://lrc.salemstate.edu/hispanics/other/Young_Americans_Geographically_Illiterate_Survey_Suggests.htm.

Rodriguez, Cindy L. "Celebrating Pura Belpré Award Winners: Spotlight on Julia Alvarez." Latinxs in Kid Lit, April 14, 2016. https://latinosinkidlit.com/2016/04/14/celebrating-pura-belpre-award-winners-spotlight-on-julia-alvarez/.

Ruiz, Pedro, Regine Latortue, and Nicole Rosefort. *Resource Guide for the Education of New York State Students from Caribbean Countries Where English Is the Medium of Instruction*. State Education Department, Albany, New York. https://docs.steinhardt.nyu.edu/pdfs/metrocenter/nbm3/english_caribbean_students.pdf.

Ryan, Pam Muñoz. *The Dreamer*. Scholastic, 2012.

Salkey, Andrew. *Hurricane*. Oxford UP, 1964.

Saltzman, Mark. "Caribbean Amphibian." *Sesame Street*, first performed 1986.

Sands-O'Connor, Karen. "Repeating or Renewing Island? Andrew Salkey and Philip Sherlock." Theracetoread, April 12, 2018. https://theracetoread.wordpress.com/2018/04/12/repeating-or-renewing-island-andrew-salkey-and-philip-sherlock/.

Smith, Sherri L. *Orleans*. Penguin, 2013.

Smith, Zadie. "Zadie Smith: By the Book." *New York Times*, November 17, 2016. www.nytimes.com/2016/11/20/books/review/zadie-smith-by-the-book.html.

Stone, Kyla. *No Safe Haven*. Paper Moon Press, 2018.

Strachan, Ian Gregory. *Paradise and Plantation: Tourism and Culture in the Anglophone Caribbean*. U of Virginia P, 2002.

Taylor, Frank Fonda. *To Hell with Paradise: A History of the Jamaican Tourist Industry*. U of Pittsburgh P, 1993.

Verbinski, Gore, director. *Pirates of the Caribbean: At World's End*. Walt Disney Pictures and Jerry Bruckheimer Films, 2007.

Verbinski, Gore, director. *Pirates of the Caribbean: Dead Man's Chest*. Walt Disney Pictures and Jerry Bruckheimer Films, 2006.

Walcott, Derek. "The Antilles: Fragments of Epic Memory." The Nobel Prize, Derek Walcott Nobel Lecture, December 7, 1992. https://www.nobelprize.org/prizes/literature/1992/walcott/lecture/.

Wolk, Steven. "Reading Democracy: Exploring Ideas That Matter with Middle Grade and Young Adult Literature." *English Journal*, vol. 103, no. 2, November 2013, pp. 45–51.

Woolf, Nick. "2x10 Relationship Building: How to Do It (and Why It Works!)." Panorama Education. https://www.panoramaed.com/blog/2x10-relationship-building-strategy#:~:text=At%20its%20core%2C%20the%202x10,for%2010%20consecutive%20school%20days.

Zong, Jie, and Jeanne Batalova. "Caribbean Immigrants in the United States." Migration Policy Institute, February 13, 2019. https://www.migrationpolicy.org/article/caribbean-immigrants-united-states-2017.

PART 3

PICTURE BOOKS AND PUBLISHING

CHAPTER 13

Publishing Children's Literature in the Caribbean
Four Authors' Perspectives

Betsy Nies and Melissa García Vega

The editors posed five questions to four children's book authors to gain greater insight into the process of writing and publishing books for children in the Caribbean, the ins and outs of self-publishing, and the challenges faced in the region for creating a thriving Caribbean children's publishing industry. Here are the participants:

Joanne Gail Johnson is the writer, director, and producer of *Sally's Way* (2015), Trinidad and Tobago's first-ever feature-length family and children's film, which earned six awards, including the 2015 People's Choice Award for Best Narrative Feature at the Trinidad and Tobago Film Festival. She served as the editor of Macmillan Caribbean's Island Fiction series (2006–2009), which brought the region's first "tween" novellas for reluctant readers to market. A published children's book author herself with several trade books, illustrated readers, and anthologized stories with Macmillan, she served as the founding regional adviser of the Caribbean South chapter of the Society of Children's Book Writers and Illustrators from 2006 to 2012.

María Teresa Marichal-Lugo (more commonly known as Tere Marichal-Lugo) is a well-known, prolific Puerto Rican playwright, storyteller, puppeteer, producer, and writer and illustrator of children's books. Her children's television show *La casa de María Chuzema* ran daily on Puerto Rican educational television between 1987 and 2009. As a playwright and puppeteer, she has toured the island, spoken at conferences, and provided workshops for teachers and children. Her children's books were initially published by Camera Mundi, a provider of educational material for Puerto Rico's school systems, and more recently in the El Nuevo Día series published by Grupo de Diarios América, Puerto Rico. Currently, among her other endeavors, Tere self-publishes picture books, plays, and craft books for children, covering such diverse subjects as protecting the environment, building global unity, and retelling indigenous myths.

Ada Haiman, a retired professor of English at the University of Puerto Rico, earned her PhD in 2006 from the same institution; her dissertation examines the relationship between dominant discourses and childrearing, specifically the unconscious parenting ideologies oppressing child protagonists in Caribbean fiction. Such research informs her own line of books, which challenge such traditional messaging. Her self-published picture books—a series launched in 2014 with *Tulipán: The Puerto Rican Giraffe*—address questions about race, identity, class, education, and injustice. For example, she questions the limiting educational beliefs that inform standardized testing to explore a more validating narrative of a child's informal as well as formal learning. Atabey Sánchez-Haiman served as the illustrator for her first book; Roberto Figueroa illustrated the remainder: *Tulipán the Puerto Rican Giraffe Thinks about Grades* (2016), *Tulipán the Puerto Rican Giraffe Rejects a Hair-Raising Lie* (2017), and *Tulipán the Puerto Rican Giraffe: A Christmas Story* (2018). All the books in the series have editions in Spanish and English.

Diane Browne is an established writer of children's stories and books who has both self-published and published with such reputable companies as Harcourt Brace, Heinemann Caribbean, Carlong Publishers, Arawak Publications, and Blue Banyan Books, in addition to the Ministry of Education in Jamaica. A number of her stories, published as supplementary reading material, are used in primary schools in Jamaica. She considers this an important aspect of children's literature, as for many children, these will be the only books they will ever own.

She has done author readings and presented papers on the importance of indigenous children's literature at international conferences in the United

Kingdom, the US, and Jamaica. Her research into the significance of and exposure to local children's literature in schools is reflected in her master's thesis (2003): "'I Will Not Look at Books the Same Way Again': Teachers' Feelings about the Use of Caribbean Children's Literature," completed at the University of the West Indies. She has won numerous awards for her work.

Q: What prompted you to start writing picture books for children? Are there issues particular to the region that may have informed your decision?

Joanne: There was, and still is, a deep longing to see the people around me lifted up and reflected in authentic ways. I felt conviction that my esteem for our land, our people, our diversity, our beauty is worth expressing and sharing and exporting. As a child, I dressed up and enlivened characters from my imagination. I spoke into the air elaborate scenes and bowed to listening audiences invisible to my family. When I looked up from the pages of the British or American published books and authors I devoured, I did not feel alienated; it was the very contrast that deepened my connection with Home and defined our uniqueness. This early kind of international exposure through the imaginations of others, broadened my horizons. [But] during the 1980s, and throughout my ten years as a primary school classroom teacher, . . . I developed an inevitable concern over the dearth of original content for and from the Caribbean. I think the questions germinating in me by then had been with me since childhood, but could finally be articulated: *Why not us? Why not me? If not me, then who?*

Reading aloud in other islands or at any venue across my country, it's apparent that no matter who we are, regardless of any differences, we want the stories and storytellers somehow to make our children's lives and world better. Today, I still see the diversity in our regional market as a strength, and a potentially unifying one. With free and easy access to democratizing technologies, this era has handed us the tools to mobilize almost any inner vision that we dare to dream and share.

Tere: *Tengo una responsabilidad con mi patria, todo lo que hago tiene una razón política, cultural y social. Todo lo que significa ser antillana, caribeña, puertorriqueña e isleña es muy importante para mi y trato de que todo lo que hago tenga ese sello. . . . Cuando vives en una colonia no puedes perder el tiempo en bobadas. Soy independentista y socialista y eso implica una gran responsabilidad porque tienes que hacer camino para los que vienen. Así veo la vida.*

Comencé a trabajar directamente con niños en 1977 y ofrecía talleres de teatro de títeres y talleres de reutilización de desechos sólidos. Escribía obras para el teatro de títeres y puedo decir que este tipo de teatro me fue llevando a la narrativa.... Desarrollé el taller Los Nuevos Alquimistas, donde transformábamos la basura en arte. El tema ambiental siempre ha estado presente en mi trabajo. El programa que tuve por veinticinco años estaba directamente unido a la Educación Ambiental y recibí muchos premios por mi trabajo educando sobre el tema. Muchos de los personajes que creé para el teatro de títeres, se transformaron en personajes de carne y hueso en el programa. Hasta la Sra. Contaminación estaba en el programa. Todos los temas de los que se habla tanto hoy, nosotros los desarrollamos como cuento y pudimos explicar hace veinte años lo que era el calentamiento global.[1]

I have a responsibility to my homeland. Everything I do has a political, cultural, and social reason. Everything that means being Antillean, Caribbean, Puerto Rican, and islander is very important to me, and I try to ensure that everything I do has that seal. When you live in a colony, you cannot waste your time on silly things. I am an *independentista* [an advocate for Puerto Rican independence] and a socialist, and that implies a great responsibility because you have to make way for those who come. This is how I see life.

I started working directly with children in 1977 and offered puppet theater workshops and solid waste upcycling workshops. I wrote plays for the puppet theater, and I can say that this type of theater led to narrative.... I developed the workshop the New Alchemists, where we transformed garbage into art. The environmental issue has always been present in my work. The [television] program that I had for twenty-five years [*La casa de María Chuzema*, WIPR-TV] was directly linked to environmental education, and I received many awards for my work educating on the subject. Many of the characters I created for the puppet theater were transformed into flesh-and-blood characters in the program. Even Mrs. Pollution was in the program. All the topics discussed so much today, we developed them as a story, and we explained twenty years ago what global warming was.

Ada: I must begin with a shout-out to Tere. I was part of her group that narrated stories for children in public plazas. She encouraged me to write my own story—thus the first Tulipán came into being. My dissertation on the discourses of childhood informs this series. When writing the dissertation, I realized that adults are complicit (though unconsciously so) in the invalidation of the mind and thinking of the child. Dominant ways of childrearing stress obedience over dissent, i.e., the child is not taught to question, but to obey. Because adults are set in their default ways of thinking, I took Tere's invitation as an opportunity to share my concerns directly with the children who, less socialized in the dominant ways of thinking and doing, were more open to seeing alternatives and questioning. Like the others in this conversation, children are at the center of my interest. Their ideas and voices will mark the future; therefore, if we can engage them in questioning the world, we are on the road to transforming it.

Diane: I smiled with recognition at the statement by Tere: "When you live in a colony, you cannot waste your time on silly things." I think we all write with a degree of urgency to see that our children have books that help them to value their identity and the validity of their own environment.

When I was a child, I was a voracious reader. Even as I read Nancy Drew, like everybody else, I longed to see characters that reflected us and our reality. When my girls were little, I more so wanted them to be able to see themselves in books, and that is what started me writing.

In 1979 I won the prize for a story for UNESCO's Year of the Child. Then I joined a project at the [Jamaican] Ministry of Education to write supplementary readers for children in government primary schools. The idea of the Dr. Bird Reading Series (1980) was that the books would be presented just as storybooks without activities to make the children like reading more. This project would let the children see themselves in the pages of a book. This has been my passion. So yes, the issues particular to this region informed my decision.

Consequently, one of the sessions I have in my workshops is the responsibility of the children's writer in postcolonial (colonial) territories: authenticity, culture, values, respect for all ethnicities, the environment in small island states, etc. This is merely the backdrop to the story; for having considered all variables, we must then turn to writing a great story.

Q: When you are composing a picture book, what criteria (such as aesthetics, illustrations, or language rhythm) do you consider? Whom do you imagine as your audience?

Joanne: When I'm authoring entirely from my own creative inspiration, the most important and consistent responses for me relate to authenticity, relevance, and purpose. The work emerging may be a screenplay, a song, a poem (long or short), a chapter, or picture book. The most fixed elements for me are writing visually and writing through character. These elements are essential to the work, whether I'm writing a Caribbean book or not.

Writing visually is vital for young readers and for our era and it's essential for the illustrations, which are ultimately what attract our young readers, who are only just learning to read. In the marketplace, too, illustrations are what ultimately sell the book to kids. So it becomes hugely important along the way. But again, unless you're an artist with a unique illustrative style and "voice," editors just want to see text on a page, or these days, in an email. You can offer a few notes or illustrative ideas if it helps communicate an element that is directly connected to the story, but editors and publishers know their markets and are usually very clear on what they want and why they want it.... Often a house has a stable of known artists with whom they've established working relationships. So, unless you know how to truly illustrate and lay out a story, and not just "add pictures," in terms of submissions—don't bother....

Typically, as a work takes form, I will use the process of rewrites to address elements so crucial to producing marketable picture books: lexical level, word count, vocabulary, syntax, semantics, etc. With dialogue and dialect, I don't think we're producing our best work when we just write the way we speak. I use flavor and rhythm during direct speech. Characters should not all sound the same. My guide for dialect is—can the sentence meaning be understood if all the dialect words are removed? Unique vocabulary or slang can be understood through context, repetition, and illustration.

Tere: *Cuando hago un libro con dibujos, tomo en cuenta el tema, la cultura, la época histórica, los personajes, el punto de vista que quiero enfatizar, los colores y formas que me inspira el cuento. Hago un mapa bastante grande y analizo dibujos, cuadros, plantas, fotos . . . es una experiencia muy intensa. A veces termino el libro y algo me dice que tengo que hacerlo de nuevo y lo hago. Ya no trabajo con prisa. Yo escribo porque quiero decir algo. Siempre he conocido miles de niños, no solo en P.R. he contado cuentos en México, Cuba, Santo Domingo y tener un programa de tv te acerca a miles de niños. He ido a cientos de escuelas, de salones, de plazas, comunidades, en diferentes épocas y momentos históricos. Todo me ayuda a conocer más la voz que busco cuando escribo para niños. Imagino a mi audiencia como gente sin prejuicios....*

Busco emocionar, sensibilizar, arropar, jugar, descubrir. No quiero ser un libro de recetas para alcanzar un mundo mejor o un libro de instrucciones para que alguien me hable de lo que piensa. Tiene que haber belleza, juego, ingenio, sal, arena, ola, color, ritmo, baile, recuerdos, añoranzas, ternura. Pienso en esto y en muchos recuerdos cuando escribo, ilustro, y cuento. . . .

Hago libros de diferente manera. Ahora publicaré una colección donde no hay fronteras; son cuentos de justicia social que vengo trabajando desde hace muchos años. . . . Hice la Colección Pachamama de cuentos ambientalistas. Hice la Colección Teatro de papel—para técnica kamishibai. Me gusta experimentar y aprender nuevas formas de decir y contar.

When I make a book with illustrations, I take into account the theme, the culture, the historical era, the characters, the point of view that I want to emphasize, the colors and shapes that the story inspires. I make a fairly large map and analyze drawings, pictures, plants, photos . . . It is a very intense experience. Sometimes I finish the book and something tells me that I have to do it again, and I do it. I don't work in a hurry anymore. I write because I want to say something. I've always met thousands of children, not just in Puerto Rico. I have told stories in Mexico, Cuba, Santo Domingo, and having a TV show brings you closer to thousands of children. I have gone to hundreds of schools, classrooms, squares, communities, at different times and historical moments. Everything helps me to know more the voice that I look for when I write for children. I imagine my audience as people without prejudice.

I am looking to excite, sensitize, clothe, play, discover. I don't want to . . . [make] a recipe book to reach a better world or an instruction book for someone to talk to me about what they think. There has to be beauty, game, ingenuity, salt, sand, wave, color, rhythm, dance, memories, longing, tenderness. I think about this and many memories when I write, illustrate, and tell.

I make books in a different way now. I will publish a collection where there are no borders; they are stories of social justice that I have been working for many years. I wrote the Pachamama Collection of environmental stories and produced a paper theater collection to be used with the [Japanese] Kamishibai technique. I like to experiment and learn new ways of saying and telling.

Ada: Rhythm is important in terms of flow and reader appeal. I realize my books are a little text heavy . . . so I add repetition, formulaic language, and dialogue, among other devices, to create fluidity. I do not illustrate; I have an illustrator. I do not design the book; I have a graphic designer. Their help and input are invaluable. I also have outside readers whose feedback is instrumental to refining the text. Like the Dr. Bird Reading Series mentioned by Diane, I do not prepare an activity book, which would certainly enhance marketing, because I feel it would predetermine interpretation. I want to know what the reader thinks. It is that dialogue that will give voice to the children. I feel the children intuit the dissonance, the prejudice. I want to validate these intuitions and, through that validation, give them a voice.

My intended reader is the child; unfortunately, you cannot get to the child without the mediation of the adult (unless of course the child is independently browsing and choosing). Puerto Rico has very few public libraries; therefore, children do not usually freely choose their reading material. It is not an easy trick to write for the child in such a way that your counterdiscourse is not censored by the adult in charge.

Tulipán [the protagonist of the Tulipán series] is a Puerto Rican giraffe, and the text is situated in Puerto Rico. The discourses disturbed in these books are more widespread than on this one island: identity, grades, race, class. For example, the Tulipán about grades has caused quite a fuss in adult circles, even in progressive circles that advocate for educational change. There is a reluctance to question the dominant multiple-choice testing if the adult reader's children are getting A grades. Tulipán questions the validity and reliability of multiple-choice testing. Faith in these tests is so ingrained that many adults will not entertain such a counternarrative because it disrupts their faith in their own merit. It may be the case that on other Caribbean islands, where oral exams and written exams are customary, the criticism of multiple-choice testing would be more welcome or understood. Such is not the case here. My goal is that the children begin to question, to doubt popular assumptions, and to validate their own conclusions. I don't imagine an audience without prejudice. On the contrary, I assume the dominant belief system is in play and has great sway. I want to disturb this system.

Diane: I tend to have with me an inner voice that speaks to me all day at odd times, through which my theme appears and characters speak. Once that character or theme has alerted me and a setting inserts itself, I begin to write. Then for children's picture storybooks, I go for the rhythm, created by repetition, alliteration, etc. The first draft may be written with the character, his or her concerns, and a draft plot, which could simply be how we get to the end of the story, the resolution. And the rhythm and refrain has to get us there, as well as the illustrations, for that is what will engage the reader. The refrain can be a powerful tool for me. For years I wanted to do the "hair" book, you know, the "accept our hair" book. Everybody is now doing the hair book. When I did *Abigail's Glorious Hair* (2016), I found that accepting our hair was already a given. It was about the female ritual of combing our hair, so the refrain became "Mum's fingers are going through my hair, one, two, twist; one, two, twist; one, two, twist . . . and love flows through her fingers and I feel snug and safe." It's almost like lullaby. I can often see the illustrations in my head as I write. Authenticity and purpose, as mentioned by Joanne, are already in the bedrock of the story. My target audience is the child, the reader from any ethnic group and social level. This may in some cases only be revealed by the illustrations. I write for the children, but as Ada reminds us, there are also the gatekeepers.

One of my stories illustrates the impact of gatekeepers. While walking around in front of my house [one] evening (one of my sporadic exercise attempts), a character turned up saying "tell my story":

> I said, "Don't be mad, you are a girl with an afro and you want to do ballet. You will ruin my reputation as a writer of authentic stories for our children in the Caribbean."
>
> "No!" she persevered.

So eventually Safiya's story was written: a short, chunky girl, quite unlike her mother, who has gorgeous, long mahogany legs and long black hair on top of her head in a dancer's knot. Safiya embarrasses her Afro-centric family by doing a ballet dance at the school concert. As you can imagine, there are many themes interwoven, including the ability to be oneself. A teacher told the marketing department of the book's publisher that he didn't like the story because the child is too "out of order" (naturally, she speaks up for herself and actually thinks). On the other hand, a mother whose child was seriously ill told me that someone had told her to buy this book as the stories are uplifting. So sometimes we will avoid controversial topics and at other times we will nudge the readers into an unfamiliar world.

Q: What particular challenges have you faced in terms of publishing for children, or what issues might a Caribbean writer face when trying to find a publisher?

Joanne: In 1998, in my first query letter . . . I targeted Macmillan Caribbean in the UK. Of all the books I pored over in the national children's library, they seemed to be the only publisher on the planet investing a sustainable and progressive interest into our region. . . . My first poem, *Go Barefoot*, was published as a part of a stepped reading series, Ready

Go. . . . I went on to write four illustrated readers for the higher-level series Hop Step Jump, several anthologized stories, two trade books, and eventually was developed the Island Fiction tween novel series that simultaneously published in print and on e-book in 2009. Internet technologies began to flourish and facilitated my earliest dreams and ideas. I set up and independently paid for the first dedicated website (no free blogs and Instagram pages yet!) for Caribbean children's books and marketed not only my books but other children's books and authors in the Macmillan Caribbean catalogue.

At this time, I also volunteered to found and run a Caribbean South chapter of the most internationally respected professional organization in our industry, the Society of Children's Book Writers and Illustrators (SCBWI). I wanted to see the growth of the publishing industry through children's books but soon found that I spent more time demystifying children's book publishing than contributing to an industry. We were hyperfocused on writer's groups and blind to the work of professionalization that would build an authentic children's publishing industry.

One solution to some of the challenges has been by way of literary festivals and awards. Prizes may motivate seasonal, event-based activity and are helpful, but may be more effective if the aim for quality was able to target a resource of more flourishing quantity. With the recent closure of the Burt Award, for example, the approach of gatekeeping sponsorships may not be authentically sustainable. . . . We need a robust industry infrastructure that exists entirely to sustain working professionals whose daily bread depends on children's book publishing, and whose independent companies combine to publish a profitable slate of new work annually.

Tere: *Publiqué con editoriales pero un día, hace doce años, me cansé de tanta reunión absurda y me volví independiente. Aprendí a hacer mis libros, trabajar los programas de edición, Photoshop. . . . Ya he publicado más de treinta libros para niños. . . . Creo en la democratización de la palabra y he enseñado a otros a hacer sus libros. . . . Conozco gente maravillosa en dos editoriales y las quiero mucho, pero sigo siendo independiente. . . . Cuando dibujo pienso en la cara de algunos niños y luego cuando cuento lo que he dibujado o escrito me encanta verlos. A medida que pasa el tiempo me identifico más con mi esencia y mi cultura. A veces pienso: si escribieras en inglés o no vivieras en una colonia todo sería diferente, pero no es cierto. Uno tiene lo que uno busca y siempre he encontrado lo que realmente necesito.*

I published with publishers but one day, twelve years ago, I got tired of so many absurd meetings and became independent. I learned to make my books, work the editing programs, [and use] Photoshop. . . . I have already published more than thirty books for children. . . . I believe in the democratization of the word and have taught others to make their books. . . . I know wonderful people in two publishing houses and I love them very much, but I'm still independent. . . . When I draw, I think of some children's faces, and then when I narrate what I have drawn or written, I love to see them. As time goes by, I identify myself with my essence and my culture. Sometimes I think: if you wrote in English or did not live in a colony everything would be different, but it is not true. You have what you are looking for and I have always found what I really need.

Ada: I self-publish; I have not even considered a commercial publisher. I see my work more as a public service than as a commercial venture. I think a child's intelligence and awareness of the social problems that affect society is underestimated. They live in this world and see how it works. I am sure they are aware of its contradictions. I want to validate those ideas that they may be reluctant to voice or do not know how to articulate. Finding a publisher in this rarefied and competitive market is not easy. Joanne's work in advancing diversity in children's literature is important. As she so aptly stated (a statement many would take issue with), she was not alienated by the British or American books she read as a child; on the contrary, they deepened her sense of self by contrast, but, the dearth of local literature must be addressed to underscore Chimamanda Ngozi Adichie's warning about a single story.

Diane: Publishing in this region is affected by three main things that are intertwined: (1) limited disposable income, (2) competition from overseas publishers whose books are often remainders, therefore they can undersell anything we produce locally, [and] (3) economies of scale; our books are expensive anyway because the print runs are low. Many of the publishers who operate in this region have traditionally been textbook publishers. That's where the money is, the secure market. When they do children's lit, they may also hope that CSEC [Caribbean Secondary Education Certificate] or the schools will adopt them for literature, or if a picture book, then early childhood, which has very little money.

Carlong in Jamaica, a successful textbook publisher, decided by way of "putting back," so to speak, to do a children's literature series called the Sand Pebbles. The books are lovely, but they don't make any money from them.

Indeed, many of the lovely children's picture books Macmillan once had in the region seem to be no longer in our bookshops. Hence my MEd study; the teachers had never seen the beautiful Caribbean picture books that I had collected over the years. So publishing children's literature is extremely challenging for the individual or the publisher. A young publisher, Tanya Batson Savage of Blue Banyan Books, has developed quite a list of YA books and picture storybooks. I am hoping that she can keep on going. And I know that there are other publishers like this in the region.

Q: What do you see as the risks and rewards of self-publication?

Joanne: Self-publishing best suits those who know their way around publishing, and who have access to infrastructure for promoting and distributing their work. Those who have a strong niche audience who already demand and pay for their content and can use social media tools to build, sustain, and convert a tribe into paying consumers. Figuring out your distribution and sales (not just focusing on "getting published" or "getting into print") are the most democratizing actions a self-publisher can take toward building a sustainable career in children's book publishing.

If you can cost and sell your first print run to pay for itself and the next run or a new title, and you stir up enough demand for a second print run, you're on your way to a successful self-publishing venture. Otherwise, your money may be put to better use by supporting yourself to spend more time writing and submitting, to meeting with agents or editors over time. At least, if you're looking for a serious career as a children's book author and/or illustrator.

Tere: *Siempre he vivido al borde del abismo; estoy acostumbrada. No lo veo como un riesgo. Soy aventurera y no le temo a no tener "la estabilidad" que este sistema colonial le hace creer a la gente que tiene.... Si me encantaría estar tres meses creando sin tener que salir a buscar el dinero para la renta y la comida y crear a mis anchas, pero no me quejo. Tal vez la falta de ayudas, de solidaridad, de dinero es lo que hace que siga viviendo al borde del abismo y no le tengo miedo a lo que venga. Decidí ser escritora, contadora de cuentos, ilustradora, titiritera, dramaturga... ¿Qué más recompensa que ser libre?*

I've always lived on the edge of the abyss; I'm used to it. I do not see it as a risk. I am adventurous and I am not afraid of not having the "stability" that this colonial system makes people believe it has. Yes, I would love to spend [time] creating without having to go out to look for money for rent and food and create at ease, but I do not complain. Perhaps the lack of aid, solidarity, money is what keeps me living on the edge of the abyss, and I am not afraid of whatever comes. I decided to be a writer, storyteller, illustrator, puppeteer, playwright ... What more reward than being free?

Ada: The only risk in my venture is to not break even.... The rewards are many. First, the delight in writing. Foremost, when the child responds with curiosity, identification, and validation. I have had the satisfaction of a few children saying they identified or felt validated by the book (not in those terms, of course). An added pleasure is when an adult gets it and responds critically (vs. courteous platitudes), and a lively discussion ensues.

Diane: When you self-publish, your main challenge is cost and marketing. If it's a children's picture book, good illustrations can be very expensive. I have self-published four books (two on Amazon, two as hard copies). I've worked both in the private and public sectors of publishing, so as Joanne indicated, I know my way around publishing, which helped.

I recall when we thought that getting a book on to Amazon was the Holy Grail of self-publishing. Not so. The two self-published books on Amazon have had no sales to speak of. We do not have a significant Caribbean children's book presence on Amazon. I now consider Amazon a place to put a book, like on a shelf. Other books for which the copyright has reverted to me after small publishers may effectively have closed, are put there as well.

On the other hand, I self-published *Abigail's Glorious Hair* and *The Happiness Dress* children's picture books as hard copies in 2016 because I was determined to put them out. We had a successful launch, and sales were brisk. But I still didn't make enough to do a second print run. Economies of scale were wrong, I knew. I printed a run of 2,500 each (5,000 would have been the practical thing, but I didn't have the money). Consequently, I was delighted when Blue Banyan Books took them over in 2018. So apart from money, marketing and distribution become a challenge.

Having a publisher is much easier, although you may not have control over the illustrations; they will do the brunt of the promotion and marketing. The rewards are when people love the books. So with *Abigail's Glorious Hair*, a friend told me that her nieces knew they were beautiful but now they believe it (postcolonial syndrome can affect us all). Many people love this book; it is as if it has given us permission to love ourselves as we are.

Q: What potential for growth and opportunities do you see for locally publishing original picture books in the spirit of "own voices"? As Summer Edward notes in volume 2 of this anthology, "Young adult author Corinne

Duyvis coined the term 'own voices,' first using it in a Twitter thread on September 6, 2015. 'Own voices' books are those in which the protagonist and the author share a marginalized identity."[2] A call for what is now termed "own voices" signals a desire to change a history of domination by the majority, who have spoken for those on the margins.

Joanne: The questions we are asking are still too much about the individual author. We tend to focus on learning about the creativity aspects, and we hope for the individual breakthroughs for success. The best potential for growth lies in a collaborative organization that collectively lobbies both government and private sectors to implement new policies and practices that will professionalize the domain. We need to always be learning about the industry globally—study peaks and troughs, trends, etc. Timing is sometimes everything, even over talent. Our goal should be to create a regional industry that can sustain a relative number of creatives outside the advertising industry, and specifically, with the possibility of a living wage and lifetime careers in the field of children's book publishing. This includes those working in legal, finance, print design, etc.

We rely on academic discussion and not enough on business models to initiate real-world change. Public policy combined with corporate antitrust regulations and oversight would prohibit booksellers from also winning public tenders for schoolbooks as well as serving our small markets as printers or publishers while denying fair employment to our working creatives. We need to clamp down on piracy, which is a big problem for our publishing industries, and open up transparency and accountability on public tenders. The work now is bigger than, and at times has nothing to do with, the creative work of a single children's book.

Textbook tenders and commissions can sustain several independent houses, and they should have to compete over time as well as commit to publishing several trade books and procuring original intellectual property and licensing copyrights legally and independently. Books that make it to the school's lists should not be tied into this model of private sector procurement and public sector guarantees. There must be fair play and healthy risk in the market if the consumer, our reading audience, is to get a say in likes and dislikes.... We should be asking the questions, I think, that will direct us to solutions for getting independent publishers set up and sustainable.... Also, we often ask about authors and not illustrators. A flourishing picture book sector would employ our artists and greatly improve the quality of visual artists and children's book publishing through increased opportunities and fair competition. A flourishing nonfiction sector especially of children's book publishing would employ photographers and license photographs, while solving the problem of illustration expense.

Tere: *Mira yo creo que hay espacio para todo. Lo importante es no empujar al otro con el codo y aprender a ser solidarios, algo que en el caribe es difícil porques somos islas-colonias y el colonizado desconfía mucho, pero se que algún día existirá una unión antillana y todos los isleños nos uniremos. No hay duda que en PR debemos escribir más sobre nosotros y nuestra cultura, nuestras voces, nuestra historia. Si no se fomenta la lectura, los niños que van a recibir nuestros libros van a ser los mismos privilegiados de siempre o sea aquellos que han tenido la suerte de crecer en un hogar donde se fomenta el amor a la lectura. Tiene que haber una apertura y los libros de los escritores puertorriqueños deben estar en todas las escuelas, pero todo en la isla es política y la política normalmente no tiene cultura.*

Look, I think there is room for everything. The important thing is not to push the other with one's elbow and learn to be supportive, something that in the Caribbean is difficult because we are island colonies and the colonized distrust a lot, but I know that one day there will be an Antillean union and all the islanders will join. There is no doubt that in Puerto Rico we should write more about ourselves and our culture, our voices, our history. If reading is not encouraged, the children who receive our books will be the same [who are] privileged as always, those who have been lucky enough to grow up in a home where the love of reading is encouraged. There has to be an opening, and Puerto Rican writers' books must be in every school, but everything on the island is political and politics usually has no culture.

Ada: I must confess I have thought little about the publishing industry. That said, Joanne's thoughts on publishing and diversity ring true to me. We cannot become fixated on individual authors—organization and solidarity are the keys to building a flourishing children's book industry. This is echoed by Tere, who adds the issue of accessibility. We must encourage publishing and reading, but that doesn't resolve the question of how the poor access books. Puerto Rico is in dire need of a fully developed public library system to serve the reading public and entice the nonreading public.

Diane: Unless and until the governments, the private sector, and the parents believe in importance of our children's literature, children's book publishing is not really sustainable from an economic point of view. I know that may sound harsh. Economies of scale, lack of disposable income, and a culture of nonreading in Jamaica (you know, punishment being go to your room and read a book) would be our main challenges. We have had more publishing projects and author groups across the region and in Jamaica than you can imagine. We have had regional workshops funded by international organizations out of which should come an anthology, and nothing happens. I have been involved with some with high hopes, only for these hopes to be shattered. And I am not indulging [in] that myth that our children don't read. They would if they had access to the books.

And yet, after all these years, I have run into adults, a nurse, a policeman, a teacher in training, who mention how much the Dr. Bird Reading Series meant to them. Jamaicans overseas write me to ask how they can get hold of these books for their children. I direct them to the section in government, but I don't know how they'll get them because the government does not sell books.

However, Bookfusion (a relatively new organization here) does have some of these which you can read free online; they have music and "read along" with some of their storybooks. So this is actually a very positive development.

I am so sad that the Burt Award for the Caribbean no longer exists. Some very outstanding books were done and my hopes soared yet again. I love these books. Here again we depend on outside funds, which can disappear. A grade 7 student wrote me to say they were reading *Island Princess in Brooklyn* [2011; Carlong Sand Pebbles series] at her school and the book is "amazing." I was so thrilled. It is a popular book. So we can't give up, can we?

Right now, we may think of technology (e.g., video games) as one of the challenges we writers face. But perhaps we can challenge the younger generation of writers to use technology and the emotions the coronavirus has stirred up to create their own approach to sensitize our people in validating our "own voices."

Q: Is there advice you would like to share with aspiring writers?

Joanne: Honor your intuition, your inner teacher. Commit to writing only what is true for you. I believe life itself will reflect to what degree you are being authentic. Don't take anything personally. Grow, grow, grow and follow your inner GPS. Treat every opportunity as your one "big thing." The opportunity you've been waiting for all your life. If you can't feel that way, maybe you need to say no to it. Maybe you're not thinking big enough. No small step is insignificant. Even if you dream of writing an award-winning best seller, treat the stepped reader that will pay you as respectfully as that, or accept the offer to write a school play with the same commitment to the long-term success you desire. Here and now, honor your work, yourself, and your audiences in this way.

Tere: *Debe existir más comunicación entre las islas. Tenemos que lograrlo. Tenemos que hacer un encuentro de escritores e ilustradores infantiles de las islas. CuentoIsla 2020.*

No soy buena dando consejos, pero comparto consejos que yo me he dado a mi misma:

- *Si sabes que eres escritor, sigue escribiendo.*
- *No creas que eres genial. Amarra el ego.*
- *Lee en voz alta. Te darás cuenta si el texto fluye. Si vuela, si es lo que debe ser.*
- *No compartas nada hasta que de verdad esté bien escrito. Si tienes que escribirlo 100 veces pues dale. Hay tiempo.*
- *Busca un editor o sea una persona que tenga estahabilidad y nunca publiques a menos que esa persona te lea y te ayude. Cuatro ojos ven mejor que dos. Todos los grandes escritores han tenido editores. ¡Aprende a escuchar sin sentirte herido! La arrogancia pesa.*
- *Uno sabe lo que uno es. No deben existir escondites. Sabes que eres porque te da pasión.*
- *Hay muchas formas de publicar tu libro de forma independiente. Investiga antes de publicar. Visita blogs, mira lo que se está publicando, dialoga con otros escritores, compara, comparte.*
- *Compratus ISBN.*
- *Escribe de vez encuando a mano, eso libera la mente.*
- *Trabaja con mapas mentales. Ayuda a descubrir.*
- *Aprende con maestros en la red. No esperes a que nadie teenseñe. Se hace de noche y todavía sigues esperando.*

There must be more communication between the islands. We have to achieve it. We have to convene a meeting of children's writers and illustrators of the islands. Story Island 2020.

I am not good at giving advice, but I share advice that I have given to myself:

- If you know you are a writer, keep writing.
- Don't think you're great. Tie [control] the ego.
- Read aloud. You will notice if the text flows. If it flies, it is as it should be.
- Do not share anything until it is really well written. If you have to write it one hundred times, then do so. There is time.
- Find a publisher or a person who has this ability, and never publish unless that person reads and helps you. Four eyes see better than two. All great writers have had editors. Learn to listen without feeling hurt! Arrogance weighs.
- One knows what one is. There should be no hiding places. You know you are because it gives you passion.
- There are many ways to publish your book independently. Research before posting. Visit blogs, see what is being published, dialogue with other writers, compare, share.
- Buy your ISBN.
- Write from time to time by hand; that frees the mind.
- Work with mind maps.
- Learn with teachers on the net. Don't wait for anyone to teach you. It's getting dark and you're still waiting.

Ada: The advice I would give is—if you are interested in children and their development, critically observe them and their context, pick something you think will respond to their doubts about the world, and write about that so they feel free to openly question. Help them develop their voice as the first step in a process of change.

Diane: All the other participants' comments are important; especially I was struck by Tere's point that all great writers have editors, Joanne's "committing to writing only what is true for you," and Ada's point that the writer should "pick something you think will respond to their (the children's) doubts about the world and write about that so they feel free to openly question." I love that!

I would add to these, "Read!" It is astonishing how many people want to write but don't read. Also, you have to want to do writing and be willing to rewrite. You will not make money from it, but we need some people in each generation to add to this writing, to this chronicle of our lives.

Notes

1. Translations provided by the editors.
2. For more on the term "own voices," see the discussion by the organization We Need Diverse Books at https://diversebooks.org/why-we-need-diverse-books-is-no-longer-using-the-term-ownvoices/.

CHAPTER 14

Creating Picture Books
Reflections of Edwidge Danticat, Olive Senior, and Junot Díaz

Betsy Nies and Melissa García Vega

In the following conversation, three internationally known, deeply accomplished authors talk about their reasons for writing for children. They highlight the connections between their literature for adults and for children, and reveal insights into reasons why writers must bridge that divide.

Edwidge Danticat, originally from Haiti, has won multiple awards for her literature for adults, including both the American Book Award and (twice) the National Book Critics Circle Award. Her book *Breath, Eyes, Memory* (1994) won the Oprah Book Club Selection in 1998. She also writes books for children. In 2005, she published *Anacaona: Golden Flower, Haiti, 1490*, part of the Scholastic Royal Diary series targeting children grades 4 through 6. This diary chronicles the life of a fifteenth-century Taíno poet and ruler of a province in what today is Haiti. *Eight Days: A Story of Haiti* (2010), illustrated Alix Delinois, details a young boy's memories of everyday life as he lies trapped beneath the rubble of Haiti's largest earthquake. *Mama's Nightingale: A Story of Immigration and Separation* (2015), with Leslie Staub, shares the trauma a young girl experiences when her Haitian mother is detained in the US for not having proper documentation. Her young adult book *Untwine* (2015) addresses the impact of grief on coming of age. Her most recent book, *My Mommy Medicine* (2019), with Shannon Wright, narrates the comfort mothers can provide when their babies feel sick.

Olive Senior, originally from Jamaica, is an accomplished poet, novelist, short story writer, and nonfiction writer; and beginning in 2012, a children's book author. Among her many awards, she received the Commonwealth Writers' Prize in 1987, for *Summer Lightning and Other Stories* (1986), which, with her book of poems *Gardening in the Tropics* (1994), was integrated into Caribbean secondary school curricula. Ms. Senior won the Musgrave Gold Medal awarded by the Jamaican Ministry for Education, Youth, and Culture in 2005 for her literary output, for capturing the language and culture of her homeland. Based in Canada, she has published three picture books: *Birthday Suit* (2012), illustrated by Eugenie Fernandes, and *Anna Carries Water* (2013) and *Boonoonoonous Hair* (2019), both illustrated by Laura James.

Junot Díaz, born in the Dominican Republic and raised in New Jersey, published his first book of short stories, *Drown*, in 1996, and in 2007 *The Brief Wondrous Life of Oscar Wao*, winner of the 2008 Pulitzer Prize. Recipient of a MacArthur "Genius" Fellowship among many other awards, Díaz published his first book for children in 2018, titled *Islandborn*. Illustrated by Leo Espinosa, the picture book addresses the situation of an immigrant who is too young to remember her country of origin. It also addresses the complicated process of addressing historical trauma in books for children. Díaz is currently the fiction editor at the *Boston Review* and the Rudge and Nancy Allen Professor of Writing at the Massachusetts Institute of Technology.

Q: What prompted you to start writing for children?
ED: I started writing for children when my daughters were born. There were stories I wanted to tell them, things I wanted them to know right away, so I started writing children's books with them in mind as my primary audience. I also remember my love of reading initially being sparked by a children's book: Ludwig Bemelmans's *Madeline*, which my uncle gave me as a gift when I was four years old. I know firsthand how important reading the right book, at the right time, can be for a child, and what a life-transforming event that can be.
OS: I have to confess that I had no plans to write specifically for children, although a lot of my adult fiction is centered around children. I write out

of ideas that come to me, and several came as stories for children—hence my three children's books. That said, I am always conscious of the need for stories that reflect Caribbean culture, and I love the idea that picture books give us the opportunity to do this in words and images.

JD: It was my goddaughters. They kept asking me to write books that they could read. This was back when they were younger and of course I promised them I would, but I couldn't come up with anything for years and years. I'm such a slow, unproductive writer. I only hit upon something worth working on *after* they were fully grown.

Q: Are there cultural or social reasons you consider your work particularly important for a young audience?

ED: I think it's important for children to see some version of themselves in books, especially when living in countries where they are considered "minorities." I think having books by and about us can definitely help our children to appreciate who they are. It's often said that you have to be able to imagine something before you can decide to do it. Books in which we're at the center of things, doing things, can help our children fully imagine the endless possibilities of who they are and who they can be.

OS: I absolutely agree with Edwidge. I would go further and say that I also want children of what might be the majority culture to learn something about ours, especially to counter the stereotypes.

JD: I'm in complete agreement here with both, Edwidge and Ms. Senior.

Q: When you are composing a picture book, what criteria (such as aesthetics, illustration, or language rhythm) do you consider?

ED: This is a personal bias, for sure, but I want my picture books to have very lively and vibrant images. I want them to look colorful and bright, even when the subjects are not such happy subjects. My inspiration is Haitian art. I want all my picture books to tell as much of a story with the images as with the words.

OS: I don't really "compose" a picture book. I write the story in the expectation that my publisher will find an illustrator who will create images that will both reflect and extend the story. I have been very fortunate so far in the choices my publishers have made. The illustrations by Eugenie Fernandes (*Birthday Suit*) and Laura James (*Anna Carries Water* and *Boonoonoonous Hair*) have both deepened and extended the universe of the stories. They are bright and colorful, reflecting the Caribbean. Although the illustrators are chosen by the publishers, I make sure I have a say in the final product, because the images represented are as important as the words.

JD: Like my *compatriotas*, I also wanted the art to replicate the Caribbean's visual vibrancy. But I've always been obsessed with the clean, expressive lines of the "retro" style from the fifties and sixties that I grew up in—"midcentury modern" as it is formally called. I loved that style as a kid but was always looking for people in the drawings who looked like me. Which was why I wanted *Islandborn*'s art to be drawn in that style—a way to redress a historical absence. I explained to my publisher what I wanted and was elated when the brilliant Leo Espinosa came on to draw the book.

Q: Do you discuss with your illustrator ways to reflect certain themes? If so, how?

ED: The theme is the text. I like to respect the illustrator, to see what their vision of the text is. Often they come up with something much more appropriate than I do. I ask to look at sketches before the final images and I offer some suggestions about the look of the characters and places, but after perhaps an initial conversation. I like to leave it up to the illustrator to come up with their vision of the book, though I certainly do share, as Junot mentioned, my preferences in general. It's always wonderful, though, to see what emerges out of that convergence of my vision and the illustrator's. For example, for *My Mommy Medicine*, I sent the illustrator a picture of my younger daughter, Leila, and said I'd love the little girl to look like this, because I wanted the book to also be a keepsake for Leila when she's older, something she can tell her children about, and I was very happy with how that turned out. It was a visually beautiful book that also ended up having that personal angle for our family.

OS: I leave it up to the illustrator to choose how to interpret the story. I usually see the illustrations at the storyboard stage, and then I am able to make any necessary comments so adjustments, if necessary, can be made before the final work, where I will "proofread" both text and pictures. I see the process as a collaboration between writer, illustrator, and publisher, and all of us need to be happy with the result. I do like the way Laura James's images reflect and respond to my stories while assuming a life of their own, enriching the overall reading experience. The illustrations for *Anna Carries Water* brilliantly convey the countryside. For me, the setting for *Boonoonoonous Hair* could be anywhere, but she chose a city setting with scenes as variable as the hairstyles. The visual puns are all hers—the hairstyles on the paintings of well-known ladies on the museum walls or the lion's mane reflecting the protagonist's own mane. In my first book, *Birthday Suit*, the artist, Eugenie Fernandes, also created an exciting tropical backdrop teeming with life. In the seaside setting, the same creatures keep popping up from page to page—crabs, fish, seabirds, an impudent cat, and the face of a female sun (wearing a hair ribbon!) showing herself on every page with a different expression that comments on the action. I'm afraid I can't take credit for any of the illustrations, but I enjoy looking at them as much as the children do.

JD: Leo is from Colombia; he grew up in the Caribbean aesthetic so he got my vision right away and expanded it with his own genius. The only advice I gave was around hair and haircuts.

Q: You have each had several read-aloud engagements with children throughout the United States, Canada, and the Caribbean. What is it like to read aloud in all of these different settings?

ED: I've read to children in tent camps after the earthquake of 2010 in Haiti. We did this via a program called Li, Li, Li. I've read to children in immigration detention centers. I have read to children at my local library. Each time it's wonderful to see how the children seem to, for a moment, slip away from their location to fall into a book. I love the questions the children ask afterward. Like you, they always want to know about the illustrations, for example. They always ask whether I illustrated the book myself.

OS: I've read in Canada and the Caribbean and Europe. I am about to have my first reading in the USA at the Bronx Library. I find that children will always be engaged in a good story, wherever they are, and whatever the topic. But they are more likely to be less shy and have lots of questions and comments if they are prepared beforehand, for instance, if the teacher has already shared the book with the class. Then they also come prepared to cross-examine the author.

JD: I don't know what it is about me, but I've had a couple of readings where the kids took over the stage and took the mike from me.

ED: Those are the best kinds of readings.

Q: When you compose, who do you imagine as your audience?

ED: I think of my children first. I often get them to edit the books for me and tell me what they like and dislike. I think of all kinds of children, from every place in the world potentially reading the book. I don't think Ludwig Bemelmans was thinking of a child like me when he wrote *Madeline*, but it found me somehow in Haiti and helped me to see another path to storytelling. So, I'd love any child who has access to books to be able to read my books.

OS: To be honest, I don't think of an audience when I am composing. I usually lose myself in having fun as the story unfolds in my mind, thinking up rhymes and rhythms, joyful words and playful scenarios—even if the subject matter is serious. It is this playfulness that I enjoy in the writing and which I hope the children enjoy in the reading. I do of course want children of my culture to read my books and see themselves reflected, but I don't limit my writing to any demographic—a good story will find readers anywhere. As Edwidge says, *Madeline* found her, as *Alice in Wonderland* found me as a child and never went away.

JD: I don't have any children but I've been surrounded by children my whole life, even now. I write to the children in my life, but what I've discovered is that these kids are way more sophisticated than I was at their age. Parents tend to think their kids can't handle certain themes, but the truth is it's often the parents that can't handle the themes that their kids are willing to wrestle with.

Q: What connections do you see between your literature written for children and for adults?

ED: I address the same themes in both types of books—immigration and separation in *Mama's Nightingale*, mother/daughter relationships in *My Mommy Medicine*, history in *Anacaona: Golden Flower*, and grief in *Untwine*. I try not to talk down or water things down for my young readers. The main difference for me is the age of the narrators. Of course, the writing veers younger because they are younger. A younger narrator will tell a story differently than an older one, but that's about it.

OS: The themes in my adult fiction might be darker and the conclusions less easy, but all my protagonists seem on the path to taking charge of a situation, so it often is about learning lessons (adults) or mastering a lesson (children). My picture books do reflect my desire as a poet to play with language—rhythms and rhymes come naturally to me even when I'm ostensibly writing prose. I use a fair amount of Jamaican Creole in my adult work but write the children's books in English, though I introduce Jamaican words (e.g., *boonoonoonous*) or phrases. There are also glimpses of the oral culture, for instance in *Anna Carries Water*; the children fetching water place a piece of leaf in their containers to prevent the water from spilling as they walk—a practice from my own country childhood. But all of these elements arrive naturally and reflect who I am rather than any considered effect. The constraints are with keeping the intended ages in mind and the small number of words you have to work with.

JD: My adult writing tends to be bleak—only the good humor and intelligence and hopefulness of the narrators keep it from being totally nightmarish. When I wrote my children's book, I dropped the bleakness, stressed the hopefulness, and found myself tapping deeper into my sense of whimsy.

Q: Ms. Danticat and Mr. Díaz—you both address disturbing historical topics in your work for children. Ms. Danticat, you treat the violence of Spanish colonialism in *Anacaona: Golden Flower*, the 2010 earthquake in *Eight Days: A Story of Haiti*, and sadness about immigration and separation in *Mama's Nightingale*. In *Anacaona: Golden Flower*, you provide information about Anacaona's death in the afterword—she was hung by the Spanish—but you choose to focus instead on the body of the work on her life, love, and daily thoughts and dreams. At the same time you don't veer away from sharing the image of the Spanish gutting a pregnant Taíno woman.

Mr. Díaz, in *Islandborn*, you allude to the reign of Rafael Trujillo, the brutal dictator of the Dominican Republic from 1930 until 1961. Figured as a giant green bat-like creature who threatens those on the island, Trujillo hovers in the background of Lola's story, the protagonist who wants to discover where she's from. She asks the janitor Mr. Mir (perhaps a reference to Pedro Mir, the acclaimed Dominican poet who resisted the oppression of Trujillo) about the island, but he shares with her the terrors of the monster only after she questions him twice. You put in other cues for the adult reading audience. Mr. Mir holds a framed picture of the Mirabel sisters and their driver, who were murdered by Trujillo's thugs, in the illustration with the sign "Salcedo," the home of the sisters' birth.

Ms. Danticat and Mr. Díaz, how do you approach writing history—particularly historical trauma or the generational silences that surround traumatic events—for children? What difficulties do you face when narrating such histories and realities for young audiences? What function do you see these books serving educationally, socially, or emotionally?

ED: These days young people have instant access to horrors we can't necessarily protect them from. As much as I try, I can't keep my daughter from seeing the police killings of Black men, women, and children on video. These things, which are much more visually graphic than the historical horrors we describe in our stories, are constantly played on a loop on the news as though they are part of an endless present. So there is really no way to protect young people anyway. They can easily look up anything. I think it's crucial for us to tell our side of the story, to help our children understand the story of the person dying or being massacred, be it in the present or in the past. Otherwise, they might only have the prevalent narrative and fully believe that. I think it's important to break those silences around our versions of these stories in order to counter those that are out there. This seems more necessary than ever right now. Imagine all the cleaning up we'll have to do when the history of this time is written, this moment of constant lying and "alternative facts." What will history make for us? What will my children's children be told? It's important for us to tell the stories that might be ignored or left out otherwise. I hope my books, both for adults and children, will do that.

JD: History's power should never be underestimated. But many of us children of the diaspora are often at a greater disadvantage than most. We often don't know the sources or the causes of the historical flows that surround us because we are not always taught the histories of back home. In the case of the Dominican Republic, the Trujillo dictatorship wounded Dominican society deeply, a wound that never healed. And as a child I certainly came up against that wound time and time again and yet never understood it, never could name it. In my generation, many of us were never encouraged to ask any questions about the past. Silence always. But fortunately, things are somewhat different with the newer generation. More questions are being asked by young people, and that's good for everyone. I wish I'd had the space growing up to ask the questions that burdened me, and so I tried to give little Lola the opportunity I never had. What I decided in the process of writing *Islandborn* was that children are hurt more by silence than they are by difficult truths. So I went with the difficult truth.

Many of us immigrants are from places we don't remember or remember dimly, and yet those places nevertheless have a powerful hold on us. How do we make sense of that tenuous connection, how do we form selves from those gaps? These are questions every immigrant must answer for themselves, and I hope that *Islandborn* can be of service in that dialogue.

CHAPTER 15

Making Memories or *Pesadillas*?
Junot Díaz's *Islandborn*

Megan Jeanette Myers

A metaphorical monster—with wings, hollow eyes, and sharp teeth—lurks in the memories of Dominicans living in the US diaspora and manifests on the pages of Junot Díaz's first foray into children's literature. Díaz's *Islandborn* (2018) outlines the Dominican immigrant experience in the United States through the eyes of Lola, an Afro-Dominican elementary-aged protagonist living in Washington Heights, Manhattan. The book shares the problem the young girl encounters as she attempts to draw a picture of her "first country," the Dominican Republic, for a class assignment. Unlike her peers who are "from somewhere else" and have vivid memories of their native countries, Lola moved to the US as a baby and admittedly remembers nothing about the Dominican Republic, referred to exclusively as "the Island" in *Islandborn*. In order for Lola to complete her homework, she interviews her family and members of her community in an effort to assemble her own understanding of her birth country.

This chapter builds on American author and activist bell hooks's "politicization of memory" to explore how the memories of an immigrant community serve to "illuminate and transform the present" ("Choosing the Margin" 147) of the young Dominican American protagonist. The motive behind politicizing memory is to provide space for those without a history or access to their respective (trans)national histories to create and envision their own version of the past garnered from collective, community-based sources. Lola, encouraged by her class assignment to politicize her own memory as an immigrant youth, builds on the memories of her neighbors and family members in the Dominican community of Washington Heights to create—through the completed illustration she shares with her elementary school class—her own version of the Dominican Republic and its history. More than the country's history, Lola attempts to capture the essence of the island-nation; she delves into the sounds, smells, and tastes of the Island as relayed to her by the multicultural community that surrounds her in Washington Heights. This chapter not only explores how the young protagonist of *Islandborn* develops an understanding of her transnational and cross-cultural identity vis-à-vis an analysis of hooks's politicization of memory but also assesses how metaphorical "monsters"—the negative elements of history often hidden from children—emerge in *Islandborn* and addresses how scholars identify the potential of culturally diverse children's literature to enhance readers' cross-cultural identity.[1]

In her essay "Choosing the Margin as a Space of Radical Openness" in *Yearning: Race, Gender, and Cultural Politics* (1990), hooks differentiates between nostalgia and the politicization of memory by classifying nostalgia as a "useless act" (147) that disregards the future. A politicization of memory instead draws from the past and is future oriented. hooks grew up as a young Black girl in racially segregated rural Kentucky. Her upbringing and experience resisting racism in the southern US in the mid-twentieth century informs her writing. In particular, her theory of politicized memory constitutes a personal reflection on marginalization and her own conscientious effort to use memory constructively. The forward-looking perspective of hooks's politicized understanding of nostalgia and memory lends itself to an analysis of children's literature, as characters in children's books, especially in culturally diverse children's literature, often re-create or reimagine their diverse backgrounds in order to establish a sense of self. In this way, children's literature, and more specifically picture books, can encourage the development of a positive identity formation (Hall 80).

hooks, like Díaz, is also a children's book author. Her own poetic picture book, titled *Skin Again* (2004), featuring illustrations by Chris Raschka, celebrates diversity and makes a conscientious effort to destabilize the notion of skin color as signifier.[2] *Skin Again* encourages children to talk about race and identity not only with words but also through Raschka's illustrations.

Raschka first utilizes different colors and shapes to show full portraits of kids with different skin colors, and then he moves to patchwork-style imagery to focus on what is inside of the children—their dreams and desires. hooks's book not only offers a model within children's literature of Molly Bang's confirmation in *Picture This* (1991) of the importance of shapes and lines to induce meaning and evoke emotion, but it further addresses the importance of "seeing" diversity in the field. If racially diverse children are absent from the picture books that children of color encounter, they can develop a "zero image" of themselves, as Carolyn Gerald asserted in the 1970s in her oft-cited article "The Black Writer and His Role" (359). Gerald suggests that Black youth are bombarded with white-controlled imagery, a fact that has been reiterated in conversations about culturally diverse children's literature; only in recent years has there been a push for the genre to "incorporate stories of many races and cultures" (Hill 445).

In the case of *Islandborn*, Leo Espinosa's illustrations pair well with Díaz's narrative, as his colorful vision of the Dominican Republic and the Dominican diaspora (represented by Washington Heights) capitalizes on the picture-book layout and uses color and illustrations to take "advantage of specific aspects of their format in order to expose, push against, and even break longstanding forms of social and political oppression" (Papazian 170). Bang's aforementioned *Picture This*, centered on the emotional content of images, delineates how shapes and lines form the essence of graphic stories. A discussion of how illustrations evoke emotion clearly relates to children's literature, given the sensitivity of youth to illustrations and the fact that "they are subject to the impression illustrations create. The images these children soak up remain with them for the rest of their lives" (Roethler 96). While this chapter focuses primarily on the text itself, the importance of the visual experience of *Islandborn* via Espinosa's illustrations is paramount to any analysis of the work. For example, the multiculturally minded picture book highlights the diverse range of skin tones; the illustrations of the Afro-Dominican Lola and her classmates and neighbors further emphasize the variation of human skin color. Thus, the pictures included in *Islandborn* prove that just as "stories can generate an attitude that does not see race as a barrier" (Steiner, Nash, and Chase 88), so too can illustrations. Espinosa's graphic additions to Lola's story emphasize the rich diversity of New York City's barrios in a way that allows for all young readers, regardless of race, to envision themselves as a part of such multicultural and inclusive communities.

hooks's own foray into picture books allows for an interesting comparison with Díaz's similarly minded *Islandborn*, but her understanding of memory also serves as an ideal means to comprehend Lola's conundrum in the book. Lola's struggles to remember her first country in *Islandborn* begin with what hooks identifies as "a struggle for memory against forgetting" ("Choosing the Margin" 205). Lola asks her teacher in her diverse school, where every kid "was from somewhere else," "Miss, what if you don't remember where you are from? What if you left *before* you could start remembering?" The teacher responds by directing Lola to her community and the people who surround her who do remember. In the moments following the teacher-student interaction, Lola decides that she will draw, both literally and figuratively, from the memories of others to create her vision of her first country. Lola's conception of her native Dominican Republic stands for politicized memory by the ways it uses the past—imparted to her through the memories of her neighbors and family—to purport a vision of the Island influenced by the diaspora and to reflect elementary-aged Lola's forward-thinking and youthful approach to history. Lola's illustrative representation of her first country is both "a conceptualization of the past and subsequent attitude toward the present" (Arapoglou 123). The pages to follow explore how Díaz utilizes Lola's illustration-based class assignment as a jumping point to insert references to the Dominican Republic's dictatorial past vis-à-vis the Monster figure—a visual that clearly links to the infamous twentieth-century Dominican dictator Rafael Leónidas Trujillo.[3] This horrific Monster, though, is not as nightmarish as it first appears and instead serves as a signpost for the Dominican Republic's resilient history and the country's important heroes and heroines. Furthermore, these pages explore how Lola's vision of her first country constitutes a community-built memory that "illuminate[s] and transform[s] the present" (hooks, "Choosing the Margin" 147).

The connection between memory and location(s) in *Islandborn* proves key to an analysis of the work. While the illustrations and imagery in the book initially center on the US Dominican diaspora, this focalization on the Washington Heights community quickly merges with visual and textual representations of the Island itself. Espinosa's illustrations envision a colorful, inviting *Dominican American*—as opposed to just Dominican or just American—community. Espinosa's graphics offer a Caribbean versioning of the metropolitan New York streets. On Lola's walk home from school with her cousin in the book's first pages, the brownstones are met and exceeded in stature by multicolored palm trees. Furthermore, an array of tropical-looking plants frames the bottom of the page spread. Espinosa's Washington Heights is unmistakably Caribbean; the colorful plants, alongside Lola's neighbors in scarves and winter hats, offer an interesting paradox for young readers comparing Lola's two countries. As Zhihui Fang confirms, picture books "strongly or sometimes completely rely on illustrations to serve these functions of a setting" (131), and in *Islandborn*, the clash between the cold city streets and the Caribbean flora and fauna introduces readers to the unique setting in a way that the text alone could not.

For young Lola, remembering her first country runs parallel to appreciating and conjuring a better understanding of her second country, too. hooks discerns in "Choosing the Margin" that "home" is an ever-mutating signifier:

> At times, . . . home is no longer just one place. It is locations. Home is that place which enables and promotes varied and everchanging perspectives, a place where one discovers new ways of seeing reality, frontiers of difference. One confronts and accepts dispersal and fragmentation as part of the construction of a new world order that reveals more fully who we are, who we can become, an order that does not demand forgetting. (205)

hooks clarifies the synergy between location and memory; while notions of home shift endlessly, the fragmentation of the self that results from displacement and decolonization also serves as a reminder not to forget previous home(s). The importance of remembering and acknowledging one's roots and history guides *Islandborn* and registers as a common theme in culturally diverse children's literature. Scholar Rudine Sims Bishop's seminal article "Mirrors, Windows, and Sliding Glass Doors" references the importance of "mirror books" in children's literature, emphasizing the need for children to see their faces and situations reflected in the pages. Such "mirroring" helps children to identify with their own culture and also those of others. Building on Bishop's widely cited work and critiquing the idea that such literature should seek solely to affirm readers' own identities, Christopher Myers espouses that children are more "outward looking" than credited and "see books less as mirrors and more as maps. They are indeed searching for their place in the world, but they are also deciding where they want to go. They create, through the stories they're given, an atlas of their world, of their relationships to others, and of their possible destinations." Myers refers to

Figure 15.1. Illustration by Leo Espinosa, copyright © 2018 by Leo Espinosa; from *Islandborn* by Junot Díaz. Used by permission of Dial Books for Young Readers, an imprint of Penguin Young Readers Group, a division of Penguin Random House LLC. All rights reserved.

children's search in literature for directions that tell them where to go and the steps needed to arrive at a specific (literal or figurative) destination. This road-map perspective reflects in *Islandborn* as Lola, thanks to the collective memories of her neighbors and family members, acquires an "atlas" to her world: a bicultural space from which two distinct cultures and geographies emerge. Lola traverses her Washington Heights community in order to uncover the essence of her native Dominican Republic; her map or atlas expands beyond the US. Díaz positions the Afro-Dominican Lola on two maps: on the Island and in the US diaspora. In this way, the book explores the meaning of *dominicanidad* for Lola and her community and, as Díaz comments in an interview on *Latino USA*, in doing so defies the need to be on the Island in order to understand what it means to be Dominican. Thus, Lola can remember her first country—the Island—regardless of her physical location on another island, Manhattan. Given its geographic distinctiveness, *Islandborn* functions as a "culturally specific" picture book, as opposed to culturally neutral or culturally generic, in which the author identifies characters as members of a given cultural group (Bishop, "Multicultural Literature"). hooks's interest in the "politics of location" ("Choosing the Margin" 203) and the shifting meaning of "home" aligns with Díaz's conjuring of an off-Island *dominicanidad* expressed through Lola's identity exploration. Importantly, hooks connects the fragmentation born of the multiplicities of home to memory. She confirms, "Our struggle is also a struggle of memory against forgetting" (205). Situated in the US diaspora and distanced geographically from the Dominican Republic, Lola also struggles to not forget, to see herself on the Island. The young Afro-Dominican battles against forgetting what she does not remember smelling, tasting, hearing, or seeing as a baby, and throughout this struggle—of which the readers are onlookers—she realizes that the Island is in her. Lola's *abuela* reminds her, "Just because you don't remember a place doesn't mean it's not in you," and Lola concludes in the book's final pages, "The Island is me." In recognizing that her first country is indeed an integral part of her, she also acknowledges the Dominican Republic's dictatorial past and accepts that the good and the bad Island memories form part of who she is.

Alongside subtle references to the Dominican Republic's political turmoil, which plagued the nation for most of the twentieth century, *Islandborn* also deals with themes of immigration and self-identity, themes often overlooked in children's literature. Numerous studies confirm the lack of culturally diverse children's literature and prove the need for books like *Islandborn* that depict, in text and illustration, the reality for US immigrant families and children as well as the hardships these often marginalized groups face (Boyd, Causey, and Galda).[4] *Islandborn* not only falls into the category of culturally diverse children's literature but also aligns in many ways with the subgenre of Trujillo narrative for its aforementioned embodiment, in Monster form, of the Island's infamous twentieth-century political tyrant. Literary critic Ana Gallego Cuiñas defines Trujillo narrative as any novel written after the decades-long reign of the Dominican dictator that reflects on his regime. While Díaz wrote *Islandborn* for an elementary-aged audience, the picture book's relation to this particular subgenre of historical narrative, more specific to the history of the Dominican Republic than the more general "dictatorship narrative," casts the book as one that reflects on the postcolonial dictatorial history of the Island. Díaz carefully positions *Islandborn* as a book that incorporates, albeit to a mild degree, a representation of the "Trujillo phenomenon" (Gallego Cuiñas 12) and a vision of the country's dictatorial past consumable for children.[5] While other Latino/a writers, including Judith Ortiz Cofer, Pat Mora, Gloria Anzaldúa, and fellow Dominican American Julia Alvarez, have also published books intended for children and adolescents, Díaz's purposeful inclusion of Trujillo—vis-à-vis a metaphorical, winged Monster—proves unique.

Moreover, *Islandborn* does more than just tell about the "Monster," but the Monster also fills—literally and figuratively—the pages. As Lee Galda and Kathy G. Short confirm,

> Children need the ability to *see* in the fullest sense and to recognize the significance of what they are seeing. . . . Picture books offer a unique opportunity for children to develop visual literacy because they are able to return to the visual images in books to explore, reflect, and critique those images. As children explore illustrations and develop the ability to read images, they will attain deeper meanings from literature and an awareness of how visual images are used in their own meaning making. (506)

The first illustration of the green, winged Monster, toward the end of the book, could be chilling for young readers—hollow eyes, big teeth, a large wingspan, and sharp claws all add to the figure's strong visual presence, which turns the whole sky a dark green. But the Monster disappears from the pages

Figure 15.2. Illustration by Leo Espinosa, copyright © 2018 by Leo Espinosa; from *Islandborn* by Junot Díaz. Used by permission of Dial Books for Young Readers, an imprint of Penguin Young Readers Group, a division of Penguin Random House LLC. All rights reserved.

as quickly as it appeared. In the following page, the green sky has already faded to blue, beams of sunlight shoot out from the horizon, and the once-frightening claws of the Monster poke out from the calm waters, resembling small green islands in the distance. The illustrations shift from evoking chaos to calm more swiftly than the text is able, confirming for readers, from the simple turn of a page, that the Monster is defeated.

The Monster whose presence permeates the pages of *Islandborn* perhaps does not come as a surprise, given that Díaz is no stranger to science fiction. Díaz's 2012 story in the *New Yorker* titled "Monstro" takes place in the near future on the island of Hispaniola. In "Monstro," an epidemic that turns humans into zombie-like monsters threatens not only the island of Hispaniola but health and safety on a global scale. Díaz centers the quickly spreading disease, coined "La Negrura" (the Blackness), in Haiti, the reported first site of infection (or ground zero), but ends the story with a detonation event that spreads the disease, which "respect[s] no kind of boundaries," even more widely. Aside from the obvious delineation of zombie monsters that dominates "Monstro," the author's Pulitzer Prize–winning novel, *The Brief Wondrous Life of Oscar Wao*, contains ample references to the science fiction genre and also utilizes monster figures, notably in the form of faceless men, as literary models of the connections between science and magic or between humans and monsters. According to scholar Ramón Saldívar, Díaz's election to include monsters—in the form of zombies or faceless men—not only offers a unique critique of racism and postcolonialism but also serves as a signpost for "imaginary history" or "historical fantasy" (382, 387). In other words, Díaz uses nonhuman, often science fiction–inspired "monsters" to tackle the pain evoked by the processes and lived realities of colonialism, immigration, and marginalization. While Saldívar's delineation of Díaz's narrative as imaginary history or historical fantasy excludes *Islandborn*, given its later publication date in 2018, the children's book also toys with the connection between history and fantasy and utilizes fantastical creatures like the green, winged Monster to approach the history of the Island. Through the Monster, Díaz responds to the call for "a more balanced, complete, accurate, and realistic literature that asks even young readers to grapple with sometimes wrenching issues" (Nieto 188).

Díaz's decision to include the Monster, his nod to the Dominican Republic's dictatorial past, in part is a refusal to leave children (to a certain extent) out of difficult or painful discussions about their past and background. Díaz addresses the politics of innocence in children's literature in the aforementioned interview with María Hinojosa:

> I think that there is a tendency to think that children are innocents and that's what they should consume.... [F]or those of us who come from the kind of post-colonial traumas, they don't allow us to fully explore the kind of traumas that our young people are carrying within them and should have an opportunity to work through.

In the same interview, Díaz recognizes that the delivery of or introduction to historical trauma is unique when it pertains to children, and this recognition reflects in *Islandborn* not only in the metaphorical Monster's embodiment of Trujillo but also in the book's final and overarching message that instead focuses on the brave heroes who defeat the Monster. Díaz's references to the Monster, detailed in the following paragraph, include overt mentions of the heroes who overcome it. Moreover, Díaz also offers his readers other examples of the Island's reality and history—from bats native to the island to destructive hurricanes—that either become woven into the Island's essence in quotidian and familiar ways or are overcome by the Dominican community.

The Monster in *Islandborn* first emerges from the memories of the superintendent of Lola's apartment building, Mr. Mir. When Lola relays to him what others have shared with her about the Island, the following conversation ensues:

> "I see," Mr. Mir said. "So no one told you about the Monster."
> Lola's eyes got wide. She shook her head *no*.
> "Even those who know don't always want to talk about HIM."
> Mr. Mir turned toward the old worn map he had of the Island. "Our Island has always been a beautiful place. It was when I was your age, and it is today. But even the most beautiful places can attract a monster. A long time ago, long before you were born, that's exactly what happened: A monster fell upon our poor Island."

The capitalization of "HIM" confirms that the Monster personifies a historical, male figure. Moreover, the word "Monster" itself is almost always capitalized, assertively positioning the metaphorical creature as a proper name. Mr. Mir clarifies to Lola from the first mention of the Island's Monster that the metaphorical figure's existence had real consequences on the Island and that his memory and recollection of the Monster is distinct from, for example, Lola's cousin's recollection of "blanket bats." The first and largest illustration of the winged, green Monster in the book (and the only visual in which the creature appears to be "winning") accompanies text, in Mr. Mir's words, that contextualizes the reach of the Monster's power for young Lola: "It was the most dreadful monster anyone had ever seen. The whole Island was terrified and no one could defeat it." Mr. Mir continues filling in historical gaps for the young Lola as his story progresses. He offers Trujillo as another reason (aside from the reason Lola's mother provided for why her own family moved away from the Island—a hurricane) for why Dominicans left the Island: "For thirty years the Monster did as it pleased. It could destroy an entire town with a single word and make a whole family disappear simply by looking at it."

The allusion to the destructive Monster in *Islandborn* acknowledges what critics refer to as *la sombra* or the shadow of the dictator in Dominican and Dominican American literature. Literary critic Neil Larson also confirms the permanency of representations of Trujillo in Dominican literature, a repetition that does not escape Dominican American literature, including Díaz's work. As Claudia Milian asserts, "The shadow of Trujillo's dictatorship follows Díaz's subjects" (189). While Trujillo's shadow persists even in Díaz's first children's book, the dictator is a minor character. Just as Jennifer Harford Vargas describes the representation of Trujillo in *The Brief Wondrous Life of Oscar Wao*, in *Islandborn*, too, the dictator remains "a minor, flat character" represented by other characters and prevented from "focalizing the narrative" (205).

Albeit a "minor character" in *Islandborn*, the book's allusion to Trujillo is unmistakable. The message that resonates with readers, however, is not the suffering of the Island at the hands of the Monster, but instead the slaying of the Monster and the (female) heroes who destroyed him. Mr. Mir explains that heroes, tired of being afraid, rose up to fight the Monster. Mr. Mir identifies the heroes to Lola as "strong smart women just like you, Lola, and a few smart young men, too." While Mr. Mir's mention of the heroes initially portrays the Monster's demise as anonymously female-led, the illustration on the following page shows Mr. Mir holding a framed photo of three young women and one man in front of a sign marked "Salcedo." To anyone familiar with Dominican history, the three women and the man are the Mirabal sisters (originally from Salcedo) and their driver, whom Trujillo murdered in a staged car accident. Notably, Espinosa's illustrations confirm this suspicion.

In addition to the "Salcedo" geographical tag, one of the girls in the photo has long braids, just as the youngest Mirabal sister, María Teresa, always wore in her hair. Brutally assassinated on the way to visit their incarcerated husbands, in jail for outwardly resisting the Trujillo regime, the death of the three sisters—María Teresa, Patria, and Minerva—enraged the Caribbean nation and paved the way for Trujillo's own assassination just a few months later.

This historical reference, although subtle, represents another signpost of Díaz's narrative style transferred to children's literature; numerous scholars have analyzed, for example, the myriad historical references in *The Brief Wondrous Life of Oscar Wao*. While many of the historical asides in Díaz's prize novel appear in the form of footnotes, constituting what some scholars have alluded to as "the footnote condition," in *Islandborn*, Espinosa's illustrations, in the form of inclusions like that of the Mirabal sisters' photo, take the place of these textual add-ons. Monica Hanna notes that Díaz's footnotes are more "traditionally historical" than the "characters' lived experiences of history" (504); the photo of three women in front of the Salcedo sign, whom readers can assume to be the Mirabal sisters, also veers from the characters' experience of history (or Lola's experience of history) and instead alludes to the national history of the Dominican Republic. In some ways, though, the illustrations do more than footnotes can. The illustrations evoke emotion. Dark colors, like the deep green of the Monster, for example, "help create and maintain an eerie feeling" (Fang 132). Further, Espinosa's purposeful implementation of color also signals a racially diverse community. The visual portrayal of Lola's neighbors and schoolmates in Washington Heights celebrates the range of skin color and a diverse cast of characters. Thus, the illustrations in *Islandborn* serve to visually represent a racially diverse diasporic community. While Díaz's novels, like *The Brief Wondrous Life of Oscar Wao*, often include overt references to history and the racial, social, cultural, and political intricacies of the Dominican Republic and the Dominican diaspora, in *Islandborn*, it's the visual clues—as opposed to footnotes—that offer readers additional information that might not be included in the body text.

The superintendent's name also recognizes one of the Island's national heroes: the Dominican poet and writer Pedro Mir. The Dominican Congress named Mir, whose verses opposing the Trujillo regime caused him to seek political exile in Cuba for nearly two decades, poet laureate of the Dominican Republic in 1984. *Islandborn*'s insistence on national heroes—from writers to organizers (of both genders)—asserts the legacy of the Island as brave

Figure 15.3. Illustration by Leo Espinosa, copyright © 2018 by Leo Espinosa; from *Islandborn* by Junot Díaz. Used by permission of Dial Books for Young Readers, an imprint of Penguin Young Readers Group, a division of Penguin Random House LLC. All rights reserved.

and heroic, convincing Lola that even the worst monsters can be defeated. Lola's *abuela* confirms the same when her granddaughter prods her about the Monster. While she admits that sometimes the Monster was scary, she ends the conversation—like Mr. Mir—by highlighting the heroic side of history: "But we were also brave." The references that resonate strongly with the reader, in textual and visual form, assert the Island's legacy, a legacy that Díaz classifies as one in which "people overcome monsters" (Díaz, "Portrait Of: Junot Díaz"). This legacy of national heroes rising above and defeating oppressive political tyrants manifests in *Islandborn* as one that speaks to and for other nations in addition to the Dominican Republic, expanding to the postcolonial and postdictatorial past of Latin America at large. Díaz highlights this inclusivity by referring to the Dominican Republic exclusively as "the Island" in the book, hinting at the fact that the history *Islandborn* relays is a shared one. With reference to the linkages between hooks's politicization of memory and Díaz's children's book, Lola's reflection on her past—a past that is communal in nature and belongs to her family, her community, and her birth country—allows her to better understand herself and how memories of the Dominican Republic inform both her present and her future. Utilizing the moniker "the Island" allows for and encourages other readers to relate to the story and find their own respective (national) histories within it. The allusion to the Monster also functions as an extended metaphor capable of embodying countless political "monsters." While immigrant experiences vary widely in terms of geographic, racial, and historical contexts, Díaz's election to use a monster figure relatable for all children and to label the Dominican Republic broadly as "the Island" allows for more children to relate to the story and locate their respective "first country" within it.

Without mention of the Monster, Lola's Island visualization may have included only music, mangoes, and *agua de coco*.[6] Moreover, without Mr. Mir's memories, not only the Monster but, more importantly, the Monster's demise would have remained hidden from Lola. The rising up of Dominican men and women—characterized by Mr. Mir as strong, smart, and brave—succeeds in banishing the Monster. In this way, Mr. Mir's memory of heroes, as opposed to the Monster himself, is the final story Lola records. While the tale of the Monster is nightmarish, this memory of a nation's heroes overshadows it. Díaz's green Monster, then, has multiple connotations in the book. The inclusion of the green, winged creature is not intended to induce *pesadillas* or nightmares, but instead to reveal other (heroic, proud) memories that have come to define the Island. In a similar way, the picture book offers other examples of possibly frightening memories (and accompanying images) coupled alongside joyful and peaceful ones.

Similar to the Monster, but more relatable for kids, the book also mentions a scary hurricane. Espinosa's artistic rendering of the hurricane makes explicit the destruction that such natural disasters can cause, with cars and houses flying through a dark gray sky, but Lola and the matriarchs of her family, her mother and her *abuela*, are the most prominent illustrations on the page. Here, Espinosa's image sends a message that family is the stronger force.

Díaz narrates the natural disaster as the motive behind Lola's mother's emigration to the US, but this memory, much like that of the Monster, appears positioned alongside a story of bravery and perseverance. Lola's mom recalls the moment the abrasive hurricane blew through her town: "And you know what? You never cried once. You were such a brave little girl." In a similar way, Espinosa's visualization of the memories of Lola's family and community allows for a recontextualization of the past. The "blanket bats" that Lola's cousin remembers about the Island, for example, prove that things or memories are only frightening if one approaches them in this way. While bats are categorized traditionally as creepy, unsanitary virus carriers, in *Islandborn* the smiley, colorful, print-laden bats appear friendly and form part of the essence of the Island. Early in the story, Lola's older cousin remembers bats that were "as big as blankets," but these "blanket bats" are only referenced once in the text; however, they reappear on nine page spreads after their first mention. Thus, Espinosa's repeated inclusion of the happy and brightly colored mammals on nearly every page functions as a makeshift game for young readers who can spot the bats peeking through barbershop windows and skirting through palm trees. Espinosa's representation of the blanket bats is comforting both in his literal interpretation of Díaz's blanket bats—little bat heads with blanket wings—and also because the recurring figures might resonate more with young readers than would the Monster. The illustrations, then, offer a varied understanding of the author's analysis of (collective) memories, which veer away from nightmarish images, and the blanket bats and use of bright colors help to override the imagery of the giant winged Monster, which appears shrunken and pushed to the margins in the book's final pages.

The memories, good and bad, that surface in Lola's hand-drawn homework assignment appearing in the final spread of the book encourage an exploration of the young Afro-Dominican's identity. Lola's drawing, her at-first anxiety-producing homework assignment, fills the page spread with blue-skinned baseball players and musicians, a smiley-faced empanada, an array of friendly blanket bats, giant whales, and dolphins, and a man on a *moto* hugging a mango. Notably, the Mirabal sisters and Lola's *abuela* also appear on the page. The women are drawn chasing away the Monster, relegated to the far-right corner of the page, with arrows, butterflies, and music. The way Lola envisions her first country reflects a "mythico-historical" record that privileges both fact and fantasy (Suárez-Orozco 70). A cultural narrative that represents equal parts myth and reality dominates the collective memory Lola records from her family and neighbors in Washington Heights. This intertwinement between two juxtaposed approaches enables what Saldívar refers to as "historical fantasy" in Díaz's literary corpus, and the phrase on the back cover of *Islandborn*, "Memory is magic," further emphasizes this relationship.

The three words "Memory is magic," printed in the colors of the Dominican flag (red and blue),[7] perhaps not only reference the play between official historical discourse and metaphorical, even science fiction–like inclusions in the picture book of monsters and blanket bats but also speak to the ability of memories to transform Lola's present reality. *Islandborn* succeeds in emphasizing the ability of transnational memories, garnered from collective sources, to allow Lola to envision and write (or draw) her own understanding of reconciliation with the past. hooks describes a similar moment for her as a young girl in "A Memory of My Girlhood," a story included in her autobiographical collection *Bone Black: Memories of Girlhood*:[8] "We have broken the leg of another doll. We have cracked open the head of an antique doll to see what makes the crying sound" (24). In this story, hooks describes how as a child she destroyed the white dolls, Barbies with blonde hair, because they looked nothing like her. The memories of the Dominican diasporic community of Washington Heights enable and encourage Lola, in a sense, to do the very same—to "crack open the head"—to access her history and to uncover her own historical reality. In doing so, Lola finds herself and finds the Island within her. Lola's community—understood as both on- and off-Island—is the bridge that allows her to see herself as part of a shared history; it is the communal nature of memory that allows the main character to triumph over the "struggle for memory against forgetting" (hooks, "Choosing the Margin" 205). Lola verbalizes the importance of collective memory on the first pages of *Islandborn* when she notes, "I should draw from their memories." In both a literal and a figurative sense, Lola "draws" from the memories of her family and neighbors, partaking in collective memory and bearing witness to generations of historical and political trauma.

The day following the heavy conversation between Lola and Mr. Mir, Lola passes Mr. Mir on her way to school as she clutches her book of Island illustrations tightly. As he wishes her good luck, she shouts back to him, "Thank you, Mr. Mir, slayer of monsters." Given the significance of Mr. Mir as an eponym, a nod to the Dominican poet laureate, does recognizing the superintendent in this way imply that one can slay monsters with words? With illustrations? This interaction between generations emphasizes the power of collective memory and suggests that words and art can help to destroy political monsters like Trujillo. Had Mr. Mir not shared the legacy of the Monster with Lola, it is possible no one would have. Díaz's election to include Trujillo, albeit in the form of a metaphorical Monster, speaks to the idea of "counter-storytelling" in children's literature, given that Díaz shares stories about the Dominican Republic that are not often shared with young audiences (Solórzano and Yosso). By implementing counter-storytelling strategies and allowing children to gain access to their own historical realities, Lola's illustration constitutes a visualization of politicized memory. Lola builds on collective memory to understand her history and herself, envisioning her own version of the past to "transform the present" (hooks, "Choosing the Margin" 147) and move through the world with an anchor to her first country's history, one that includes monsters but does not end with them.

Díaz's *Islandborn* presents an Afro–Dominican American protagonist whose doors are opened to her past. Despite the fact that bats, hurricanes, and even a Monster emerge through these metaphorical doors, the representation of politicized memory that materializes in the picture book gives the young protagonist the tools to confront her past with a positive and forward-thinking mentality. While at first glance the young protagonist Lola is unsure of her ability to draw her "first country" for her school assignment, her family and surrounding community succeed in sharing collective memories that model the shared experiences and solidarity of diverse and transnational communities. At the same time, Lola's lesson about her birth country—imparted by her family, Mr. Mir, and others—highlights the importance of depicting such diverse communities in children's literature and demonstrates how the power of community and the memory of national heroes and heroines can squelch even the scariest of monsters.

Notes

1. While definitions of diverse or multicultural children's literature vary, the Cooperative Children's Book Center (CCBC) defines multicultural literature as "books by and about people of color." The CCBC also annually publishes statistics on the number of multicultural books published in the US; this resource is made available for free on the CCBS's website. These open-access statistics build on Nancy Larrick's seminal 1960s article in which she highlights the disparity between white characters and characters of color in published children's books. While the CCBC primarily uses the term "multicultural literature," I have elected to use the term "diverse children's literature" throughout this chapter in an effort to differentiate between the terms "multicultural" and "diversity." As Rose Casement confirms, by using the term "diversity," we can "create a lens that will offer a way to more intentionally include multicultural literature that avoids stereotypes" while also reflecting "the diverse world that children live in" (7).

2. hooks and Raschka also paired up on other children's books prior to *Skin Again*, including *Happy to Be Nappy* (1999) and *Be Boy Buzz* (2002).

3. When referring to *Islandborn*, all mentions of the Monster (in singular form) are capitalized to reflect the repeated capitalization of the term in the text.

4. We Need Diverse Books is a grassroots organization focused on addressing the lack of nonmajority narratives in children's literature. See https://diversebooks.org/.

5. The subgenre of Latino/a dictatorship novels also fits with the emphasis on Trujillo in Díaz's literary corpus. Jennifer Harford Vargas defines these novels as works that "collectively re-conceptualize dictatorial power by constructing intersectional analyses of authoritarianism, imperialism, heteropatriarchy, and racism in the hemisphere" (222).

6. Evident from the mention of *agua de coco*, the code switching in *Islandborn* helps the picture book obtain cultural and linguistic authenticity. Another word used in the same way in the text is *güira*, a musical instrument. *Islandborn* also uses other untranslated Spanish words such as *prima* ("cousin"), *abuela* ("Grandma"), and *agua* ("water"). Lourdes Torres describes this type of code switching as "Easily Accessed." Easily accessed code switching commonly includes proper names like *mamá* or common Hispanic foods. Torres notes that writers using code switching in this way "may not wish to alienate monolingual English readers" (79).

7. Gretchen Papazian addresses how picture books use color in different ways, in particular to talk about culture and race, and notes that some use "flag color" (177) to encode meaning.

8. *Bone Black*, an autobiographical memoir, narrates the power of memory and the construction of self but also delves into themes such as race consciousness and gender bias.

Works Cited

Arapoglou, Eleftheria. "Enacting an Identity by Re-Creating a Home: Eleni Gage's *North of Ithaka*." *Identity, Diaspora and Return in American Literature*, edited by Maria Antònia Oliver-Rotger, Routledge, 2015, pp. 118–33.

Bang, Molly. *Picture This: Perception and Composition*. Little, Brown, 1991.

Bishop, Rudine Sims. "Mirrors, Windows, and Sliding Glass Doors." *Perspectives: Choosing and Using Books for the Classroom*, vol. 6, no. 3, Summer 1990, pp. ix–xi.
Bishop, Rudine Sims. "Multicultural Literature for Children: Making Informed Choices." *Teaching Multicultural Literature in Grades K–8*, edited by Violet J. Harris, Christopher-Gordon Publishers, 1992, pp. 37–54.
Boyd, Fenice B., Lauren L. Causey, and Lee Galda. "Culturally Diverse Literature: Enriching Variety in an Era of Common Core State Standards." *Reading Teacher*, vol. 68, no. 5, February 2015, pp. 378–87.
Casement, Rose. "Differentiating between the Terms 'Multicultural' and 'Diversity': Broadening the Perspective." *Language Arts Journal of Michigan*, vol. 18, no. 1, Spring 2002, pp. 5–8.
Cooperative Children's Book Center. "Multicultural Literature." ccbc.education.wisc.edu/books/multicultural.asp.
Díaz, Junot. *The Brief Wondrous Life of Oscar Wao*. Riverhead, 2007.
Díaz, Junot. *Islandborn*. Illustrated by Leo Espinosa, Dial Books, 2018.
Díaz, Junot. "Monstro." *New Yorker*, May 28, 2012, www.newyorker.com/magazine/2012/06/04/monstro.
Díaz, Junot. "Portrait Of: Junot Díaz." Interview with María Hinojosa, *Latino USA*, April 6, 2018. latinousa.org/2018/04/06/junotdiaz/.
Fang, Zhihui. "Illustrations, Text, and the Child Reader: What Are Pictures in Children's Storybooks For?" *Reading Horizons*, vol. 37, no. 2, 1996, pp. 130–42.
Galda, Lee, and Kathy G. Short. "Visual Literacy: Exploring Art and Illustration in Children's Books." *Reading Teacher*, vol. 46, no. 6, March 1993, pp. 506–16.
Gallego Cuiñas, Ana. *Trujillo: El fantasma y sus escritores; Historia de la novela del trujillato*. Mare & Martin, 2006.
Gerald, Carolyn F. "The Black Writer and His Role." *The Black Aesthetic*, edited by Addison Gayle Jr., Doubleday, 1971, pp. 349–56.
Hall, Katrina Willard. "Reflecting on Our Read-Aloud Practices: The Importance of Including Culturally Authentic Literature." *Young Children*, vol. 63, no. 1, January 2008, pp. 80–86.
Hanna, Monica. "'Reassembling the Fragments': Battling Historiographies, Caribbean Discourse, and Nerd Genres in Junot Díaz's *The Brief Wondrous Life of Oscar Wao*." *Callaloo*, vol. 33, no. 2, Spring 2010, pp. 498–520.
Harford Vargas, Jennifer. "Dictating a Zafa: The Power of Narrative Form as Ruin-Reading." *Junot Díaz and the Decolonial Imagination*, edited by Monica Hanna, Jennifer Harford Vargas, and José David Saldívar, Duke UP, 2016, pp. 201–27.
Hill, Rebecca A. "The Color of Authenticity in Multicultural Children's Literature." *Voya*, vol. 34, no. 5, December 2011, pp. 445–47.
hooks, bell. *Bone Black: Memories of Girlhood*. Henry Holt, 1996.
hooks, bell. "Choosing the Margin as a Space of Radical Openness." 1990. *Yearning: Race, Gender, and Cultural Politics*, Turnaround, 1991, pp. 203–9.
hooks, bell. *Skin Again*. Illustrated by Chris Raschka, Hyperion/Jump at the Sun, 2004.
Larrick, Nancy. "The All-White World of Children's Books." *Saturday Review*, September 11, 1965, pp. 63–65, 84–85.
Larson, Neil. "¿Cómo narrar el trujillato?" *Revista Iberoamericana*, vol. 54, no. 142, January–March 1988, pp. 89–98.

Milian, Claudia. "Latino/a Deracination and the New Latin American Novel." *Junot Díaz and the Decolonial Imagination*, edited by Monica Hanna, Jennifer Harford Vargas, and José David Saldívar, Duke UP, 2016, pp. 174–200.

Myers, Christopher. "The Apartheid of Children's Literature." *New York Times*, March 15, 2014. https://www.nytimes.com/2014/03/16/opinion/sunday/the-apartheid-of-childrens-literature.html.

Nieto, Sonia. "We Have Stories to Tell: A Case Study of Puerto Ricans in Children's Books." *Teaching Multicultural Literature in Grades K–8*, edited by Violet J. Harris, Christopher-Gordon Publishers, 1992, pp. 173–201.

Papazian, Gretchen. "Color Multiculturally: Twenty-First-Century Multicultural Picturebooks, Color(ing) Beyond the Lines." *Children's Literature*, vol. 46, 2018, pp. 169–200.

Roethler, Jacque. "Reading in Color: Children's Book Illustrations and Identity Formation for Black Children in the United States." *African American Review*, vol. 32, no. 1, Spring 1998, pp. 95–105.

Saldívar, Ramón. "'Chiste Apocalyptus': Prospero in the Caribbean and the Art of Power." *Junot Díaz and the Decolonial Imagination*, edited by Monica Hanna, Jennifer Harford Vargas, and José David Saldívar, Duke UP, 2016, pp. 377–89.

Solórzano, Daniel G., and Tara J. Yosso. "Critical Race Methodology: Counter-Storytelling as an Analytical Framework for Education Research." *Qualitative Inquiry*, vol. 8, no. 1, February 2002, pp. 23–44.

Steiner, Stan F., Claudia Peralta Nash, and Maggie Chase. "Children's Books: Multicultural Literature That Brings People Together." *Reading Teacher*, vol. 62, no. 1, September 2008, pp. 88–92.

Suárez-Orozco, Marcelo M. "Everything You Ever Wanted to Know about Assimilation But Were Afraid to Ask." *Daedalus*, vol. 129, no. 4, Fall 2000, 1–30.

Torres, Lourdes. "In the Contact Zone: Code-Switching Strategies by Latino/a Writers." *MELUS*, vol. 32, no. 1, Spring 2007, pp. 75–96.

ABOUT THE CONTRIBUTORS

María V. Acevedo-Aquino is assistant professor of early childhood at Texas A&M University–San Antonio. Her research interests focus on global and multicultural children's literature (especially stories portraying the lives of Latinxs), intercultural understanding of young children, and story, inquiry, and play as transformative experiences in early childhood education.

Consuella Bennett is assistant professor of English at Morehouse College in Atlanta. Her areas of research and publication are mainly in Caribbean literature and linguistics, particularly in Caribbean creole languages as both vestiges of colonialism and defiance of it.

Florencia V. Cornet holds a PhD in comparative literature with specialization in comparative Black gender studies, Black diaspora studies, and cultural studies. Her areas of teaching, publishing, and research specialization include Latin American, Caribbean, and US Afro-Latino/a cultures; gender studies in global perspective; and studies in global Blackness. She is a faculty member at the University of South Carolina in Columbia.

Stacy Ann Creech is a Dominican doctoral candidate in English at McMaster University, Canada, specializing in transatlantic literature in the long eighteenth century. Her research and teaching interests include Black diaspora literature and theory, Black feminism, Latin American/Latinx studies, and Caribbean studies.

Zeila Frade holds a PhD in Spanish literature from Florida International University. Her research focuses on Cuban children's literature before and after 1959. Currently she is adjunct professor of Spanish at Montclair State University.

Melissa García Vega teaches at Lehman College, the City University of New York. Her research interests examine children's literature with emphasis on the Caribbean region, multilingual learners, and the global context. She has published on Caribbean children's literature in the *Journal of West Indian Literature*. A former elementary school teacher, she now teaches literacy and child development in the Early Childhood and Childhood Department at Lehman College.

Ann González (PhD 1983) is professor emeritus of the University of North Carolina at Charlotte, where she taught in the Department of Languages and Culture Studies for thirty years and chaired from 2015 to 2020. She specializes in Latin American literature and Hispanic children's literature. Her latest books are *Postcolonial Approaches to Latin American Children's Literature* (Routledge, 2018) and a textbook on children's literature: *Introducción a la literatura juvenil hispana* (Panda Publications, 2014).

Louise Hardwick is professor of Francophone studies and world literature at the University of Birmingham (UK), and associate fellow of Homerton College, University of Cambridge. She has published extensively on various aspects of Francophone cultures, including the monographs *Childhood, Autobiography and the Francophone Caribbean* (Liverpool University Press, 2013) and *Joseph Zobel: Négritude and the Novel* (Liverpool University Press, 2018). Her research has been funded by major EU and UK research grants, most recently through an AHRC Early Career Leadership Fellowship for her work on Joseph Zobel (www.josephzobel.wordpress.com).

Barbara Lalla's five novels include *One Thousand Eyes* (2021), *Grounds for Tenure* (2017), *Uncle Brother* (2014), *Cascade* (2010), and *Arch of Fire* (1998). At the University of the West Indies, she has taught and published on Caribbean language history, literary discourse, and the rereading of other canons. Scholarly publications include *Caribbean Literary Discourse: Voice and Cultural Identity in the Anglophone Caribbean* (coauthored with Jean D'Costa and Velma Pollard, 2014); *Methods in Caribbean Research: Literature,*

Discourse, Culture (coedited with Nicole Roberts, Elizabeth Walcott-Hackshaw, and Valerie Youssef, 2013); and *Postcolonialisms: Caribbean Rereading of Medieval English Discourse* (2008).

Megan Jeanette Myers is associate professor of Spanish at Iowa State University. Myers is the author of *Mapping Hispaniola: Third Space in Dominican and Haitian Literature* and coedited the multimodal anthology *The Border of Lights Reader: Bearing Witness to Genocide in the Dominican Republic*.

Betsy Nies has been exploring the field of Caribbean children's literature for the past decade, speaking at conferences, publishing, and noticing gaps in scholarly research that overlook the Caribbean as central to the field of children's literature. She has published on Caribbean children's literature in the international journals *Amaltea: Revista de Mitocrítica* and *Children's Literature in Education*, and reviewed Caribbean literature for *Wasafiri: International Contemporary Literature*. A former elementary school teacher, she now teaches children's, young adult, and US ethnic literatures as an associate professor at the University of North Florida in Jacksonville.

Karen Sanderson-Cole is a lecturer in the Department of Modern Languages and Linguistics at the University of the West Indies, St. Augustine, Trinidad. Caribbean literature is her first love, but she has published several articles in the areas of autobiography and the postgraduate university experience, as well as teaching and learning at the tertiary level.

Karen Sands-O'Connor is a leading expert on Black British children's literature. She works with UK national organizations, including Seven Stories, the Chartered Institute of Library and Information Professionals (CILIP), and the British Library on issues of diversity. In addition to her most recent academic monograph, *Children's Publishing and Black Britain, 1965–2015* (Palgrave Macmillan 2017), she writes a regular column for *Books for Keeps* and contributes to the Centre for Literacy in Primary Education's Reflecting Realities reports.

Geraldine Skeete teaches in the Literatures in English program in the Faculty of Humanities and Education at the University of the West Indies, St. Augustine. Among her publications is the coedited book *The Child and* *the Caribbean Imagination*. Her areas of interest are Caribbean literature, the short story form, literary linguistics, and the scholarship of teaching and learning.

Aisha T. Spencer is a senior lecturer in language and literature education in the School of Education, at the University of the West Indies, Mona Campus. Her research areas include Caribbean literature, literature education, and gender studies.

INDEX

ABC de Puerto Rico (Deliz), 93
Abigail's Glorious Hair (Browne), 163, 204–5
Adichie, Chimamanda Ngozi, 215, 249
Afro-Trinidadians, 171
agency, 95
Alegría, Ricardo, *La historia de nuestros indios*, 93
alienation, 228–29
Allen-Agostini, Lisa, *Home Home*, 77
Alonso, Dora, 86–87
Alvarez, Julia, 26; *Before We Were Free*, 26, 163
Amazon, 251
Anansesem, 13, 95
Anansi (Anancy), 7, 73, 78, 166, 177, 190, 199
androcentrism, 93
Anglo-American roots, 101
Anthony, Michael, 23, 54, 156; *The Year in San Fernando*, 156
anti-Blackness, 102
Antología puertorriqueña: Prosa y verso para lectura escolar (Fernández Juncos), 92
Anuario iberoamericano sobre el libro infantil y juvenil, 96
Arawak Publications, 240
archipelago, 91–95
Arnold, Sarah Louise, *Stepping Stones to Literature: A Second Reader*, 92
Arroyo Pizarro, Yolanda, 94; Cátedra de Mujeres Negras Ancestrales, 94

Aruba: Charuba (publisher), 42; children's literature, 41; Munye Oduber-Winklaar, 43; National Public Library, 42; Olga Buckley, 42–43
Asperger's syndrome, 79
attention-deficit/hyperactivity disorder, 120

Backfire (Giuseppi and Giuseppi), 125–52
Baksh, Iman, 8; *Children of the Spider*, 78, 165; *The Dark of the Sea*, 79
Bang, Molly, 268
Baptiste, Tracey, 8; *The Jumbie God's Revenge*, 80; *The Jumbies*, 26, 224–26
Barbados, children's authors from: Austin Clark, 127; Shakirah Bourne, 79. *See also* Drayton, Geoffrey
Barrios Llorens, Rossana, 96
basal readers (Jamaica), 190, 207
Bébel-Gisler, Dany: *Grand-mère, ça commence où la Route de l'Esclave?*, 64–65; *Grand-mère, pourquoi Sundari est venue en Guadeloupe?*, 65
Before We Were Free (Alvarez), 26, 163
Belize, Zee Edgell, *Beka Lamb*, 159–60
Bennett, Louise ("Miss Lou"), 23–24, 74–75, 140, 190, 192; *Children's Jamaican Songs and Games*, 75
Bernier-Grand, Carmen, 94, 97; *In the Shade of the Níspero Tree*, 94
Binch, Caroline, 162, 181

biodiversity, 114
Bishop, Rudine Sims, 212, 270
Blackness (in the Dominican Republic), 100–101
Blue Banyan Books, 240
Bocas Lit Fest, 161
Brathwaite, Kamau, 4, 11; Caribbean Arts Movement, 75; nation language, 23, 207
Breinburg, Petronella, 75
Br'er Rabbit, 57
British education system, 174, 176
British history, Black, 175
Britons, Black, 175, 181
Brodber, Erna, 192
Browne, Diane, 13, 26, 240–56; *Abigail's Glorious Hair*, 163, 204–5; Dr. Bird Reading Series, 243; *The Happiness Dress*, 251; "'I Will Not Look at Books the Same Way Again': Teachers' Feelings about the Use of Caribbean Children's Literature," 241
Buckley, Olga, 43
Burt Award, 77–80, 248, 254

Cadilla de Martínez, María, *Juegos y canciones infantiles de Puerto Rico*, 92
Callender, Kacen, 78
Camera Mundi, 240
canon, Caribbean literary, 3
Capote, Renée Méndez, 86
Caribbean: Anglophone, 10–11; Dutch, 13; Francophone, 13, 53–71; Spanish-speaking, 13–14; stereotypes in literature, 175, 180, 193, 220–33, 260; stereotypes in media, 212–14
Caribbean Arts Movement, 11, 75
Caribbean Examination Council (CXC) in fiction, 164
Caribbean Secondary Education Certificate, 148
Carlong Publishers, 240, 249, 254
Casas, Bartolomé de las, 102
Cassá, Roberto, *Los Taínos de la Española*, 103
Centro para el Estudio de la Lectura, la Escritura y la Literatura Infantil (CELELI), 96
ceremony, religious, 101

Chamoiseau, Patrick, 55, 58, 62; *Au temps de l'antan*, 62, 64; Creole folktales, 66–67; and Édouard Glissant, 64; Émerveilles, 62–63; *La commandeur d'une pluie*, 64; *Manman Dlo contre la fée Carabosse*, 62; *Veilles et merveilles créoles*, 64
Chansky, Ricia Anne, *Mi María: Puerto Rico after the Hurricane*, 95
Child and the Caribbean Imagination, The (Rampaul and Skeete), 12
Children of the Spider (Baksh), 78, 165
Children's Jamaican Songs and Games (Bennett), 75
children's literature: Anglophone Caribbean, 72–82; contemporary Caribbean, 28; Dutch Caribbean, 35–52; Francophone Caribbean, 53–71; language arts classroom (Jamaica), 188, 190, 201; primary classroom (Jamaica), 191
Chinese diasporic community, 141
Clark, Austin, 127
class, 93
classroom: democratic, 216; multicultural, 216, 220
climate change, 95
code shifting (switching), 167, 284n6
colonial(ism), 20, 100, 275; and curricula, 193; educational system, 171, 187; history, 100, 184; ideologies, 93; status, 91
communal activism, 95
Conde, Eric González, 88
Condé, Maryse, 13, 56–58; childhood memoir, 57; children's literature praxis, 59
corporal punishment, 144
Costa Rica, children's authors from: Carlos Rubio, 120; Lara Ríos, 120. *See also* Duncan, Quince; Gutiérrez, Joaquín; Lyra, Carmen
Costa Rican children's literature, 118–21; Atlantic coast, 119; Black child protagonist, 119; Black storyteller, 120; *campensinos*, 119; diversity and inclusion, 120; indigenous teenager as protagonist, 120; Jamaican Blacks, 119; national identity, 119
Craig, Christine, 25
Creole: Anglophone Caribbean, 20, 23, 73, 138; in *Backfire*, 136–37; Barbadian, 143;

in *Beka Lamb*, 159–61; bilingual children's book, 61; *Children of the Spider*, 165; in education, 16, 21, 176; fiction, 23; folktales, 61; Francophone children's literature, 61, 66; Geoffrey Drayton, 156–57; in Grace Hallworth's children's stories, 178; for instruction, 139; Jamaican, 21, 164–65, 207–8, 263; patios (Jamaican), 174, 177–78; poems, 190; poetry, 23; stereotypical labels, 184; stigmatization, 139; in Trinidadian readers, 138–39, 142; in US classrooms, 219; versus Standard English, 153–69; young adult literature, 77, 164. *See also* Bennett, Louise; Papiamentu/o
créolité movement, 58
creolization, 9; in Dutch Caribbean literary works, 37
CSEC (Caribbean Secondary Education Certificate), 249
Cuba: Anita Arroyo, 84; Barcardí Moreau, 85; children's literature, 19, 83–89; Cuban Revolution (children's literature), 86–88; Hilda Perera, 84; José Martí, 92; republican era, 88; republic authors, 84–85
Curaçao: children's literature, 41, 49; Loekie Morales, 44; May 30, 1969 uprising, 41, 45–46; National Public Library, 41; young adult literature, 45–47
curricula/um: Caribbean, 3; colonial, 20; colonialism and, 193; Dominican Republic, 105–6, 109–11; junior secondary, 24, 129, 195; language arts, 185, 195; literature, 197–98; objectives, 190; primary, 194–95; Roman Catholic Church, 105; secondary (postcolonial), 6, 22–24, 146; US multicultural literature, 25, 216–31

Da Matas, Jarrel, 12
"Dan is the Man (in the Van)," 127
Danticat, Edwidge, 27, 58, 258–65; *Anacaona: Golden Flower*, 263–64; *Eight Days in Haiti*, 163, 264; *Mama's Nightingale*, 60, 263–64; *My Mommy Medicine*, 261, 263
Dark of the Sea, The (Baksh), 79
D'Costa, Jean, 192; *Caribbean Literary Discourse*, 138; *Sprat Morrison*, 21, 158; *Voice in the Wind*, 157–58, 166
deafness, 166

decolonization, 7; Dutch Caribbean, 36, 39
De Jesus, Wanda, 96
de Jesús Galván, Manuel, *Enriquillo*, 102
Delacre, Lulu, 97
de la Cruz, Verónica, *La gran Victoria*, 95
Delgado, Luis Cabrera, 87
delinquency, 144
Deliz, Monserrate, 93
DeLoughrey, Elizabeth, 103
depression, 27
dialogue, 246
Díaz, Enrique Pérez, 87–88
Díaz, Junot, 27, 259–65; *Islandborn*, 27, 264, 266–86
Díaz Alfaro, Abelardo, *Terrazo*, 93
diaspora (Caribbean), 4, 9; African, 6; Black, 7; to Canada, 77
didacticism, 103
Diekmann, Miep, 40, 45
difference, physical or neurological in fiction, 78–79, 180
disability, 87
disasters, 18
discourse of assimilation, 92; national, 103–5
dissonance, 246
diversity in children's books, 114, 120, 268; definition, 284n1; lack of, 126
divorce, 88
domestic conflict, 100
Dominica, *I am Dominica/Mwe sé Donmnik*, 61
Dominican Republic: African, 100, 103–5, 107; African ancestry, 112; African heredity, 101; African influences, 108; African roots, 115; artists, 101; Black character, 114; Blackness, 101, 105–6, 112; Catholicism, 105–6; children, 100; children's literature, 20, 100–117, 266–84; colonialism, 100–101; cultural traditions, 114; curriculum, 107, 111; diaspora, 265; discrimination, 107; educational laws, 109; Educational Reform Act, 1993, 111, 115; educational system, 104–7; empire, 100; Haitian occupation, 101, 105–6; history, 278; imperialism, 100, 108, 115; independence, 105; Indigenous, 101–3; Ministry of Education, 112; national identity, 20, 101, 107; national imaginary,

110; nationhood, 111–12; racial imaginary, 105; representations of mixed race, 114; resistance to colonialism, 114; Spanish, 100, 102, 104; Taíno, 101–4, 114; whiteness, 112; whitening, 106; US occupation, 101, 108. *See also* Trujillo, Rafael

Dominican Republic, children's authors from: Leibi Ng, 113; Rafael Peralta Romero, 114. *See also* Alvarez, Julia; Díaz, Junot; Grimaldi Silié, Eleanor; López, Margarite Luciano; Ortea, Virginia Elena

Drayton, Geoffrey, 156–57

Duncan, Quince, 10, 20, 120

Dutch Caribbean (and Caribbean Dutch): children's books, 38; relationship to Netherlands, 36

Dutch language (in the Caribbean): in Caribbean children's literature, 39; instruction, 16, 39; language of status, 39

Duyvis, Corinne, 252

dystopian fiction, 80

Edgell, Zee, *Beka Lamb*, 155

Edith Jackson (Guy), 76

education, 3; Black British as "subnormal," 176; British, 172; colonialism, 19, 125, 187; colonial secondary school education, 127; junior secondary school, 129; US, 221

Edward, Summer, 13, 115, 251

El Nuevo Día (series), 240

empire, 100

environmental education, Educación Ambiental, 242

environmental literature, 66, 80, 93, 95

enslaved Africans, 103

Espinosa, Leo, 269, 271, 279

Etienne-Manley, Mara, 61

European colonizers, 101, 102

Fanon, Frantz, *Black Skins, White Masks*, 5

fantasy: *Children of the Spider*, 78, 165; Dutch Caribbean children's books, 48–49. *See also* speculative fiction

Feliciano Mendoza, Ester, 93

Fernández Juncos, Manuel, 92

Ferré, Rosario, *El medio pollito*, 93

Figueroa, Roberto, 240

folklore, 6, 12–13, 176, 192, 193; African, 8; Anglophone Caribbean, 73; Ciguapa, 113; collective history, 67; as colonial children's stories, 154–55; Costa Rican, 119; Creole, 24, 57, 66–67; Dominican, 113; duppy, 164; in environmental fiction, 80; in fiction, 79–80; folktales, 175–76, 178, 180–81; French Caribbean, 66–67; Puerto Rican, 92; *Ti Bolom*, 162; Trinidadian, 171, 224–26; West Indian, 176

foreign, 100

Freire, Paulo, 5, 189; critical literacy, 6; *Pedagogy of the Oppressed*, 5, 191

Freire de Matos, Isabel, *ABC de Puerto Rico*, 93

Friends, The (Guy), 76

García Vega, Melissa, 12

gatekeepers, 247

Gegele, A-dZiko, 165

gender inequality, 78; gender (in)equality, 144

Gibson, Tamika, 78–79

Giuseppi, Neville and Undine, 125–53

Glissant, Edouard, 7, 9; *Poetics of Relation*, 9; *tout-monde*, 63–64

Godreau, Isar, *Arrancando mitos de raíz*, 94

González, Ann, 113

Goyco, Carlos, Libros787 online bookstore, 95

Grand-mère, ça commence où la Route de l'Esclave? (Bébel-Gisler), 64–65

Grand-mère, pourquoi Sundari est venue en Guadeloupe? (Bébel-Gisler), 65

Grimaldi Silié, Eleanor, 113–14

Grupo de Diarios América, Puerto Rico, 240; Francophone Caribbean, 65–66

Guadeloupe, 56, 61, 64; children's publishers, 66; folklore, 67; racism, 62. *See also* Bébel-Gisler, Dany; Condé, Maryse; Pineau, Gisèle

Gutiérrez, Joaquín, 118–20

Guy, Rosa, 192

Guyana, children's authors from: Beryl Gilroy, 75; David Makhanlall, 73; Grace Nichols, 25, 192; Ian Robertson, 143; John Agard, 25, 192. *See also* Baksh, Iman

Haiman, Ada, 11, 26–27, 240–56
Haiti, 56; children's authors diaspora, 60; conflict with Dominican Republic, 101, 105; *Eight Days: A Story of Haiti*, 163; history, 101, 105; Maryse Condé, 59; representations of in children's literature, 59–60
Haiti, children's authors from, Émille Ollivier, 56. *See also* Danticat, Edwidge; Laferrière, Dany
Haïti chérie (Condé), 59
Hallworth, Grace, 24, 170–83; *Buy a Penny Ginger*, 173, 181; *Cric Crac*, 177–78; *Down by the River*, 180–82; folktales, 176, 178; *Going to School*, 179; *Listen to this Story*, 176–77; *Mouth Open, Story Jump Out*, 178; *My Mind Is Not in a Wheelchair*, 180; nursery rhymes, 180–81; *Rhythm and Rhyme*, 181; *Stories to Read and Tell*, 174
Harcourt Brace, 240
Heinemann Caribbean, 240
Hillhouse, Joanne, 78
Hodge, Merle, 23, 125–26; on Creole, 138; *Crick Crack Monkey*, 127; *For the Life of Laetitia*, 160
Home Home (Allen-Agostini), 77
homophobia, 77
homosexuality, 87
hooks, bell, 59, 216, 267, 269–70, 280; *Skin Again*, 267
Hosein, Kevin Jared, 79
Hostos, Eugenio María de, 92
Huggins, Sujin, 8, 12–13, 192
Hugo le terrible (Condé), 59
human exploitation, 94
Hunt, Peter, 9, 153; *Understanding Children's Literature*, 9
hurricane, fictional, 281

identity, 5, 14, 103; Afro–Puerto Rican, 94; Caribbean, 184; cultural, 7; diasporic, 62; European, 114; national, 93, 100; neocolonial, 45; positive picture books, 267; postcolonial national, 102; Taíno, 114
Iguana's Tale: Crick, Crack Stories from the Caribbean (Sherlock), 73

Ilán ilán (Feliciano Mendoza), 93
illiteracy, 25, 110, 187
illustrations: in picture books, 268; in readers, 140
immigration in fiction, 265; Caribbean to US, 25, 211; Dominican Republic to US, 228–29, 272; French Caribbean to France, 66; Haiti to US, 60; *Islandborn*, 266–84; and self-identity, 272; Windrush generation, 11, 75, 173, 179, 221
imperialism, 91, 93, 100
incarceration, 88
Incubadora de Literatura Infantil y Juvenil de Puerto Rico, 96
independence, 7, 20; children's literature, 20, 192; Jamaican, 186
independence movements, 125
indigeneity, 100
indigenous people, representations of as childlike, 155
Indio/a, 103
Indo-Caribbeans, 180
Indo-Trinidadians, 171
Island Princess in Brooklyn, 254

Jacobs, Debbie, 80
Jamaica, 11; Bookfusion, 254; Carlong Sand Pebbles series, 249; classrooms, 186–95, 203; curriculum, 186–95, 203; Dr. Bird Reading Series, 243; education, 19, 184–209; English, 219; English into French writers, 60; Ministry of Education, 21, 195, 242–43
Jamaica, children's authors from: A-dZiko Gegele, 165; Diana McCaulay, 80. *See also* Browne, Diane; D'Costa, Jean; Reid, Victor; Salkey, Andrew; Senior, Olive; Sherlock, Sir Philip
James, C. L. R., 126, 147
James, Cynthia, 3, 11, 73, 171, 192
jíbaro, 94
Jiménez, Marilisa, 97
Johnson, Joanne Gail, 26, 239–57; *Go Barefoot*, 247; *Hop Step Jump*, 248; Island Fiction tween novel series, 248; *JoJo & Gran Gran*, 62; People's Choice Award for Best Narrative Feature at the

Trinidad and Tobago Film Festival, 239; Sally's Way, 239
Joseph, Lynn, A Wave in Her Pocket, 8
Jóvenes del 98 theater company, 96
Jumbie God's Revenge, The (Baptiste), 80
Jumbies, The (Baptiste), 26, 224–26

Kamishibai, 93
Keens-Douglas, Paul, 23, 75, 140

La casa de María Chuzema, WIPR-TV, 240–42
Laferrière, Dany, 56, 60–61; Je suis fou de Vava, 60
Lamming, George, 54
landscapes, 92
language, official, 91
language arts, 185; classroom, 188, 194; primary school, 185; secondary school, 185
La planète Orbis (Condé), 59
La Rose, John, 11, 75
Latin American education, 92
Lázaro, Georgina, 95
Lebacs, Diana, 45–48
Legend of the St. Ann's Flood, 80
lexical level, 244
libraries: Anglophone school, 18; colonialism, 18; Dutch Caribbean, 15, 42–43; El Centro para el Estudio de la Lectura, la Escritura y la Literatura Infantil (CELELI), 96; Francophone school, 18; national children's library, 247; public Francophone, 66; Puerto Rico Necesita Biblioteca, 96; Trinidad and Tobago (children's), 172
library service, 172
Libros787 (online bookstore), 95
literacy, 184, 186–88, 190–91, 197–98, 202–3; studies, 185
literary festivals and awards, 248
Lloyd, Errol, 75
local literature, 249
Lopez, Marco, 95
López, Margarite Luciano, 113–14
López Baralt, Mercedes, Mitos del pueblo Taíno: Libro de colorear, 103
Los Cuentacuentos de Puerto Rico (Marichal-Lugo), 96

"lost" Natives, 102
Lovelace, Earl, 139
lullaby, 247
Lyra, Carmen, 118–20

Macmillan Caribbean, 12; Macmillan Caribbean's Island Fiction series, 239, 247
Mama Wata/Mama D'Leau, 79–80
marginalization, 267
"María Generation," 95
Marichal-Lugo, Tere (Marichal-Lugo, María Teresa), 26, 93, 239–56; Carla feliz, 93; Colección Pachamama, 245; La casa de María Chuzema, 240; La cucarachita Martina y el huracán, 95; Los Nuevos Alquimistas, 242; Mrs. Pollution, 24; Pancha la planchadora, 93
Marronage, 104
Marti, José, 83–84, 86, 92
Martínez-Roldán, Carmen, 97
Martinique, authors from. See Chamoiseau, Patrick; Zobel, Paul
Martorell, Antonio, ABC de Puerto Rico, 93
Maximin, Daniel, 56–57
McCaulay, Diana, 80
Medina, Carmen L., 97
Mejorar la raza (Arroyo Pizarro), 94
memoir, childhood (Francophone), 58
memory, collective, 95, 282–83; fragmentation, 272; politicizing/politicization of, 266–70, 280, 283; transnational, 282
México, 244
Mighty Sparrow (Slinger Francisco), 127
migration, 7, 211; in Backfire, 138; in Dutch young adult books, 46; in picture books, 60
Milagros Torres-Rivera, Carmen, 12, 19
military occupations, 93
Mills, Therese, 192
Ministry of Education in Jamaica, 240
Mir, Pedro, 278, 280
Mirabel sisters, 277–78, 282
Mis cantares (Rodríguez de Tió), 92
Mitos del pueblo Taíno (López-Baralt), 103
Mohr, Nicholasa, 97
Monpierre, Roland, 65
Morales, Loekie, 44, 48–50

Moya Pons, Frank, *The Dominican Republic: A National History*, 102
multivocality, 165
muteness, 166
mystery, 79

Naipaul, V. S., 139
narrative(s): cultural, 100; postcolonial, 103
nation, 101
nation language, 23, 263
Netherlands: language use in Caribbean, 36; neocolonialism, 38
Netherlands Antilles, 15. *See also* Dutch Caribbean
New Day (Reid), 74
Ng, Leibi, 113
Nieto, Sonia, 97
NourbeSe Philip, Marlene, *Harriet's Daughter*, 76
nursery rhymes, 170, 181

oral tradition (literature), 6, 93, 171, 181; Dutch Caribbean, 39, 43; stories, 95
orature, 3, 23
Ortea, Virginia Elena, *Risas y lágrimas*, 104
Ortiz Cofer, Judith, 97
Otra maldad de Pateco (Vega), 94
Oublié, Jessica, 65–66; *Péyi an nou*, 65; *Tropiques toxiques*, 66
"own voices," 252, 257

Palmer, C. Everard, 73
Pané, Ramón, 102
Papiamentu/o: Catholic children's literature, 38; in children's literature, 37–42, 45, 48–49; education, 16; in library collections, 16, 42; as resistance to colonization, 38, 41; in young adult literature, 37, 47
Pastrana Andino, Isset, *Mi isla bella*, 95
patriarchy, 93
pedagogy, 5; ecosocialist, 5; literary, 184, 195; reading, 187–88, 190–91; skills (-based), 187
Pelo bueno (Arroyo Pizarro), 94
Pépin, Ernest, 56–57
Peralta Romero, Rafael, 114
phenotypical descriptions, 103
Photoshop, 248

Picó, Fernando, *The Red Comb*, 94
picture books: *Abigail's Glorious Hair*, 163, 204–5, 246; *Birthday Suit*, 205–7, 262; *Boonoonoonous Hair*, 260–61; *Calling the Water Drum*, 60; Caribbean, 25–26; *Carla feliz*, 93; *Eight Days: A Story of Haiti*, 163; *En la bahía de Jobos: Celita y el Mangle Zapatero*, 94; *I am Dominica/Mwe sé Donmnik*, 61; *Islandborn*, 27, 264–65; *La cucarachita Martina y el huracán*, 95; *La gran Victoria*, 95; *A Long Way from Home*, 202–3, 207–8; *Look Back!*, 162; *Mi isla bella*, 95; *My Mommy Medicine*, 261; *Pancha la planchadora*, 94; *Pelo bueno*, 94; *Por ahí viene el huracán*, 94; *The Red Comb*, 94; *Skin Again*, 167; *Thiago y la aventura del huracán*, 94; Tulipán: The Puerto Rican Giraffe series, 240; *Y llegaron los esclavos*, 94
Pineau, Gisèle, 60; *L'exil selon Julia*, 61–62; *Un papillon dans la cité*, 61–62
Piñeiro de Rivera, Flor, 93; *Un siglo de literatura infantil puertorriqueña*, 96
plazas, 244
Plummer, Janet, 202, 207–8
poem, 203
pollution, Jessica Oublié, 66
polytheism, 101
poverty, 179
Pratt, Mary Louise, 102
pregnancy, illegitimate, 143
protagonists, Afro-Caribbean, 9
Puerto Rico: Afro–Puerto Rican, 94; colonialism, 19–20, 91; education, 19; English-only, 19; Puerto Rico Oversight, Management, and Economic Stability Act (PROMESA), 91
Puerto Rico and diaspora, children's authors from: Abelardo Díaz Alfaro, 93; Ana Lydia Vega, 94; Antonio Martorell, 93; Carmelina Vizcarrondo, 92; Eric Velasquez, 97; Esmeralda Santiago, 97; Ester Feliciano Mendoza, 93; Eugenio María de Hostos, 92; Fernando Picó, 94; Georgina Lázaro, 95; Isabel Freire de Matos, 93; Isar Godreau, 94; Isset Pastrana Andino, 95; Laura Rexach Olivencia, 94; Lola Rodríguez de Tió,

92; Lulu Delacre, 97; Manuel Fernández Juncos, 92; María Cadilla de Martínez, 92; María Rijos Guzmán, 94; Nicholasa Mohr, 97; Ricardo Alegría, 93; Rosario Ferré, 93; Sarah Louise Arnold, 92; Verónica de la Cruz, 95; Wanda De Jesus, 96; Yolanda Arroyo Pizarro, 94. *See also* Bernier-Grand, Carmen; Haiman, Ada; Marichal-Lugo, Tere; Rosario, Rubén del

publishers, Caribbean children's books, 95; Arawak Publications, 240; Black British, 75; Blue Banyan Books of Jamaica, 81, 240; Camera Mundi, 240; Carlong Publishers, 240; Cuban, 86, 244–45; Dutch Caribbean, 42–45; educational, 26; El Nuevo Día, 240; French Caribbean, 66; Grupo de Diarios América, Puerto Rico, 240; Harcourt Brace, 240; Heinemann Caribbean, 240; *Jamaica Gleaner*, 172; Lilac Publishing, 95; Macmillan Caribbean, 172, 191; school texts, 172; self-publishing, 95; Tanya Batson Savage, 250

Puerto Rico Strong, 95

race, 88, 100; constructions, 103; and diversity, 93–94; racial imaginary, 101–2; mixed-, 103–4

racism, 267

rafters, 88

Ramchaud, Kenneth, 127

Rampaul, Giselle, *The Child and the Caribbean Imagination*, 12

Ramsawack, Al, 73

reader-response theory, 134

readers, school: Anglophone junior secondary, 24, 129; Anglophone secondary, 22; middle-grade, 6; *Nelson's New West Indian Readers*, 132

reading, 187–91, 194–96, 204

realism in fiction, 78

Reid, Victor, *Peter of Mount Ephraim: The Daddy Sharpe Rebellion*, 74, 130

religiosity, Afro-Caribbean, 7

Renadío del cantar folklórico de Puerto Rico (Deliz), 93

resilience, 95

Rexach Olivencia, Laura, *Por ahí viene el huracán*, 94

Rijos Guzmán, María, *Y llegaron los esclavos*, 94

Ríos, Lara, 120

Rodríguez de Tió, Lola, *Mis cantares*, 92

Ronda del mar (Feliciano Mendoza), 93

Rosenblatt, Louise, 134, 144–45, 189, 197–98, 201–2

Rosselló, Ricardo, 95

Rubio, Carlos, 120

Ruby (Guy), 76

Saint Lucia, *JoJo & Gran Gran*, 62

Salkey, Andrew, 11; *Anancy's Score*, 73; Caribbean Arts Movement, 75; *Drought*, 76; *Earthquake*, 76; *Hurricane*, 26, 221–23; *Riot*, 76

Sánchez-Haiman, Atabey, 240

Sands-O'Connor, Karen, 108

Santiago, Esmeralda, 97

Schwarz-Bart, Simone, *Ti Jean l'horizon*, 67

schools, primary (Trinidad), 194

science fiction: *La planète orbis*, 59; *Skylarking*, 60

self-publishing (children's books), Dutch Caribbean, 40, 48

Selvon, Sam, 23, 139

Senior, Olive, 27, 77; *Anna Carries Water*, 260–61; *Birthday Suit*, 205–7, 260, 262; *Boonoonoonous Hair*, 260–61; "Colonial Girls School," 127; *Talking of Trees*, 127

Sherlock, Sir Philip, 73; *Anansi the Spider Man*, 73, 173–74

Sint Maarten, 43–44; children's literature, 44, 49; Geraldine Skeete, 12, 24; Loekie Morales, 44, 48–50

Sixty-five (Reid), 74

skin color, 268, 278

slavery, children's books, 49; *Grand-mère, ça commence où la Route de l'Esclave?*, 64–65

Smith-Dennis, Colleen, *Inner City Girl*, 78

social hierarchy, 103

Society of Children's Book Writers and Illustrators, 239; Caribbean South chapter, 239

sociogeny, 5
Spain (Spanish) clergy, 102; conquerors, 102
speculative fiction, 48, 78
Spencer, Aisha, 12, 25
storytelling, 171
subordination, 94

Tai: El pequeño Tayno, 103
Taíno, 14, 101, 102; Arawak, 10, 102; Enriquillo, 103; in children's literature, 103; history in children's books, 104; as noble, 103; physical descriptions, 103
teacher preparatory program, 3, 6; institutions, 195
teachers, 6, 185–86; and language awareness, 218; lower secondary school, 185–86; primary, 185–86, 191, 194–96, 241
technology in fiction, 78
Terrazo (Díaz Alfaro), 93
territory, 91
testing: in fiction, 77; fourteen-plus examinations, 129; junior secondary school examination, 129; postcolonial, 22; and reading practices, 25, 196
Thiago y la aventura del huracán (Arroyo Pizarro), 94
Ti Jean, 67
tout-monde, 63
trauma: historical, 276, 283; postcolonial, 276
trickster, 73, 177
Trinidad and Tobago: Black Power revolution, 147; Caribbean literature curriculum, 126; Chinese, 141, 171; colonial education, 126–27; as colony, 171; education plan (post-independence), 20–21, 129; folklore, 170; independence, 161; junior secondary school, 24, 129, 149; national identity, 21, 161; National Library, 12; Port of Spain Children's Library, 12; primary school, 145, 149; secondary school, 145–46, 149, 161, 172; Standard English (Trinidadian), 160; storytelling, 134
Trinidad and Tobago, children's authors from: Joanne Gail Johnson, 26, 239–57; Lynn Joseph, 8; Tracey Baptiste, 224–26. See also Allen-Agostini, Lisa; Gibson, Tamika; Guy, Rosa; Hallworth, Grace; Hodge, Merle; Hosein, Kevin Jared; NourbeSe Philip, Marlene; Palmer, C. Everard
Trujillo, Rafael: contact with US military, 108; dictatorship, 101, 231; in fiction, 227–28, 265, 269, 272–74, 276–77; impact on education, 106–7, 109–10
Tulipán: The Puerto Rican Giraffe (Haiman), 240
Tulipán the Puerto Rican Giraffe: A Christmas Story (Haiman), 240
Tulipán the Puerto Rican Giraffe Rejects a Hair-Raising Lie (Haiman), 240
Tulipán the Puerto Rican Giraffe Thinks about Grades (Haiman), 240
Twitter, 252

UNESCO's Year of the Child, 243
United States: Caribbean American children's books, 26; multicultural literature curricula, 26
University of Puerto Rico, 95; Mayagüez, 95; Rio Piedras, 96
University of Sagrado Corazón, 95
University of the West Indies, 22, 127
Un siglo de literatura infantil puertorriqueña, 96

Vega, Ana Lydia, 94
Vega, Jonathan A., 95
Velasquez, Eric, 97
Venegas Pérez, Ita, 96; *Jóvenes del 98*, 96
Vizcarrondo, Carmelina, *Poemas para mi niño*, 92

Year in San Fernando, The (Anthony), 156
Y No Había Luz (theater company), *El centinela de mango*, 96
Yo opino (Venegas Pérez), 96
young adult literature (Caribbean), 3, 6; Anglophone Caribbean, 76–81, 160–65; Dutch Caribbean, 37, 39, 41, 45–46; French Caribbean, 67
young adult literature, diaspora, 226–29, 231–33
Young Warriors, The (Reid), 74

Walcott, Derek, 214
West Indian Folktales (Sherlock), 73
Windrush generation, 11, 75, 173, 179, 221
working class, 143
Wynter, Sylvia, 5, 8

Zobel, Joseph, 54–55, 57; *Diabl-là*, 65; *Et si la mer n'était pas bleue*, 59; *La Rue Cases-Nègres*, 54–55, 57, 65

www.ingramcontent.com/pod-product-compliance
Lightning Source LLC
Chambersburg PA
CBHW021954220426
43663CB00007B/814